Maximizing Your ERP System

Maximizing Your ERP System

A Practical Guide for Managers

Scott Hamilton, Ph.D.

McGraw-Hill

New York   Chicago   San Francisco   Lisbon   London
Madrid   Mexico City   Milan   New Delhi   San Juan
Seoul   Singapore   Sydney   Toronto

567890 BKM BKM 0987

ISBN-13: 978-0-07-140611-6

ISBN-10: 0-07-140611-5

Library of Congress Cataloging-in-Publication Data

Hamilton, Scott.
    Maximizing your ERP system : a practical guide for managers / by Scott Hamilton.
       p. cm.
    ISBN 0-07-140611-5 (hardcover : alk. paper)
    1. Business planning.   2. Business logistics.   3. Manufacturing resource planning.
I. Title.
    HD30.28 .H354   2002
    658.4′012   dc21

2002010790

Contents

Preface

Maximizing Your ERP System focuses on the management of manufacturing and sales operations using an ERP software package, especially in smaller autonomous sites. This reflects the author's bias in experience and interest. The advantages of smaller firms, in comparison to large firms, are often intangible. One advantage is the ability to "put ones arms around" the firm's customers, products, people, and business processes, as well as ERP system usage.

Focus on Smaller Manufacturing Sites

Manufacturing sites can be segmented into large, medium, smaller, and very small based on the number of employees per site, as shown in Figure 1. For our purposes, smaller manufacturing sites range from 25 to 250 employees. They represent 17 percent of the approximate 700,000 U.S. manufacturing sites, based on Dun & Bradstreet data for the year 2002. The estimated number of worldwide manufacturing sites is approximately 2 million, so smaller manufacturers represent approximately 340,000 sites worldwide.

Within the U.S. manufacturing sector, an ERP software package is used in the majority of large and medium-size sites. Estimated usage in smaller manufacturing sites ranges from 20 percent to 50 percent, and less than 10 percent in very small manufacturers. As a site grows beyond 25 employees, the increasing need for coordination justifies the investment in an ERP system with more comprehensive capabilities in manufacturing planning and control. Very small manufacturing sites often use an accounting package with limited manufacturing capabilities. This may be explained in part by their limited budget. From a functionality point of view, even the very small manufacturing sites require ERP system capabilities. System-savvy executives at many start-up firms, for example, ensure they start with a solid ERP system as a foundation for growing the business. In addition to most start-up firms, the vast majority of the smaller (and very small) manufacturers operate as a single site.

A manufacturing company may consist of multiple sites. Many of these companies have a bias toward autonomous operations, where an individual site operates as a stand-alone business unit. A typical example involves a remote site in another country. These sites closely resemble a smaller autonomous manufacturer, with limited requirements for centralized reporting or coordination. Variations of multisite operations involve increasing levels of coordination and ERP system complexity. For simplicity's sake, this book focuses on single-site autonomous operations.

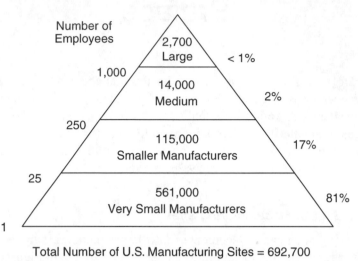

Total Number of U.S. Manufacturing Sites = 692,700

Figure 1 Number of U.S. Manufacturing Sites

Focus on Manufacturing and Sales Operations

An ERP system supports multiple functional areas, including manufacturing and sales operations, accounting, and human resources. This book focuses on manufacturing and sales operations, which includes the engineering, cost accounting, procurement, production, sales and marketing, distribution, customer service, field service, and quality functions. While critical, the accounting and human resource applications within an ERP system fall outside the scope of this book and the author's areas of expertise and field experience. The book does cover integration points with these applications. Figure 2 illustrates the segmentation of major ERP applications and the book's focus on manufacturing and sales operations.

An ERP system provides transaction processing and a common database to model operations within a manufacturing firm, and supports several levels of decision making. Figure 2 illustrates the classic segmentation of levels of decision making. Operational planning and control, for example, involves scheduling material purchases, production, and sales order shipments. Strategic and tactical planning, on the other hand, involve developing game plans for each product (or product family) on the basis of actual or projected demands and constraints. These game plans drive supply chain activities in procurement, production, and distribution.

Modeling the operations within a manufacturing firm, such as defining the way products are really built and recording activities about demands and supplies, represents the basics of an ERP system. When done correctly, these provide the foundation of information for decision support. Many companies stumble

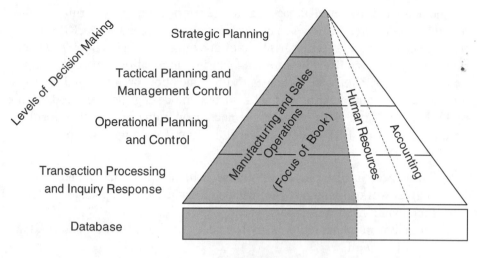

Segmentation of Major ERP Applications

Figure 2 ERP Systems and Decision-Making Framework

over these fundamentals, thereby limiting the usefulness with which an ERP system can support decisions.

A comprehensive treatment of ERP systems, especially the aspects of manufacturing and sales operations, should include several topics not covered in this book. These topics include the implementation process for an ERP system, considerations about the MIS function, and the impact of international business on ERP systems. Book length constrains coverage of these topics in a single volume.

Focus on ERP Software Packages for Smaller Manufacturers

A generalized ERP software package can handle a large proportion of information system requirements for the majority of smaller manufacturers, as confirmed by field experience in firms across many industries and manufacturing environments. An internally developed system offers the appeal of a tailored solution, but typically encounters problems with development expense (both initial and ongoing), technology upgrades and functional enhancements, and lack of integration, quality, documentation and support. There are also problems with some ERP software packages, such as dead-ended package (or vendor), software quality and support, out-of-date technology platform, and limited functionality (especially for manufacturing and sales operations). Too much functionality can also be a problem, especially when the system becomes too complex and requires extensive implementation assistance.

The baseline of understanding an ERP system is often gained through a previous ERP package implementation. This baseline has proven effective in how people learn and use an ERP package, where people employ a learning method termed *anchor and adjustment*. The explanation of a generalized ERP software package can provide a similar baseline of understanding. This book's explanations of a generalized design for manufacturing applications reflect a composite of current ERP software packages. It illustrates how an integrated ERP system models a manufacturing business, such as modeling the way products are really built and sold. This provides the anchor or frame of reference for those unfamiliar with an ERP system, and a straw man for comparison purposes to identify:

- Differences in ERP packages to model critical functionality, and suggest work-around or customized approaches when a package lacks functionality.
- Variations in manufacturing environments, and how they are modeled in an ERP system.
- The incremental impacts of new manufacturing practices and information technologies on ERP system functionality.
- Common problems (and their suggested solutions) in operations and ERP system usage.

The baseline of understanding represents the ground floor of a three-story building. The second story consists of taking action on common problems to improve system effectiveness. The third story consists if improving business practices and extending ERP applications to improve firm performance. Knowledgeable executives can focus on the second or third stories. But they often have to walk inexperienced members of their management team through the first (and second) stories to take action and improve practices.

Case Studies and Action Research on ERP System Usage

Explanations of ERP system usage need to reflect a contingency-based approach that accounts for variations in manufacturing environments and system capabilities. This book employs contingency-based frameworks to account for major variations, and provides illustrative case studies of both major and minor variations. It includes directly identified case studies, as well as indirectly referenced case studies embedded in sections labeled "common problems related to *x*," "other considerations related to *x*," and "variations in environments." In addition, major variations in system capabilities are highlighted as an "ERP design issue." The case studies draw on the author's firsthand experience across more than a thousand firms in various manufacturing environments.

Consulting engagements involve collaborative diagnosis and suggestions for organizational change that solve immediate practical problems. They also represent a form of action research, especially when the same diagnostic methodology is applied across hundreds of firms. The methodology employed by the author involved interviews with the most knowledgeable individuals and a focus on representative products to diagnose areas of ERP system usage. Multiple consulting engagements with the same firm provided opportunities for more in-depth analysis, and a longitudinal approach to action research. The book's coverage of major and minor variations in manufacturing environments and system capabilities reflects the frequency distributions of phenomena observed by the author.

In one of his humorous reflections on life, Ben Franklin once said, "I don't know how it is, but I meet with nobody but myself that's always in the right."[1] This book reflects a limited viewpoint that provides practical suggestions for maximizing your ERP system. Hopefully, they are mostly in the right.

[1]H. W. Brands, *The First American: The Life and Times of Benjamin Franklin,* New York: Anchor Books, 2000, p. 690.

Acknowledgments

Many people offered their time and expertise to review various sections of the book. In particular, I would like to thank Holly Bruce, Jon Chalmers, Tom Cory, Garth Geoghen, Greg Hillenbrand, Laura Hutter, Paul Kohler, Patty Martin, Jim Morrison, Ron Mussaw, Sid Perera, Dave Rorke, Terry Peterson, Tom Pick, John Pohl, Gary Rushlo, Mel Stuckey, and Jim Williams. My appreciation also applies to those involved in publishing the book, including Catherine Dassopoulos, Jan Degross, and Emily Autumn.

Maximizing Your ERP System

Part 1

Introduction

The benefits of an ERP (Enterprise Resource Planning) system justify significant investment by manufacturing firms. However, many firms do not achieve the potential benefits because of ineffective system usage. Suggestions for maximizing system usage depend on the manufacturing environment and system capabilities. This book provides diagnostic frameworks and practical suggestions for more effective system usage, particularly for smaller manufacturers.

The diagnosis of major variations in manufacturing environments and ERP system designs provides the starting point for a contingency approach to prescribing appropriate suggestions. The first chapter introduces several major variations that form the basis for subsequent suggestions in the rest of the book. It also includes a summarized explanation of an ERP system for coordinating supply chain activities.

The scope of ERP systems has evolved over time, where the evolution has been driven by new business practices and information technologies. The second chapter identifies several trends affecting manufacturers and describes the impact on ERP systems. The explanations highlight extensions to the basic ERP framework for management planning and control.

The initial and ongoing investments in an ERP system can be based on quantifiable bottom-line benefits as well as integrative effects. The third chapter describes the tangible and intangible benefits, and the costs, of an ERP system using illustrative examples of a smaller manufacturer.

Chapter 1

Overview

Most manufacturers do not effectively use their ERP (Enterprise Resource Planning) system to run the business. They do not achieve the potential benefits—quantifiable bottom-line benefits or intangible benefits—of their initial and on-going investment. In many ways, these manufacturers are paying more for the lack of effective systems, in measures that include excess inventory, excessive expediting, and poor customer service. These represent significant costs for ineffective ERP usage.

Variations in successful systems can be attributed to several critical success factors involving the implementation process and system usage. From a usage viewpoint, characteristics of an effective ERP system reflect the extent it

- defines the way each product is *really* built
- identifies *all independent demands* for products or (stated differently) explicitly defines customer requirements impacting supply chain activities
- defines *realistic* game plans and delivery promises
- provides schedules *actually used* to coordinate supply chain activities
- provides *correct* accounting of results and *useful* management information

The five characteristics cited above reflect the basics of running a manufacturing business: structuring the manufacturing database, developing sales and operations plans, processing sales orders, coordinating and executing activities to plan, and integrating systems and information. They also reflect the basic manufacturing equation: define what you plan to produce (the sales and operations plan), the resources you need (the bills of material and routings), and the resources you have (inventory and capacity), then determine what needs to be done (supply chain activities) to meet the plan and satisfy customer requirements.

Practical suggestions to maximize usage of an ERP system can be organized around these five characteristics. The suggestions are specifically addressed to the management team responsible for implementing and using the ERP system. While the suggestions apply to firms of any size, this book focuses on smaller manufacturers and autonomous plants of larger firms. These firms have unique attributes, such as a limited management team and a Management Information Systems (MIS) budget, affecting system implementation and usage.

Suggestions concerning ERP system usage depend on the manufacturing environment and the firm's particular system. Major variations in manufacturing environments and system design provide a framework for a contingency approach to suggested ERP usage. A diagnosis of major variations represents the first step in understanding how to maximize your ERP system.

Bridging the Theoretical and Detailed Viewpoints on ERP System Usage

Most textbooks, seminars, and business school curricula cover the theoretical viewpoints of ERP. Theoretical understanding, especially of the terminology and conceptual frameworks, is critical to effective usage of ERP systems. Many manufacturing executives lack a theoretical understanding of ERP, often exemplified in attempts to "replicate the way we currently do business." In contrast, ERP software vendors provide detailed viewpoints of system usage, typically embedded in the system's user manuals, training materials, online help, and work flows.

Detailed viewpoints reflect the underlying design of an ERP system. Each software package differs in implementing the terminology and conceptual frameworks, sometimes varying significantly from the theoretical viewpoints. This makes it more difficult to bridge the two viewpoints. One approach taken here highlights the key variations in design issues, and builds on the generally accepted approaches, to provide practical guidance for different situations. In particular, many situations require a contingency approach to usage suggestions.

Variations in Manufacturing Environments Affecting ERP System Usage

Much of the variation in manufacturing environments and ERP system usage can be attributed to several basic factors. These factors include the approach to defining products, the need to anticipate demands, the type of linkage between sales orders and supply orders, the extent of lean manufacturing practices, and the need for advanced scheduling capabilities. These basic factors provide a high degree of explanatory value in a contingency approach for suggestions on system usage. They reflect major factors—but not all factors—of consideration.

Approach to Defining Products: Standard Versus Custom Product

ERP systems employ two basic approaches to defining a product: a standard product approach and a custom product approach. Many manufacturers require both approaches to defining their products, reflecting a mixed-mode environment.

- ◆ *Standard Product.* A standard product has an item master record, and a predefined bill of material and routing for a manufactured item. A standard product approach applies to items with repeat requirements and inventory.

♦ *Custom Product.* A custom product has a single item master record (identified as a custom product or model item) that serves as the starting point for defining configurations. Each configuration is normally defined in the context of a quotation or sales order line item. The custom product approach applies to items with one-time requirements (or combinations of many predefined options) and no requirement for inventory.

The approach for modeling a specific product may not be clearcut or it may change over time. For example, the standard product approach can be used to model a custom product with limited combinations of options or with requirements for forecasting and stocking a particular configuration. A custom product approach may be used in the prototype phases of building a standard product item, with a switch in approach after stabilization of product designs. A standard product may evolve into many variations, which can be modeled as options of a custom product. The choice of approach may be constrained by capabilities within an ERP system. Limited capabilities for custom products, for example, may involve single-level configurations and lack of inventory visibility on completed configurations.

The choice of defining a product using a standard or custom product approach impacts every aspect of ERP system usage. Beyond the differences in the manufacturing database, it impacts sales and operations planning, sales order processing, the nature of supply orders for coordinating supply chain activities, and cost accounting.

Production Strategies and the Need to Anticipate Demands

Production strategies reflect the extent to which material supplies must anticipate actual demands. They are typically categorized into make-to-stock or make-to-order. Make-to-stock only applies to standard products, whereas make-to-order applies to both standard and custom products. Variations of the make-to-order production strategy reflect the delivery lead-time to produce an item from stocked material. Figure 1.1 illustrates variations in production strategies in terms of delivery lead-time, which reflects the elapsed time between sales order entry and delivery at the customer ship-to location. An item's delivery lead-time may encompass segments of design, procurement, production, and shipping lead-times in the cumulative manufacturing lead-time.

Make-to-Stock (MTS) A make-to-stock item reflects a standard product already designed and in finished goods inventory in anticipation of actual demands. The item can be shipped immediately upon entry of a sales order. Delivery lead-time can be as short as the shipping lead-time, typically consisting of the shipping preparation time plus transportation time.

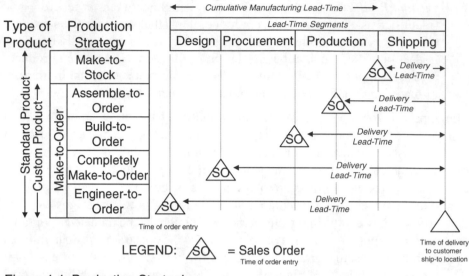

Figure 1.1 Production Strategies

Make-to-Order (MTO) A make-to-order item reflects a standard or custom product only produced upon entry of a sales order. Variations of the make-to-order strategy involve two factors: the level of stocked components and visibility of the item's sales order backlog.

- *Assemble-to-Order (or Configure-to-Order).* Purchased materials and manufactured intermediates are replenished in advance of actual demand. Sales orders drive the remaining production activities, typically consisting of final assembly or finishing operations.
- *Build-to-Order.* Only purchased materials are replenished in advance of actual demand. Sales orders drive the production activities of the item.
- *Completely Make-to-Order.* Nothing is replenished in advance of actual demand. Sales orders drive production and procurement activities since the sales order backlog exceeds the cumulative manufacturing lead-time of the item.
- *Engineer-to-Order.* Sales orders drive the product design and the subsequent procurement and production activities.

The term make-to-order refers to all four variations. Shorter delivery lead-times stemming from just-in-time (JIT) and lean manufacturing practices facilitate make-to-order production strategies.

The need to anticipate demands must consider visibility of the sales order backlog and the appropriate planning horizon for an item. The shortest planning horizon for material represents the cumulative manufacturing lead-time for a saleable item. Resource requirements, such as equipment, people skills, head count, facilities, and finances, generally require a longer planning horizon. Forecasts provide one method of anticipating demand; demand variations may be anticipated using inventory plans. Other methods of anticipating demand for stocked material include order point logic and/or Kanban inventory.

The choice of an item's production strategy has an incremental impact on ERP system usage. It primarily impacts the sales and operations planning process and the definition of appropriate supply and demand management policies for the item.

Linkage between Supply Orders and Sales Orders for Make-to-Order Items

A make-to-order production strategy involves an additional consideration: the need for direct linkage between a sales order and its supply order(s). A custom product, for example, requires direct linkage between the sales order and the supply order to build the configuration. With direct linkage for a manufactured configuration, a sales order typically has one custom product manufacturing order that is automatically updated by changes to the sales order quantity, date, or configuration. The changes can also automatically update multiple linked supply orders in a multilevel configuration.

Supply orders for a make-to-order standard product may involve direct linkage or indirect linkage to a sales order.

- *Indirect Linkage.* MRP (materials requirement planning) logic uses indirect linkage so that one supply order may cover the demands for one or more sales orders. The supply order due date is indirectly linked to the sales order ship dates. The suggested order quantity reflects lot-sizing considerations in MRP logic. With indirect linkage, pegging information identifies the relationship between supply chain activities and customer demand.
- *Direct Linkage.* Direct linkage ignores MRP logic. As a general rule, one final assembly manufacturing order covers one sales order. Changes to the sales order quantity or date result in automatic updates to the manufacturing order; they may also update multiple linked supply orders for make-to-order components. Direct linkage provides visibility of customer demand to supply chain activities.

The concept of direct linkage for standard products has been implemented differently in ERP systems. One approach identifies the need for direct linkage in the item master; another designates the need for direct linkage on the sales order line item. One approach automatically creates directly linked supply orders; another allows manual assignment to an existing supply order. Some ERP systems support only a single-level direct linkage; others support multilevel linkage. Some systems only support direct linkage; others only support indirect linkage.

Forecasts can be used to anticipate demands for make-to-order standard products, regardless of linkage approach. That means forecasted demands for a make-to-order item blow through to the level of stocked components, whereas actual demands result in supply orders. These supply orders may be automatically generated based on direct linkage to a sales order, or suggested on the basis of indirect linkage.

The need for direct linkage has an incremental impact on ERP system usage. It primarily impacts the supply management policies for an item and the nature of the final assembly schedule for make-to-order standard products.

Extent of JIT and Lean Manufacturing Practices

Just-in-time and lean manufacturing practices focus on simplifying operations and reduced lead-times, with the flexibility to support make-to-order production strategies. These practices typically involve changes in factory layout that simplify material flow and routing operations (often reflected in dedicating a manufacturing cell to each product family) resulting in reduced manufacturing cycle time. They may also entail orderless coordination of supply chain activity using Kanbans (or other signals) rather than orders, schedules, and action messages.

With an orderless environment, the Kanban trigger and quantity can be directly linked to sales orders (for noninventoried items) or indirectly linked to demands for replenishing inventory of standard products. An item's Kanban trigger and replenishment quantity can be automatically updated based on the dynamically calculated projected daily usage quantities. Production completions result in backflushing of materials and resources, while supplier receipts represent releases against blanket purchase orders. The accounting of results focuses on actual versus planned production rates, and possibly period costing.

Most firms involved in orderless manufacturing also require some order-based coordination capabilities. They may be just starting implementation or have partial implementations with a subset of the factory and products. Certain activities require order-based coordination, such as custom product configurations, new product development, and repairs, even in completely orderless environments.

JIT and lean practices still require effective sales and operations planning, and realistic game plans and delivery promises. Each game plan reflects changing demand patterns and constraints, and drives supply chain activities using Kanbans to represent master schedules and final assembly schedules.

Need for Advanced Scheduling Capabilities

More advanced scheduling capabilities tend to be required when the manufacturing environment involves dynamic changes, multiple scheduling constraints, or more complex scheduling rules.

- *Stability of Manufacturing Environment.* Stability reflects the number and size of near-term changes in demands and available capacity.
- *Number of Scheduling Constraints.* Scheduling constraints may focus on a single manufacturing process (the pacemaker or bottleneck resource) or encompass multiple resources and multiple parallel legs.
- *Complexity of Scheduling Rules.* Scheduling rules may optimize sequencing based on setup considerations, resource capabilities, or other factors. Even a single manufacturing process can have complex scheduling rules.

The need for advanced scheduling capabilities is directly affected by the extent of JIT and lean manufacturing practices. These work simplification efforts may result in short manufacturing cycle times, a reduced number of scheduling constraints, and elimination of complex scheduling rules. For example, simplified scheduling rules (such as lead-time offsets) may be used for nonconstrained production resources, with inventory buffers at constrained resources to avoid production disruptions. In other cases, scheduling of supply chain activities involves the calculation of Kanban triggers and replenishment quantities, and releases to production within the limits of production rates.

Basic scheduling capabilities are often built into MRP logic. Calculations of variable lead-times on manufacturing orders, for example, reflect simple models of available capacity and linear scheduling of operation sequences using infinite loading. MRP logic may generate daily schedules reflecting simple rate-based scheduling assumptions. The planning fence for an item represents an approximation of constraints for planned orders. Available-to-promise logic provides a simple form of forward finite scheduling for making sales order delivery promises. Simple capable-to-promise logic, reflecting variable lead-time calculations, also provides a form of forward finite scheduling.

Other Variations in Manufacturing Environments

Other factors contributing to variations in manufacturing environments include project manufacturing and multisite operations. Project manufacturing capabilities provide one method to support multilevel linkage between demands and supplies. Multisite operations may have coordination requirements ranging from the simple to complex. At one end of the spectrum, a company with autonomous manufacturing plants simply requires a consolidated general ledger. At the other end of the spectrum, a company with a network of distribution centers fed by manufacturing plants requires much greater system functionality.

Other variations in environments reflect the extent to which a firm has embraced the trends affecting manufacturing and ERP. In addition to lean manufacturing, these trends include customer-oriented strategies, virtual manufacturing, e-business, and supply chain management initiatives.

Design Issues That Affect ERP System Usage

Usage of an ERP system is shaped (and limited) by the system design. The primary engine for coordinating supply chain activities represents one of the most critical design issues. Other design issues are more subtle and embedded in the system. Some of the major differences in system design, designated "ERP design issues," are highlighted in breakout boxes throughout the book. The design of a system can make it easier to use and implement, impacting the economic justification for ERP investment.

Primary Engine for Supply Chain Coordination

The design of most ERP systems involves several software programs to coordinate supply chain activities. Separate programs may be used to calculate material and capacity requirements and to suggest recommended actions for production, procurement, distribution, customer service, quality and cost accounting. Other programs may be used to perform finite scheduling, calculate backflushing, and handle closures of supply orders, sales orders, and shipments. Still other programs may be used to calculate production and vendor schedules, daily usage rates and Kanban replenishment signals, and anticipated expirations of lots, purchase contracts, and sales quotations.

The primary engine for coordinating supply chain activities typically includes MRP logic. A narrow viewpoint of MRP logic focuses on calculations related to material requirements planning for order-based manufacturing environments. A broader viewpoint of MRP logic encompasses calculations for all of the issues mentioned above. A bill of resources approach to routing data, for example, enables MRP logic to calculate both material and capacity requirements. Other capabilities can be incorporated in MRP logic to handle orderless manufacturing, rate-based scheduling, custom products, and basic scheduling capabilities.

Even with a broader viewpoint, the term *MRP logic* is too limiting to describe the primary engine for coordinating supply chain activities. The primary engine involves several ERP design issues and can be supplemented by event managers, work flows, and other applications.

Illustrations of ERP Design Issues That Affect Usage

Philosophical differences in ERP designs become apparent in how a system supports different types of manufacturing environments. Several differences have already been covered, such as the ability to support standard and custom products, direct and indirect linkage in supply orders, order-based and orderless manufacturing, project manufacturing, and multisite operations. Design issues impacting how to structure the manufacturing database, for example, include the following:

- Item identification and the significance of revision levels and multiple units of measure
- Bills of material definitions based on an operation-centric versus a material centric approach, and the approach to managing bill changes (e.g., component date effectivity versus parent revision level effectivity)
- Routing definitions based on a bill of resources versus a separate routing data approach, and modeling available capacity using simplistic versus comprehensive approaches
- Managing external production using a subcontract item versus outside operation approach
- Variations of replenishment methods, such as the support for fixed versus dynamic daily usage rates, fixed versus variable lead times on manufacturing orders, MRP versus rate-based scheduling logic, and order-based versus orderless (Kanban) replenishment
- Product costing using a standard versus an actual costing approach
- Handling inventory of custom product configurations, supporting multilevel configurations, and storing custom product configurations in separate files (versus the item master and bill of material files)

Variations of philosophical differences in ERP software packages can frequently be traced to their origins, such a standard versus custom product orientation. Differing design philosophies within the same ERP system may emerge as it matures. Internal inconsistencies in system design often reflect a "design by committee" or "bolt-on capability."

Trends and the Impact on ERP System Design

The scope of ERP systems has evolved over time. The evolution has been driven by the emergence of new business practices and information technologies. These business practices include supply chain management, customer-oriented strategies and customer relationship management (CRM), just-in-time (JIT) and lean manufacturing, virtual manufacturing, and "demassified" multisite operations. Information technologies affecting ERP include e-commerce, computer integrated manufacturing (CIM), and advanced planning and scheduling (APS). These driving forces or trends represent natural extensions to an ERP system rather than replacements, since they build on the basic ERP framework for management planning and control. New terms are often coined to reflect these extensions, such as ERP II and ECM (electronic commerce management). ERP will be used as a broad umbrella term throughout this book.

Focus on ERP Usage in Small Manufacturers

Characteristics of smaller manufacturers, and autonomous sites of larger firms, affect the nature of ERP system usage and implementation. Firms with 25 to 250 employees can be considered smaller manufacturers, and these firms often operate as a single site. Smaller manufacturers can be characterized by the feasible time period for a complete ERP implementation (less than 6 months), the number of MIS personnel (less than five people), the number of buyers and planners (less than five), and the size of the executive team (less than 20).

Smaller firms are often characterized by a lack of internal expertise in MIS and ERP, and by budgetary constraints on ERP expenditures. The lack of expertise necessitates an ERP system with a simpler design. Budgetary constraints necessitate a reasonably priced ERP software package running on standardized hardware, minimal software customization, and minimal external assistance. One measure of system complexity is the ratio between expenditures on external assistance (for consulting and training) and the software package purchase price, where the ratio should be less than one. Ratios greater than one reflect greater complexity in the ERP software package.

Smaller firms generally have the same requirements as larger firms for modeling the manufacturing enterprise and coordinating supply chain activities. However, their size generally means that most firms do not have a network of distribution centers or field service offices. Their position within their industry and their purchasing volumes often make procurement EDI (electronic data interchange) unnecessary.

Overview of an ERP System

The basic architecture for an ERP system consists of 12 business functions utilizing a common manufacturing database, as shown in Figure 1.2. This top-down model shows how aggregate plans (the business, sales, and production plans) drive the detailed plans for coordinating supply chain activities. The accounting function tracks the financial implications of supply chain activities. The common database master files and the 12 functions are described briefly here and explained further in subsequent chapters.

Common Manufacturing Database

Each business function builds on the foundations of a common manufacturing database. The heart of the common database consists of several master files about customers, vendors, products, inventory locations, and general ledger accounts. Information about products is particularly relevant for further explanation, since it models many aspects of the manufacturing enterprise.

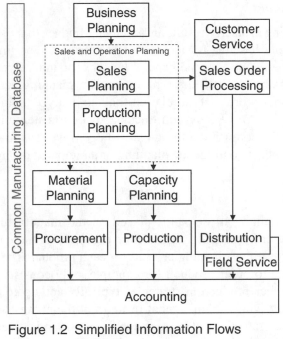

Figure 1.2 Simplified Information Flows
for ERP

Product data about standard products consists of master files about items, bills of material, resources, and routings. The item master identifies every standard product, from raw materials to saleable end items. Bills of material reflect the product design. Bill information gets used for product costing, material planning, material usage reporting, lot tracking, and stages of manufacturing. Planning bills can be used for forecasting and production planning of standard products. The resource master identifies each internal resource used in the manufacturing process, such as machines, manufacturing cells, labor, and tools, and information about costs, capacity, and scheduling characteristics. It may also identify external resources such as subcontractors. Routings reflect the process design of internal and outside operations, and routing information is used for product costing, capacity planning, production scheduling, labor and machine reporting, and shop floor tracking.

Product data about custom products consists of configurations and planning bills. A custom product configuration is normally defined in the context of a quotation or sales order. It defines a one-time bill of material and routing that gets used for costing and pricing and the other purposes cited above (such as material and capacity planning, scheduling, and so forth). Planning bills can be used for forecasting and production planning of custom product components, as well as option selection to create a configuration.

Business Planning

Business planning typically results in an annual budget that establishes the financial plan and a baseline for measurement purposes. The financial plan, for example, may be defined for the general ledger accounts representing revenue and cost of sales by product line. These financial planning activities typically employ spreadsheets or other simulation tools to analyze assumptions and the impact on budgets. An ERP system tracks actual costs stemming from supply chain activities for comparison to budget. Budget revisions may be developed periodically to reflect contingency planning or anticipated changes.

Sales Planning

Sales planning defines all demands placed on the manufacturing enterprise, both actual sales orders and forecasts. These demands form the primary input to the sales and operations planning process for each product. The sales plan for a completely make-to-order product, for example, only consists of sales orders. Products with other production strategies typically anticipate actual demands using forecasts, driving replenishment of items at the highest stocking level in the product structure. Sales orders consume forecasts, and demand management policies govern interactions between actual and forecasted demands. Inventory plans can be used to anticipate demand variability. Product families and planning bills support aggregate forecasts and inventory plans related to standard and custom products.

Production Planning

Production planning provides a game plan for each product that coordinates supply chain activities to meet demands. The approach to formulating each game plan is contingent on the type of product and production strategy, and the nature of supply orders for make-to-order products. A product's game plan consists of master schedules for stocked items and final assembly schedules for make-to-order items and configurations. Coordination efforts in production and procurement typically focus on supply orders, while efforts in distribution, field service, and customer service focus on sales orders.

Production planning formulates realistic game plans based on analyzing constraints identified by capacity and material planning. Infinite capacity planning identifies potential overloaded periods requiring adjustments to capacity or loads. Material planning identifies potential shortages requiring expediting. Finite scheduling (accounting for capacity and material constraints) may be used to identify potentially late or impossible deliveries to meet demands. A production plan (or rate) may be used to represent aggregate available capacity, such as a dedicated manufacturing cell producing all items within a product family.

Each game plan provides the basis for making delivery promises. Availability for a make-to-stock product, for example, is reflected in its inventory and master schedule. Availability for a make-to-order product is reflected in its stocked components, production capacity, and possibly the uncommitted production plan as an aggregate measure of available resources. Sales orders consume availability.

Sales Order Processing

A key step in sales order processing—accept order—captures actual demands, whatever the format of order entry (ranging from manual entry by internal personnel to electronic transfer). Other steps involve configuring the order (such as the configuration for a custom product), making delivery promises, and monitoring order status. It may involve quotations (especially custom products and sourcing in multisite firms).

Sales order designations may affect an item's demands and supply chain activities. For example, a sales order may be designated as cancelled or hold, or as an addition to forecast. It may involve allocations, shipment authorization, or a final assembly designation for direct linkage with a supply order.

Sales order entry can trigger communication of needed actions to other functional areas. These include actions for distribution (to ship product), manufacturing (to final assemble products), procurement (to purchase material), field service (to perform service tasks), and customer service (to review holds).

Customer Service

The scope of customer service extends across the entire customer relationship life cycle, covering every customer contact. Several key events across the life cycle, such as quotations, sales orders, shipments, and returned goods, represent basic transactions in an ERP system. Recommended actions for customer service include reviewing quotations about to expire, sales orders exceeding availability or placed on hold, and past-due shipments. Other required activities for customer service (stemming from customer contacts and support incidents) include followup calls, meetings, and sending requested information. These activities are often coordinated through a customer relationship management (CRM) system.

Capacity Planning

Capacity planning can be used to support sales and operations planning (to make game plans realistic) and production scheduling. Infinite capacity planning uses proposed schedules (extended by routing information) to calculate loads and identify potential overloaded periods for each resource. In overloaded situations, the courses of action include increasing available capacity (by overtime, additional equipment and personnel, and other measures) or reducing loads (by rescheduling, alternate operations, and other measures). Finite capacity planning, also termed *finite scheduling,* treats the available capacity as a given constraint to identify late and unscheduled orders.

Material Planning

Material planning is based on the master schedules and final assembly schedules for each game plan. It calculates material requirements based on the bills of material, and suggests changes to existing supply orders or new planned supply orders (reflecting item planning parameters). It communicates recommended actions to planners and buyers, and provides the basis for production and vendor schedules (or Kanbans), to synchronize supplies to meet demands.

Procurement

Procurement involves identifying and qualifying vendors, as well as negotiating agreements. Procurement may start with requests for quotes. The vendor agreement may be formalized as a purchase contract or a blanket purchase order. The supplier relationship may involve close working ties that focus on quality at the source, thereby eliminating receiving inspection.

Procurement also involves daily coordination of external suppliers, through purchase orders and vendor schedules, to align supplies with demands. Procurement activities involve different types of purchases, from normal and subcontracted standard products to outside operations and those related to custom product configurations. The approach to procurement activities is contingent on the type of purchase. Daily coordination can also be accomplished through visible replenishment techniques such as Kanbans.

Receiving activities encompass purchase order receipts and other types of receipts. The receiving activities vary slightly by type of purchase, such as receiving a standard product item into inventory (or receiving inspection) versus receiving an outside operation or nonstock material into work-in-process (for a custom product configuration). Receipt transactions provide the basis for measuring vendor performance (in terms of delivery, quality, and price), and automatically building a buy-card history.

Production

Production and production activity control involve daily coordination of internal resources through a production schedule and manufacturing orders to align supplies with demands. Production activities involve different types of manufacturing orders, from normal orders (with indirect linkage) to custom product and final assembly orders (with direct linkage to sales orders). Coordination can also be accomplished through daily schedules or visible replenishment techniques such as Kanbans. The approach to coordination and execution of production activities is contingent on the type of production. For example, a normal manufacturing order must be received into inventory whereas a custom product manufacturing order can be shipped from work-in-process (due to direct linkage).

A manufacturing order defines the quantity and dates for producing an item. On a given order, the order-dependent bill and routing may be modified to reflect material substitutions or alternate operations. Material usage and labor and resource expenditures are reported against the manufacturing order. As an alternative to picking material components prior to starting production, the materials (and resources) may be auto-deducted after completion of an operation or receipt of the parent item. Reporting actual material and resource consumption provides the basis for measuring progress, efficiencies, and actual costs. Actual costs can be compared to standard costs for calculating variances for standard products or for calculating profitability on a custom product configuration.

A production schedule (or dispatch list) coordinates operations performed at each resource, and identifies the parent item and order. A router or traveler (of detailed process instructions for each operation) can also serve as a coordination tool, especially in custom product environments.

Quality management considerations related to production are frequently expressed in factors for item yield, component scrap percentages, or operation yield percentages. Quality considerations may also mandate lot-trace and serial-trace requirements, as well as receiving inspection requirements.

Distribution

Distribution focuses on outbound shipments for sales orders, including packaging, shipping, and transportation activities, that represent the completion of supply chain activities. This typically involves a sales order packing list, a bill of lading and package labels (for the shipment), and an invoice. The approach to these distribution activities is contingent on the type of sales order. For example, standard products may have standard pack sizes and require advanced ship notices (ASN) with bar-code labels for shipment from inventory. A custom product configuration may specify packaging variations and be shipped from work-in-process. Distribution may also be involved with shipments related to purchase orders, such as sending supplied material to subcontractors or returns to vendor.

Variations in distribution environments include sales order allocations, special orders, truck-loading considerations, drop-shipments, and specialized documents.

Field Service

Field service involves daily coordination of personnel to perform field service tasks driven by sales order demands. Service work orders and schedules provide coordination of field service activities. A service work order identifies the required resources, material, tools, and documents needed to perform the task, although some cases require after-the-fact identification. Reporting actual material and resource consumption provides the basis for measuring actual costs and comparison to planned costs. Reporting completion of the service work order can trigger invoicing.

Accounting

Accounting uses shipment data for generating invoices, receipt data for validating vendor invoices, labor data for payroll, and costed manufacturing transactions for updating the general ledger and tracking actual costs versus budget. From a cost accounting viewpoint, the cost of sales for a given shipment typically reflects standard costs for a standard product and actual costs for a custom product. Variances can also be calculated for standard product items, including manufacturing variances and purchase price variances.

Organizing Focus of the Book

The book is organized into eight parts. The "Introduction" includes three chapters providing an overview of ERP, the trends impacting ERP applications, and the economic justification for investing (and reinvesting) in an ERP system.

The second part explains approaches to "Structuring the Manufacturing Database" with an integrative viewpoint for both standard and custom products. It addresses how to define the way each product is really built. Five chapters are devoted to standard products, covering items, bills of material, routings, planning data, and product costing. A sixth chapter covers custom products, and builds on the concepts explained in the previous chapters. This segmentation reflects an integrative viewpoint rather than a bias toward standard products.

The third part uses an integrative framework for explaining a contingency approach to "Sales and Operations Planning" for different manufacturing environments. It addresses how to define realistic game plans and delivery promises and includes three chapters. The first chapter covers the prerequisites of identifying demands and demand management, the second summarizes the integrative framework illustrated by two case studies, and the third provides additional case studies.

The fourth part covers "Sales Management" with two chapters about sales order processing and customer service. It addresses how to explicitly define customer requirements impacting supply chain activities.

The fifth part covers "Executing Supply Chain Activities," reflecting the emphasis of this book on supply chain management. It addresses how schedules are actually used to coordinate supply chain activities. It contains six chapters covering procurement, inventory control, production, distribution, field services, and quality. The quality chapter summarizes practical implications of quality concerns across the entire ERP system.

The sixth part covers "Accounting and Reporting" with a focus on the financial impacts of sales and operations. It contains two chapters about cost accounting and management reporting, and addresses how to provide correct accounting and useful management information.

The seventh part covers "Variations in Manufacturing Environments," which extends the explanations of basic ERP for single-site operations to other environments. It contains chapters about managing multisite operations and project manufacturing.

The concluding part summarizes the significance of a contingency approach to ERP systems for various audiences.

Chapter 2

Trends Affecting
Manufacturers and ERP

The evolution of ERP systems has been driven by the emergence of new business practices and information technologies. These have been supported by the growing maturity of the manufacturing profession, and by the evolving development of commercially available software packages.

New business practices include supply chain management, customer-oriented strategies and customer relationship management (CRM), just-in-time (JIT) and lean manufacturing, virtual manufacturing, and "demassified" multisite operations. These new business practices sometimes represent a reformulation and synthesis of previous ideas, or current themes in the literature. New information technologies include e-commerce, computer integrated manufacturing (CIM), and advanced planning and scheduling (APS).

The commercially available software packages reflect variations in origins and orientation, as well as software maturity. Although progress has been made to standardize vocabulary and conceptual frameworks for generally-accepted manufacturing practices, the underlying design of each ERP software package reflects wide variations in interpretation of these practices.

Supply Chain Management

Supply chain management (SCM) emphasizes the need to model the manufacturing enterprise from the perspective of the supply chain in order to synchronize supplies with demands and respond to change. An ERP system provides the tools to model various supply chain scenarios. The supply chain model for a particular manufacturing enterprise reflects the company's product and industry and its position within the supply chain. Supply chain models range from simple to complex. The two supply chain models shown in Figure 2.1 help illustrate the impact on an ERP system.

+ *Simple Model.* The simple manufacturing enterprise buys items from external suppliers and internally produces items for direct sale and shipment to customers. The ERP system must handle buy and make items at a single-site operation.

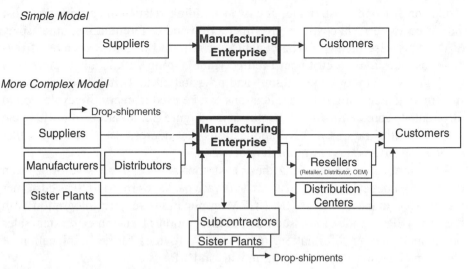

Figure 2.1 Supply Chain Models

◆ *More Complex Model.* The complex manufacturing enterprise buys items from external suppliers, authorized distributors, and sister plants. In addition to internally produced items, it supplies components for external production at subcontractors and sister plants. It sells and ships products direct to customers and through multiple sales channels, such as resellers, distributors, and original equipment manufacturers (OEMs). It involves multiple sites, with inventory at distribution centers replenished from manufacturing plants. Sales orders can be shipped from designated sites, requiring visibility of available inventory across the distribution network. Items may also be drop-shipped from subcontractor sites.

Initiatives in supply chain management have created other requirements for ERP applications. For example, an ERP system must handle inventory stocked at customer sites and supplier's material stocked at the manufacturing enterprise.

The supply chain perspective has helped expand the scope of ERP beyond coordination of internal production activities to align supplies with demands. On the demand side, supply chain management concepts intersect with the philosophy of customer-oriented strategies and e-business.

Customer-Oriented Strategies and CRM

ERP applications have evolved to cover the entire spectrum of customer service, beginning with the customer's initial contact with the firm. It continues through product acquisition and ends when the customer terminates product usage. The steps in the customer relationship follow a predictable pattern, termed the *customer relationship life cycle.*

Customer-oriented strategies focus on building relationships with the most valued customers via cost-effective interaction and differentiating some aspect of the enterprise behavior. The benefits are reflected in future streams of revenue (as measured by customer lifetime value), along with loyalty, referrals, a willingness to pay price premiums, and a hesitation to switch to competitors. Information technology (IT) applications can be used in every life cycle step to differentiate interactions with the customer. Figure 2.2 identifies the life cycle steps with illustrations of ERP applications that address each step. Note that some applications support more than one step.

ERP applications addressing these customer service steps have often been developed independently, such as the software packages referred to as customer relationship management (CRM). CRM applications require integration with the other ERP applications, such as the integration of customer master, sales order, and product information. (Chapter 14 provides further explanation of CRM applications and its integration with an ERP system.)

A customer-oriented strategy can also be employed when the customer and manufacturer are closely linked in a partner relationship. The customer benefits from improved customer service, a reliable source of supply, and possibly lower costs. Lower costs may be achieved because of cost efficiencies, and the long-term commitments expressed in extended contracts and stable demand patterns.

Life Cycle Step	Illustration of ERP Application	
1 Initial Contact	Lead Tracking	
2 Establish Requirements	Quotation Rules-Based Configurator Sales Forecast Customer Schedule	
	For Product	*For Service*
3 Process Sales Order	Product Availability Sourcing (Ship-From)	Service Availability
4 Coordinate Supply	Production Schedule Procurement Schedule Distribution Schedule	Service Delivery Schedule
5 Ship or Deliver Item	Ship Product Shipment Status	Deliver Service Delivery Status
6 Integrate/Monitor Usage	Track Customer Inventory	Field Installation Services Phone Support Services
7 Upgrade and Maintain	Spare Parts	Field Maintenance Services
8 Transfer or Dispose	Warranty Tracking Returned Goods Rentals/Leases, Loaners	Service Agreement Tracking
9 Accounting	Invoice and Payment Account and Project Status	

Figure 2.2 ERP Applications across the Customer Relationship Life Cycle

JIT and Lean Manufacturing

A just-in-time (JIT) or lean manufacturing strategy focuses on simplifying operations and eliminating waste and promotes a flexible manufacturing organization that can produce to exact customer demand. This has also been termed a *demand-pull* or *flow manufacturing strategy*. To be successful, a JIT approach requires several changes in business structure, responsibility, and processes. A JIT approach also requires changes in an ERP system, such as the applications for product and process design, demand management, production, procurement, and cost accounting.

JIT Impact on Product and Process Design

Changes to factory layout are reflected in definitions of new resources, such as a manufacturing cell, assembly line, or other group of people or equipment. These resources have different cost structures and routing operation times. Changes to routings include date effectivities for phasing in factory layout changes, faster run rates reflecting process improvements, and elimination of inspection operations and setup time. Changes in process design often result in significantly reduced production lead-times (e.g., from weeks to days or even hours), thereby impacting approaches to sales and operations planning and to production scheduling.

An ERP system requires new replenishment methods to support JIT approaches to replenishment. A dynamically calculated daily usage rate, for example, provides the basis for Kanban replenishment quantities and trigger points. These may be expressed in electronic signals, or visual signals such as empty containers or Kanban cards.

JIT Impact on Demand Management

Demands within ERP—stemming from sales orders, forecasts, and inventory plans—can be used to calculate the projected daily usage rates for stocked items. This demand rate (also called takt time) can fluctuate over time, requiring a dynamic daily usage rate. Sales orders trigger production of make-to-order items. In the simplest form of JIT, you only enter sales orders and record shipments, where the shipments trigger auto-deduction of material components and resource usage.

JIT Impact on Production

A JIT production environment often synchronizes production activities using replenishment signals, thereby eliminating traditional coordination tools such as manufacturing orders, production schedules, and recommended planner actions. In this orderless environment, visual or electronic signals communicate the need for replenishment of stocked items and for make-to-order items. Completions can result in auto-deduction of materials and resources.

The simplification efforts typically simplify the nature of production scheduling, especially when production lead-times (or manufacturing cycle times) can be reduced to hours (or days). In many cases, production of various items within a product family involves a single linear flow and a single constraining resource or pacemaker. Previous upstream activities are paced accordingly and production operates at a continuous flow. The production rate (or work released to production) should match the demand rate. An inventory buffer or time buffer is typically defined for the pacemaker resource to ensure continuous operation.

Most firms involved in JIT manufacturing require ERP applications that can support both orderless and order-based production. These firms are just starting JIT implementations, or have partial JIT implementations with a subset of the factory and products. Even manufacturers with complete JIT implementations may have some order-based activities, such as custom product configurations, engineering projects, new product development, and repairs.

JIT Impact on Procurement

JIT can also synchronize procurement activities using electronic or visual replenishment signals. For example, the supplier may access his version of an electronic Kanban board to coordinate replenishment. A vendor schedule can be used to communicate long-range requirements to a supplier.

CASE STUDY A JIT Demand-Pull Scenario

An industrial products manufacturer initiated its JIT efforts by constructing a manufacturing cell for producing similar products that were a subset of all items being produced. It also had a dedicated feeder line producing an intermediate item. As shown in Figure 2.3, suppliers replenished floor stock inventory for the manufacturing cell and feeder line based on electronically communicated Kanbans. The end-item gets produced to actual sales orders, and the shipment transaction backflushes floor-stock material based on the end-item's bill of material.

An interdisciplinary product team took responsibility for all products built in the manufacturing cell. These responsibilities included all supply chain activities, from product/process design to supplier relationships and customer requirements. For example, this team coordinated work simplification efforts for internal production (and defined the corresponding bill and routing information), and established Kanban replenishment with suppliers for floor stock inventory (and defined the appropriate item planning parameters). They also defined the demand rates and production rates.

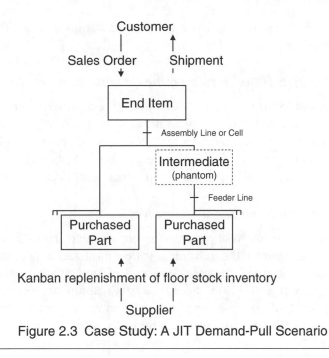

Figure 2.3 Case Study: A JIT Demand-Pull Scenario

ERP and Virtual Manufacturing

Virtual manufacturers contract with suppliers for outsourcing almost all manufacturing activities. A virtual manufacturer takes responsibility for the complete product design for documentation and costing purposes. Depending on the scenario, the bill defines reference information for a buy complete item, the supplied material for a subcontract item, or the internal production activities for a make item.

These bills can be used for cost rollup and material planning calculations. Other impacts on an ERP system include tracking kits of components as well as direct-ship components to the subcontractor. Multiple levels of subcontractors may be used. The ERP system may need to recognize different costs for an item stocked in two locations, handle sales orders that designate the ship-from location, and communicate shipping requirements to the different locations.

Demassified Multisite Operations

Many firms with multisite operations are adopting a management bias toward small autonomous business units, rather than a large centrally managed organization. These thrusts to demassify the organization have been coupled with efforts to push decision making down in the organization, empower the local management team, reduce corporate staff, and eliminate layers of management.

Associated with this general trend is decentralization of the ERP systems and the MIS function.

The Advantages of Decentralizing the Organization

The movement to smaller plants has an objective of fostering an entrepreneurial spirit and ownership within the plant management and employees. The smaller size reduces bureaucracy. Decisions are delegated to personnel who best understand the local operation and can create the best solutions to problems in the shortest time. Decentralizing helps middle managers become profit-oriented.

Decentralizing Information Systems for ERP

The availability of low-cost easy-to-implement micro-based ERP systems has enabled and accelerated the movement to decentralize. Compared to mainframe centralized applications, these systems can be implemented faster and at less cost. Less MIS expertise is required for system administration and end-user decision support tools (such as spreadsheets and report writers) make users less dependent on MIS staff for customizations. In particular, an autonomous ERP system fosters the sense of ownership within plant management, giving them greater control of the tools to plan and control their business. Standalone ERP applications work best in autonomous manufacturing sites with minimum coordination between sites. They may be deployed at remote sites of larger firms, such as an offshore manufacturing plant. A standalone ERP application facilitates the acquisition and divestiture of an autonomous site, since the system and site stay together. With a centralized ERP system, a newly acquired unit must convert from an existing information system to a system that meets central specifications. Divesting a business unit using a centralized ERP system creates issues for ongoing system usage at the divested site.

E-Business (or E-Commerce)

An ERP system provides the foundation for many electronic business applications, termed *e-business* or *e-commerce* applications. E-business applications differ slightly between business-to-business and business-to-consumer relationships.

- Business-to-consumer (termed B2C) relationships do not generally involve negotiation and collaboration. One example involves an online catalog of standard products, or custom products with predefined options, with fixed prices. Orders are often placed by one-time customers, with payment by credit card.
- Business-to-business (termed B2B) relationships generally involve negotiation and collaboration, covering issues such as product specifications,

delivery, and price. One example involves an electronic marketplace or trading exchange, where a web site enables companies to buy and sell from each other using a common technology platform.

Collaboration in a business-to-business relationship (sometimes termed C-Commerce) can be carried out within a framework that integrates the firms' business processes and manages knowledge across organizational boundaries. Collaborative product development, for example, may involve multiple trading partners providing components. Work flow capabilities, with access to technical documents and drawings and electronic signoff procedures, can facilitate this collaboration.

E-business applications represent 24/7 availability for customers and suppliers, and reduced personnel requirements for handling inquiries and coordination. On the customer side, for example, customers can place orders and check status at any time of the day without waiting for normal business hours or availability of customer service personnel.

EDI Applications

EDI standards have been developed for U.S. markets in various industries, such as automotive and retail industries. Other standards apply in European and Asian markets. The core concept is that basic transactions in supply chain activities can be replaced by electronic communication. Some of the basic transactions, shown in Figure 2.4, include releases for shipment and shipping schedules (from the customer) that represent demands, and advanced ship notices upon shipment to customers. Each transaction has been identified by an ANSI identifier, such as the 856 transaction for an advanced ship notice transaction.

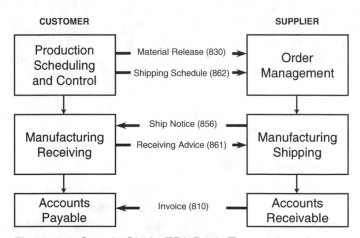

Figure 2.4 Supply Chain EDI: Basic Transactions for
Scheduling and Delivery

An EDI transaction requires a mapping between the standard transaction format and the transaction format in an ERP system. The vendor schedule in one ERP system, for example, can be generated as standard EDI transactions and subsequently translated into a customer shipping schedule in a second ERP system. The standard EDI transaction format provides a bridge between two different ERP systems.

Quotes and Sales Orders

E-business can facilitate collaboration between the customer and sales (or the sales channel). This step in sales order processing, termed *configure order,* often precedes the actual sales order. It can be structured around the key constructs in an ERP system, such as quotations and sales orders. It can support attachments to the quote or order, such as text or other objects, which flow through to an ERP system for specifying customer requirements.

The customer can obtain quotes and enter sales orders directly, typically via the shopping cart analogy. To load their shopping cart, a user can directly identify items, select from catalogs, select from user-defined templates or previous orders, or use expert assistance to guide them to the correct product. The system provides availability and pricing information, and access to product pictures, specifications, and other descriptive information. The system may identify previous purchases and suggest related purchases (for up-selling and cross-selling purposes). The user can save the cart (with a user-specified description) for subsequent use.

A custom product can also be configured without personal assistance. A rules-based configurator can prompt the user through a decision-tree of questions and provide pricing information based on responses. The configuration can be saved as an item in the shopping cart and revised as needed.

Each item in a shopping cart represents a line item on a quote, and the check out process converts the cart contents to sales order line items. The check out process enforces credit management policies and payment methods, such as credit card processing. The system prompts established customers for ship-to and bill-to information, and gathers additional information to process orders from guest or new customers. Confirmations can be sent via e-mail about the quotations, sales orders, and shipments.

Status of Orders and Account

A customer can verify their order and account status without requiring assistance from customer service personnel. Order status typically identifies the quotes and unshipped orders and enables the user to change information. Linkages to carrier web sites can augment shipment information for the specified tracking number.

Request for Quotes and Electronic Marketplaces

E-business enables a manufacturer to electronically communicate requests for quotes to suppliers and to obtain and store the responses. An electronic marketplace or trading exchange provides one solution approach. A buyer firm can publish product requirements and demand schedules, request quotes from supplier firms, and then review the bids and select the supplier.

An electronic marketplace can facilitate more than just requests for quotes. It may offer additional services, such as logistic or transportation services and payment services, to help complete a transaction. It may support community activities, like distributing industry news, sponsoring online discussions, and providing research information about the industry.

Vendor Schedules

E-commerce enables a supplier to review and download requirements (e.g., for released purchase orders and projected orders). In JIT operations, the vendor schedule may take the form of a Kanban board.

ERP and Computer Integrated Manufacturing

Individual standalone IT applications for structured tasks have been reasonably easy to justify and implement in a specific functional area. Some examples are a computer-aided design (CAD) system in design engineering and a statistical process control (SPC) application in quality management. Efforts to link these standalone applications to ERP are termed *computer integrated manufacturing* (CIM). The relationship between CIM applications and an ERP system can be demonstrated by examples of data exchanges that loosely couple the parts of the system.

- Computer-aided design applications require item data from an ERP system and provide item and bill of material data to an ERP system.
- Shop floor data collection applications require information about manufacturing orders and routings from an ERP system. They provide material movement and labor time transactions to an ERP system. Labor transactions may also feed a time and attendance system or a payroll application.
- Quality management applications, such as an SPC and laboratory information management system (LIMS), can provide detailed tracking of manufacturing processes. For example, quality data may be collected about defects and reason codes, or about product attributes. This quality data can supplement standard ERP functionality, such as lot- and serial-tracking and inspection requirements.
- Automated material handling systems require information about picking and shipping schedules from an ERP system and provide material movement data to the ERP system.

- Automated assembly systems and flexible manufacturing systems require ERP information about the manufacturing schedule and product and process design, such as routing details, tools, component parts, and identification of numerically controlled machine programs. They provide information about manufacturing events, such as units completed and scrap.
- A sales forecasting system may be as simple as a standard micro-based software package, or a customized decision support application. An ERP system maintains historical sales data about bookings, shipments, invoices and returns that provide key inputs to generating a statistical forecast, and the resulting forecast provides the primary inputs to ERP for a sales plan and inventory plan.

Several approaches can be taken to link CIM applications with an ERP system. Tools provided by the ERP software vendor and the software's database management system facilitate (or constrain) the approaches for integrating CIM applications. Ideally, the tools should enable you to extend and supplement ERP functionality without affecting source code, so that you can easily upgrade to new releases from the ERP software vendor. The tools include:

- *Open Data Base Connectivity (ODBC) Design.* An ODBC design within an ERP system makes it easy to access the data with off-the-shelf industry-standard decision support tools, such as spreadsheets and report writers. A data export capability provides the additional benefit of extracting ERP data for use in an external application.
- *Data Import.* Data import capabilities can be used to initially load the ERP database with data from existing systems. The same tool also enables other applications to update the ERP database, such as data collection systems and rules-based configurator packages.
- *Event Manager.* Events within an ERP system can be monitored so that additional applications are launched or personnel get notified as a result of the event. Events occurring outside ERP may also be monitored to trigger actions.

Before undertaking significant capital outlays for CIM integration, it is critical that business processes be reengineered and simplified. The cost and difficulty of integrating a CIM application increase as the level of integration becomes more extensive.

ERP and Advanced Planning and Scheduling

Many ERP systems employ MRP logic as the primary engine for coordinating supply chain activities. Advanced planning and scheduling (APS) logic represents a major change from traditional MRP logic for scheduling purposes. To explain the differences, it helps to understand the starting points of MRP logic and APS logic.

Summary of MRP Logic

MRP logic uses backward infinite scheduling to explode demands for make items through the bills and generate production schedules. This is a simplified explanation of MRP logic, but sufficient to highlight two underlying assumptions about infinite resource capacity and no material constraints.

- *Infinite Resource Capacity.* MRP logic assumes a manufacturing order can be completed by its due date regardless of resource capacity considerations. In overloaded periods, schedulers must adjust available capacity or reschedule loads to make the schedule feasible. Alternatively, the demands (such as sales orders) must be adjusted.

    A related assumption is that a manufacturing order has a fixed lead-time regardless of lot size, current production loads and available resource capacity. In some ERP systems, MRP logic calculates a variable lead-time and operation due dates that reflect considerations of available capacity. These calculations generally reflect simplistic scheduling rules and simplistic models of available resource capacity. MRP logic may also support rate-based (or daily) schedules that support the same concept of a variable lead-time. However, the simplistic approaches to variable lead-times and daily schedules can still result in schedules reflecting an underlying assumption of infinite capacity.

- *No Material Constraints.* MRP logic assumes a manufacturing order can start (and finish by its due date) regardless of material availability. This means schedulers must expedite material to make the schedule feasible. Alternatively, demands (such as sales orders) must be adjusted to make the schedule feasible.

MRP logic, especially with variable lead-time and rate-based scheduling calculations, provides a simple yet sufficient model of production activities to synchronize the supply chain in many environments. Sales order delivery dates reflect availability (thereby aligning demands with supplies and minimizing expediting), capacity planning anticipates overloaded periods, and material planning identifies the need for expediting.

Summary of APS Logic

APS logic uses finite scheduling based on capacity and material constraints to synchronize activities in the supply chain. In the context of production activities, APS automatically schedules manufacturing orders (and operation due dates) based on comprehensive models of available resource capacity, detailed routing information, and finite scheduling rules.

- *Models of Resource Capacity.* APS logic uses comprehensive models of available resource capacity. Machine and labor capacity can be expressed in terms of shift patterns (or shop calendars) of available hours, where labor capacity also requires the available headcount by shift. Each shift can have a different efficiency, and each machine and labor type may have different capabilities (or skill sets). Some machines can process multiple items at once (such as ovens and slitters), which means they also have a capacity limit of weight, volume, width, or other dimension.
- *Detailed Routing Information.* APS logic performs scheduling based on detailed routing information. Routing information minimally specifies the operation sequence, a primary resource, and processing time for each operation. Additional routing information may include machine-specific processing time, setup time (and setup matrices), secondary resources (such as labor and tools), parallel operations, alternate operations, and other aspects of production activities. Using an operation-centric view of the bill of material for an item, APS logic considers material constraints based on material tied to an operation.
- *Finite Scheduling Rules.* APS logic provides various scheduling rules to optimize objectives, such as minimizing flow time, minimizing tardiness, maximizing utilization, or completing highest priority work. For example, forward finite scheduling minimizes tardiness. APS logic can consider alternate operations, machine-specific run rates, and sequencing-specific setup times to automatically schedule orders and meet due dates. The finite scheduling rules may be based on attributes of the manufacturing order (such as priority) or of the operation (such as setup time or campaign sequencing).

APS logic schedules the start of an operation when all required materials and resources are available. APS logic typically treats scheduled receipts and purchasing lead times as a given constraint, rather than assuming that material can be expedited. APS logic can be extended to synchronizing procurement activities.

The APS logic underlying a specific schedule can be very complex. This means the scheduling person requires easy drill-down to the scheduling exceptions and rationale. Schedules automatically generated by APS may need manual overrides. APS logic can generate schedules that do not meet due dates, which means demands must be adjusted to align with the schedule (such as revising sales order delivery promises).

APS applications have been maturing so that they are becoming easier to implement and use, as well as less expensive. However, the comprehensive modeling and finite scheduling logic have a degree of complexity that makes APS difficult to implement. In addition, APS logic can have difficulties with some ERP capabilities such as component date effectivities. The focus on manufacturing orders that seem to run counter to JIT philosophies involving orderless manufacturing. APS logic has been incorporated into some ERP systems as the primary engine for coordinating supply chain activities. Many ERP systems provide APS logic as a supplement to MRP logic, such as a finite scheduling module. The case study highlights some of the issues in integrating APS logic with MRP logic.

CASE STUDY Integrating MRP Logic and an APS Application

One ERP software vendor integrated a standalone APS application with its ERP system, where the level of integration evolved through several design iterations. The ERP system acted as the master database for resources, bills and routings, manufacturing orders (generated by MRP logic), and inventory and purchases. This data was replicated in the APS application, where the APS application supported comprehensive models of resource availability.

The ERP application supported infinite capacity planning to identify overloaded periods for key resources. Resource availability was then modified in the APS application.

The APS application performed finite scheduling using resource and material constraints, and generated detailed production schedules for each resource. It uploaded the resulting schedule to the ERP system for coordinating procurement activities and making delivery promises. Actual production activities reported in the ERP system provided the basis for calculating remaining work in the APS application.

Integration between the APS application and the ERP system covered most of the manufacturing issues. For example, the integration handled phantoms, planned manufacturing orders, bill of material dependencies, parallel and alternate operations, operation attributes (such as setup matrices), split operations (across multiple machines), and updates to the order-dependent bill in the ERP system. Difficulties were encountered in handling component date effectivities (since they were not recognized in the APS application) and capable-to-promise calculations across a multilevel bill (since MRP logic was required to calculate multiple manufacturing orders prior to downloading them to APS).

APS Logic and the Theory of Constraints

The theory of constraints (abbreviated as TOC) is a management philosophy that focuses attention on the constraining resource within a production process and the desired goal. As a simplified explanation, TOC starts with the production rate of the pacemaker resource and a time buffer or inventory buffer to protect the constraining resource from disruptions. The production rate and buffer reflect the family of items produced by the resource. Operations at prior (and subsequent) resources are synchronized to the pacemaker resource, resulting in the timely release of materials to support scheduling at the pacemaker. The production schedules for resources involved in prior operations ensure that releases match the production rate (or capacity) of the pacemaker resource. Improvement activities focus on the constraint. This approach has been coined "drum-buffer-rope," since it focuses on the pacemaker's schedule (the drum), its buffer, and the pull-through effect (the rope) on other activities.

APS logic and the TOC approach both employ detailed routing data to schedule orders through the pacemaker or bottleneck resource. They provide almost identical solutions to a single-operation production process. Differences between APS logic and the TOC approach include the need for routing data for other nonconstrained resources, reporting requirements, and the use of inventory buffers.

- ◆ APS logic uses routing data for other nonconstrained resources to synchronize prior and subsequent operations (via backward and forward finite scheduling), whereas the TOC approach employs simplistic rules such as lead-time offsets. It could be argued that simple routing data for APS logic accomplishes the same purpose as lead-time offsets and provides additional benefits in costing and capacity planning.
- ◆ APS logic requires reporting of actual work performed (such as unit completions by operation) to calculate remaining work at nonconstraining resources, whereas the TOC approach does not.
- ◆ APS logic generates detailed schedules for every resource and focuses on schedule adherence, whereas the TOC approach focuses on the schedule and inventory buffers at the constraining resource.

Some environments require more advanced scheduling capabilities. These environments can be characterized by multiple potential constraining resources (dependent on the product mix), multiple parallel legs (rather than a single linear flow), products with widely varying time requirements for the pacemaker resources, or resources with varying capabilities. APS logic provides these scheduling capabilities, whereas a TOC approach becomes more difficult.

Evolution of ERP Software Packages

ERP software packages have evolved over time to support a wide variety of manufacturing environments and business practices. They have also evolved in terms of ease-of-use and ease-of-implementation. The starting points for ERP can be traced to early accounting systems that handled sales order processing, basic purchasing functions and inventory, and also to early bill of material processing logic.

Variations in ERP software packages can frequently be traced to their origins. This includes an accounting versus manufacturing orientation, a standard versus custom product orientation, a discrete versus process orientation, a mainframe versus microcomputer origin, and a standard package versus toolkit orientation.

Variations in ERP software packages can also be traced to their maturity and the use of third-party applications. An ERP software package matures over time with additions of new modules and functionality by the software vendor. Increased functionality frequently reflects increased complexity, especially when new functionality runs counter to the package's fundamental design. This sometimes results in multiple mutually exclusive versions of software modules. Increased complexity makes it very difficult to reengineer the software package to a simpler fundamental design. New initiatives in an ERP package are often constrained by concerns about upgrading the installed base, upgrading the technology foundation, or the expense of rewriting the entire system. New initiatives are also constrained by the sheer complexity of an existing ERP system. Hence, new initiatives often take the form of third-party packages that are unencumbered by concerns about an installed base or technology platform. Limitations in connectivity tools and in the package's fundamental logic typically constrain approaches to third party packages.

ERP and Generally Accepted Manufacturing Practices

Generally accepted accounting practices have been consistently implemented in most ERP systems. Generally accepted manufacturing practices, in contrast, have not been widely agreed-upon and consistently implemented. This has been complicated by the different ways in which a given ERP system simulates or models a manufacturing business. The conceptual framework underlying the design of an ERP system may provide an overly complex approach to needed functionality, or even ignore needed functionality. Extensions to the framework to support new business practices—such as orderless environments—may be cumbersome and overly complex, rather than natural extensions that reflect simple symmetric solutions. Explanations in this book are based on conceptual frameworks that reflect generally accepted approaches taken in most ERP systems and the body of knowledge represented by APICS (American Production and Inventory Control Society).

The relevant chapters in this book provide explanations of generally accepted approaches for each concept. This includes comparisons to alternative approaches taken in some ERP systems. The key point is that each ERP system can provide different solution approaches to handling various manufacturing practices.

Chapter 3

Justification of ERP Investments

The expected return on investment provides the cost justification and motivation for investing in ERP. There are quantifiable benefits as well as intangible benefits in the ERP investment decision. The quantifiable benefits have a bottom-line impact on profitability and asset turnover and a potential effect on stock value.

This chapter discusses the quantifiable and the intangible benefits of an ERP system, comparing firm performance before and after implementing ERP. These benefits were previously described in *Managing Information: How Information Systems Impact Organizational Strategy* (G. Davis and S. Hamilton, Business One Irwin, 1993). Other scenarios are encountered in justifying ERP investments. For example, a firm may be considering replacement versus upgrade or reimplementation of an ERP software package.

There are significant costs for not successfully implementing an ERP system. Manufacturers often pay more for the lack of systems than they would have paid for improved systems. They carry excess inventory or provide poor customer service, for instance. Manufacturers also may invest in ERP without gaining the benefits because the systems are partially implemented, unsuccessfully implemented, or usage deteriorates over time.

Quantifiable Benefits from an ERP System

Studies that surveyed manufacturers about the impact of ERP systems on firm performance indicate that company size and industry do not affect the results. Benefits have been indicated for large and small firms, whether they make standard or custom products or are in discrete or process manufacturing environments. This section explains the quantifiable benefits in terms of several areas of improvement.

Typical Benefits

The most significant quantifiable benefits involve reductions in inventory and in material, labor, and overhead costs, as well as improvements in customer service and sales.

Inventory Reduction Improved planning and scheduling practices typically lead to inventory reductions of 20 percent or better. This provides not only a one-time reduction in assets (inventory typically constitutes a large proportion of assets), but also provides ongoing savings of the inventory carrying costs. The cost of carrying inventory includes not only interest but also the costs of warehousing, handling, obsolescence, insurance, taxes, damage, and shrinkage. With interest rates of 10 percent, the carrying costs can be 25 percent to 30 percent.

ERP systems lead to lower inventories because manufacturers can make and buy only what is needed. Demands rather than demand-insensitive order points drive time-phased plans. Deliveries can be coordinated to actual need dates; orders for unneeded material can be postponed or canceled. The bills of material ensure matched sets are obtained rather than too much of one component and not enough of another. Planned changes in the bills also prevent inventory build-up of obsolete materials. With fewer part shortages and realistic schedules, manufacturing orders can be processed to completion faster and work-in-process inventories can be reduced. Implementation of JIT philosophies can further reduce manufacturing lead times and the corresponding inventories.

Material Cost Reductions Improved procurement practices lead to better vendor negotiations for prices, typically resulting in cost reductions of 5 percent or better. Valid schedules permit purchasing people to focus on vendor negotiations and quality improvement rather than on expediting shortages and getting material at premium prices. ERP systems provide negotiation information, such as projected material requirements by commodity group and vendor performance statistics. Giving suppliers better visibility of future requirements helps them achieve efficiencies that can be passed on as lower material costs.

Labor Cost Reductions Improved manufacturing practices lead to fewer shortages and interruptions and to less rework and overtime. Typical labor savings from a successful ERP are a 10 percent reduction in direct and indirect labor costs. By minimizing rush jobs and parts shortages, less time is needed for expediting, material handling, extra setups, disruptions, and tracking split lots or jobs that have been set aside. Production supervisors have better visibility of required work and can adjust capacity or loads to meet schedules. Supervisors have more time for managing, directing, and training people. Production personnel have more time to develop better methods and improve quality and throughput.

Improved Customer Service and Sales Improved coordination of sales and production leads to better customer service and increased sales. Improvements in managing customer contacts, in making and meeting delivery promises, and in shorter order-to-ship lead-times, lead to higher customer satisfaction and repeat orders. Sales people can focus on selling instead of verifying or apologizing for late deliveries. In custom product environments, configurations can be quickly identified and priced, often by sales personnel or even the customer rather than technical staff. Taken together, these improvements in customer service can lead to fewer lost sales and actual increases in sales, typically 10 percent or more.

ERP systems also provide the ability to react to changes in demand and to diagnose delivery problems. Corrective actions can be taken early, such as determining shipment priorities, notifying customers of changes to promised delivery dates, or altering production schedules to satisfy demand.

Improved Accounting Controls   Improved collection procedures can reduce the number of days of outstanding receivables, thereby providing additional available cash. Underlying these improvements are fast, accurate invoice creation directly from shipment transactions, timely customer statements, and follow through on delinquent accounts. Credit checking during order entry and improved handling of customer inquiries further reduces the number of problem accounts. Improved credit management and receivables practices typically reduce the days of outstanding receivables by 18 percent or better.

Trade credit can also be maximized by taking advantage of supplier discounts and cash planning, and paying only those invoices with matching receipts. This can lead to lower requirements for cash-on-hand.

ERP System Benefits on the Balance Sheet

Benefits from improved business processes and improved information provided by an ERP system can directly affect the balance sheet of a manufacturer. To illustrate this impact, a simplified balance sheet is shown in Figure 3.1 for a typ-

	Current	Typical Improvement	Benefit
Current Assets			
Cash and Other	500,000		
Accounts Receivable	2,000,000	18%	356,200
Inventory	3,000,000	20%	600,000
Fixed Assets	3,000,000		
Total Assets	$ 8,500,000		$ 956,200
Current Liabilities	xxx,xxx		
Noncurrent Liabilities	xxx,xxx		
Stockholder's Equity	xxx,xxx		
Total Liabilities and Equity	xxx,xxx		

Figure 3.1 Summarized Balance Sheet for a Typical $10 Million Firm

ical manufacturer with annual revenue of $10 million. The biggest impacts will be on inventory and accounts receivable.

In the example, the company has $3 million in inventory and $2 million in outstanding accounts receivable. Based on prior research concerning industry averages for improvements, implementation of an ERP system can lead to a 20 percent inventory reduction and an 18 percent receivables reduction.

- *Inventory Reduction.* A 20 percent inventory reduction results in $600,000 less inventory. Improved purchasing practices (that result in reduced material costs) could lower this number even more.
- *Accounts Receivable.* Current accounts receivable represent 73 days of outstanding receivables. An 18 percent reduction (to 60 days' receivables) results in $356,200 of additional cash available for other uses.

ERP Benefits on the Income Statement

A simplified, summary income statement for the same $10 million manufacturer is shown in Figure 3.2. For many manufacturers, the cost of sales ranges from 65 percent to 75 percent of sales (the example will use 75 percent). Using industry averages for each major benefit, the improved business processes and associated information system almost double the current pretax income.

- *Inventory Reduction.* A 20 percent reduction in the current inventory of $3 million results in ongoing benefits of lower inventory carrying charges. Using a carrying cost of 25 percent results in $150,000 in lower carrying charges each year, identified here as part of the administrative expenses.
- *Material Cost Reductions.* A 5 percent reduction in material costs because of improved purchasing practices results in annual savings of $225,000.
- *Labor Cost Reductions.* A 10 percent reduction in labor costs because of less overtime and improved productivity results in annual savings of $100,000.

		Current	Typical Improvement	Benefit
Sales		$ 10,000,000	10%	
Cost of Sales		7,500,000		
Material	4,500,000	60%	5%	$ 225,000
Labor	1,000,000	13%	10%	$ 100,000
Overhead	2,000,000	27%		
Administrative Expenses		2,000,000		$ 150,000
Pretax Income		$ 500,000		$ 475,000

Figure 3.2 Summarized Income Statement for a Typical $10 Million Firm

- *Increased Sales.* Improvements in customer service typically lead to a 10 percent sales increase; this is not shown in the figure.

Annual benefits totaling $475,000 in this example almost equals the current pretax income of $500,000.

ERP Impact on Key Financial Ratios

Ration analysis provides another way to look at the impact of an ERP system. Three ratios illustrate the effect, two related to liquidity and one to operating performance.

- *Inventory Turnover (Cost of Sales/Inventory).* Low inventory turnover can indicate possible overstocking and obsolescence. It may also indicate deeper problems of too much of the wrong kind of inventory. High turnover indicates better liquidity and superior materials management and merchandising. Given the example $10 million company, the current number of inventory turns is 2.5. With a 20 percent inventory reduction, the number of inventory turns increases to 3.1.
- *Days of Receivables (365 * 1/(Sales/Receivables)).* This ratio expresses the average time in days that receivables are outstanding. It is a measure of the management of credit and collections. Generally, the greater the number of days outstanding, the greater the probability of delinquencies in accounts receivable. The lower the number of days, the greater the cash availability. With an 18 percent reduction in receivables, the current days receivable of 73 days can be reduced to 60. This means $356,200 is available for other purposes.
- *Return on Assets (Profit Before Taxes/Total Assets).* This ratio measures the effectiveness of management in employing the resources available to it. Several calculations are necessary to determine the return on assets. In this example, the return on assets can be improved from 5.9 to 12.9 by effectively implementing an ERP system.

Performance evaluation based on ratio analysis can also use comparisons between one's own company and similar firms in terms of size and industry. The Annual Statement Studies[1] provide comparative ratios for this purpose. The same three ratios for inventory turnover, days receivable, and return on assets will be used for this comparative ratio analysis. To perform the analysis, the median and upper quartile ratios for firms in the same industry need to be identified.

---

[1]Robert Morris Associates, the national association of bank loan and credit officers, publishes the Annual Statement Studies. The Statement Studies contain composite financial data on manufacturing industries broken down by four-character Standard Industrial Classification (SIC) codes. For each industry, it displays a common-size balance sheet and income statement, with each item a percentage of total assets or sales, respectively. Ratios are also calculated, and each ratio has three values: the upper quartile, median quartile, and lower quartile.

These roughly correspond to average and good performance. By comparing the ratios with your firm's current performance, you can calculate how much better your company should be performing to be competitive. The same analysis can be performed using the BenchmarkReport.com web site.

Using the inventory turns ratio for the example $10 million manufacturer, assume the Annual Statement Studies indicate that the median and upper quartile are four and six turns for other firms in the same industry. Average performance of four inventory turns translates into an expected inventory of $1.875 million ($7.5 million divided by four). If the example firm had this ratio, it would have had $1.125 million less in inventory. With inventory carrying costs at 25 percent, this would produce savings of $281,250 each year.

For the days receivable ratio, assume the Annual Statement Studies indicate that 60 and 50 days are the median and upper quartile. The days receivable in the example $10 million manufacturer is currently 73 days; an improvement to 60 days would reduce receivables by $356,200 (using a daily sales rate of $27,400 and a 13 day reduction). This means that cash is available for other purposes.

Note that the return on assets ratio is 5.9 for the example company. Assuming the Annual Statement Studies indicate the return on assets is 10 and 15 for firms in the same industry at the median and upper quartiles, improving the return on assets to equivalent levels would mean increased profits and/or asset turnover.

ERP Impact on Stock Price

If the integration and improved information of an ERP system results in a better balance sheet and increased profits, these improvements should impact stock price for the company. Although stock price is affected by a variety of factors, the typical effect of improved profits and balance sheet ratios can be estimated. We will use the example $10 million manufacturer and typical benefits already described, and assume 100,000 shares outstanding and an existing stock price of $30 per share. With a price to earnings multiplier of 6, the stock price for the example company could be increased from $30 to $58.50 per share.

These calculations suggest that ERP systems can lead to significant impacts on financial results, including the balance sheet, income statement, key ratios, and stock price.

The Intangible Effects of ERP

The intangible or nonfinancial benefits of an integrated ERP system can be viewed from several perspectives. For illustrative purposes, the discussion will focus on the benefits for accounting, product and process design, production, sales, and MIS functions. From the overall company standpoint, ERP provides a framework for working effectively together and devising a consistent plan for action.

Each of the intangible effects could be quantified in terms of cost savings. Duplicate data maintenance, for example, requires personnel time in entering data (and possibly managerial time in determining which set of data should be used for decision making). Expediting efforts have a visible effect of consuming personnel time. These quantified cost savings can also be used to show impacts on financial results.

Effects on Accounting

With a common database from ERP, accounting no longer requires duplicate files and redundant data entry. Product costing, for example, can be performed using accurate and up-to-date product structures. Product costing simulations can be used to analyze the impact of changing material costs, labor rates, and overhead allocations as well as planned changes to bills and routings. Differences between actual and standard costs are highlighted as variances. Order-related variances help pinpoint problem areas.

Customer invoices can be based on actual shipments (without duplicate data entry), which helps speed invoice processing. Payables can use purchase order and receipt data for three-way matching with supplier invoices.

As manufacturing transactions are recorded, the financial equivalents are automatically generated for updating the general ledger. This provides a complete audit trail from account totals to source documents, ensures accurate and up-to-date financial information, and permits tracking of actual versus budgeted expenses. Detailed transaction activity can also be easily accessed online for answering account inquiries.

Since manufacturing transactions automatically update the general ledger, time-consuming manual journal entries can be eliminated. Period-end closing procedures can be performed in hours or days, rather than weeks. This reduces clerical accounting work and improves the timeliness of financial reports.

Financial reports can be easily customized to meet the needs of various decision makers. Financial projections can be based on detailed ERP calculations for future requirements. Cash planning, for example, can account for current and projected sales orders and planned purchases, as well as current receivables and payables. Decision support tools (such as spreadsheets, graphics packages, and data managers) can use the financial data maintained in the ERP database.

Effects on Product and Process Design

The product structure database offers engineering much greater control over product and process design, especially in terms of engineering change control.

Planned changes can be phased in and emergency changes can be communicated immediately.

ERP systems offer numerous analytical tools for the engineering function. When diagnosing the impact of changes to materials and resources, for example, engineers can check where-used information to identify the affected products. Lead-time reduction efforts can use critical path analysis of item lead-times in multilevel bills to focus attention on those key components affecting cumulative manufacturing lead-time. Costed multilevel bills can be used to focus cost reduction efforts on high value items. Bill comparisons can be used to highlight differences between products, or between revisions of the same product (e.g., to identify upgrade kit requirements).

ERP systems support custom product configurations. Rules-based configurators reduce the need for expert assistance from engineers and ensure sales personnel (or even customers) can develop timely, accurate configurations. Cost estimates and pricing for custom product configurations can also be quickly calculated.

Effects on Production and Materials Management

ERP systems help establish realistic schedules for production and communicate consistent priorities so that everyone knows the most important job to work on at all times. Visibility of future requirements helps production prepare for capacity problems, and also helps suppliers anticipate and meet needs. As changes to demands or supplies do occur, ERP helps identify the impact on production and purchasing.

Finite scheduling capabilities in ERP ensure production activities are scheduled based on capacity, tool, and material constraints. Scheduling rules help minimize setup times and optimize sequencing. Changes in factory demands, as well as changes in available machine time, labor headcount, skill levels, tools, and material can be immediately simulated to assess the impact on production and purchasing.

ERP helps eliminate many crisis situations, so people have more time for planning and quality. Buyers can spend more time in vendor negotiation and quality improvement. When the shortage list is no longer used to manage the shop, the quality of working life can improve.

Effects on Sales

Customer service can be improved by making valid delivery promises and then meeting those promises. Custom product quotations can be developed faster and more accurately, which improves job estimating. Delivery lead-times can be shortened and customer inquiries on order status can be answered immediately.

E-commerce capabilities enable customers to place orders and check status over the Internet at any time. In addition to customer convenience, this reduces the time requirement for sales and customer service personnel.

Effects on the MIS Function

An ERP system implemented as an integrated software package offers several advantages to the MIS function. The software package can offer a growth path from simple to comprehensive applications built on top of a database management system. It provides an upgrade path to technology and functional enhancements supported by the software vendor. It can reduce the development time and cost for software, documentation, and training classes. These costs would be incurred before the firm can start obtaining the benefits of an ERP system. It permits the MIS staff to focus their attention on organizational change and servicing user needs for customization and professional assistance.

Costs of Implementing an ERP System

ERP implementation costs can be divided into one-time costs and ongoing annual costs. Both types of costs can be segmented into hardware, software, external assistance, and internal personnel.

One-Time Costs

Software   The cost of an ERP software package varies widely, ranging from $30,000 for micro-based packages to several million dollars for some mainframe packages. The number of concurrent users generally drives the software costs, so that smaller systems cost less. For illustrative and general guideline purposes, the software package costs range from $50,000 to $200,000 for smaller manufacturers. In addition to the ERP software package, one-time costs may include systems software, development of customized software, or integration with other applications.

Hardware   Hardware selection is driven by the firm's choice of an ERP software package. The ERP software vendor generally certifies which hardware (and hardware configurations) must be used to run the ERP system. Hardware may need to be replaced or upgraded. As a general rule, small- to medium-size manufacturers already have microcomputers and a local area network, so that a micro-based ERP system built on *de facto* standards requires little additional investment in hardware.

External Assistance   External assistance includes the consulting and training costs to implement the ERP package. The software vendor, reseller, or independent consulting group may provide external assistance. The amount of external assistance required is dependent on several factors, such as the complexity of the ERP package, the experience and knowledge of internal personnel, and the extent to which external personnel are used in place of internal personnel to implement the system.

A general guideline for these costs has been a ratio with the cost of the ERP software package. A comprehensive micro-based ERP package typically has a 0.5 to 1.0 ratio; the manufacturer requires $.50 to $1.00 of external assistance for each dollar of software package costs. The elapsed time for implementation of the entire ERP application typically is 4 to 6 months. Many of the mainframe ERP packages have a 3 to 5 ratio for the costs of external assistance. The software package typically costs more, and the elapsed time for implementation is 9 to 24 months.

Internal Personnel   Internal personnel time reflects the time commitments for the implementation project team, the executive steering committee, the users in various functional areas, and MIS personnel. The time commitments include training classes, development of internal procedures for using the system, developing customized reports and applications, preparation of the data, meetings with external consultants, and team meetings. A general guideline for internal personnel costs can also be expressed as a ratio with the ERP software costs, where a typical ratio is 0.5 to 1.0.

The one-time costs for implementing an ERP system can be simplistically estimated using typical ratios with ERP software costs. These ratios are summarized in Figure 3.5 for one-time and ongoing annual costs, along with example calculations for a $100,000 ERP software package.

The one-time and ongoing annual costs for hardware are not included in the example. In many cases, the use of *de facto* standard hardware means that a firm already has the hardware for an ERP system. The example shown in Figure 3.3 indicates an estimated $300,000 for one time costs and $65,000 for annual costs related to an ERP system.

Ongoing Annual Costs

Software   Ongoing software costs should include the annual customer support agreement with the ERP software vendor. This customer support typically provides telephone assistance and software upgrades and is priced around 15 percent to 20 percent of the software price. Upgrades to system software releases will also be required.

The upgrade path for new releases of the ERP software package is critical. New releases contain enhancements for functionality and bug fixes, and ensure that the software runs on the latest technology platform. From the user's point

One-Time Costs	Ratio to Software Purchase Cost	Example ERP System
ERP Software	1	$100,000
Hardware	-	-
External Assistance	.5 to 1.0	$100,000
Internal Personnel	.5 to 1.0	$100,000
	Total One-Time Cost	$300,000

Annual Costs	Ratio to Software Purchase Cost	Example ERP System
ERP Software	.25	$25,000
Hardware	-	-
External Assistance	.1 to .2	$20,000
Internal Personnel	.1 to .2	$20,000
	Total Annual Costs	$65,000

Figure 3.3 Estimating Costs for Implementing a New ERP System

of view, the upgrade path enables the manufacturer to take advantage of hundreds of labor-years of development efforts undertaken by the ERP software vendor (and other technology vendors) with minimal investment. From the vendor point of view, it is much easier to support users on the latest releases. However, user changes to source code and other user customizations can make it very expensive or even impossible to upgrade. Additional costs must then be incurred to ensure the customizations work with the latest upgrade. As shown in the example estimates in Figure 3.3, a ratio of .25 has been used for total annual costs related to ERP software.

A phased implementation approach may mean that additional software must be purchased. A data collection system, for example, may be implemented as part of a second phase.

Hardware Ongoing hardware costs will reflect new requirements specified by the ERP vendor to run the software.

External Assistance External assistance should be used as part of a continuous improvement program to effectively use an ERP system application for running the company. Training and consulting can focus on improved business processes, new or poorly used software functionality, and training of new personnel. A phased implementation approach requires additional assistance at each phase. Additional customizations may be required, especially with evolving user sophistication. As shown in the example estimates in Figure 3.3, a ratio of 0.1 to 0.2 could be used for total annual costs related to external assistance.

Internal Personnel The implementation project team does not necessarily end its responsibilities at time of system cutover. A phased implementation approach and continuous improvement efforts will require ongoing time commitments. Employee turnover and job rotation will also require ongoing training efforts. The nature of the ERP software package (and associated system software and hardware) typically mandates the number and expertise of MIS personnel needed for ongoing support. This support may range from a part-time clerical person (for administering a micro-based ERP package) to a large group of MIS experts (for some mainframe ERP packages). As shown in the example estimates in Figure 3.3, a ratio of 0.1 to 0.2 could be used for total annual costs related to internal personnel.

Replacing or Reimplementing an ERP System

An investment analysis focusing on ERP benefits frequently applies to those firms initially justifying an ERP implementation. It can also be used to justify a reimplementation when the initial efforts have failed to produce desired results. The breakout box describing classifications of ERP success identifies situations where the ERP implementation falls short of producing desired benefits.

Classifications of ERP Success

Several measures have been used to gauge the successful implementation of an ERP system. The impacts on business performance and bottom-line results provide the best measure of success. Another measure of success is the degree to which the formal ERP system is used to run the business. Four classifications, termed Class A through Class D, have often been used to characterize success. Field surveys about ERP success indicate approximately 10 percent of firms achieve Class A status, 40 percent are Class B, 40 percent are Class C, and the remainder (10 percent) are failures.

Class A User. The formal ERP system is effectively used to run the entire company. The manufacturing database defines the way products are really built and efforts have been undertaken to simplify factory layouts and business processes. The ERP system defines realistic agreed-upon S&OP (sales and operations planning) game plans that cover all demands, sales orders have realistic delivery promises, and the schedules are actually used to coordinate supply chain activities. Coordination efforts reflect action messages, with a manageable number of exceptions. The ERP system correctly updates accounting and provides useful management information. The ERP system typically reflects the latest releases from the software vendor.

Class B User. The formal ERP system is partially effective in being used to run the entire company. It defines S&OP game plans, but they typically lack company-wide agreement and completeness. Supply chain activities are frequently initiated that do not reflect schedules from the ERP system and the volume of action messages frequently makes them difficult to use. Unrealistic delivery promises on many sales orders contribute to the problem, and also create a larger-than-necessary volume of exception conditions requiring expediting. Some informal and/or parallel systems are employed to manage expediting outside the formal system. While the manufacturing database provides a reasonably complete and accurate model of how products are really built, there are just enough exceptions to make some people question the formal system. The accounting applications are closely coupled to operational reporting, but sufficient exceptions exist to make some financial impacts suspect.

Class C User. The formal ERP system is only used in part of the company, typically in recording information about sales orders, shipments, purchase order receipts and accounting applications. The manufacturing database provides an incomplete or inaccurate model of how products are really built. S&OP game plans are typically nonexistent and unrealistic delivery promises are made on many sales orders. Several informal or parallel systems are required to coordinate procurement and production activities, typically with excessive expediting efforts and duplicate data maintenance. The accounting applications are not closely coupled to the activities reported in production.

Class D User. The formal ERP system is not used to run any part of the company, and might be "running" only in the MIS function. Informal and parallel systems are being used to manage the business.

Many manufacturers think they need a new system when they really need to upgrade and reimplement their current ERP software package. They can be characterized as a Class B or Class C user, and are not achieving the possible benefits—both quantifiable and intangible. The costs to reimplement an ERP system should be significantly lower than implementing a new system. The users have familiarity with system usage and should know the system strengths and weaknesses. Many firms can live with the shortcomings of their existing system. External assistance from the software vendor or consultants can help develop solutions to shortcomings, and should in any case be part of continuous improvement efforts. With a solid understanding of the reimplementation costs and shortcomings, the investment decision should be justified on the basis of benefits.

Many manufacturers are faced with decisions about replacing their current ERP software package or homegrown system. The replacement decision can stem from any number of situations. The current ERP software package is no longer supported, is too expensive to maintain, is heavily customized and cannot be upgraded, runs on old technology, is too complex and expensive to implement, and so forth. A homegrown ERP system provides partial solutions or nonintegrated solutions, is not on the right technology platform, is unfamiliar to current staff and cannot be supported or upgraded, and so forth. The investment decision in these cases tends to use cost comparisons between alternatives.

The starting point for cost comparisons should be the previously discussed classification of costs, both one-time and ongoing annual costs. The following case study illustrates the use of cost displacement as the basis for ERP investments.

CASE STUDY Cost Displacement as the Basis for ERP System Replacement

Several autonomous plants of a multisite manufacturing firm implemented a standalone micro-based ERP package at each site because it was a cheaper alternative than the corporate standard. The corporate ERP system was a complex mainframe system that required very high levels of external assistance, large expenses for customizations, and high charge-out rates from the corporate MIS function. The one-time and ongoing costs for the corporate system were two to three times higher. The plant management even argued (successfully) that they could implement the new system in 3 months, obtain the benefits over a 6-month payback period, and ultimately throw it away in 2 years when the corporate MIS function was finally ready to implement the mainframe system at their plants. Three years after these plants successfully implemented the single-site ERP system the plants are still using the system while other sites within the company have struggled to even partially implement the mainframe system. The cost displacements (and benefits) have been estimated to be more than one million dollars.

Part 2

Structuring the Manufacturing Database

The manufacturing database provides the foundation for using ERP to plan and control a manufacturing enterprise. It contains information about product and process design. Product information is used for engineering specifications, product costing, material planning (for procurement and production), reporting material usage, tracking stages of manufacturing, lot tracking, and sales pricing. Process information is used for production process specifications, calculating value-added costs, capacity planning, production scheduling, labor and machine reporting, and shop floor tracking. The functional areas involved in these tasks (engineering, costing, procurement, production, quality, sales, and so forth) have responsibilities for maintaining segments of this common manufacturing database.

A basic success factor is the extent to which an ERP system defines the way each product is really built. This involves item differentiation, realistic planning data, and complete and accurate information about bills, configurations, and costs. There are many common problems associated with this basic success factor that will be highlighted in this section.

Some companies use an ERP system with a common manufacturing database, but various functional areas still use standalone applications and databases that are poorly integrated. Tremendous expense and effort is incurred in maintaining duplicate data and in reconciling differences (and errors) in data. The death knell for effective use of an ERP system is typically heralded by use of multiple non-integrated systems to get the job done.

The wide-reaching implications and breadth of the manufacturing database requires segmentation for explanatory purposes. One approach would be to segment the explanation by functional area, but this misses the point on the integrative nature of a common manufacturing database. The approach taken here segments the explanation between standard products and custom products. Starting with standard products, the explanations cover items, bills of material, routings, planning data, and product costing (with a focus on standard costing approaches). Custom products are then discussed, along with variations, such as methods to create a configuration, estimate the costs, and determine prices. Effective use of a planning bill for forecasting, production planning, and option selection is also covered.

Chapter 4

Items

The item master contains information about every material item, from raw materials and purchased parts through intermediate manufacturing levels to end-items. While item identification would seem to be an easy task, it is often the source of problems in ERP implementations. The item master also involves several design issues in ERP systems, such as variations in revision level significance.

A comprehensive model of the manufacturing enterprise involves material and other types of items, such as resources, tools, and documents. They can be considered different item types in the item master, although some ERP systems use different master files.

This chapter reviews item identification issues and several ERP design issues related to material items. It also introduces other item types. Subsequent chapters cover item master information related to costs and planning data.

Item Identification for Material Items

Item identification represents the very basics of a manufacturing database. The lack of item differentiation often causes problems in modeling the way products are really built and effectively coordinating supply chain activities. This section covers several considerations in policies regarding item numbering, including unit of measure considerations and suggested approaches for adding new items.

Item or Part Numbering

The item number (or part number) for a standard product provides a unique internal identifier for each material item. Several considerations may affect policies on item numbering.

Significant Versus Nonsignificant Item Identifier   The item number can be nonsignificant or partially significant, but should be as short as possible for internal identification purposes. Significant digits typically reflect an item's attributes or components, resulting in a longer identifier. Significant digits tend to become outdated due to evolving requirements. A suggested approach is to use the item description and/or item attributes for identifying significance, with the ERP system providing item finder or search capabilities based on description and attributes.

In some cases, significant or extended item numbers have been firmly established within a company or industry. The significant or extended item number often reflects requirements for sales or procurement purposes, and may be handled by customer (catalog) items or vendor items. Alternatively, the extended item number may reflect a smart part number that identifies selected features and options in a custom product configuration. The smart part number may provide a fast means of entering a sales order and a shorthand communication method for understanding product content. The custom products chapter (Chapter 9) provides further explanation.

Interchangeability   Items not completely interchangeable require different identifiers. Interchangeability is affected by differences in form, fit, or function. Some changes in characteristics, exemplified by differences in lot attributes, do not require a different item number. That is, lots are used to differentiate an item's supplies and replenishment logic treats the lots as interchangeable.

Stages of Manufacturing   Any stage in the manufacturing process that must be stocked (or purchased or sold) requires an item number. The item number can be used for physical inventory counts. While routing operations are generally used to reflect various steps in the manufacturing process, the stocking level consideration may mandate a separate item (with its own bill of material) for a given step. A phantom item can identify a nonstocked manufacturing stage, such as a parts kit or a transient subassembly. A by-product or coproduct item may be needed to track material generated by a manufacturing process. A subcontracted item identifies a stage of manufacturing completed by an external vendor, with a bill of material that must be supplied to the vendor. The case studies on item numbering (see the breakout boxes) illustrate differentiation in stages of manufacturing.

Other Item Identifiers for Sales and Procurement Purposes   An internal item number can be associated with other item identifiers for sales and procurement purposes. A saleable item, for example, may have an associated customer item number for each customer, or sales catalog numbers that apply to any customer. A purchased item may have one or more manufacturers' parts numbers and an associated vendor item number for each supplier. An ERP system provides mapping capabilities that solve several item identification problems, including unit of measure conversions and differing item descriptions.

CASE STUDY Item Numbering for a Plastics Manufacturer

A process manufacturer of a plastic compound started with a simple item numbering scheme when they implemented their ERP system. As shown in the left side of Figure 4.1, the end-item compound was produced on an extrusion machine from several ingredients.

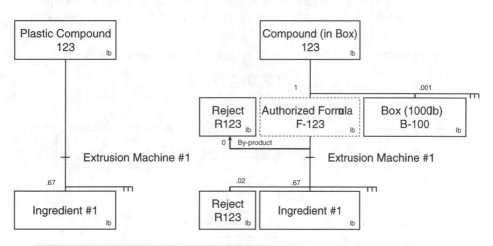

	Simple Scheme	Comprehensive Approach
Parent Item	The parent item (the compound) defined the ingredients for a bulk item with no packaging components. The compound was sold in pounds, but each packaging variation (such as 1,000 pound boxes, 200 pound drums, and bulk) was priced differently. This made it impossible to create a price book tied to the packaging variation. It also made it difficult to communicate the customer's desired packaging to shipping and production and to track finished goods inventory by packaging variation.	The existing parent item represented an authorized recipe for bulk compound, which became a phantom component to the new items defined for each packaging variation of the material. Each new item had a unit of measure in pounds. In this way, a sales order could specify the sales price per pound, and the desired packaging variation.
Packaging	Packaging materials were not identified as items and were not included in the bill of materials. This made it difficult to plan replenishment of packaging materials. The product costs were also understated because they did not include packaging material.	A new item was defined for each packaging material and the appropriate packaging components were defined in the bill of material for end-items. In this way, product costs included packaging and MRP logic calculated the packaging requirements.
Reject Material	Each production run resulted in rejected material that could be used in the next production run. The same item number was used for the rejected material, which caused problems in tracking inventory and MRP calculations.	A new item was defined for each compound's rejected material. The rejected material was defined twice in each compound's bill: once as a normal component and once as a by-product component. This approach identified the amount of rejected material consumed in production and received from production.

Figure 4.1 Case Study: Item Numbering for a Plastics Manufacturer

This simple scheme encountered several problems (in parent item variations, packaging, and reject material) that were solved with a comprehensive approach to their item numbering.

CASE STUDY Item Numbering for a Fabricated Products Manufacturer

A manufacturer of fabricated items produced cylinders from various castings and used a simple item numbering scheme when they initially implemented their ERP system. As shown in the left side of Figure 4.2, one of the end-items (Cylinder #100) required three

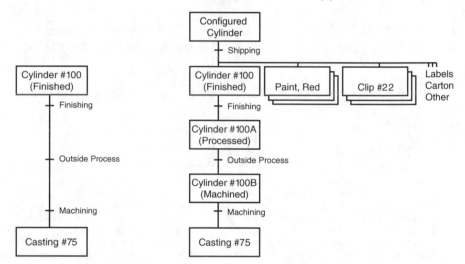

	Simple Scheme	Comprehensive Approach
Stages of Manufacturing	The end-item (the cylinder) went through three operations: machining of a casting, then an outside process performed by a subcontractor, then a finishing operation. The inventory and costs at each stage of manufacturing could not be identified, especially for the machined item sent to the subcontractor.	Two additional item numbers identified the intermediate stages of manufacturing: one for the internally machined item and one for the processed item completed by the subcontractor.
Shipping Configuration	The sales order for an end-item (cylinder) included textual instructions about painting, additional parts (such as clips), labels, and packaging. The shipping area was responsible for these details, but many errors occured, especially when a customer changed their instructions. Inventory management and replenishment of these items were poorly coordinated.	The sales order identified a custom product item, where option selection (from the planning bill) was used to define customer requirements about painting, additional parts, labels, and packaging. The configuration clearly specified customer requirements for coordinating shipping activities. The planning bill improved inventory replenishment and material usage could be reported against the configuration.

Figure 4.2 Case Study: Item Numbering for a Fabricated Products Manufacturer

major operations to be manufactured from a given casting (Casting #75). This simple scheme encountered several problems (in identifying stages of manufacturing and coordinating shipping activities) that were solved with a comprehensive approach to item numbering.

Unit of Measure Considerations

Most manufacturing environments should employ a single unit of measure (UM) for each internal item. This unit of measure applies to inventory, bill component quantities, costing, material planning, and recording material transactions. The single UM eliminates confusion, such as bills expressed in one unit of measure and costs expressed in another. The single UM typically reflects the dominant perspective of inventory quantity or bill component quantity.

The internal item can be mapped to vendor items, customer items, or catalog items with different units of measure. Each level in a bill can also reflect a unit of measure conversion. For example, a component measured in kilograms may be used to make an item measured in liters or pieces.

Some manufacturing environments may require more than one internal unit of measure. Requirements for multiple UM often reflect dimensional items, weight or volume and potency, a dual UM for sales, and packaging variations. However, multiple units of measure become increasingly complicated. They can impact the required quantity of a component item, inventory stock status, supply orders, receipt and issue transactions, demands, replenishment logic, costs, and prices. An additional complication involves unpacking inventory in one UM for shipment or usage in another UM.

An item's unit of measure should be subject to a decimal precision rule to avoid problems in having infinitesimal inventory quantities stemming from inventory transactions or auto-deduction. This decimal precision rule does not affect how many decimal places are used for component quantities in the bill of material

Item Attributes

Item attributes help differentiate items and serve multiple purposes, especially in peripheral support for managing supply chain activities. Some of these attributes are discussed below, grouped by functional area of interest.

Engineering and Quality Data   Engineering may maintain information about many attributes of an item, such as the item drawing, classification codes, and item description(s). Item attributes can be used for finder purposes, requiring standardization of codes and descriptive text. The item description, for example, requires standardization of nouns, adjectives, dimensions, and any abbreviations. Extended descriptions and multiple descriptions (e.g., for multiple languages) may be required.

Attributes of an item can be an object, such as a CAD drawing, a digitized picture, a scanned image, a video clip, or word-processing documents about item specifications and inspection procedures. These attributes are often embedded in product data management (PDM) or manufacturing execution system (MES) applications within an ERP system. They provide information to production or suppliers for engineering and quality purposes.

Shipping Data   Item shipping data includes information that supports a standard pack approach to shipments, such as item weight and volume, the item count per package, and a freight classification code. An ERP system can automatically generate packaging labels and a bill of lading based on the standard pack information. A pick-and-pack approach to shipments (e.g., with mixed items in a box) can use the weight information.

The weight and volume information can also be used during sales order processing to calculate a cumulative weight and volume for an order. They may be used for pricing or to plan truckload shipments. The cumulative weight and volume information can also be used for a purchase order.

Sales and Sales Analysis Data   Item classification codes and other attributes provide the basis for segmenting and analyzing sales history. An attribute may reflect a grouping of products into a product family. The term *product family,* however, has a special significance with respect to planning bills and MRP logic.

Item attributes for sales purposes include other identifiers, such as the UPC (universal product code), ECCN (export commodity control number), and HTS (harmonized tariff system) numbers. Other attributes include country of origin information.

Text and Other Objects Related to Items

Textual information and other objects provide critical communication in an ERP system. The term *objects* represents a wide variety of computer-readable data, including drawings, scanned images, video clips, and text files. Both text and objects represent attributes of an item. They can also represent attributes of many other things within an ERP system, such as bill of material components, routing operations, customers, vendors, quotations, sales orders, purchase orders, manufacturing orders, shipments, and transactions (such as inventory adjustment transactions).

Every ERP system provides support for text, but the implementations vary widely in their flexibility and comprehensiveness. Three considerations include:

◆ *Master Text.* Master text has a user-assigned identifier, with an unlimited amount of predefined textual information. The user can assign one or more text identifiers to an item (or customer, sales order, or other construct), and the system automatically tracks text where-used information. Changes to the master text affect every where-used instance. A variation to master text supports the concept of a text template.

- ◆ *Free-Form Text.* Free-form text does not require pre-definition and a user-assigned identifier. It can supplement the capabilities of master text.
- ◆ *Text Characteristics.* The characteristics of master text and free-form text include selective carry-forward (e.g., from the item to the sales order line item), selective usage (e.g., internal versus external), and selective printing (e.g., by document type).

Item Status

An item status field reflects a critical policy affecting how an ERP system should handle the item. The item status typically identifies whether an item should be treated as active (production), preproduction, being phased out, or obsolete. Other user-definable values may be possible. An ERP system uses item status to provide soft warnings on transactions for the item, recommend suggested actions, and even prevent transactions via hard warnings. Item status is typically used in conjunction with an engineering change order (ECO) approval process to add new items and to phase out or obsolesce old items.

Adding New Items and an ECO Approval Process

Most companies require a standard procedure for adding new items to the item master. The procedure ensures justification for assigning a new item number, thereby avoiding redundant numbers. It also ensures complete definition of critical item master information. This standard procedure is typically referred to as an engineering change order (ECO) or engineering change notice (ECN) approval process.

An ECO approval process consists of several approval steps, with a sign-off requirement by relevant functional areas at each step. The approval process typically requires completion of standardized forms, such as an impact analysis or the required fields of critical information. A template can be established for a standardized approval process, so that a new ECO inherits the template and standardized forms. Multiple templates may be established to reflect different types of approval processes. For example, separate templates could be defined for adding manufactured and purchased items, and for adding saleable items.

The ECO approval process also applies to the bill of material and routing data for an item. The chapters on bills of material (Chapter 5) and routings (Chapter 6) provide additional suggestions about using an ECO approval process.

Recommended Action Messages Related to Engineering

Approval steps in the ECO approval process provide the foundation for communicating several recommended actions related to engineering. The recommended action may notify needed approval (or past-due approval) for a given step; it can also communicate a rejected ECO. Other recommended engineering actions can be considered, as illustrated in Figure 4.3.

Recommended Engineering Action Message	Message Filter
Take action on step in ECO approval process	Look ahead days
Follow-up on past-due step in ECO approval process	Days late
Follow-up on rejected step in ECO approval process	Reason code
Incomplete or missing data in item master	Item attribute value
Incomplete or missing data in bill of material	Item attribute value
Incomplete or missing data in routing	Item attribute value
Review configuration for custom product	Configuration attribute value

Figure 4.3 Summary of Engineering Action Messages

ERP Design Issues Related to Material Items

Item master capabilities vary between ERP systems in several areas. These include variations on revision level significance, primary source of supply, the phantom item concept, and the alternate item concept.

Item Identification and Revision Level Significance

ERP systems support differing perspectives on how a revision level should be treated for item identifier purposes. A revision (rev) level generally represents a level of documentation, and several terms (such as rev level or engineering change level) refer to the same concept. The perspectives can be viewed as a continuum concerning the significance of the revision levels for item identification. With low significance, the revision level differentiates supplies but does not affect interchangeability. Higher significance reflects the degree to which supplies cannot be treated as interchangeable.

Rev Level as an Item Descriptor   The revision level acts as an item descriptor field (indicating only the current level of documentation) and is not used to differentiate inventory. An item's authorized revisions may be defined. An item's revision level can act as a descriptor field on a supply order.

Rev Level to Differentiate Supplies   The revision level differentiates supply orders and inventory, where order receipts update inventory by rev level. The ability to differentiate supplies is equivalent to a lot number, where supplies are treated as interchangeable.

Rev Level to Differentiate Supplies and Versions of a Bill   The revision level differentiates supplies and also identifies versions of a bill. The revision level of a parent item may provide the basis for managing bill changes, with date effectivity tied to the item's authorized revisions. Planned manufacturing orders may inherit the parent item's revision level (and associated bill) that is in effect as of the order start date. Calculations of standard costs are based on one version of the bill.

In addition to bill versions, a separate routing revision level may identify versions of a routing. Planned manufacturing orders may inherit the item's routing revision level (and associated routing) that is in effect as of the order start date. Separate versions of a routing and bill often reflect the need to identify an alternate operation (or group of operations), where the alternate operation may require different material because of machine characteristics.

Rev Level to Differentiate Demands and Supplies (with Partial Interchangeability)   Partial interchangeability between revision levels introduces greater complexity. Given a sales order demand with a specified revision level, for example, one or more revision levels of supply may be considered suitable to ship to the customer. This requires sharing or suitability rules with respect to supplies, since they are not completely interchangeable. A typical example involves a spare part for warranty and upgrade purposes that must be differentiated by rev level. A sales order requirement for the spare part may specify a rev level, but several rev levels will actually serve the customer's purpose.

Rev Level and Item Number Define a Unique Identifier   Revision levels are not interchangeable; they uniquely define the item's inventory, supplies, demands, bills (and bill components), and costs. This is equivalent to embedding the revision level in the item number.

A comparison between revision level perspectives, shown in Figure 4.4, highlights the interchangeability of supplies and the ability to differentiate supplies and demands. The identification of bill versions reflects an additional consideration, especially when managing bill changes with parent revision level effectivities.

The first perspective on item identification—revision level acting as an item descriptor—provides the simplest viewpoint. It is the one used in this book.

Primary Source of Supply

An item's primary source of supply, often referred to as a make/buy code, is one of the basic planning parameters. It is reflected in the item's bill and routing, lead-time, and lot-sizing logic; it affects the type of suggested supply orders, definition of value-added costs, and calculation of total costs. The primary sources of supply include buy, make, and subcontract.

		Revision Level Significance				
		Descriptor Only	Differentiate Supplies	Differentiate Supplies + Bill Versions	Differentiate Supplies and Demands	Unique Item/Rev Identifier
	Treatment of Supplies	←——— Completely Interchangeable Supplies ———→			← Partial →	← Not Interchangeable
Ability to Differentiate	Supply Order	By Rev Level	By Rev Level	By Rev Level	By Rev Level	By Rev Level
	Inventory		By Rev Level	By Rev Level	By Rev Level	By Rev Level
	Demand				By Rev Level	By Rev Level
	Bill - Parent Item - Component			By Rev Level		By Rev Level By Rev Level
	Costs					By Rev Level

Figure 4.4 Perspectives on Revision Level Significance

- *Buy.* The item normally gets replenished by purchasing it from an external vendor.
- *Make.* The item normally gets replenished by producing it internally using material components and operations defined in the item's bill and routing.
- *Subcontract.* The item normally gets replenished by purchasing it from an external vendor, who produces it using a kit of supplied material defined in the item's bill.

Designation of an item's primary source of supply does not preclude other sources. A make item, for example, may be intermittently purchased or subcontracted because of capacity constraints. Some ERP systems support date effectivities for the primary source (reflected a planned change) and/or multiple primary sources (with mix percentages).

There are other sources of supply. In a multisite operation, for example, material at one site may be replenished from another site (on a transfer complete basis or a subcontracted basis) as described in the chapter on multisite operations (Chapter 23). Other sources include customer-supplied material and by-products, as described in the bills of material chapter (Chapter 5).

Managing External Production Activities Using Subcontracted Items Versus Outside Operations

ERP systems provide two basic approaches (a subcontract item versus an outside operation approach) to managing external production with supplied material. Both approaches are needed in an ERP system. The subcontract item (with a kit of supplied material) represents a bill of material approach, whereas an outside operation represents a routing approach. Figure 4.5 illustrates a comparison of the two approaches.

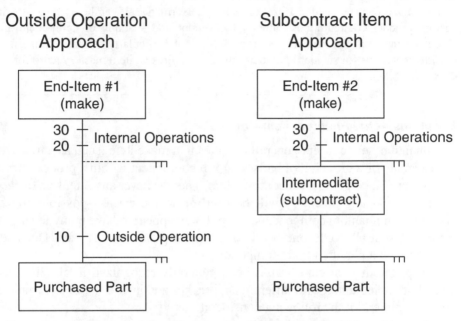

Figure 4.5 Comparison of Outside Operation Versus Subcontract Item Approach

Outside Operation Approach. An outside operation is defined in the context of a make item's routing, shown as Operation 10 for End-Item #1 in Figure 4.5. The routing operation defines a purchase cost, quantity (and UM), turnaround time, and approved vendor. The outside operation approach requires coordination between two streams of activities: one for the manufacturing order operation and one for its related purchase order. It often applies to one-time production at an external vendor, and works better when a single component must be supplied.

Subcontract Item Approach. A subcontract item is defined in the item master, with a primary source of subcontract. It represents one outside operation, with a bill defining a kit of supplied material, shown as Intermediate in Figure 4.5. The item defines the purchase cost, UM, turnaround time, and approved vendors. The subcontract item approach combines the concepts of a purchase order and a manufacturing order operation. It applies to recurring production of a standard product at an external supplier, especially when multiple components must be supplied.

The subcontract item approach provides several advantages. The biggest advantage is a single coordinating mechanism for two streams of related activities: one for the manufacturing order operation and one for its related procurement. The subcontract item approach supports vendor schedules, blanket purchase orders, and a buy card history for the subcontract item. It provides an explicit definition of the supplied component(s) and the other materials to be furnished by the vendor. It supports planned bill changes and a pick list and packing list to send supplied material. It tracks external work-in-process, material shortages, and component scrap, and it supports physical inventory counts for material at vendors. It provides a complete lot/serial genealogy for materials sent to (and received from) a vendor. It tracks vendor performance. It can be used to support custom product configurations built by the vendor and stocking of component and parent inventory at the vendor. The approach is not particularly suitable to one-time outside operations for standard products, since it requires an item master record for the subcontract item.

Variations of the Phantom Item Concept

The phantom item concept generally applies to a make item, such as a transient subassembly or a grouping of parts, that is a component within a product structure. It can also apply to a subcontract item. There is never any intention to keep inventory, and any inventory will be used up at the earliest possible convenience. With phantom components, the bill may appear to have many levels but there is essentially only one level for material planning purposes. Demands blow through a phantom to its components.

The phantom item concept has been generally recognized in all ERP systems, but implemented with different approaches and interpretations. Variations reflect treatment of the following considerations

- A component item may be changing from normal to phantom in an effort to flatten the bill for planning purposes, or the component item may be considered a phantom in one product structure and normal in another. These cases argue for designating phantoms at the bill component level rather than the item master level.
- A material item can be stocked, costed, priced, sold, purchased, and manufactured. The phantom designation should not limit these capabilities.
- MRP netting logic considers a phantom component's inventory and scheduled receipts and blows through any unmet demands without suggesting a separate supply order.
- In MRP logic, unmet demands blow through a phantom to its component materials *and* its routing operations, and the phantom item's lead-time is ignored. This approach supports modularized routings.
- The initial creation of an order-dependent bill typically reflects inventory of a phantom component so it is used up. That is, the order-dependent bill contains the phantom item (for the inventory quantity). This approach may cause problems when the inventory is used elsewhere since the order-dependent bill still has a requirement for the phantom.
- The initial order-dependent bill reflects blow though logic on unmet demands for a phantom component, so it includes the phantom's material

components and routing operations (with their specified operation sequences). This approach may affect scheduling or auto-deduction based on operation sequence numbers, especially when it causes duplicates in sequence numbers.

The phantom item concept can be used to support make-to-order environments, where an end-item is produced to actual demand but other demands (such as forecasts) blow through to the highest stocking level in the product structure. A make-to-order production strategy also applies to make-to-order components of the end-item. The intention is to generate final assembly supply orders to cover sales order demand. This represents two exceptions to the phantom concept: selective creation of a supply order (to cover sales order demands) and lead-time consideration. This case argues for designation of a final assembly planning policy for an item.

The phantom item concept applies to an item sold as a kit of parts, where any demands blow through to the components (and supply orders do not apply). The sales order for the item can be shipped without requiring inventory for the item, and the shipment triggers auto-deduction of the kit's components. This case argues for designation of a kit planning policy for an item.

This book views the phantom item concept as an item master and a bill component policy. In terms of an item master policy, the designated planning policy—of normal, final assembly, and kit—supports make-to-order standard products requiring a supply order to cover sales order demands and the sale of kits. In terms of a bill component policy, the designated component type—of normal and phantom—supports cases of an intermediate component that can vary between normal and phantom.

Variations of the Alternate Item Concept

The alternate item concept has several interpretations. An alternate item from a manufacturing perspective, for example, may indicate the need to use up inventory of an old item. It may be designated for an item (or bill component) for MRP logic purposes, or only information purposes. An alternate item from a sales perspective, on the other hand, may identify a similar product. It may be displayed during the order entry process based on availability of the original item.

Other Types of Items

The item master applies to more than standard product material items. The item master can define family items for standard products or custom products. The item master can also be extended to define nonmaterial items such as resources, tools, documents, and field service tasks. Some ERP systems provide a separate master file for each of these item types.

Resource Items

A resource item typically represents a capacity-constrained internal production capability, such as an individual machine, manufacturing cell, or a pool of interchangeable people (or machines) with the same capabilities. Internal resources have capacity limitations expressed in hours of availability and costs expressed per hour of operation. In some cases, a resource item may be used for just cost allocation purposes. Some ERP systems provide a separate work center master file to model resources.

A second category of resource items represents an external production capability with subcontractors. An external resource represents a vendor performing outside operations, or a subcontractor providing value-added services on supplied material. External resources may have capacity limitations expressed in hours of availability. Vendors identified as external resources may also need to be identified in a separate vendor master.

A resource item cannot be stocked, since its availability expires as time elapses. A resource item can only be a component of another item, and it cannot be directly purchased, manufactured, or sold. It can be indirectly sold, typically as a resource component in a custom product configuration. A resource item can have another resource component for the purposes of calculating aggregate capacity requirements. Further discussion of resource items is provided in the chapters covering resources and routings (Chapter 6) and product costing (Chapter 8).

Tool Items

A tool item typically represents a reusable mold, fixture, or jig. A tool's inventory may be tracked via tool crib management (for issues and returns), or inventory tracking may be ignored. Inventory is typically serialized when multiple tools exist for the same purpose. A tool item has properties similar to a material item, but also like a resource item.

- As a material item, a tool has a unit of measure of piece or each. It can be identified as a bill component for items requiring the tool, typically with a per order quantity. An order's pick list identifies when to issue the tool (for tool crib management purposes). A tool can be purchased or manufactured. A manufactured tool can have a bill and routing, and a manufacturing order (and rework order) applies to the tool.
- As a resource item, a tool typically has a unit of measure in hours and a capacity limitation expressed in hours of availability (typically 24/7). Its available time can be reduced by maintenance or calibration requirements. It can be identified as a requirement for an item's routing operation, and it can act as a constraining resource. You can optionally assign hourly costs to allocate tool usage costs to operations requiring the tool.

In addition, you can optionally define an hourly sales price to calculate quoted prices for custom product configurations requiring the tool.

A serialized tool has special properties that differentiate it from other resources. A given serialized tool may have a capacity limitation expressed in usage hours (or usage cycles). This requires projections and tracking of cumulative usage for the purposes of scheduling maintenance and calibration.

The chapter on resources and routings provides further discussion of a reusable tool as resource item. Some tools reflect a *consumable* item that does not get reused, so that the tool more closely resembles an MRO (maintenance, repair, and office) item.

Document Items

A document that can be inventoried and costed (such as manuals and labels) should be treated as a material item. In contrast, a document item is only used for information purposes; it is not costed or inventoried. A document item typically identifies the instructions for producing a material item, or an engineering change order (ECO) that affects the item. A document defining manufacturing specifications, for example, would be identified as a component for every item impacted by the specifications. Planned changes in the bill can be used to show a change in the specifications. As another example, a specific ECO would be identified as a component for every item impacted by the ECO (with appropriate effectivity dates). Where-used information for the document item identifies the affected items, and the order-dependent bill and printed pick lists identify the specifications (or ECOs) that apply to a manufactured item.

Service Items and Field Service Tasks

The item master can be extended to define saleable service items requiring materials and resources. The typical examples involve field service tasks such as equipment installations or maintenance. A service task requires materials, resources, and tools, where the components provide the basis for costing and pricing the service. The services may be standardized (with a standard bill and routing) or customized (with a configuration). This argues for two types of service items: a standard service item and a custom service item.

Demands for saleable services can be forecasted to anticipate material and capacity requirements. A sales order can be taken for the service item (or task), which results in a work order for performing the service. The work order is directly linked to the sales order (and the customer). You can report material usage and resource time against the work order and against work order completion. These aspects of service items are similar to material items, but there are several key differences. A service item cannot be stocked; a completed work order can trigger an invoice (rather than reporting a receipt and shipment); and the work order(s) must be directly linked to a sales order.

Note: Maintenance tasks represent another type of service item. These service tasks involve nonproduction material commonly referred to as MRO (maintenance, repair, and office) material. MRO items can be make or buy. Buy items require approved vendors, price quotes, and a buy card history. Inventory may be maintained with specified replenishment methods and actual usage reported. MRO items also consist of consumables such as drills, saw blades, and adhesives. Maintenance tasks reduce availability of resources, such as preventive or emergency maintenance on production equipment. Maintenance tasks and MRO items are frequently managed by a separate maintenance management application. Further explanations of maintenance tasks are considered outside the scope of this book.

Family Items

A family item serves as the parent item for a planning bill for either standard products or a custom product. A planning bill is also called a *super-bill*. A family item is used for planning purposes and cannot be stocked. A custom product family, termed a *model* in some ERP systems, can also serve as the starting point for defining a configuration.

Effective use of a family item and planning bill requires an understanding of supply/demand terminology, so that a brief introduction is deemed necessary at this point. Supply orders for a family item represent its production plan. MRP logic can calculate planned supply orders for the family item based on forecasts, and these can be firmed (but never opened or released) to indicate manual overrides to the item's production plan. MRP logic uses the production plan and the family item's planning bill to calculate component requirements that are termed production forecasts.

A family item can be used for either forecasting or production planning purposes, or both.

- ♦ *Forecasting Purposes of a Family Item.* A family item (and its planning bill) provides a simplified method for forecasting many items with related demands. A sales order consumes the family item's forecast, or the saleable item's production forecast, based on demand management policies for the saleable item.
- ♦ *Production Planning Purposes of a Family Item.* A family item provides a simplified method to represent a capacity constraint. For example, it may represent a dedicated manufacturing cell producing a family of standard product items or a custom product family. In this way, sales order delivery promises can be based on availability of the cell's uncommitted capacity using available-to-promise (ATP) logic for the family item's

production plan. Sales orders must consume the family item's production plan to correctly calculate ATP.

Standard Product Family Items

The family item represents a generic make item and is typically used for forecasting purposes. The planning bill provides the basis for breaking out the family's aggregate forecast into production forecasts for family members. The family members must have related demands and reasonably stable mix percentages. A family of similar end-items may also share a common production process and/or common raw materials. A standard product family can optionally represent all items produced in a common production process in order to support ATP logic for the family's production plan.

A planning bill for a standard product family item is explained in Chapter 5, while the chapter covering sales and operations planning (Chapter 11) provides a further explanation about using planning bills.

Custom Product Family Items

A custom product family item (or model item) typically represents a generic make item, and serves as the starting point for defining a configuration. It could be a buy, subcontract, or transfer item (rather than a make item). A custom product family item can optionally serve as the parent item of a planning bill.

Starting Point of a Configuration   A custom product item specified on a sales order (or quotation) line item provides the starting point of a configuration. The configuration can have a user-defined item number and description. The configuration's components consist of materials and resources, which can be used for estimating costs and prices. A component can be another custom product item with its own configuration. Each sales order configuration drives a supply order reflecting the family item's primary source (such as a manufacturing order for a make item), and the supply orders represent a final assembly schedule.

Parent Item of a Planning Bill   A custom product family may optionally have a planning bill. Forecasted demands for the family item can be used to anticipate component requirements prior to obtaining a sales order for a configuration. The planning bill may also be used as the basis for option selection to create a configuration. Chapter 9 on custom products explains a planning bill, while Chapter 11 covers sales and operations planning and illustrates uses of the planning bills.

Regardless of the planning bill, a custom product family can optionally represent all items produced in a common production process in order to support ATP logic for the family's production plan.

Common Problems Related to Material Items

Problems in Using Different Item Identifiers

A common problem in item master information involves the use of other item identifiers and units of measure for engineering, sales, and procurement purposes. An ERP system provides several solutions to these problems.

Manufacturer's Part Number A manufacturer, and the manufacturer's part number and description, can be defined for an internal purchased item. In some cases, multiple manufacturers (and their associated part numbers) must be defined because they provide an interchangeable part. This approach eliminates the need for using the manufacturer's part numbers as the unique identifier. Information about the manufacturer's part number can be used by procurement for sourcing a buy item, or for providing information to a subcontractor about required components. With industry standards on manufacturers' part numbers (such as electrical/electronic parts and chemicals), the information can also be used for sourcing items via manufacturing exchanges on the Internet.

Vendor Item Numbers A vendor item number and the manufacturer's part number are typically the same, but may differ when purchasing a manufacturer's part number from a distributor. An internal item number can be mapped to one or more vendor item numbers (and manufacturer's part numbers). The mapping can account for the vendor item description, its unit of measure with conversion factor, and a revision level. Receipt transactions can be recorded for either the internal item or vendor item, using the associated unit of measure to record the receipt quantity. The vendor item information can appear on external documents (such as purchase orders), while the internal item information appears on internal documents (such as receivers and labels). This approach eliminates the need for using vendor item numbers for the unique identifier.

Customer Item Numbers ERP systems can provide a mapping between an internal item and each customer item. The mapping accounts for the customer item description and its unit of measure with conversion factor and revision level. The customer item number can be used for sales order entry and can be displayed on external documents (such as order acknowledgements, packing lists, and invoices), while internal item information appears on internal communications (such as pick lists for shipping).

Sales Catalog Item Numbers ERP systems can provide a mapping between an internal item number and sales catalog numbers. For sales and marketing purposes, a sales catalog number provides creative approaches to item identification, typically with significant digits. The mapping may support different units of measure (with conversion factors) for the purposes of pricing and shipping. The sales catalog item number can be used for sales order entry and displayed on external documents (such as order acknowledgements, packing lists, and invoices), while internal item information appears on internal communications (such as pick lists for shipping). This approach eliminates the need for changing internal items to support sales and marketing requirements.

Problems in Differentiating Items

Some ERP software packages lack the functionality to handle situations requiring differentiation of an item's bills, demands, supplies, costs, or prices. Separate item numbers may be needed to provide differentiation.

New Versus Used Material   Different item numbers can differentiate between new and used material of the same item. Another variation may be needed to differentiate used material that has been refurbished. Each item can have a different cost, bill, supplies, and demand. In some process manufacturing environments, a production run can generate reject or by-product material that can be folded into the next production run. Different item numbers can differentiate between the good and the rejected material.

End-Item Packaging Variations   Variations in packaging for an end-item may require different item numbers, especially when costs, prices, bill structures, demands, or supplies must be differentiated. Examples include an item sold in a 12-pack and a 24-pack, and a chemical compound sold in boxes and drums.

Approved Manufacturers   Different item numbers can be used to differentiate between approved manufacturers for the same item. A typical example occurs in electronics manufacturing, when customers mandate the use of a specific manufacturer's part number for a component. The different item numbers support tracking of supplies and demands for each manufacturer's part number, even though they might be considered interchangeable for other purposes.

Separate Service Parts Inventory   A separate service parts inventory (for sales purposes) may require differentiation of demands and supplies, otherwise replenishment logic treats them as interchangeable with inventory used for internal manufacturing purposes. The service parts inventory for an item sometimes requires special packaging for sales purposes, which justifies a separate item number (with different costs and a bill of material specifying the packaging).

Customer-Supplied Material   Different item numbers can differentiate between internal and customer-supplied material of the same item. The customer-supplied item typically has a zero cost.

Potency and Grade   Different potencies or grades of an item may or may not require different item numbers. Saleable end items, such as different grades of integrated circuit chips, generally require different item numbers (and sales prices). A component material, such as a beverage ingredient with different alcoholic potencies, generally requires different lots (with lot attributes for potency) for the same item number. Some ERP systems recognize a lot's potency in replenishment logic, whereas other ERP systems assume a standardized potency.

Authorized Recipes   Some ERP systems lack the functionality to handle situations requiring multiple versions of an item's bill and/or routing. These versions reflect authorized recipes or master routings. Separate item numbers provide one method of defining each authorized recipe, where an authorized recipe item is a phantom component in a product's bill of material.

Unit of Measure Problems for Internal Items

Some manufacturing environments may require more than one internal unit of measure. Multiple units of measure become increasingly complicated when they must be differentiated in versions of a parent item's bill, the required quantity of a component item, inventory stock status, supply orders, demands, costs, and prices. Inventory in one UM may need to be unpacked for shipment or usage in another UM. Other UM situations reflect dimensional items, weight/volume and potency, a dual UM for sales, and packaging variations. Some ERP systems provide elegant solutions to these situations, while other ERP systems provide work-around solutions because they are constrained to a single internal UM.

Multiple UM for an Item   A given item may have multiple units of measure, where a user-defined table defines the authorized units and conversion factors.

Dimensional Items (Length and Area)   Some items can be measured in pieces as well as dimensions, such as bar stock (length) or sheets (area). One or more standardized dimensions is typically purchased or manufactured, and manufacturing processes may result in reusable remnants or drop-offs of variable dimensions. This requires that the ERP system be able recognize quantity (pieces) and dimensions in terms of inventory stock status, costs, bill quantities, supply orders, and by-products.

Volume, Weight, and Potency   Some items can be measured in volume and weight, such as a liquid containing particles of a solid. Items may also be measured in volume and potency, such as a liquid containing an active ingredient.

Dual UM on Sales Orders   A dual unit of measure may be required for sales orders and pricing purposes. A turkey producer, for example, produces various standard weights, such as 8-, 10-, and 12-pound turkeys. Sales orders are expressed in "eaches," but invoices (and pricing) are based on actual weights shipped.

Bulk Packaging Variations and Sales UM   Some process manufacturers produce and sell a bulk item by weight or volume, but inventory the same item in several packaging variations (such as boxes, drums, barrels, and totes) that do not affect pricing. A sales order for the bulk item, for example, specifies the required weight of the bulk material and the desired packaging (drums, for instance). Inventory of the bulk item, however, is stocked in various packaging variations (totes and barrels, for instance) that do not match the customer's desired packaging. This creates complexities in checking availability during order entry, and sometimes means the inventory of bulk material may need to be repackaged.

Chapter 5

Bills of Material

Bills of material provide a model of the product design for manufactured and subcontracted items. In a simple manufacturing environment, the product design may be modeled with a single-level bill of material, consisting of a parent item and its material components. In more complex environments, the product design requires a multilevel bill of material reflecting different stages of manufacturing. The common database about bill information is used for product costing, material planning, material usage reporting, lot tracking, analyzing variances, and tracking progress through stages of manufacturing.

A manufactured item must reflect concurrent product and process design considerations in its bill of materials. For a bill, concurrent design impacts the operation sequence assigned to material components, component date effectivities, and the approach to defining planned scrap. Planned scrap, for example, can be defined by operation yields or by a component scrap percentage. The approach to planned scrap reflects a larger issue about the approach taken by an ERP system in defining a bill.

An ERP system typically employs one of two basic approaches in defining a bill of material. The two approaches can be termed *operation-centric* and *material-centric*.

- ◆ *Material-Centric Approach.* A single-level bill consists of a parent item and its material component items. An operation sequence number provides a loose coupling between a material component and its routing operation
- ◆ *Operation-Centric Approach.* A single-level bill consists of a parent item and its operations, with material components tied to an operation. An operation sequence number provides tight coupling between a material component and its routing operation. At the extreme of an operation-centric approach, a parent's routing operations must be defined (with operation sequences) before a material component can be defined for an operation.

The bill for a manufactured item may use either approach, whereas the material-centric approach applies to bills for a subcontracted, purchased, and product family item (planning bills). Hence, an ERP system must support both approaches.

ERP DESIGN ISSUE

Operation-Centric Versus Material-Centric Approaches to Defining a Bill of Material

There are two fundamentally different approaches to defining a bill of material: an operation-centric approach and a material-centric approach. Most ERP systems support just one of the two approaches. Differences between the two approaches affect how an ERP system handles planned scrap, external production, material required dates, yield and inspection, and the scheduling and reporting of production activities. Figure 5.1 summarizes these differences.

The most marked differences between an operation-centric and material-centric approach often manifest themselves in scheduling and reporting material issues/receipts in production.

- With respect to scheduling, most APS (advanced planning and scheduling) systems take an operation-centric approach to the bill of materials. A material requirement (constraint) doesn't exist unless it is tied to an operation, and APS logic does not understand bill dependencies without operations. In contrast, the material-centric approach uses the bill of material to define bill dependencies.
- With respect to material receipts for a manufacturing order, an operation-centric approach typically uses the units completed at the final operation to receive parent items into inventory. It may require an initial operation to even issue

	Operation-Centric Approach	Material-Centric Approach
Planned Scrap	An operation's planned yield percentage defines the proportional scrap for related material components (with a per item quantity). The impact of cumulative operation yield percentages on material requirements can be automatically calculated.	A planned scrap percentage is defined for each material component. This ignores the relationship between an operation's yield and its related components, and it is difficult to account for the cumulative effect of operation yields.
External Production	An item's routing may contain one or more outside operations, with a purchase cost and turnaround time assigned to each outside operation. It is difficult to identify the semi-finished item being supplied to the vendor.	A subcontract item represents one outside operation. The bill for the subcontract item explicitly defines the supplied material, and the subcontract item has a purchase cost and lead time.
Material Required Date	An operation's start date defines the required date for any related material components.	The order start date defines the required date for material components, although each component can have a lead time offset (expressed in working days) to indicate delayed requirements. This means a component's required date can get decoupled from the operation requiring the component.
Yield, Inspection and Replenishment Logic	Replenishment logic for a manufactured item can use the cumulative operation yield percentages to determine item yield, and each operation's yield can be used to factor up requirements for material needed at the operation. Duration of the final inspection operation(s) defines the inspection lead time.	Replenishment logic can use the item's yield percentage to factor up planned order quantities (to cover demands). Item yield typically applies to a purchased item. It can also apply to a manufactured item, where it represents an equivalent scrap percentage for all bill components. After receipt into inspection, replenishment logic assumes availability after the item's inspection lead-time, and calculates an expected good quantity based on the item's yield.
Reporting Activities	Reporting unit completions by operation provides the basis to compare expected and actual quantities for good and bad units, and to calculate variances by operation. Reporting bad units explicitly identifies scrap by operation. An initial operation may be required to report material issues, with a final operation to report parent receipts.	Reporting parent item receipts provides the basis for comparison to the order quantity and yield variances. Reporting of unit completions by operation does not create variances, although it can trigger usage of auto-deduct components and indicate remaining work on an operation.

Figure 5.1 Operation-Centric Versus Material-Centric Approach to Defining a Bill of Material

components to the manufacturing order. In contrast, the material-centric approach does not require any operations to receive parent items from (or issue component materials to) a manufacturing order.

Critical Information in a Bill of Material

The critical information for defining a bill of material is similar for both the operation-centric and material-centric approaches to bills. Several fields for each component represent the critical information. These fields identify the component's operation sequence, required quantity, a find number and the component type. The fields also include in-effect and out-effect dates when using component effectivity dates to manage changes to a bill, as discussed in the section on managing changes to a bill of material.

Operation Sequence

A material component's operation sequence (in a bill for a manufactured item) provides the linkage to the routing operation requiring the material. The operation sequence is typically a numeric field, and may be used for scheduling and/or backflushing purposes (as explained further in the next chapter on routings). In a bill for other types of items, such as subcontract item or a family item (with a planning bill), the operation sequence has no particular significance. It is often identified as a zero in these cases.

Required Quantity

The required quantity of a material component is normally the amount needed to build one parent item. This is called a per item quantity. The quantity can also be expressed per order, which means the component quantity will be the same regardless of the manufacturing lot size. A quantity type field can be used to specify whether the quantity is per item or per order.

Some environments require additional component material because normal manufacturing practices result in scrapped components. The additional requirements for component scrap can be modeled with either a material-centric approach, an operation-centric approach, or a combination of approaches.

Material-Centric Approaches to a Component's Planned Scrap One or more approaches can be used to define planned scrap for a material component.

- *Identify a planned scrap percent for a component.* This approach assumes proportional scrap for the component and provides differentiation between true and scrap requirements.
- *Identify a second occurrence of the component with a per order quantity.* This approach models a fixed amount of scrap, and provides some differentiation between true and scrap requirements.

◆ *Increase the required per item quantity for a component.* This approach assumes proportional scrap, and makes it impossible to differentiate true requirements from scrap requirements.

Operation-Centric Approach to Planned Scrap   The operation-centric approach only applies to components of a manufactured item with routing operations. It identifies an operation yield percent for a routing operation, which assumes proportional scrap for any components associated with the operation sequence. This provides good differentiation between true and scrap requirements. It also models environments with multiple operations having differing operation yields, with a cumulative effect on required component quantities for each operation. Operation yields do not affect requirements for any component with a per order quantity.

Combination Approach   A combination of the operation-centric and material-centric approaches may be required to model some production activities. The scrap percentage defined for a specific component represents a requirement above and beyond that associated with operation yields. An operation with a 90 percent yield, and a related component with a 10 percent scrap rate, for example, would result in a required component quantity reflecting a 22.2 percent scrap rate.

Find Number

A component's find number field can serve several purposes, and has various synonyms such as point of use field. In a traditional application, the find number is a sequential counter of components, typically tied to the find number on drawings. In more creative applications, the find number field provides segmentation of bill components or provides abbreviated information for manufacturing purposes.

The find number field may be treated as part of the unique identifier for a bill component, along with component item number and operation sequence. In this way, you can define multiple occurrences of the same component and operation sequence. For example, the component quantity for a given operation may be changing so that two occurrences will be required: one occurrence to phase out the old component quantity and another occurrence to phase in the new quantity.

Component Type

A component type field defines the nature of the component material, and provides the basis for how an ERP system should handle costing, material planning, printed pick lists, and issuing material to production. The three basic types of material components include normal, reference, and phantom.

Normal Component Most material components will be identified as a normal component. An ERP system can include it in cost roll-up calculations, material requirement calculations, and printed pick lists. The material can be issued to production or auto-deducted.

Reference Component A material item designated as a reference component typically represents material that is not issued to manufacturing. An ERP system does not include it in cost roll-up calculations or material requirements calculations, and it is not issued to (or auto-deducted for) an order. A reference component often represents low-cost expensed material that is not costed, planned, or inventoried. It may represent material components that have a required quantity of "as required." Reference components are copied to an order-dependent bill, and can appear on printed pick lists for reference purposes.

A reference component can also represent an item not supplied to a subcontractor, whereas normal components are supplied to the vendor. The reference components communicate the materials that the subcontractor must obtain to manufacture the item.

Phantom Component. The need for designating a phantom component type (rather than an item master designation) was explained in the previous chapter. With a phantom component, requirements can blow through to lower-level components. The order-dependent bill and printed pick list reflect the phantom's components.

By-Products and Coproducts

Some manufacturing processes result in other materials in addition to the desired parent item. These materials are referred to as by-products or coproducts. One approach to supporting requirements for by-products and coproducts involves using the component type field to identify which items get created as a result of producing the parent item. The term *by-product component* or *coproduct component* is somewhat misleading, since the item is actually received from (rather than issued to) an order.

By-Product Component A by-product component typically represents recoverable high-value waste (such as precious metals in a plating operation or rejected compounds), usable secondary products from a grading operation, and usable components resulting from a strip-down process. Another example includes a temporary, removable component that is subsequently replaced by the real item. The component quantity of a by-product material represents the percentage (or ratio) of expected by-product receipts per one parent item. As a general rule, a bill of material is not defined for a by-product item. In cases where the material is also required to produce the parent, it appears twice in the bill of material, once as a required normal component and once as an expected by-product component.

MRP logic calculates a scheduled receipt (rather than a requirement) for by-product material, and each by-product has a separate supply order. A by-product does not appear on a pick list. Cost roll-up calculations can subtract costs for a by-product component. Some ERP systems attempt to model a by-product component using a negative component quantity. While this approach may provide correct cost calculations, it generally fails to recognize the scheduled receipts and the pick list implications.

Coproduct Component A coproduct material component is similar to a by-product. In comparison to a by-product, the item designated as a coproduct component has a bill of material with a coproduct component of the other item. One coproduct example is family tooling, where one mold or production run produces multiple items. Each parent item has normal material components and a by-product component for the other parent item. Coproduct components involve circular bill logic. An order for one parent item creates scheduled receipts for the other coproduct item. Materials are issued to one order.

The component quantity of a coproduct material represents the percentage (or ratio) of expected receipts per one parent item. MRP logic can create planned orders for either parent item based on replenishment calculations, and calculate a planned scheduled receipt for the related coproduct material(s). Cost roll-up calculations subtract the coproduct costs, just like a by-product component.

Customer-Supplied Material

Customer-supplied material is used in some manufacturing environments to produce the parent item. One approach to supporting this requirement involves using the component type field to identify the need for customer-supplied material. The component type can model how the firm handles customer-supplied material. Some firms only want reference information about customer-supplied material, while others want detailed tracking.

Materials management of customer-supplied material is ignored in some instances, typically because material tracking involves more effort than it is worth. In these cases, the customer-supplied material may be identified as a *reference* component in the parent item's bill. Other manufacturers have focused only on the requirements for customer-supplied material, typically because the scheduled receipts are outside of their control. In these cases, the customer-supplied material can be identified as a *normal* component in the parent item's bill, and receipts recorded as inventory adjustments.

Many situations need visibility of scheduled receipts and material tracking of customer-supplied material. In this case, the item can be specified once in the bill of material (with a customer-supplied material component type) to define the requirement and the expected receipt. Requirements, receipts, and inventory of the customer-supplied material can be tied to a supply order for the parent item. The component appears on a pick list and can be issued to the parent item's supply order.

Managing Changes to a Bill of Material

Many manufacturers have dynamic product designs, where changes are driven by product improvements, marketplace requirements, and other considerations. Identification of planned bill changes in an ERP system enables the firm to communicate the anticipated impact across multiple functional areas. Cost accounting can anticipate cost implications. Sales can anticipate pricing and availability implications. Materials management can anticipate new requirements in replenishment decisions (and use up old material). Production management can anticipate capacity and scheduling requirements.

Various methods have been used in ERP systems in defining planned bill changes. The most commonly accepted method uses component effectivity dates to phase-in and phase-out changes to components in a bill. This ERP design issue affects how planned changes are communicated, and directly impacts the basis for creating an order-dependent bill. An order-dependent bill supports one-time changes to a bill of material.

One-Time Bill Changes and the Order-Dependent Bill

An item's bill of material differs from an order-dependent bill of material for the item. An ERP system can create a copy of an item's bill of material for a manufacturing order or subcontract purchase order. The term *order-dependent bill* refers to this copy. It can be modified to reflect one-time material substitutions or other changes without affecting the item's bill of material. The copy reflects the components in effect as of the order start date when using component effectivity dates to manage planned changes.

ERP DESIGN ISSUE

Variations in Managing Changes to Bills of Material

Manufacturers have employed a variety of methods to manage planned changes to a bill of material. Component effectivity dates represent the most commonly accepted method, the method easiest to understand and use, and the one used throughout this book. Other methods include parent revision level effectivity, end-item serial number effectivity, and engineering change order (ECO) effectivity.

Component Effectivity Dates. A component's in-effect and out-effect dates indicate planned engineering changes to the parent item's bill of material. A typical change involves phasing in a new component, phasing out an existing component, or changing a component's quantity by phasing out the current quantity and phasing in the new quantity. By phasing in and phasing out changes, a complete history of an item's bill of material can be maintained. You can view a historical bill, the current bill, or a future bill by viewing a bill of material as of a specified date. Immediate changes should be defined with an in-effect date of today's date, and may require changes to the order-dependent bill for existing orders. Corrections to errors in a bill can be entered directly (e.g., as deletions or changes), but this eliminates the possibility of viewing a historical bill.

Cost roll-up calculations consider the bill components in effect as of a specified target date. This supports calculations of projected costs as well as historical costs. MRP logic uses order start dates as the basis for considering which bill components are in effect. Order-dependent bills initially reflect the components in effect on the order start date.

Parent Revision Level Effectivity. The revision level of the parent item has date effectivities to indicate planned engineering changes. In one variation of this method, each revision level is associated with a different version of the parent item's bill of material. The bill for one revision can be copied to another revision of the item, and then modified. This approach makes it difficult to view a complete history of bill maintenance in one place.

Cost roll-up calculations consider the bill version in effect as of a specified target date. This supports calculations of projected costs as well as historical costs. MRP logic creates planned manufacturing orders using the revision level in effect as of the order start date. Users can manually specify a revision level on a manufacturing order, thereby determining which version is used as the basis for the order-dependent bill regardless of order start date.

Component Serial Number Effectivity (Tied to End-Item Serial Numbers). A component's in-effect and out-effect serial numbers indicate planned engineering changes to a parent item's bill based on a serialized end-item. A serialized end-item, for example, could be an automotive part that requires bill changes based on cumulative shipments. As another example, a serialized end-item could reflect the tail number on an airplane, either for initial manufacturing or for repair-and-overhaul purposes. This approach also requires component date effectivity, since the bill components may require a planned change for a given end-item serial number.

By phasing in and phasing out changes, a complete history of an item's bill of material can be maintained. A bill of material can be viewed as of a specified end-item serial number and date. Cost roll-up calculations specify a target end-item serial number and date. Demands for an end-item (and its serial number) are carried through material requirement calculations to determine the appropriate bill components as of a given date.

ECO Effectivity. An engineering change order (ECO) defines the impact on new items, new bills, and bill changes. Upon ECO approval for a specified in-effect date (and an optional out-effect date), the ERP system updates the item master and bill of material information. In one variation of this method, the updates are closely linked to the ECO so that changing just the in-effect date of an ECO creates a mass change to the bills of material.

Updating Bills and an ECO Approval Process

Most companies involved in standard products manufacturing require a procedure for adding and updating bills of material. This typically requires coordination with the procedure for adding new items. The procedure ensures definition of a complete and accurate bill of material for new products, and calculation of the product costs. For changes to existing bills, the procedure identifies a planned cutover for new components (or changes to existing components) in the bills. It may involve changes to order-dependent bills related to existing supply orders, and considerations about using up supplies of an outdated item. This standard procedure is typically referred to as an ECO approval process.

An ECO approval process typically consists of several approval steps, with a sign-off requirement by relevant functional areas at each step. A template can be established for a standardized approval process, and multiple templates are typically required to model different types of engineering changes (such as a new product versus an emergency change). Each approval process typically requires completion of standardized forms, such as an impact analysis of current supplies when engineering changes require old material to be used up. A new ECO inherits a user-defined template and standardized forms.

The ECO approval process may be loosely or closely linked to the item master and bills. An ERP system that manages bill changes using an ECO effectivity approach provides this linkage, so that the ECO approval can automatically update bill of material information. With other approaches, approval of an ECO must be followed by manual updates to the bills of material.

Note: Updates to planning bills do not typically require an ECO approval process, since they reflect a tool for forecasting and;shor production planning purposes.

Tools for Maintaining and Analyzing Bills

ERP systems provide multiple approaches for making bill maintenance easier. These approaches include copying one item's bill to another item, and making mass changes to a component based on its where-used information. A mass change, for example, can replace one component with another component in all bills or for selected bills. Other mass changes can be used to phase out one component and phase in the replacement item, to delete a component, or to change a component's quantity.

ERP systems also provide tools for analyzing bills of material. A summary of tools is provided below, including tools related to product costing.

Where-Used An item's where-used information identifies the potential impact of an engineering change to bills of material. It can be viewed through a single-level or multilevel where-used inquiry.

Where-Used via the Supply/Demand Schedule   An item's supply/demand schedule provides where-used information relative to supply orders and their order-dependent bills via pegging to the source of manufacturing demands. Depending on the ERP system, the pegging of where-used information can be single-level or end-level.

Summarized Bill   A summarized bill can be viewed for a specified parent item, effectivity date, and proposed build quantity. A summarized bill totals the requirements for multiple occurrences of a component, thereby ignoring differences reflecting bill structuring approaches. The calculation of component requirements (based on the proposed build quantity) can be compared to inventories to assess the quantity of needed material (and the projected cost of needed material).

Bill Comparison   A bill comparison between an item's bills for two different dates (or two different revision levels) can identify the differences in components. The bill comparison can be based on regular bills or summarized bills, where summarized bills eliminate differences due to bill structuring approaches. For example, this information can define requirements to upgrade an older product version to a new version. A bill comparison can also be made between two different items (and specified effectivity dates) to identify differences or similarities in components. This information could be used to eliminate an item with a similar bill.

Costed Bill   A costed bill can be viewed for a specified parent item, effectivity date, and cost type, either as a single-level or multilevel costed bill. Costs for each bill component are extended by the bill quantity and item costs, and optionally factored by scrap and yield percentages. A costed bill helps focus efforts concerning cost reduction on the components contributing the most to product costs.

Lead-Time Analysis   A lead-time analysis views a multilevel bill of material turned sideways for a specified parent item (and effectivity date). It depicts component lead times across the cumulative manufacturing lead-time, and can identify components on the critical path. Figure 5.2 provides an example product and two formats for lead-time analysis: an indented bill and a Gantt chart. Lead time analysis helps focus efforts concerning lead time reduction on the critical path components, and provides a key decision support tool for determining the highest stocking level for a make-to-order production strategy.

Exposure Profile   An exposure profile combines the features of costed bills and lead-time analysis. It provides a graphic summary of accumulated costs incurred across the cumulative lead-time for a specified parent item (and effec-

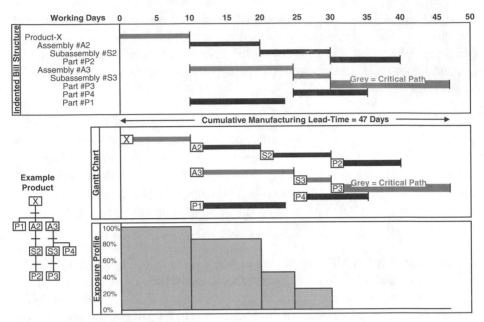

Figure 5.2 Examples of Lead-Time Analysis

tivity date). The graphic summary depicts a bar chart with the bar height representing accumulated costs (or percent of total costs), as illustrated in Figure 5.2. The right side of the bar chart identifies the costs incurred for the first receipt of purchased material, while the left side identifies 100 percent of the parent's total costs. The bar heights across the cumulative lead-time reflect step-function increases in accumulated costs corresponding to major intermediate items in the bill of materials. An exposure profile helps focus efforts concerning lead time reduction on the critical path components, especially high-value components. It also provides another viewpoint on stocking levels for a make-to-order product.

Cost Estimate by Lot Size   A cost estimate by lot size provides a per unit cost estimate for several user-defined lot sizes. It can be viewed for a specified item, effectivity date, and cost type. The per unit costs reflect per order component quantities and setup times amortized across the different lot sizes. The information helps in creating price quotes for different quantity breakpoints, and in setting an item's planning data about optimal lot sizing.

Other Considerations in the Bill of Material

This section explains a number of considerations involved in defining bills of material. Most of these reflect requirements for modeling different manufacturing environments.

ERP DESIGN ISSUE

Engineering Bills Versus Manufacturing Bills

Some environments require a separate database of engineering items and bills of material that can be maintained independently from the manufacturing item master and bills of material. The engineering database typically focuses on a subset of item master and bill of material information, since it does not have to model the manufacturing operations. The same tools for maintaining and analyzing the manufacturing bills apply to the engineering bills. The tools should also be extended to provide bill comparisons between engineering and manufacturing bills, and copying between manufacturing and engineering bills. Engineering items and bills can be promoted (or copied) to the production items and bills based on user-specified rules (such as completeness of information). This provides the basis for retaining "as originally designed" information for subsequent comparison to "as designed by manufacturing" and "as built" information.

Several problems are typically encountered in maintaining a separate set of engineering items and bills. While the design is being developed using engineering items and bills, procurement (and production) may require information in the manufacturing database to procure (and produce) long lead-time materials. The design may require several iterations of prototypes requiring procurement (and production) of one-time items prior to settling on a final design. Even when the final design (defined in the engineering database) has been promoted to the manufacturing database, the manufacturing perspective (about stages of manufacturing, phantoms, operation sequences, routing operations, and so forth) typically requires significant changes to the engineering bills. The manufacturing database will also evolve to correctly reflect changes in the bills and routings. The manufacturing database must be constantly updated to accurately reflect current conditions, and the gap between the two databases will grow over time. Therefore, there are strong arguments against the use of a separate engineering database.

Low Level Code and Circular Logic Check

MRP logic uses an item's low-level code to correctly perform level-by-level netting logic. The low-level code is automatically updated based on bill of material maintenance. Items at the top level of product structures, or not used in any bill, have a low level code of 0. Component items have a low-level code of 1 or more depending on their relative position in product structures. Cost roll-up calculations use the low-level code in reverse.

Bill maintenance involving a new component is automatically checked for circular logic to prevent situations where an item gets made from itself. Circular relationships create difficulties in MRP logic and cost roll-up calculations. The two exceptions to circular logic include coproduct components and rework manufacturing orders in which a component item can be the same as the parent item.

Reference Designators for Bill Components

In some manufacturing environments such as PC board assembly, the components must be placed in specific locations on the parent item. These environments require supplemental bill of material information called *reference designators,* which typically are specified on the parent item's drawing. For a material component with a quantity greater than one, multiple reference designator locations must be specified. The locations may be individually specified (e.g., R1, R2, R3), or specified as a range (e.g., R1-3).

The ERP system should enforce rules about reference designators. For example, the number of specified locations should equal the component quantity. Duplicate reference designators should be prohibited, since only one item can fit in the location. Duplicates should be allowed when the components' date effectivities do not overlap.

CAD Capabilities and the Bill of Material

A CAD (computer-aided design) software package provides and uses information defined in a bill of material. Viewer capabilities in a CAD package enable users to "red line" or annotate a copy of the drawing and send proposed changes to engineering via e-mail. These proposed changes may go through an ECO approval process before updating the bills of material.

A CAD package can be closely integrated to the bill of material information. This integration may enable CAD drawing information to be used for updating a new bill of material (via data import). Most of the critical information can be updated, such as the component, quantity required, find number, and even reference designators. Some information may be maintained manually to reflect manufacturing engineering concerns, such as operation sequences, scrap percentages, and date effectivities. Incremental updates to bill information from a CAD package become more difficult than adding new bills.

Bill of Material for a Subcontract Item

A subcontract manufacturer is supplied with a kit of component materials, and produces the parent subcontracted item. The subcontractor may need to obtain some components. The bill of material for a subcontract item consists of normal components (for those items supplied to the vendor) and reference components (for those items procured independently by the vendor). In this way, the bill of material provides a complete definition of material requirements.

Bill of Material for a Buy Item

A manufactured item may be designed and then purchased complete from a vendor. Relative to the design, a bill of material can provide the basis for estimating costs and then communicate the product design to the vendor. A buy item may also be manufactured in-house (on an intermittent basis) based on its bill and routing. Opening a manufacturing order for the buy item creates an order-dependent bill. MRP logic considers this supply order in its netting logic, but only generates planned purchase orders based on the item's primary source.

Bill of Tools

A bill of tools can be used for reference information, or to support tool crib management. A tool component in a bill identifies the need for a reusable tool. Since a tool item has a unit of measure of piece or each, the component's required quantity is expressed per order. The component type is tool, and component date effectivities can indicate tool changes. Where-used information identifies parent items produced with the tool, and a supply order's pick list identifies when to issue the tool.

In support of tool crib management, a tool component identifies when the tool must be issued to a supply order. The expected tool return can be identified with a second occurrence of the tool component using a component type of tool return. A tool return acts like a by-product, so that it can be received back in the tool crib after order completion (and MRP logic can identify scheduled receipts of the tool).

Bill of Documents

A bill of documents can be used for reference information. Since a document item has a unit of measure of each, the component's required quantity is expressed per order. Component date effectivities can indicate changes in applicable documents. Where-used information identifies parent items affected by the document, and a supply order's pick list identifies applicable documents.

Bills of Material for Field Service Tasks

A standardized field service task can have a bill of materials normally used to perform the task, such as equipment installations or maintenance. One aspect of field service requires identification of material requirements for upgrade kits. An upgrade kit represents the difference in bill components for a parent item built for two different effectivity dates (or two different revision levels). A comparison bill identifies the differences in bill components.

Some field service environments require bill of material information about an installed unit of equipment. Field service tasks for maintenance and upgrades result in changes to the unit's bill of material. These environments require a separate database containing the bill for each installed unit.

Manufacturer's Part Number for Bill Components

A bill of material may be required with the manufacturer and manufacturer's part number displayed for each component item. For example, this provides component information to a subcontractor who needs to obtain the correct manufacturer's part numbers.

Component Usage Policies

A component's usage policy can be issue or auto-deduct to reflect how you primarily report material consumption of its inventory. A backflush location is generally specified for auto-deducted components. A component's usage policy (and backflush location) can default from the item master and be overridden within the bill. In this way, multiple occurrences of a given component (such as multiple usage points in an assembly line) can have different backflush locations.

Food Products and Government Labeling Requirements

Selected food products require special package labeling that is related to the bill of material. One example is the FDA requirement for nutritional labels for a parent item, where the nutritional values are derived from bill components. Another labeling example involves the list of ingredients in descending sequence of product content.

Process Manufacturers and Nonlinear Component Quantities (Batch Formula)

A linear relationship between a component and parent item is assumed when specifying the component quantity per one parent item. A nonlinear formula must be specified when batch size affects the proportion of ingredients. A typical example occurs in food manufacturing when the mix of ingredients depends on batch size.

Planning Bills and Standard Products

A planning bill provides a simplified approach for forecasting many items with related demands and an alternative to forecasting them independently. An aggregate forecast for the family item provides fewer management control points than independent forecasts. In addition, the family item may represent all items produced with a common production process, such as items produced in a dedicated manufacturing cell.

A planning bill is defined just like a normal bill of material. Each component's required quantity identifies a product mix percentage that reflects a probability of sale. A planning bill works best when product mix percentages are reasonably stable, or at least stable over time periods of 3 months or longer. Anticipated changes to a component's mix percentage can be defined using multiple occurrences of the component in the planning bill, where each occurrence defines the appropriate date effectivities. Changes in mix percentages may stem from several factors. These factors include introductions and/or deletions of items to the product family, or from changing demand patterns that reflect promotions, trends, seasonality, or other reasons. The sum of the components' mix percentages is typically 100 percent for any given date. Component mix percentages can be used in cost roll-up calculations to provide an average per-unit cost of the product family.

The planning bill for some environments must handle different units of measure (UM) for the family item and the family members. A beer manufacturer, for example, may forecast a type of beer (a family item) in barrels that is sold in differing packages, such as 12-packs, 24-packs, and half-barrels. An additional component field is required in the planning bill to define the UM conversion factor (also termed a typical configuration quantity). The UM conversion factor reflects the ratio between the component's UM and the family item's UM. The ratio would be 0.5, for example, when you have a family item expressed in barrels and a planning bill component for a half-barrel container.

Several types of manufacturing environments can effectively use a planning bill. The following case study involves a product family of spare parts where demands are related to a population of previously sold equipment.

CASE STUDY   Planning Bill for a Family of Spare Parts

A planning bill can represent a logical grouping of service parts sold as replacements in supporting many units of similar equipment in the field. The family item represents the type of equipment and a model year. Several family items (and planning bills) are typically required to represent the combinations of model years and equipment types.

Each component identifies a service part with a per item required quantity reflecting the probability of replacement in the field units in a given month. The probability may be an estimated projection for service parts related to newly introduced equipment, or it may be a historically derived probability. The sum of probabilities does not have to add up to 100 percent. A component's date effectivities can be used to reflect changes in replacement probability. The replacement probability may change as the equipment type ages and as better field statistics are obtained about actual component replacements. A monthly forecast for the family item represents the equipment population at that point in time. This monthly forecast drives monthly requirements for the matched sets of spare parts in the planning bill.

Chapter 6

Resources and Routings

Routing information provides a model of the process design for a manufactured item, where routing operations define the resources required at each step in the item's production process. In addition to specifying product design, this information is used for calculating value-added costs, determining capacity requirements, scheduling production activities, reporting actual work performed and unit completions, tracking progress of production activities, and analyzing variances.

Some manufacturers do not require routing information, such as virtual manufacturers using subcontractors. Other firms use minimal routing information for just costing, capacity planning, and basic scheduling purposes with no reporting of actual work performed. These firms may be involved in orderless manufacturing with auto-deduction of material and resources.

The large majority of manufacturing firms can obtain significant benefits from routing information when it models the way manufactured products are really built. This does not necessarily require a comprehensive model of every operation, detailed measurement of required operation time, or voluminous data collection for reporting production activities. Auto-deducting resources can minimize reporting about actual work performed. Efforts to simplify factory layout can simplify routings. Simplified routings and approximate times are easier to maintain and usually sufficient to obtain the majority of benefits.

The routing for a manufactured product is closely linked to its bill of material. An operation sequence number typically defines the link between a routing operation and its required material components. This applies to both operation-centric and material-centric approaches to defining a bill of material, as described in the previous chapter. This chapter explains routing information by building on the operation-centric approach for make items and the material-centric approach for subcontract items.

ERP systems have taken different approaches to modeling resources and routing operations. One design issue involves managing external production activities using a subcontract item versus outside operation approach (as described in Chapter 4). This chapter covers other design issues, such as the approaches to modeling available capacity and the significance of operation sequence numbers in scheduling logic. A basic design issue that must be addressed up front is the approach to modeling routing operations. Two common approaches—termed the *bill of resource* and the *separate routing data* approaches—have been used in ERP systems. The breakout box explains these two approaches and identifies the advantages of the bill of resources approach. The explanations about routing information in this book will build on the bill of resources approach, but the concepts and discussion apply to both approaches.

ERP DESIGN ISSUE

Modeling Routing Operations Using a Bill of Resources Versus Separate Routing Data

There are two fundamentally different approaches to defining routing information for a manufactured item. These approaches, termed the bill of resource and the separate routing data approaches, are explained below. An ERP system generally takes only one approach, but both approaches work.

Bill of Resources Approach. A routing operation is defined as a resource component in the item's bill, using resource items defined in the item master. This approach provides several advantages in simplicity and symmetry:

- ◆ Maintain material and resource item information on the same screens
- ◆ Maintain bill and routing information on the same screens
- ◆ Use the same tools for analyzing where-used data and making mass changes
- ◆ Perform a single cost roll-up calculation, since the same data structure defines bills and routings
- ◆ View costed bill and routing information on the same screen
- ◆ Maintain the order-dependent bill and routing on the same screen
- ◆ Perform a single planning calculation for material and capacity requirements, since the same data structure defines bills and routings
- ◆ Support scheduling logic that simultaneously considers resource and material constraints

Separate Routing Data Approach. Routing operations and work centers are defined in separate files from items and bills. This approach requires two different sets of maintenance and inquiry screens. It requires two cost roll-up calculations (for calculating the value-added costs based on routings and rolled costs based on bills), and two planning calculations (for calculating material plans based on bills and capacity plans based on routings). The separate data structures make it more difficult to simultaneously consider resource and material constraints in scheduling logic.

Brevity in terminology highlights differences in the two approaches. One approach uses the term bill of material and routing, whereas *bill* expresses the same concept in the other approach. Other examples include order-dependent bill, costed bill, bill comparison, summarized bill, and item where-used. If for no other reason than brevity, this book uses terms from the bill of resources approach to explain concepts and practicalities related to routing information. The terms routing and routing operation will also be used for brevity's sake.

Routing information starts with the resource master. These may be internal resources such as machines, tools and labor, or external resources (subcontractors) providing value-added to supplied material. Internal and external resources can be conceptualized similarly, but differ significantly in routing information about costs, time requirements and scheduling logic. Outside operations also have related procurement activities. This chapter first covers internal resources and routing information for internal operations, and then covers external resources and outside operations.

Resource Master: Internal Resources

Internal resources typically reflect single machines or labor pools of people with similar skills. These types of resources have a physical identity and operate under capacity constraints, expressed in hours of availability. Other types of resources have a logical rather than a physical identity. A dummy resource, for example, may be used for scheduling, capacity planning, or costing purposes.

This section provides a brief explanation of common resource types—categorized as single resources, pooled resources, and other—and provides guidelines for modeling supply chain activities related to internal production processes. Figure 6.1 summarizes a comparison of internal resource types. The types of resources differ in how you define available capacity and costs, the required capacity by operation, and the applicability of a production schedule.

	Type of Resource	Examples	Characteristics of the Resource			
			Capacity Constraint	Use in Costing	Required Capacity By Operation	Use in Finite Scheduling
Single Resources	Finite	Machine, Assembly Line, Manufacturing Cell	Hours	Y	Hours	Y
	Simultaneous	Oven or Slitter	Hours + Max Units	Y	Hours + Required Units	Y
	Tool	Serialized Fixture	Hours	Y	Hours	Y
	Person	Operator, Engineer	Hours	Y	Hours	Y
	Infinite	Fermentation, Burn-in (Focus on Elapsed Time)	Hours	Y	Hours	Y
Pooled	Pooled Resource	Labor with Same Skills Identical Machines or Tools (Treated as a Whole)	Hours + Avail Crew	Y	Hours + Required Crew	Y
Other	Resource Group	Interchangeable Machines (Treated as Individuals) Can specify Preferred Resource	N/A	Y (Average vs Preferred)	Hours (Average vs Preferred)	For Logic Purposes
	Department	One Department per Resource	Hours	Y	N/A	N/A
	Dummy	Creative Use for Costing or Capacity Planning	Hours or Any UM	Y	Hours or Any UM	N/A

Figure 6.1 Comparison of Internal Resource Types

Types of Single Resources

A single resource generally identifies a machine, tool, or person with capacity constraints expressed in hours of availability. Variations of a single resource reflect differences in capacity and scheduling, such as a machine that can handle several similar jobs concurrently, or a burn-in area that can handle an unlimited number of jobs. Five types of single resources are described below and summarized in Figure 6.1.

Finite Resource   A single finite resource typically represents a stand-alone machine, a manufacturing cell, or an assembly line. A cell consists of one or more machines and their operators.

Simultaneous Resource   A simultaneous resource represents a special case of a finite resource and is illustrated by an oven or slitter machine. It can concurrently process multiple operations (with similar attributes) from different orders, up to a maximum capacity. Each routing operation has attributes and an associated capacity requirement, so that a number of different operations run concurrently when the sum of their capacity requirements does not exceed the maximum.

Tool   A tool resource is identified only when it defines a critical scheduling constraint, such as a serialized, reusable fixture or mold.

Note: A single resource (for a finite, simultaneous, or tool resource) typically requires maintenance that reduces available hours. It may also require projections and tracking of cumulative usage hours (or usage cycles) for the purposes of scheduling maintenance and calibration.

Person   A person resource is identified only when scheduling requires order assignments to individual people, such as individual operators or engineers. Capacity availability of a person is limited to a single shift, unlike machines or tools. A group of people with similar skills is normally modeled as a pooled resource rather than individuals.

Infinite Resource   An infinite resource is typically used for operations with elapsed time as the primary constraint on operation duration. This includes a time period for quarantine, burn-in, fermentation, gestation, or the turnaround of inspection results. In this case, the infinite capacity viewpoint means an unlimited number of orders can be processed concurrently (ignoring space or other limitations) for each operation's duration. It can also be used to approximate the capabilities of a miscellaneous manufacturing area.

Note: A second viewpoint on infinite capacity ignores even the operation duration in that multiple concurrent orders can be processed immediately. Both viewpoints use the term infinite capacity which leads to confusion. For infinite loading purposes, an ERP system should consider operation duration in calculating a resource's capacity requirements.

Types of Pooled Resources

A pooled resource generally identifies a number of people with similar capabilities, where capacity constraints for a labor pool are expressed in hours of availability and available headcount. Each shift represents a different pooled resource. The label assigned to a labor pool (such as operators, assemblers, welders, or engineers) reflects their capabilities. The pooled resource is treated as a whole (without recognition of individuals) in terms of a single production schedule.

Routing operations for a pooled resource specify the headcount requirement as well as operation duration. The headcount (or crew size) requirement may identify multiple people to perform the task or a fraction of an individual's time, such as one person running two machines. Using headcount requirements, the schedule for a pooled resource reflects its ability to concurrently process multiple orders (each with different operation duration) within the constraints of available headcount. The schedule for a pooled resource reflects several underlying assumptions. The basic assumptions, for example, are that an operation's headcount requirement is optimal and fixed over the duration of an operation, and that work on a given operation can span shifts.

An operation's headcount requirement and duration are used in capacity requirement calculations (with infinite loading) to identify the total hours and headcount by time period. They are also used in cost roll-up calculations, along with the labor pool's average pay rate. Actual time reported against operations can use the pool's standard rate or the individual pay rates for actual costing purposes.

A labor pool is typically identified only for labor-intensive work centers, or for identifying people as a constraining resource on machine-paced operations. In most manufacturing cells and assembly lines (and even machines), labor does not require a separate resource since labor costs can be embedded in the hourly rates for the single resource.

The concept of a pooled resource also applies to a number of identical machines or tools, where individuals are not identified. The available headcount of machines or tools does not typically vary by shift, unlike a labor pool. Maintenance on the tools or machines during working hours can be modeled by a reduction in the available headcount. When scheduling requires assignment of orders to individual resources, a resource group rather than a pooled resource should be used to model the production activities.

Additional variations of a pooled resource reflect variations in capacity and scheduling assumptions. One assumption could be that work on a given operation cannot span shifts. Another assumption could involve an operation's headcount requirement: perhaps an operation's headcount requirement must be available to start the operation but can vary over the operation duration. These variations in assumptions can become extremely complex; they generally become significant only in situations requiring comprehensive scheduling logic. Each variation could be identified with a different resource type. Only one type of pooled resource is identified in Figure 6.1, which reflects the basic scheduling assumptions.

Other Types of Internal Resources

A miscellaneous manufacturing area typically represents a mixture of personnel and equipment performing multiple operations. It can be difficult to model with the constructs of single resources and pooled resource. Defining detailed routing operations for each person or machine would be overkill. An approximation of the capabilities of a miscellaneous area is generally sufficient for costing, capacity, and basic scheduling purposes. Use of a single infinite resource, or a pooled resource, provides a reasonable approximation for a miscellaneous area.

Other types of resources have a logical rather than a physical identity. They provide different ways to support scheduling, capacity planning, or costing purposes. The three resource types described below, and summarized in Figure 6.1, illustrate these differences.

Resource Group A resource group provides a logical construct to support scheduling logic for single (or pooled) resources that can be treated as interchangeable for a given operation. A resource group identifies a capability or skill set, and a resource can belong to multiple resource groups when it has multiple capabilities. Therefore, a routing operation can identify requirements for a capability (the resource group), and scheduling logic can assign a resource with the capability. An operation's required time (or run rate) reflects an average for the resource group, and is used for costing and infinite capacity planning purposes. The average run rate reflects a basic scheduling assumption, whereas more advanced scheduling logic can handle machine-specific run rates.

CASE STUDY Extruded Products and the Use of Resource Groups

An extruded products firm manufactured plastic pipes of varying diameters and colors. They had multiple extrusion machines producing different pipes from plastic pellets, resin, color, and other additives. The product structure for a given pipe, illustrated in

Figure 6.2, identified these material components and one routing operation. They initially identified a specific machine in the routing operation with an average setup time. This simple scheme worked for costing purposes, but did not support capacity planning and scheduling requirements. Schedulers used an informal system to assign machines to manufacturing orders that accounted for machine capabilities and availability, tools, operators, and sequencing to minimize setups.

A more comprehensive approach to modeling production activities was taken to support the other requirements. Three resource groups were defined (small, medium, and large diameter capabilities) and each extruder machine was assigned applicable resource groups. The routing operation now identifies a resource group, such as the small diameter resource group (shown in Figure 6.2) for producing the 1 inch black pipe. Availability of operators and tools were identified as secondary resources, since they constrained the ability to use the primary (or pacing) resource. Each operation had setup attributes (such as "1.00" inch and "black"), and associated setup matrices, that reflected variable setup times. Scheduling logic assigned manufacturing orders to machines based on availability of machines (within the resource group), operators, and tools. It also calculated variable setup times that reflect sequencing and machine-specific run rates that reflect machine assignments.

Designating a preferred resource and a resource group for the routing operation can support additional scheduling logic. In this case, an operation's required time and costing could reflect the preferred resource.

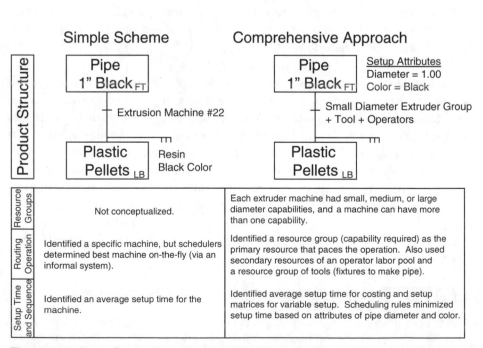

Figure 6.2 Case Study: Extruded Products and the Use of Resource Groups

Department Resource A department provides a logical construct to support aggregate capacity planning or cost allocations. One department is assigned to each resource. As a logical construct, a department does not have a capacity constraint, but available capacity may be defined for aggregate capacity planning purposes.

Dummy Resource Dummy resources provide a tool supporting creative solutions to knotty problems in scheduling, costing, and capacity planning. A dummy resource can have any unit of measure (such as weight, volume, area, or pieces), with available capacity expressed in units (or units per time period). A dummy resource's unit of measure may reflect production *output units* rather than *input units*. As an example in a chemical manufacturer, a dummy resource with a unit of measure in gallons (a volume) can be used in a bill of resources to allocate overhead costs per gallon of output and to calculate capacity requirements in gallons. A dummy resource can represent a capacity constraint that is not directly involved in the production process, but still merits consideration in the scheduling logic. Examples include warehouse or production area floor space.

A dummy resource can represent a noninventoried item such as water or power. Noninventoried material such as tap water may be a required ingredient in a bill of material. As a resource, you can calculate capacity requirements and optionally report actual usage (without having inventory). Costing information may be defined for the resource.

Resource Unit of Measure and Available Capacity

The simplest approach for a single resource (and pooled resource) uses hours for the resource unit of measure (UM), with capacity expressed in hours of availability. Other time increments could be used for the resource UM and routing operation requirements, such as run rates in seconds, minutes, or days. In contrast, a dummy resource can have any unit of measure to allocate costs, calculate capacity requirements, or support scheduling logic.

A resource's available capacity serves two major purposes: as a capacity constraint in finite scheduling and for comparisons in infinite capacity planning.

◆ *Infinite Capacity Planning Purpose.* Capacity requirement calculations (with infinite loading) are compared to available capacity to identify overloaded periods for each resource. These calculations treat every resource as an infinite resource, where the infinite capacity viewpoint means each resource can concurrently handle an unlimited number of orders (for the duration of each operation).

◆ *Finite Scheduling Purpose.* Finite scheduling logic uses capacity constraints in several situations, such as calculating a variable lead time for a manufacturing order, calculating a capable-to-promise date for a sales order, and optimizing a production schedule. Finite scheduling logic also results in capacity requirement calculations that identify resource utilization by time period (based on a comparison to available capacity).

A resource's available capacity can be modeled with a simplistic or comprehensive approach, or something in between. A simplistic approach supports infinite capacity planning. Comprehensive scheduling logic generally requires a comprehensive approach to modeling available capacity. The breakout box on modeling available capacity provides further explanation.

ERP DESIGN ISSUE

Modeling Available Capacity Using a Simplistic Versus Comprehensive Approach

ERP systems provide various approaches to modeling the available capacity of resources. They vary from a simplistic to a comprehensive model, typified by two approaches termed a *daily shop calendar* and a *shift pattern* approach. Both approaches can support infinite capacity planning and many finite scheduling situations, but a comprehensive approach is generally required to support advanced scheduling logic.

Simplistic Approach: Daily Shop Calendar. A simplistic approach to modeling resource capacity supports only daily time increments, as defined by a daily shop calendar identifying the dates of working (and non-working) days. Each resource's daily available capacity is expressed in the resource's unit of measure, which can be time (hours) or other unit (such as weight, volume, or pieces). Exceptions to available capacity are identified by dates for working and nonworking days in the shop calendar, or by changes to a resource's available capacity on a given date.

The most simplistic approach provides only one plant-wide shop calendar of working days. As a refinement, multiple shop calendars can be defined, with assignment of one daily shop calendar to a resource.

Comprehensive Approach: Shift Patterns. A comprehensive approach to modeling resource capacity supports time increments (hours and minutes) within a day, as defined by hours of operation and shift segmentation. A shift pattern specifies start- and stop-times of working (and nonworking) hours by shift, with a repeating cycle of 24-hour days across a 7-day week (or other time span). Shift patterns are defined independently of resources, and then assigned to a resource. Exceptions to available capacity are identified by one-time exceptions (expressed in terms of start and end times), and by assigning multiple shift patterns with effectivity dates to identify a planned change in resource capacity. The shift pattern approach can handle other capacity characteristics, such as differences in shift efficiencies and available head counts by shift for pooled resources.

Note: A daily shop calendar (expressed in hours) can be derived from shift pattern information by summing the available hours within a 24-hour period and subtracting (or adding) the exceptions.

In summary, support of infinite capacity planning requires a daily shop calendar in order to highlight overloaded periods. The daily shop calendar approach provides an approximation of available capacity that is sufficient for many finite- or manual-scheduling situations. Even the comprehensive approach provides only an approximation of available capacity when you consider that the dynamics of production capabilities, such as constantly changing head counts and intermittent machine availability, cannot be easily modeled without excessive efforts to update availability information.

Reporting Resource Usage

Reporting resource usage (in time and in unit completions) is critical when an operation's remaining work must be considered for scheduling, and when actual costs and operation yields are being tracked. Actual time can be reported via individual issue transactions, or the theoretical time can be auto-deducted based on unit completions reported for the operation (or subsequent operations). An operation's unit completions can be treated as information only with no back-flushing impact, or as a pay-point that triggers backflushing of auto-deducted resources and material. Some ERP systems provide policies on reporting time (issue versus auto-deduct) and unit completions (information only versus pay-point) at a resource.

Routing Operations: Internal

A routing consists of a parent item and one or more routing operation. A routing operation identifies the primary (or pacing) resource that determines operation duration and optional secondary resources. An operation sequence number uniquely identifies each operation in a routing and provides the foundation for basic scheduling assumptions. The operation sequence and designated resource(s) represent two aspects of the critical information defining an internal routing operation.

ERP DESIGN ISSUE

Operation Sequence Number and Scheduling Logic

ERP systems use operation sequence numbers to define basic scheduling assumptions. The numbering conventions are generally consistent and they are explained below. Figure 6.3 provides an example routing that illustrates operation sequence numbering. Additional features can supplement the basic scheduling assumptions, such as operation overlaps for the linear sequence assumption.

Enforced Uniqueness. Operation sequences within a routing must be unique, since duplicates can confuse scheduling logic.

Linear Sequence Assumption. Scheduling logic assumes that operations must be performed in a linear sequence based on the operation sequence, such as operations 30, 40, and 50 for the parent item shown in Figure 6.3.

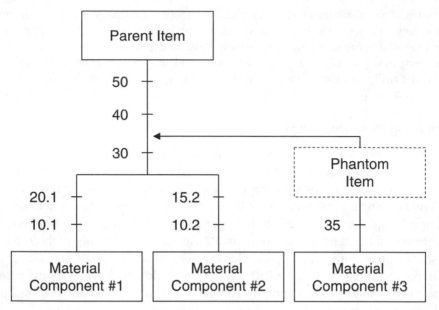

Figure 6.3 Example Routing for Operation Sequence Numbering

Parallel Path Assumption. One approach to designating parallel operations uses a suffix to the operation sequence. Scheduling logic assumes that operations identified with the same suffix (such as 10.1 and 20.1 in Figure 6.3) belong to a parallel path. Multiple parallel paths can be identified with a different suffix (such as 10.2 and 15.2 for a second parallel path). The linear sequence assumption applies to operations in each parallel path. Scheduling logic assumes parallel paths come together when it encounters a higher operation sequence without a suffix (such as sequence 30 in this example). All parallel paths must be completed before scheduling logic can schedule the start of this "next" operation.

Alternate Operation Assumption. Scheduling logic assumes that an alternate operation has the same operation sequence as the original. This often creates difficulties when the alternate consists of multiple operations (with differing operation sequence numbers).

Impact of Operations from Phantom Items. An order-dependent routing will combine a phantom's operations (with their operation sequences) and the parent item's operations. The phantom item in Figure 6.3 illustrates the impact with operation 35. The combination of operations can result in duplicate operation sequences without careful forethought in numbering assignments. The interrelationship between parallel operations, alternate operations, and operations stemming from a phantom can cause additional complexities.

Required Material Assumption. The material components for a given operation have the same operation sequence number. In Figure 6.3, component materials are tied to operations 10.1, 10.2, and 35.

Critical Information for an Internal Routing Operation

Several fields represent the critical information defining an internal routing operation for a parent item. These fields identify the operation sequence, the resource, required time (quantity), operation yield percent, and operation description. Some resource types require additional fields to specify capacity requirements. The fields also include in-effect and out-effect dates when using effectivity dates to manage changes to a routing, as discussed in the section on managing changes to a routing.

Operation Sequence   Operation sequence provides a unique identifier for a routing operation and defines the basic scheduling logic when a routing involves multiple operations.

Resource   One primary resource and optional secondary resources perform an operation. The primary resource acts as the pacing resource, so that scheduling logic uses its time requirements for determining operation duration.

Required Time (Quantity)   The required time for the operation's primary resource component defines the average run time (or run rate) to produce one parent item. It can also be stated as a fixed per order time.

Some environments need to express run time per operation UM rather than per parent. The operation processes a multiple (or fraction) of the parent's quantity. This requires two additional fields—the desired UM and a UM conversion factor—to correctly express the operation UM. The UM conversion factor is normally "1" for operation run time expressed per parent item. The operation UM affects reporting of unit completions by operation and operation yield calculations.

An operation's time requirements may also include setup, tear down, move, queue or other time element. Only setup time will be considered here. An average setup time, expressed in hours, represents a per order quantity that can be used for capacity planning and costing purposes. Scheduling logic may need to consider variable setup time based on sequencing considerations, typically using setup matrices and operation attributes.

Additional information related to required time may be necessary for some resource types. For instance, a pooled resource needs information about the required crew size (or headcount) to perform the operation.

Operation Yield Percent   An operation's yield percent defines the expected proportion of good units out of the total units processed. It affects the requirements for material components tied to the operation, and the requirements for both material and resource components tied to prior operations. It does not affect component requirements defined with a per order quantity.

Operation Description   The operation description provides textual information about how to perform an operation. The operation description may also identify required operator feedback, such as equipment settings, quality measurements, and signoffs.

Additional Information for an Internal Operation   Additional information may reflect operation attributes, text, and use of a master operation identifier.

Use of a Master Operation

The concept of a master operation is that it can be defined once and then identified for a specified operation sequence in various routing operations. Each master operation has a unique user-defined identifier, and defines all of the critical information for an internal operation. The concept of a master operation has several variations. In one case, changes to a master operation automatically update all related routing operations (identified by where-used information). In another case, information inherited from the master operation acts as a template subject to manual overrides. A master operation may have a status, date effectivities, or an alternate operation.

External Resources and Outside Operations

Each vendor performing outside operations can be viewed as a single infinite resource, which assumes they can concurrently handle an unlimited number of orders during hours of operation. This provides the simplest viewpoint when you lack the detailed knowledge and schedule responsibility of a vendor's production processes. Conversely, the vendor could be viewed as a single finite resource when you have detailed control of their schedules. These represent two types of external resources, as summarized in Figure 6.4. Other resource types may apply, such as a dummy resource.

Type of Resource		Examples	Characteristics of the Resource				
			Capacity Constraint	Purchase Cost	Turnaround Time	Required Capacity by Operation	Use in Finite Scheduling
Single Resource	Finite	Complete control of scheduling at vendor	Hours	Y	Calculated	Hours	Y
	Infinite	No control of scheduling at vendor	N/A	Y	Specified	N/A	Y
Other	Dummy	Provide visibility of vendor capacity requirements	N/A	Y	N/A	Hours or Any UM	N/A

Figure 6.4 Comparison of External Resource Types

An outside operation involves two streams of supply chain activities (for the manufacturing order operation and its related purchase order) that require coordination. The typical activities will first be summarized, and coordination issues highlighted, before explaining the critical information that defines an outside operation.

Overview of an Outside Operation and Related Purchasing Activities

The outside operation is first defined in the manufactured item's routing. Creating a manufacturing order results in an order-dependent routing with the outside operation. An ERP system can now recommend creation of the purchase order for the outside operation. The recommended action can identify the manufacturing order and operation sequence, along with a suggested purchase cost, preferred vendor, quantity, and turnaround time. After creation of the purchase order, the supplied material can be sent to the vendor, and the completed items received against the PO. Actual costs can be passed directly to the manufacturing order's operation.

Coordination issues in the two streams of activities are apparent in dual fields for costs, due dates, order quantities, completed quantities, and order closures. Multiple outside operations and direct shipments between vendors create additional coordination issues. A subcontract item approach provides a simplified coordinating mechanism in comparison to an outside operation.

Critical Information for an Outside Operation

Several fields represent the critical information defining an outside operation. These fields identify the operation sequence, resource, purchase quantity, purchase cost, operation description, and turnaround time. Additional fields can define capacity requirements for modeling a finite resource. The fields also include in-effect and out-effect dates when using effectivity dates to manage changes to a routing.

Operation Sequence   Operation sequence provides a unique identifier and defines the basic scheduling logic when a routing involves multiple operations.

Resource (Preferred Vendor)   The resource represents a subcontractor and can be used for scheduling purposes. The resource type affects an operation's routing information, such as the capacity requirements for a finite resource. A separate field identifying the preferred vendor (defined in the vendor master) is typically required in most ERP systems for procurement purposes.

Purchase Quantity   The purchase quantity is normally expressed in terms of the parent item's quantity. It may be expressed as a fixed or per order quantity.

Some environments require an operation UM (and UM conversion factor) to define the basis for a purchase quantity.

Purchase Cost   The purchase cost is defined in terms of the purchase quantity and represents the operation's standard cost.

Turnaround Time   The turnaround time for an outside operation represents an average elapsed time for the external vendor to process the order, regardless of order quantity. Turnaround time does not apply to a finite resource when scheduling logic can calculate the turnaround time.

Assigned Buyer   The assigned buyer is responsible for coordinating procurement activities and receives recommended action messages for placing the outside operation purchase order.

Additional Information for an Outside Operation   Additional information may reflect secondary resources, operation attributes, text, and use of a master operation identifier. Additional information is also required for a finite external resource, such as operation duration, setup time, move time to the vendor (for supplied material), and move time from the vendor (for returning the completed items).

Managing Changes to a Routing

Temporary changes to a routing can be identified in the order-dependent routing. Planning changes to routings may use operation effectivity dates. Several other methods can be used to define authorized variations in a production process, such as alternate operations and versions of a routing.

Routing Versus Order-Dependent Routing

An order-dependent routing can identify one-time changes to an item's routing. The order-dependent routing is tied to a manufacturing order, just like an order-dependent bill of material. It initially reflects the routing operations in effect as of the order start date (when using component effectivity dates to manage changes).

Planned Changes in Routing Operations

Changes in process design and factory layout can be identified as planned changes in a routing. The planned changes can be used to anticipate impacts on costs, capacity, and schedules. Different approaches to managing planned changes in bills were described earlier, and similar approaches can be used for routing data. The most commonly accepted method uses operation effectivity dates to phase in and phase out changes to routing operations. This approach maintains a complete history of an item's routing. Cost roll-up calculations consider the routing operations in effect as of a specified target date. This supports calculations of projected costs as well as historical costs. MRP logic uses order start dates as the basis for considering which routing operations are in effect. Order-dependent routings initially reflect the operations in effect on the order start date.

Authorized Variations in Routings

Authorized variations in a production process can be predefined using one or more approaches.

Alternate Operation   The alternate operation approach requires a predefined operation (or series of operations) to be designated for an operation in the item's routing. An alternate operation may be automatically considered in advanced scheduling logic subject to rules such as "consider the alternate only when the job would be late by 24 hours." Some ERP systems support manual selection of the predefined alternate operation in an order-dependent routing.

Version of a Routing   Multiple versions of a routing can define authorized variations in a production process. ERP systems provide different approaches to support multiple versions of a routing. One approach uses different item revision levels (or an item's routing revision level) to predefine versions of the routing. This capability may be supplemented by the "parent revision level effectivity" approach to managing bill changes. Another approach uses phantoms to identify authorized recipes.

An alternate operation or routing version often has differing material requirements. An operation-centric approach to defining the bill, with material components tied to the operation, provides one method to support this requirement.

Updating Routings and an Engineering Change Order Approval Process

Most companies involved in standard products manufacturing require a procedure for adding and updating routing information. It sometimes requires coordination with the procedure for adding new resource items. The procedure ensures definition of a complete and accurate routing for new products, and calculation of the product costs. For changes to existing routings, the procedure identifies a planned cutover date for new operations or changes to existing operations. This standard procedure is typically referred to as an engineering change order (ECO) approval process. A suggested ECO approval process was provided earlier in Chapter 5.

Tools for Maintaining and Analyzing Bills of Resources

Using the bill of resources approach to routing data, the same tools for maintaining and analyzing bills of material apply to the bill of resources. You can copy one item's bill to another item for all components or selected components. You can make mass changes to a resource component based on its where-used information. A mass change, for example, can replace one resource component with another component in all bills or for selected bills. Other mass changes can be used to phase out a resource component and phase in the replacement, to delete a component, or to change a component's quantity. You also have the same analysis tools, such as the where-used for resource items, supply/demand schedules, bill comparisons, and costed bills.

Other Considerations in the Routing

This section explains a number of considerations involved in defining resources and routings. Most of these reflect requirements for modeling different manufacturing environments.

Operation Attributes Related to Scheduling

Operation attributes can serve multiple purposes. Several attributes affect scheduling, such as an overlapping operation offset, campaign sequence value, and setup matrices.

Overlapping Operation Offset An operation's offset defines the amount of time or number of units that must be completed before the succeeding operation can start setup or processing.

Campaign Sequence Value An operation's campaign value provides one method of sequencing operations on a resource, so that operations will be scheduled in ascending, descending, or cyclical sequence.

Simultaneous Resource Attributes Concurrent operations are scheduled on a simultaneous resource (up to the resource's maximum capacity) based on the same values for matching attribute fields. In addition, an operation performed at a simultaneous resource has a required capacity attribute (and an indicator of per item versus per order quantity) so that the values can be summed for comparison to the resource's maximum capacity.

Setup Matrix Attributes A setup matrix identifier, and related operation characteristics, can be defined for each operation in order to calculate sequence-dependent setup times. The sequence-dependent setup times and a setup matrix are described next.

Sequence-Dependent Setup Times

Sequence-dependent setup times can be modeled with a setup matrix. A setup matrix reflects operation characteristics along each axis with the setup times in each matrix cell. A setup matrix identifier can be defined as an attribute for each operation performed at the resource. An operation may have one or more setup matrices that can be used to calculate a variable setup time contingent on the preceding operation. The contingencies reflect characteristics of the current job's operation compared with the preceding job's operation. These characteristics are also defined as operation attributes, so that scheduling logic can determine the appropriate matrix cell for defining setup time.

Using a Buy Item to Model an Outside Operation

When an ERP system cannot support outside operations in a parent's routing (with a purchase cost and turnaround time), an alternative approach uses buy items on the item master. A buy item is typically defined for each combination of outside operation and parent item, such as "Outside Operation X on Parent Item Y." The material component can specify the appropriate unit of measure, the turnaround time, and a purchase cost. This approach offers some advantages over an outside operation approach. For example, it supports approved vendors, a buy-card history, and a vendor schedule of planned requirements for the item. However, the approach still has coordination issues between the procurement and manufacturing activities.

Routing Information for a Subcontract Item

A routing operation is not required for a subcontract item. An optional routing operation specifying a dummy resource can be used for capacity planning purposes. The operation's required capacity defines a per item quantity, expressed in hours or other units.

The optional routing operation may be used for finite scheduling purposes, but this involves more complexity. It requires detailed information on the operation's required capacity, the resource's available capacity, and other loads placed on the external resource. It must also model the time requirements to send supplied material and receive the completed item.

Routing Information for a Field Service Task

A standardized field service task can have routing operations normally used to perform the task, such as equipment installations or maintenance. The internal resources performing the tasks typically reflect a labor pool or single resources (people) for finite scheduling purposes.

Run Rates Based on Crew Size in a Pooled Resource

Some environments have labor-intensive operations where the run rate depends on the assigned crew size. Advanced scheduling logic can use a run-time matrix to model varying run rates. For example, the run-time matrix can specify pooled resources on one axis and the crew size head count on the other axis, with the run time in each matrix cell. The run-time matrix identifier can be defined as an operation attribute. Scheduling logic initially uses the suggested crew size for a pooled resource as the basis for a run time, and then considers alternative crew sizes if the operation results in a late job.

Common Problems Related to Routings

Routing data that does not model how products are really built is frequently cited as the underlying cause of an ineffective ERP system and unusable production schedules. There are many reasons for poor routing data. Definition and maintenance of reasonably complete and accurate routing data can be aided by simplification of factory layouts, reconceptualization and simplification of routing operations, and a feedback mechanism to continuously improve routing information.

One starting point for simplification of routing operations focuses on the schedulers' requirements for production schedules produced by the ERP system. The schedulers often want just the visibility of items (orders), quantities, and due dates by work center. They work out the details of machine and people assignment, sequencing, and other scheduling issues. This helps establish the minimal level of routing information, which then provides the basis for costing and capacity planning.

Some firms do not have any routing information defined in their ERP system. The lack of routing data makes it difficult (if not impossible) for an ERP system to translate manufacturing orders into production schedules by resource. Schedulers typically use informal systems to communicate production schedules that reflect sales orders and ship dates. These firms often perceive the level of effort to define and maintain routing information as too onerous. The counter-argument is that the lack of routing data affects their ability to manage internal supply chain activities, and the level of effort can be balanced against benefits.

Chapter 7

Item Supply and Planning Data

Item supply orders and planning data provide the cornerstones for effectively managing supply chain activities. Planning data (or planning parameters) define the basic logic for material replenishment. For each item (what), the parameters define the primary source of replenishment (where), the decision-making responsibility (who), and the replenishment method (why, when, and how many).

A supply order represents item replenishment. MRP logic suggests supply orders (based on the item's planning data) to cover demands. An item's supply order defines a quantity and availability date and is indirectly linked to sales orders. The three basic types of supply orders (manufacturing orders, purchase orders, and subcontract purchase orders) reflect the three primary sources of replenishment. Other sources of replenishment reflect component materials (such as by-products and customer-supplied materials) identified in the context of a parent item's bill of material, and replenished in the context of the parent item's supply order.

Some ERP systems support direct linkage between an item's supply order and the sales order. A supply order is automatically created for each sales order rather than being suggested by MRP logic. This results in variations of the three basic supply orders.

Most ERP systems support multiple line items on a purchase order, and even delivery lines within a line item. This represents the basic structure of a purchase order. For symmetry's sake, the same structure should apply to other supply orders, such as a manufacturing order. However, many ERP systems do not support multiple line items for a manufacturing order, or the concept of a blanket manufacturing order.

This chapter begins with several ERP design issues related to item supplies, such as the structure of a supply order and direct linkage to sales orders. Other issues involve planning parameters about lead-time, daily usage rate, and order-less manufacturing. The chapter then reviews the types of supply orders and explains the critical planning data involved in modeling supply chain activities.

ERP Design Issues Related to Item Supplies

Different approaches have been taken in ERP systems to model the structure of a supply order and material replenishment. One approach uses MRP logic to suggest and manage supply orders indirectly linked to sales order demand, while another approach uses supply orders directly linked to sales orders. Orderless manufacturing environments do not use supply orders.

ERP systems also use different approaches for planning parameters underlying replenishment logic. The differences can be highlighted in terms of key planning parameters.

The Structure of a Supply Order

The global term *supply order* applies to purchase orders, manufacturing orders, and other variations of supply (such as subcontract purchase orders and rework orders). A supply order defines a scheduled receipt in terms of a specified item, quantity, and due date. The identifier for each supply order consists of two data elements: an order number and line item number. A given line item may specify multiple delivery dates, so that the unique identifier may consist of a third element: the delivery date or delivery line number. These three data elements reflect the basic structure of a supply order.

A generally accepted approach to the structure of a purchase order involves multiple line items. Variations exist for handling multiple delivery dates within a line item, especially in handling a blanket purchase order. The structure of a purchase order is reflected in its life cycle, such as an order status for each line and delivery line. In terms of symmetry, the same structure should apply to manufacturing orders. This represents the structure of the supply order and life cycle viewpoint taken in this book. For brevity's sake, the explanations often employ terminology focusing on line items rather than delivery lines within line items.

Direct Versus Indirect Linkage between Supply Orders and Sales Orders

ERP systems that handle standard products typically support indirect linkage between supply orders and sales orders. Normal MRP logic calculates planned supply orders to cover demands based on an item's planning parameters. The supply orders are indirectly linked to sales orders via dates: the supply order due date and the sales order ship date. Pegging information identifies demands stemming from sales orders. One manufacturing order, for instance, may cover the demands for multiple sales orders, and changes to sales orders may require a separate action to update the manufacturing order.

Direct linkage between a sales order and a supply order is normally associated with a custom product configuration. With direct linkage, a sales order has one custom product manufacturing order that is automatically updated by changes to the sales order quantity and configuration. The supply order can be scheduled independently (via start and end dates) from the sales order.

Some ERP systems support direct linkage for standard products. Various approaches have been used to identify the need for direct linkage. One approach identifies direct linkage via a sales order line type, while another approach designates it in the item master. Direct linkage for a make item, for example, means that a sales order has one final-assembly manufacturing order that is automatically updated by changes to the sales order quantity.

Direct linkage represents one form of a make-to-order production strategy for standard products. Replenishment of stocked material can still be based on forecasted demands for the final-assembly end-items, where forecasted demands blow through the product structure to the highest stocking level.

Fixed Versus Variable Lead-Times on Manufacturing Orders

The item master lead-time for a make item represents the average elapsed days for an average order quantity under average factory load conditions. Many ERP systems used this fixed lead-time on manufacturing orders to calculate an order start date based on its due date. A user can manually override the order start date to indicate a different lead-time. The user may also manually update operation start/end dates. This provides a sufficient model of production activities in many cases.

Some ERP systems calculate a variable lead-time on manufacturing orders to derive an order start date. The calculations account for the order quantity and routing, and generally employ simplistic assumptions about available capacities and scheduling rules. For example, the calculations treat a resource's available capacity as infinite, ignore current factory loads, and backward schedule a linear sequence of operations. This basic scheduling logic results in an order start date and typically calculates operation start/end dates for the order-dependent routing. An alternative approach to variable lead-time involves rate-based scheduling with daily schedules spread over a variable number of days. The basic scheduling logic for variable lead-time and daily schedules is often embedded within MRP logic and provides an enhanced model of production activities.

A few ERP systems support advanced scheduling (or APS) logic to calculate variable lead-times and operation start and end dates. This approach uses comprehensive models of available capacity, scheduling rules, and current factory loads. It may use forward or backward finite scheduling and consider material constraints. The advanced scheduling logic may apply to a single job or globally to all jobs. With a single job (or group of related orders in a multilevel product structure), the scheduling logic typically places the order at the end of current factory loads or at the beginning, thereby ignoring current loads. With a global approach, the advanced scheduling logic considers current factory loads and adjusts schedules for multiple orders to meet scheduling objectives.

Fixed Versus Dynamic Daily Usage Rates

An item's daily usage rate represents a key planning parameter. It can be used by MRP logic to calculate a level of safety stock or daily schedules. Order point logic can use it to calculate an order point and order quantity. The trigger point and replenishment quantity for Kanbans also reflects the daily usage rate.

Most ERP systems view an item's daily usage rate as a fixed quantity, which can be derived from average historical usage. This viewpoint ignores projections of future demand and product structure changes, as well as seasonality and trends in demand patterns. Frequent updates to the fixed daily usage rates provide a partial solution, but this does not address the fundamental limitations.

A few ERP systems support a dynamic viewpoint of a daily usage rate that reflects variable quantities derived from projected usage. An item's variable usage rate can be stated as a daily usage quantity by month and calculated by dividing projected monthly requirements by the number of working days in the month. An item's projected monthly requirements can be based on MRP calculations, which include forecasted demands for saleable items.

Order-Based Versus Orderless Manufacturing

Most firms involved in orderless manufacturing require an ERP system that can support both orderless and order-based production. These approaches are not mutually exclusive. Orderless manufacturing requires different item planning data and different approaches to reporting production activities.

Item planning data in an orderless environment reflects an order point and order quantity, typically expressed in Kanbans or some other visible signal. The Kanban trigger point and quantity are based on daily usage rates. MRP logic can be used to calculate a dynamic daily usage rate, as described earlier.

Production activities in an orderless environment can be reported for completed items (with auto-deduction of components) rather than orders. Completions may be assigned to a time period for tracking costs by period (rather than by orders).

Supply Orders

Item replenishment can be represented by a supply order. Suggested replenishment reflects an item's primary source: a purchase order for a buy item, a manufacturing order for a make item, and a subcontract purchase order for a subcontract item. There are other sources of replenishment. Some sources can be identified in the context of an item's bill of material, such as by-product and customer-supplied material components. They result in a by-product supply order and a customer-supplied material supply order, respectively. A special case of replenishment involves a rework manufacturing order.

Each supply order requires coordination of supply chain activities. Major stages in the supply chain activities reflect an order life cycle, and can be represented by an order status. The concept of order status is closely tied to the structure of a supply order. A comprehensive life cycle viewpoint involves a status for the order, for each line item (termed line item status), and for each delivery line within a line item (termed delivery line status). This represents the structure of a supply order and the life cycle viewpoint taken in this book. For simplicity's sake, further explanations of life cycle and order status focus on the line items within a supply order.

The supply chain activities differ based on the type of supply order, but order status can be symmetrical. This section summarizes the supply chain activities and order status for each type of supply order.

Supply Orders for Purchasing and Manufacturing

The basic types of supply orders—a manufacturing order, purchase order, and subcontract purchase order line item—have similar life cycles. Figure 7.1 illustrates the similarity and explains the significance of each status in an order life cycle.

Status	PO Line Item	MO Line Item	Subcontract PO Line
Planned	Suggested quantity/date Suggested vendor	Suggested quantity, date and bill	Suggested quantity, date, and bill Suggested vendor
Firm	Assign order number Assign or modify quantity/date Assign or change vendor	Assign order number Assign or modify quantity/date	Assign order number Assign or modify quantity/date Assign or change vendor
Open		Create order-dependent bill	Create order-dependent bill
Released	Print PO paperwork Authorize delivery Report receipts	Print MO paperwork Authorize production Issue material Report resource usage Reports units by operation Report receipts	Print PO paperwork Authorize production and delivery Ship supplied material Report receipts

Inventory Status   → Issue material

Status	PO Line Item	MO Line Item	Subcontract PO Line
Completed	Prevent reporting Allow reopening Ignore remaining quantity	Prevent reporting Allow reopening Ignore remaining quantity	Prevent reporting Allow reopening Ignore remaining quantity
Closed	Prevent reopening	Prevent reopening Calculate manufacturing variances	Prevent reopening Calculate manufacturing variances

Note: The diagram illustrates the significance of each status, and does not identify all impacts. For example, a line cannot be deleted after reporting activities for it, and the vendor on a PO cannot be changed once a PO line has been released.

Figure 7.1 Life Cycle of a Supply Order

Each stage (or status) in the life cycle has significance. A planned order is generated by MRP logic with a suggested quantity and date. A planned order may be *firmed* to lock in a future schedule without locking the bill through creation of an order-dependent bill. A planned order may be *opened* so that the order-dependent bill can be created and modified prior to release. A released order represents an authorization to produce or deliver the item, and the ability to print paperwork and report activities. An order can be released without progressing through all steps. Manually entered orders can be defined as firm, open, or released.

Received material goes into inventory with an inventory status. Inventory status may be on-hand, or the material may be placed in-inspection or on-hold. After receiving the ordered quantity, the order status changes to completed. The order status changes to closed after system calculation of variances. Order status can go backward by changing a completed line item to a released line item, typically to report additional supply chain activities. This is often termed *re-opening* an order.

These six stages represent the basic life cycle of a supply order line item. Each stage has significance. Figure 7.1 does not identify every aspect of significance, such as limitations on deletions after reporting activity for an order. Other stages in an order life cycle can also be considered. For example, additional stages could be defined for picked complete on a manufacturing order, or for tracking procurement activities prior to inventory receipt (such as shipped from vendor or multiple inspection stages). However, too many stages can add unnecessary complexity.

An additional status for each line item is often required to designate hold or cancelled. The hold status can prevent activities from being reported, and a cancelled status results in the supply order being ignored

A supply order line item can have multiple delivery dates, especially on a blanket order. A delivery line requires further granularity in order status. Each delivery line can have an open, released, and complete status; these stages are referred to as *delivery line status*.

Three key points must be emphasized in the order life cycle. First, the component demands for an open or released supply order reflect the order-dependent bill, whereas component demands for a planned or firm order reflect the current bill. Second, closure of a line item involves two steps: one for production activities and one for accounting. Third, all types of supply orders can have multiple lines and multiple delivery lines.

Supply Orders for By-Products (and Coproducts)

By-product and coproduct material are both replenished on a by-product supply order as a result of the production process for the parent item. A by-product supply order is closely tied to the parent item's supply order. Changes in order status, quantity, and due date for the parent item's supply order automatically update any related by-product supply order.

Supply Orders for Customer-Supplied Material

Customer-supplied material is replenished and then used in the production process for the parent item. The customer-supplied material supply order provides visibility and tracking of supplies, and is closely tied to the parent item's supply order. Changes in order status, quantity, and due date for the parent item's supply order may automatically update any related customer-supplied material supply order.

Special Case: Rework Manufacturing Order

A special case of a supply order is a manually created rework manufacturing order, or rework order for short. A rework order typically represents a situation where an item is made from itself: it is the parent item and a component of the supply order. Creating a rework order does not create an order-dependent bill, and components in the order-dependent bill must be manually added. The order status for a rework order starts with open or released, at which point it parallels a normal manufacturing order.

Supply Orders with Direct Linkage to Sales Orders

Some ERP systems support a supply order directly linked to a sales order. The supply order reflects the sales order quantity, and may even be identified with the same order number. Changes in the sales order quantity and date automatically update the supply order, although the supply order due date can be scheduled independently after it has been opened/released. Closing a sales order, or placing it on hold or cancelled status, directly affects the supply order. The type of supply order (manufacturing order, purchase order, or subcontract order) reflects the item's primary source. They are slightly different than the basic supply orders reviewed above. They can be termed *final-assembly* or finishing orders to differentiate them from the basic orders.

The direct linkage with a sales order allows a final-assembly manufacturing order to be shipped from work-in-process (WIP) without being received. Direct linkage between final-assembly orders also allows a completed item to be issued directly to the next-level final-assembly order. With direct linkage purchase orders, purchased material can be received into WIP rather than to inventory.

CASE STUDY Faking Direct Linkage between a Supply Order and a Sales Order

One manufacturer used an ERP system that only supported indirect linkage, but still needed to identify the manufacturing order associated with a sales order. A work-around approach was employed to "fake" the direct linkage. After entering a sales order for an item, a manufacturing order was immediately created with the same order number and order quantity. The manufacturing order due date was specified as the sales order ship date. This approach provided visibility of the sales order to production activities. However, changes to the sales order quantity and/or date required a separate manual update to the associated manufacturing order.

A second work-around approach was also employed that utilized the ERP system capabilities for handling custom products, since this provided direct linkage. A custom product item was defined for each standard product requiring direct linkage. Its planning bill contained just the standard product item as a phantom component. A sales order was entered for the custom product item, and automatic option selection included the standard product in the configuration. This approach provided visibility of the sales order to production activities, and changes to the sales order quantity/date automatically updated the custom product manufacturing order.

Responsibility for Coordinating Supply Chain Activities

Planner and buyer fields identify the responsibility for item replenishment, and provide the organizing focus for how ERP systems communicate the need to synchronize supplies with demands. An item can sometimes be purchased and manufactured, hence the need for separate fields to identify both a buyer and a planner. Suggestions about planned procurement for a buy or subcontract item inherit the item's buyer, which can be overridden on a purchase order. Suggestions about planned production for a make item inherit the item's planner, which can be overridden on a manufacturing order. In this way, an ERP system can direct messages concerning planned and existing orders to the relevant buyers and planners.

An ERP system communicates warnings and suggested purchasing actions to buyers for synchronizing procurement activities, and similar information to planners for synchronizing production activities. Suggested actions and warnings include releasing, rescheduling, and canceling orders, and engineering changes affecting open orders.

The effectiveness of communication can be improved by defining message filters for each buyer and planner code. Creative use of the buyer and planner codes can focus attention on problem areas, such as items with delivery or quality problems or orders requiring intense follow-up activities. A purchasing agent, for example, can employ multiple buyer codes to segment items and orders (with a different message filter for each buyer code) to focus efforts on managing external supply chain activities.

Replenishment Methods

Replenishment methods in an ERP system have traditionally focused on MRP logic, and even order point logic, to anticipate demands. These have been augmented by Kanban methods for orderless environments. There are other replenishment methods, but these represent the dominant methods employed in the vast majority of ERP systems.

An item's replenishment method represents one of the basic planning parameters for modeling supply chain activities. The term for *replenishment method* varies by ERP system and may be expressed by more than one field. Other terms include order policy or plan code. Each replenishment method requires additional planning parameters, but many of these parameters are common across methods. The review of replenishment methods starts with those based on MRP logic. This explanatory approach enables us to highlight usage of the same parameters (and even MRP logic) by other replenishment methods.

Planning Parameters for MRP Logic

Normal MRP logic generates planned supply orders to cover an item's unmet demands (a combination of actual and forecasted demands) for an item. The suggested supply orders reflect the item's planning parameters, with indirect linkage between supply orders and sales orders. The key planning parameters include the item's primary source, lead-time, daily usage rate, days of supply, and days of coverage.

Primary Source An item's primary source can be designated as make, buy, or subcontract. The item's primary source is reflected in the item's lead-time, planning parameters, bills, routings, and costs. MRP logic suggests planned orders based on the item's primary source, but this does not preclude other sources of supply.

Item Lead-Time MRP logic uses an item's lead-time to calculate the start date for a suggested supply order based on the order due date. The significance of an item's lead-time depends on its primary source.

- ◆ *Make Item.* The lead-time represents the average elapsed days to produce an average order quantity under average factory load conditions. The lead-time for a manufacturing order can reflect the item's fixed lead-time, or a variable lead-time calculated by MRP logic (as described earlier).
- ◆ *Buy Item.* The lead-time represents an average supplier notification period for releasing a purchase order. The notification period should reflect

considerations of the supplier relationship. Use of a vendor schedule and blanket purchase orders, for example, provide visibility of anticipated requirements thereby reducing the notification period in comparison to "surprise" purchase orders.

◆ *Subcontract Item.* The lead-time represents an average turnaround time to send components and receive an average order quantity under average conditions. The turnaround time should reflect considerations of the vendor relationship, as described above.

Daily Usage Rate   An item's daily usage rate can be fixed or dynamic.

Days of Supply   MRP logic uses the days of supply (also termed frequency of delivery) to calculate a suggested order quantity that covers all demands during the interval. The suggested order quantity may be subject to modifiers, such as lot size minimum and multiple. The combination of these factors is termed lot-sizing logic.

An alternative to days of supply is a fixed lot size. MRP logic suggests a supply order for the fixed lot size to cover unmet demands. It may suggest multiple supply orders if necessary to cover the demands.

Days of Coverage   MRP logic uses the days of coverage and the daily usage rate to calculate an item's inventory plan that covers variations in demand. The inventory plan has also been termed the safety stock level.

Replenishment Methods Based on MRP Logic

There are several basic replenishment methods based on MRP logic. The four covered here include a variable order quantity, a fixed order quantity, daily schedules for rate-based scheduling, and manual planning. The rate-based scheduling approach described here represents one method employed by ERP systems (there are others) that is a simple extension of MRP logic.

MRP Logic and Variable Order Quantity (Days of Supply)   MRP logic uses the days of supply to calculate a suggested order quantity to cover demands during the interval.

MRP Logic and Fixed Order Quantity   MRP logic uses the fixed lot size to calculate a suggested order quantity to cover demands.

MRP Logic and Rate-Based Scheduling (Daily Schedules)   MRP logic uses the daily usage rate (or fixed lot size) to generate a group of daily schedules, where the sum of the daily schedules covers demand. The last daily schedule meets the demand need date. A group of daily schedules can be identified as a blanket supply order with multiple delivery lines. It is sometimes termed a schedule identifier.

MRP Logic and Manual Planning   MRP logic does not suggest planned supply orders for the item, but does calculate requirements for information purposes. Supply orders must be manually created. The approach is typically used when MRP logic lacks visibility of demands. It may be used for items constituting a master schedule under manual control.

Replenishment Methods Based on Order Point Logic

Order point logic and MRP logic use many of the same planning parameters. A suggested supply order based on order point logic reflects the item's primary source and lead-time. Other common planning parameters include an item's daily usage rate, days of supply, and days of coverage.

MRP logic and order point logic differ in a supply order's *event trigger* and in the visibility of future supply orders. MRP logic considers visibility of future demands in generating planned supply orders, and the event trigger for releasing a supply is based on unmet demands. Order point logic ignores demands, and the event trigger (termed a *reorder point*) for releasing a supply order is based on supplies of current inventory. With daily usage rates, an item's reorder point and quantity can be calculated using days of coverage and days of supply, respectively.

Order point logic can be based on a fixed versus dynamic daily usage rate. As described earlier, dynamic daily usage rates can be calculated by MRP logic. A dynamic daily usage rate recognizes changing demand patterns, the impact of new items and changing product structures, and related dependent demands (reflected in bills of material).

A variation of order point logic involves *min-max* or *order up to* logic. A minimum quantity represents the item's reorder point, and the maximum represents the order up to quantity. The suggested replenishment quantity results in the maximum quantity.

Replenishment Methods Using Kanbans (Orderless Environments)

Replenishment methods in an orderless environment use Kanbans (or other visible signal such as empty containers) to communicate the need for replenishment. Calculations for the Kanban trigger point and replenishment are similar to order point logic, and based on daily usage rates. A fixed or dynamic daily usage quantity can be used, where MRP logic can calculate the dynamic daily usage rate and even generate appropriate Kanban cards.

Kanban replenishment can be triggered by an electronic signal based on the comparison between an item's inventory balance and its reorder point.

Production activities in an orderless environment are typically reported for completed items. Additional activities, such as resource time and material usage, may be optionally reported. These production activities and associated costs can be assigned to a time period, such as a week, for period costing purposes. This time period represents an additional planning parameter.

Comparison of Replenishment Methods

The basic replenishment methods reviewed above are based on MRP logic, order point logic, or Kanbans (that approximate order point logic). The MRP-based replenishment methods were further segmented into a variable order quantity, a fixed quantity and daily schedules (consisting of a fixed daily quantity for a variable number of days). Figure 7.2 summarizes a comparison of these replenishment methods.

The comparison highlights characteristics of replenishment methods, with several categories of characteristics. The first category identifies the applicable planning parameters for suggested replenishment. The second category identifies the suggested replenishment in terms of trigger, suggested quantity, and suggested start date. The third category identifies how actual activities are reported.

Each MRP-based replenishment method uses relevant planning parameters to suggest replenishment. MRP logic can also use the planning parameters to calculate an item's inventory plan based on daily usage rate and days of coverage.

Characteristic of Replenishment			Replenishment Based on MRP Logic			Order Point Replenishment	Kanban Replenishment
			Variable Quantity	Fixed Quantity	Daily Schedules		
Item Master Planning Data		Daily Usage Rate			X	X	X
		Days of Coverage				X	X
		Days of Supply	X		X	X	X
		Fixed Order Quantity		X			
		Item Lead-Time	X	X		X	
Suggested Replenishment	Trigger	Supply (Current Inventory)				X	X
		Unmet Demand (Projected Available Balance)	X	X	X		
	Quantity	Fixed Quantity		X		X	X
		Variable Quantity	X		X		
	Start Date	Today				X	X
		Calculated Start Date	X	X	X		
Reporting Activities		Report against Order	X	X	X	X	
		Report against Item					X

Figure 7.2 Comparison of Replenishment Methods

ERP DESIGN ISSUE

Replenishment for Make-to-Order Standard Products

Three factors must be considered in replenishment of a make-to-order standard product: the lead-time to produce it from stocked components, the visibility of a sold-out backlog, and the need for direct linkage between supply orders and sales orders. The backlog for a completely make-to-order standard product, for example, has future sales orders at or beyond the item's cumulative manufacturing lead-time. Only sales orders drive replenishment of a completely make-to-order product, and the concept of stocked components does not apply.

A partially make-to-order item—one produced from stocked components—has a lead-time shorter than its cumulative manufacturing lead-time. Demands must be anticipated for stocked components. MRP logic can drive replenishment of stocked components based on forecasted demand for the end-item. It explodes forecasted demand through the product structure to components at the highest stocking level, and suggests planned supply orders for these items. This argues for differentiation between normal stocked items and final-assembly items that are only built to actual sales orders.

Sales order demand for a final-assembly item triggers a supply order. A supply order can be indirectly linked or directly linked to a sales order.

The direct linkage approach ensures that a final-assembly supply order has explicit visibility of the customer requirement, and changes to sales orders automatically update related supply orders. Some ERP systems have limitations related to inventory receipts for direct-linkage supply orders, since this breaks the linkage between supply orders.

The indirect linkage approach accounts for item planning parameters, and may suggest a single supply order to cover multiple sales order demands. However, the indirect linkage approach does not provide explicit visibility of the customer requirement. Changes to sales order quantity and date will be reflected in planned supply orders, but may require a separate manual update to existing orders.

Both approaches can use MRP logic to drive replenishment of stocked items based on forecasted demand. Use of inventory plans for a final-assembly item helps anticipate demand variability in the supplies of stocked items. Forecasts and inventory plans expressed for the end-item also help anticipate demands for resources involved in producing final-assembly items.

Planning Policies and Their Impact on Replenishment

A key planning parameter identifies how an item should be treated in MRP calculations. This will be termed an item's planning policy. The basic planning policies are termed normal and final assembly. Two additional planning policies, kit and production plan, can also be identified.

Normal Planning Policy

An item with a replenishment method based on MRP logic has a normal planning policy. The normal planning policy also applies to items replenished on the basis of order point logic or Kanbans. A normal item typically represents a make-to-stock product, or any stocked component in the product structure of a make-to-order product. A normal item may also represent a make-to-order product when the sales order delivery date exceeds the item's cumulative manufacturing lead-time.

Final-Assembly Planning Policy

A partially make-to-order product requires a different planning policy than normal. The rationale was explained in the breakout box discussing replenishment of make-to-order standard products. In summary, sales order demand drives final assembly of the item, but forecasted demand can be used by MRP logic to calculate requirements for stocked components. The planning policy for a make-to-order item is termed final assembly. An ERP system typically supports one of two approaches for the item's supply order: the supply order can be indirectly linked or directly linked to a sales order. Support for both approaches would require two variations of a final-assembly planning policy.

The concept of a final-assembly planning policy has been implemented in various ways within ERP systems. For example, some ERP systems designate items as phantoms so that forecasted demands blow though to stocked components. Sales orders drive end-item replenishment, typically with supply orders indirectly linked to sales orders. A supply order is not typically generated for a make-to-order component designated as a phantom. A single supply order (for the end-item) may be sufficient for managing supply chain activities in many environments. Other environments need multiple supply orders: one for the end item and one for each make-to-order component.

Note: Some ERP systems handle the final assembly capability by designating it on a sales order line. This approach results in a single supply order directly linked to the sales order for the end-item. It does not support direct linkage to supply orders for any make-to-order components.

Kit Planning Policy

Some items are sold as a kit of parts, where a bill of material defines the components. Any demands for the item blow through to its components. A supply order is never created. A sales order for an item can be shipped without having an item inventory and it can trigger auto-deduction of the components. A kit planning policy applies to these items.

Production Plan Planning Policy

A family item can be used for aggregate planning purposes, such as forecasting or production planning. The term *production plan* only applies to family items, so the planning policy for a family item is termed production plan.

The MRP-based replenishment methods apply to family items. MRP logic can use forecasted demands for a family item to suggest a production plan, typically expressed as a planned manufacturing order. The suggested production plan can be manually overridden, which is commonly termed *firming up* the production plan. It is expressed with a firm status on the order. The production plan may be manually entered as a firm order. The life cycle for a supply order representing the production plan only has two stages: a planned status and a firm status.

Other Policies Impacting Replenishment Based on MRP Logic

Replenishment methods based on MRP logic suggest supply orders for an item based on its basic planning parameters, such as lead-time, lot-sizing logic, and planning policy. Other policies impacting item replenishment include demand management policies, a planning fence, and several quality-related policies.

Demand Management Policies   Demand management policies impact MRP-based replenishment methods, since suggested replenishment reflects demands. These policies apply to make-to-stock as well as make-to-order environments. They determine how MRP logic should treat the combination of actual and forecasted demands. One policy determines how sales orders consume forecast. Another policy, a demand fence, applies to a make-to-order item, since MRP logic only considers near-term sales orders (within the demand fence) as demands. A full explanation of demand management policies requires an understanding of forecasts and sales orders, which will be covered in Chapter 10.

Planning Fence Policy for Unrealistic Planned Orders   A planning fence is a supply management policy used by MRP logic in suggesting realistic planned orders for an item. It represents the constraint of near-term schedule stability and the agility to react to new demands. Rather than suggesting an unrealistic supply order in the near-term (within the planning fence), MRP logic schedules the planned order on a realistic date (called the demand fence date). MRP logic warns the responsible planner or buyer via a recommended action to review or release the planned order currently placed at the planning fence date. The planner or buyer can determine expediting feasibility and manually schedule the order accordingly.

A planning fence typically applies to a master-scheduled item and reflects the item's cumulative manufacturing lead-time. New supply orders for a stocked item would be unrealistic inside its planning fence. Long lead-time materials and manufacturing capacity constrain the agility to react to new demands.

A planning fence can also apply to purchased material and make-to-order products. The planning fence for purchased material represents its minimum lead-time; a planned purchase order with a receipt date inside the planning fence date would be unrealistic. The planning fence for a make-to-order product can be interpreted as the minimum delivery lead-time to produce it from stocked components (rather than its cumulative manufacturing lead-time). A planned manufacturing order with a due date inside the planning fence date would be un-realistic, since MRP logic assumes manufacturing capacity has already been committed. An item's planning fence can be determined from lead-time analy-sis, subject to several assumptions. The key assumption is that an average lead-time applies to the make-to-order end-item, and to any of its make-to-order components. This involves MRP logic concerning a final-assembly planning policy and the treatment of lead-times by blow through logic. A related assump-tion is that stocked components will be available in anticipation of demand. This involves a sales and operations planning (S&OP) game plan that anticipates de-mand and demand variability in replenishment of stocked components.

Quality-Related Policies   Several item-related quality policies impact MRP-based replenishment methods. These policies concern lot control, serial control, and expected yield percentages. The impact of these quality policies on item supplies and replenishment methods are:

- *Lot Control Policy.* Stringent lot control may require fixed lot sizes in manufacturing orders.
- *Serial Control Policy.* Stringent serial control may mandate manufactur-ing orders with a lot size of one.
- *Expected Yield Percentage.* MRP logic will inflate the quantity of a planned order by the item's yield percentage to ensure demands can be covered. MRP logic factors down the quantity of a scheduled receipt, and the quantity in receiving inspection inventory, by the yield percentage.

Chapter 20, Quality Management, provides further discussion of item quality policies.

Chapter 8

Product Costing

Product costing of standard products represents one responsibility of cost accounting. Information about product costs has a wide range of uses. These include projecting future costs, analyzing cost reduction opportunities, pricing, and profitability analysis. With a standard costing approach, the product costs provide the baseline for valuing inventory transactions and identifying variances in procurement and manufacturing. The responsibilities of cost accounting for tracking actual costs and variances are covered in Chapter 21.

Standard costing represents the dominant approach used by manufacturers of standard products, whereas actual costing typically applies to custom product configurations. This chapter focuses on explanations of a standard costing approach. With standard costing, cost calculations build on the common manufacturing database of items and bills of material, and resources and routings. This provides an activity-based costing approach based on the cost drivers for manufactured products. Stated in activity-based costing terms, activities (operations) have material and resource requirements, and activities produce an item.

An explanation of standard costing starts with an overview and summary of product costing considerations. The explanation then reviews those aspects of the manufacturing database relevant to product costing. It concludes with suggestions for maintaining standard costs, and common problems related to product costing.

Overview of Product Costing

An overview of product costing requires a basic understanding of how an ERP system supports a standard costing approach. A comparison can then be made to an actual costing approach. The logic for calculating product costs varies by type of item, as explained in a summary of product costing considerations.

Summary of a Standard Costing Approach

Standard costing is typically based on one set of cost data for all items. Each item's cost is *frozen* during a user-defined time period, such as a year or quarter. Calculations of the frozen standard costs reflect the bills and routings in effect as of a specified date, typically the first day of the frozen time period. Costs for new items can be calculated and included in the frozen standard costs without impacting costs of existing items. ERP systems use standard costs to value transactions related to material and resource usage (at standard hourly rates). Standard costs provide the basis for calculating purchase price variances upon purchase order (PO) receipt, and for calculating manufacturing variances after order closure of manufacturing orders and subcontract POs. The manufacturing variances include those stemming from component effectivity dates, where the current bills differ from those originally used in calculating frozen standard costs.

Standard costing involves multiple sets of cost data, typically termed cost types. An item can have costs for each cost type. For example, one cost type may represent the next period standard costs, so that costs can be calculated beforehand. Cost roll-up calculations are performed with the cost data within the specified cost type, using a specified effectivity date. At the end of a frozen period, the set of frozen standard costs are replaced by next period standard costs. The impact of inventory revaluation can then be communicated to the general ledger.

Summary of Product Costing Considerations

Product costing focuses on calculating the value of each material item. Cost calculations are based on an item's primary source: make, subcontract, or buy. Cost calculations for a make item, for example, use the item's bill of material and routing to calculate its total cost. Costs can be segmented by cost element. The basic cost elements include material, labor, and overhead. Additional cost elements are needed for costs associated with external production activities, typically identified by two cost elements (subcontract and outside services) to reflect the two approaches to managing external production. Each item has incremental and total costs, segmented by cost element.

A summary of product costing considerations can be explained in terms of the incremental and total costs for several types of items. The summary shown in Figure 8.1 provides an organizing focus for further explanation.

The starting point for product costing involves manually specified costs for each buy and subcontract item. These costs represent each item's average purchase cost, and they reflect incremental or value-added costs. The costs must be specified for the appropriate cost element: incremental material costs for a buy item and incremental subcontract costs for a subtract item. The values in these two cost elements provide the basis for calculating purchase price variances.

Manually specified costs are also required for internal resources and outside operations.

♦ An internal resource item typically represents a machine, a manufacturing cell, or people with similar skills in a labor pool. An internal resource involves costs, such as personnel, maintenance, supervision, and other costs, for each operating hour. The hourly rates can be expressed as in-

		Incremental or Value-Added Cost			Total Cost	
		Manually Specified Cost		Automatically Calculated	Automatically Calculated	Consideration of Overhead Allocations
	Type of Item	Significance	Applicable Cost Element	Basis of Cost Calculation	Basis of Cost Calculation	
Item Related Costs	Buy Item	Average Purchase Cost	Material	No	Purchase Cost	Material-Related Overhead
	Subcontract	Average Purchase Cost	Subcontract	No	Purchase Cost + Bill of Material	Subcontract-Related Overhead
	Make Item	-	-	Yes (based on routing)	Bill of Material + Routing	-
	Internal Resource	Hourly Costs	Labor Overhead	No	Hourly Costs	Internal-Resource Related Overhead: Labor-Related OH Machine-Related OH
	External Resource	-	-	-	-	Outside Service OH
Routing	Outside Operation	Average Purchase Cost	Outside Service	No	N/A	
	Internal Operation	-	-	Yes (Resource Hourly Costs * Operation Required Time)		

Figure 8.1 Summary of Product Costing Considerations

cremental costs for the labor and/or overhead cost elements. These will be used to calculate the value-added costs associated with an operation performed by the resource.

♦ An outside operation has a cost specified in the routing operation. It represents an average purchase cost for the value-added activities performed by the vendor (external resource), and is treated as an outside service cost element. This value provides the basis for calculating purchase price variances.

Total costs for each item can be calculated automatically, with segmentation by cost element. Total costs for a buy item are the same as its incremental purchase cost, plus any associated overhead costs. Total costs for a subcontract item reflect its incremental purchase cost and the supplied components in its bill of material, plus any associated overhead costs. Total costs of a make item reflect its incremental costs (based on its routing) and the components in its bill of material. Total costs for an internal resource item are the same as its incremental hourly costs.

Consideration of overhead allocations involves additional complexities in product costing. One method of overhead allocation involves hourly overhead costs specified for internal resources—has already been covered. As an alternative approach, an internal resource's overhead costs could be calculated based on labor costs using a specified percentage. There are other overhead allocation methods.

- Material-related overhead can be manually specified as incremental overhead costs for a buy item, or automatically calculated based on a percentage of the item's purchase cost. These overhead costs may reflect allocations of freight, material handling, landed costs, or other purchasing-related costs.
- Subcontract-related overhead can be manually specified as incremental overhead costs for a subcontract item, or automatically calculated based on a percentage of the item's purchase cost.
- Outside service overheads may be associated with an external resource, and automatically calculated based on a percentage of an outside operation's purchase cost.
- Dummy resources embedded in routing operations provide creative ways to allocate overhead costs to make and subcontract items.

Segmentation of Basic Cost Elements

The basic cost element for overhead requires further segmentation to retain the identity of cost allocations. As argued above, the segmentation may reflect overheads related to labor, resources, material, subcontract manufacturing, and outside services. Overheads are frequently segmented into fixed and variable.

Many firms require further segmentation of other cost elements. Material costs, for example, can be segmented into packaging and raw materials. An ERP system provides various ways to segment a cost element, such as separate fields, a user-defined attribute associated with item costs assigned to a cost element, or some other approach. Increased segmentation provides greater analytical capabilities, but also increases system complexity.

Cost Roll-Up Calculations

Cost roll-up calculations are performed using a specified effectivity date and cost type. Costs can be calculated on the basis of a total regeneration, a net change calculation, or a partial calculation for new items only. The cost calculations typically consider all items, although they may be performed for a single item and its associated product structure. Cost calculations retain the identity of costs for each cost element, such as the total costs for an item's material, labor, and overhead.

An ERP system's approach to modeling routing operations (a bill of resources versus separate routing data approach) affects cost roll-up calculations. The separate routing data approach typically requires two calculations: one to calculate incremental costs based on routing data, and another to calculate total costs based on the bill of material. A single cost roll-up calculation can be made with the bill of resources approach.

In addition to roll-up calculations, the cost data within a cost type can be copied to another cost type, and cost data can be exchanged between two cost types.

Item Policies in Cost Calculations

An item's total costs are typically calculated automatically and can include three factors related to quality: the item's yield percent, component scrap percentages in the item's bill, and operation yield percentages in the item's routing. There are situations in which an item's costs should be manually maintained and quality factors ignored. These situations require a separate cost calculation policy for an item, where the item's policy may differ between cost types. The following factors provide the rationale for a cost calculation policy.

- *Exclude Quality Factors in Cost Calculations.* The quality factors can be excluded from a cost roll-up calculation. A cost comparison between sets of cost data (one with and one without quality factors) provides one viewpoint on cost of quality.
- *Prevent Automatic Cost Calculation.* Some items will require manual maintenance of incremental and total costs. A new product with partially defined bills, for example, may require manual maintenance. Automatic calculations would incorrectly calculate costs.
- *Ignore the Item's Cost in Cost Calculation for Parent Items.* The costs for some items may need to be ignored. A tool item, for example, may have a bill and routing for manufacturing purposes, but the tool's calculated cost would not be included in calculations for its parent's costs.

Tools for Analyzing Product Costs

The costed bill and the detailed item cost data provide the key tools for analyzing product costs. The costed bill identifies the primary cost drivers to support cost reduction efforts. Simulated changes to item cost data (in a cost type for simulation purposes) can be used to calculate the impact on product costs. For example, simulated changes can be made to material costs and resource costs (for labor and overhead rates), and a cost roll-up calculation performed for a future effectivity date, to analyze projected future costs. Cost calculations with and without quality factors (such as yield percentages and component scrap percentages) can be compared to identify the cost of quality.

Cost Data and the General Ledger

A material item's total costs are used for inventory valuation and cost of sales. Each material item can be assigned general ledger (G/L) account numbers for inventory and cost of sales. G/L account numbers related to cost of sales must support segmentation of costs by cost element (such as material, labor, and overhead). There are other G/L account numbers related to an item, including account numbers for variances, internal work-in-process, and external work-in-process.

An internal resource item can be assigned G/L account numbers for labor and overhead. An external resource can be assigned G/L account numbers for outside services and overhead.

Building on the Common Manufacturing Database

Product costing builds on the common manufacturing database of items and bills of material, and resources and routings. The critical information relevant to product costing is summarized below.

Item Planning Data

The critical item planning data for a material item involves the primary source, planning parameters affecting accounting lot size, and yield percent.

Primary Source A material item's primary source (make, subcontract, or buy) determines the need for entering manually specified costs (and applicable cost elements), and the calculation of incremental and total costs. Costs must be specified for buy and subcontract items, and items that are by-products of a manufacturing process.

Accounting Lot Size Accounting lot size applies to a make and subcontract item to amortize per order costs related to any component. It represents the item's average order quantity. It may be specified separately, or reflect the item's planning parameters such as the fixed lot size or the daily usage rate times the days of supply.

Yield Percent An item's yield percent can be optionally included in cost roll-up calculations.

Bills of Material

The bill of material is used to calculate total costs for a make or subcontract item. Cost calculations reflect each component's type, required quantity, scrap percent, and effectivity dates. Accurate costing requires that bills reflect the way products are really built.

Component Type The component type determines whether the component costs will be included in cost roll-up calculations. Costs are added for normal and phantom components, ignored for reference and customer-supplied material components, and subtracted for by-product and coproduct components.

Component Required Quantity and Quantity Type Cost calculations reflect each component's required quantity, expressed per item or per order. The costs associated with a per order quantity are amortized over the parent item's accounting lot size to calculate a per unit cost.

Component Scrap Percent A component's scrap percent can be optionally included in cost roll-up calculations.

Component Effectivity Dates Calculations of an item's total cost reflect the components in effect as of a specified effectivity date.

Internal Resources and Operations

A routing's internal operations are used to calculate incremental and total costs for a make item. Cost calculations reflect the costs specified for internal resources, and each operation's required time for a resource. They also reflect each operation's effectivity dates and operation yield percent.

Costs for Internal Resources Costs for internal resources must be manually specified for the labor and/or overhead cost elements

Operation Required Time Cost calculations reflect each operation's required time for the primary resource and for possible secondary resources. Cost calculations include the required crew size for pooled resources. Aspects of the required time may represent a per order quantity (such as setup time), where costs are amortized over the parent item's accounting lot size to calculate a per unit cost.

Operation Effectivity Date Calculations of an item's incremental costs reflect the operations in effect as of a specified effectivity date.

Operation Yield Percent Cost calculations can optionally include the operation yield percentages.

External Resources and Outside Operations

A routing's outside operations are used to calculate incremental and total outside service costs for a make item. The incremental costs comprise an outside service cost element, and they reflect each operation's purchase cost and effectivity dates.

Purchase Cost An outside operation's purchase cost must be manually specified. It is normally defined per item for producing the parent item, although an operation unit of measure and a unit of measure conversion factor may apply. A purchase cost expressed per order is amortized over the parent item's accounting lot size to calculate a per unit cost.

Operation Effectivity Date   Calculations of an item's incremental costs reflect the outside operations in effect as of a specified effectivity date.

Suggestions for Maintaining Standard Costs

The key concept of standard costing is that an item's standard costs must be unchanged over a frozen time period. An item's standard costs during this period provide a baseline for meaningful interpretation of variances. The frozen period may be a year or any user-defined time period, and it typically aligns with the end of a financial period. For explanatory purposes in this section, we will assume the frozen period equates to one calendar year (January 1 through December 31). The suggestions cover initially setting standard costs and updating standard costs (for new items) throughout the frozen period.

Initially Setting Standard Costs

A separate set of cost data, termed *next period standard costs,* is used to develop the standard costs. The cost calculations are based on a specified date effectivity of January 1 to account for the latest available information about changes in product and process designs. At the time of cutover on January 1, the frozen standard costs are replaced with cost data from the next period standard costs. Some considerations in cutover to new frozen standard costs include:

- *Impact on Inventory Values.* A comparison between the two sets of cost data (performed beforehand) can identify the potential impact on G/L accounts for the change in inventory value. Changes in inventory value represent a standard cost variance.
- *Impact on WIP (Work-in-Process) Inventory Values.* The change in WIP values may not be recognized until after closure of a supply order, when variance analysis can recognize a standard cost variance.
- *Retain the Basis for Frozen Standard Costs.* An ERP system should automatically retain information about items and bills used to calculate frozen standard costs. This information provides the baseline for variance analysis.
- *Create a Duplicate Set of Cost Data.* One set of cost data, termed *updated standard costs,* will start off exactly the same as the frozen standard costs. This set of cost data will be used to update standard costs as time progresses.

Updating Standard Costs for New Items

As time progresses beyond January 1, the manufacturing database will be updated with new items, bills, planned changes and corrections in bills, and changes to relevant planning parameters (such as yield percent and accounting lot size). Use the cost data for updated standard costs to calculate the impact of these changes. Ongoing maintenance of the updated standard costs involves several considerations.

♦ *Correctly Model New Products and Supply Chain Activities.* Define new items and bills, define corrections and planned changes in bill components for existing items, and update item planning parameters for existing items.

♦ *Only Calculate Costs for New Items.* Cost roll-up calculations for the updated standard costs focus on new items, typically by flagging them as new until accurate costs have been calculated. Cost calculations for only new items are termed a *partial cost roll-up.* The partial cost roll-up typically uses today as the specified effectivity date, thereby accounting for the latest bill information.

New items include internal resources and material. Costs for a material item (with make or subcontract as the primary source) cannot be correctly calculated until completion of its bill and relevant item planning data. Further complications arise when it includes new components that also require complete bill or routing information. An item should remain flagged as new until accurate costs have been calculated.

♦ *Do Not Change Standard Costs for Existing Items.* This means that cost roll-up calculations for the updated standard costs should not update existing items, typically because they are not flagged as new.

♦ *Update the Frozen Standard Costs with the Updated Standard Costs on a Periodic or As-Required Basis.* The only changes in the cost data will be the costs for new items, thereby retaining frozen costs for existing items.

Near the end of a frozen period (such as December 31), copy the cost data from the updated standard costs to the next period standard costs. Modify costs for existing items, such as new purchase costs and internal resource labor and overhead rates, and perform a total recalculation of product costs (using a regeneration cost roll-up) using a specified start date of January 1. This will recalculate costs for all items based on the latest available information about product and process designs and relevant item planning parameters. The process can then be repeated for the next frozen period.

Common Problems Related to Product Costing

The common problems related to product costing involve allocations of overhead, maintenance of standard costs, wide fluctuations of raw material costs, and handling partially defined bills.

Allocating Overhead and Labor Costs When Only a Bill of Material Exists

Routing information in some manufacturers is non-existent, partially defined, or so inaccurate as to be unusable for allocating overhead and labor costs. The bill of materials may be the only source of complete and accurate information. Several approaches can be used for allocating overhead and labor costs, including:

- *Labor and Overhead Cost Allocations Based on a Percent of Material Value.* Most ERP systems support automatic calculation of material-related overheads, typically using a percent of material value. Using this approach is based on the assumption that overhead and labor costs are proportionate to material value.
- *Dummy Resources for Allocating Labor and Overhead Costs.* A dummy internal resource can be used as a component in product structures to allocate costs for labor and overhead. The dummy resource has a unit of measure (such as hours) and costs (such as hourly labor and overhead costs). As a component, the required quantity for the dummy resource approximates requirements (such as approximate hours) to produce the end-item.

Calculating Overhead Rates for an Internal Resource

A stumbling block for many firms involves the allocation of overheads, especially with manufacturing cells. One solution approach can be based on historical information. Select a specified time period such as a year. Identify all labor costs associated with operating the cell over the selected time period, and divide it by the cell's historical hours of operation. This provides an hourly labor rate. Segment overhead costs over the selected time period into directly traceable and nontraceable overheads. Using historical hours, calculate the directly traceable overheads per hour of operation. The nontraceable costs should also be calculated and placed in a separate overhead cost element. A second solution approach is based on projected requirements, where hours of operation can be projected using capacity requirements calculations based on infinite loading assumptions.

Complex Schemes for Overhead Allocations

Overhead allocation schemes often require creative use of an ERP system. Overheads can be tied to a material item (via an overhead percent, or a manually maintained value), an internal resource (via overhead costs per hour of operation), an external resource, and other items. Overheads can also be allocated with departmental resources. These approaches build on the common manufacturing database and require no additional effort to provide overhead allocations.

When all else fails, use dummy internal resources and creative bill component quantities (including per order quantities) to model a complex scheme. This requires additional data maintenance to support overhead allocations, although it may also provide capacity planning capabilities when done correctly. A difficult-to-model scheme for overhead allocations is often a signal that a simplified approach should be considered.

Handling Landed Costs for Purchased Material

Landed costs represent the overheads incurred for material purchased from foreign or overseas suppliers. These costs include the transportation costs, duties, and other fees. A simple approach to handling landed costs is to manually specify an incremental amount in an overhead cost element (in addition to the incremental material cost). In many ERP systems, this approach involves manual maintenance of the item's total costs because automatic calculations ignore a manually specified incremental overhead cost. A second approach to handling landed costs involves a routing for a purchased item, where the routing operation(s) for a dummy resource can calculate the associated overhead. This approach will be constrained by an ERP system's capabilities to support routing operations for a purchased item.

Lack of a Frozen Standard Cost and Meaningless Variances

Many ERP system users do not correctly maintain the set of data for frozen standard costs. Typically, their cost roll-up calculations during the frozen period result in cost changes to existing items (rather than just new items), which means that variances become extremely difficult to interpret. Conversely, a new item's costs have been calculated and frozen based on an incomplete bill and routing. Real confusion occurs when the frozen standard costs reflect manually entered data for costs that are normally calculated automatically, since the costs retained in the frozen bills have no correlation to reality.

A related problem is the reporting of variances in an ERP system. Some ERP systems provide a complete framework for easily analyzing and understanding supply order variances, whereas other systems provide little analysis or just enough analysis to cause confusion in understanding the details.

Wide Fluctuations in Raw Material Costs

Wide fluctuations in raw material costs are sometimes put forth to justify actual costing. In most cases involving standard products, there are only a few raw materials with wide purchase price fluctuations. One solution approach with standard costing involves frequent changes to the item's cost in the cost type for updated standard costs. This also involves marking every affected parent item as new, so that partial cost roll-up calculations automatically update product costs with each change in the component costs. This approach builds on the basics of maintaining standard costs, described in an earlier section of this chapter.

A similar situation occurs when the price of a key ingredient of purchased material fluctuates widely. The key ingredient (such as a precious metal, a chemical, or dairy fat) is not defined as an item, since it indirectly goes into purchased material. A similar solution approach can be taken. First, add a dummy material or internal resource item for the key ingredient (with a unit of measure and cost), then define it as a component in affected parent items.

Using Stubbed-In Costs for Partially Defined Bills

Cost calculations for a partially defined bill of material may use stubbed-in costs to approximate the item's total cost until the bill has been completely defined. These costs represent an approximation of the bill's undefined portions. One method for modeling stubbed-in material costs uses a dummy material item with a cost of one dollar. The dummy item gets added to the bills of material with a component quantity equal to the stubbed-in costs. A similar approach can be used with a dummy resource to model stubbed-in costs for labor and overhead.

The Cost Implications of Using a Buy Item to Represent an Outside Operation

When an ERP system cannot support outside operations in a parent's routing (with a purchase cost and turnaround time), an alternative approach uses buy items on the item master. A buy item is typically defined for each combination of outside operation and parent item, such as "Outside Operation X on Parent Item Y." The material component can specify the appropriate unit of measure, the turnaround time, and a purchase cost. The item's purchase cost must be manually specified for the material cost element (rather than the cost element for outside services) to provide the appropriate basis for calculating purchase price variances.

Chapter 9

Custom Products

A custom product configuration represents a one-time product, with a supply order directly linked to a sales order. Examples include a special item built to customer specifications, prototypes, first articles, or repairs. Other examples include assemble-to-order products with many predefined options that can be specified for a sales order configuration. A configuration may also be ordered and built multiple times. A configuration may take minutes or months to complete, depending on its complexity.

A custom product family item serves as the starting point for defining a configuration's bill and as the parent item for defining a planning bill. A planning bill for a custom product provides one approach to anticipate demands prior to a sales order, and may also support an option selection approach to defining a configuration's bill.

♦ *Configuration Bill.* A configuration's bill consists of the same components as a standard product bill, with the possibility of two additional component types: a nonstock material component and a custom product component. The configuration's bill represents an order-dependent bill with a current planned cost. For a make item, the life cycle of the configuration's supply order, termed a *custom product manufacturing order,* parallels that of a manufacturing order with an open/released status.

♦ *Planning Bill.* A planning bill (or bill of options) consists of the same components as a standard product bill, with the possibility of one additional component type: a custom product component. In a planning bill, the required quantity represents a product mix percentage (or probability of sale) and an additional field defines a typical configuration quantity. The available options may change over time. A separate supply order defines the production plan for the custom product family item. The life cycle of this supply order, termed a *production plan,* parallels that of a manufacturing order with planned/firm status.

The explanation of custom products covers these two types of bills and their associated supply orders. The explanation starts with the configuration's bill and a custom product manufacturing order, since this is common to all custom product manufacturers. Separate sections cover a planning bill and the use of a production plan (supply order) to anticipate demands. In both cases, the explanation extends the concepts presented earlier about standard products and highlights the similarities and differences.

Defining a Custom Product Configuration

A custom product family item is defined in the item master and provides the starting point for a configuration. This custom product item is sometimes called a model item. Some ERP system support a configuration method without using a custom product item, but this precludes use of a planning bill and often limits applicability of option selection and a rules-based configurator. A configuration and its bill are defined in the context of a quotation or sales order line item. They may be defined in the context of a warehouse order, which is simply a sales order for an internal customer that is subsequently changed to an external customer.

The explanation about a configuration starts with the custom product item, and then covers considerations about the configuration's identification, bills, costing, pricing, and supply orders.

Considerations about the Custom Product Item

The item master for a custom product item defines the internal unit of measure and primary source of replenishment for configurations based on the item. A configuration is generally viewed as a make item, but it could be a buy or sub-contract item based on the item's primary source. The custom product item also defines the planner (or buyer) responsible for managing supply chain activities, although this can be overridden on a given supply order. Planner responsibility will probably differ between configurations for prototypes and configurations for production.

The custom product item defines other policies related to quality, planning, and general ledger accounting. The quality policies concern lot and serial control, inspection lead time, and receiving inspection for purchased configurations. With respect to planning data, the production plan planning policy applies to a custom product item. With respect to accounting, the custom product item may define applicable general ledger accounts, such as segmenting cost of sales by cost element.

The item master for a custom product item also defines attributes applicable to all configurations based on the item, such as engineering or sales analysis attributes. Configuration-specific attributes must be defined for the sales order line item.

Several custom product items may be defined to reflect differences in product families, the primary source of replenishment, responsibility, unit of measure, quality policies, general attributes, and so forth.

Configuration Identification

The unique identifier for a configuration in most ERP systems is the combination of sales order number and line number. Some ERP systems use the combination of the model item number and a counter as the unique identifier.

A user-defined configuration part number, termed a *configuration ID,* represents an attribute of the unique identifier. It frequently represents a smart part number that communicates product specifications. The considerations about part numbering, described in Chapter 4, also apply to the configuration ID. These considerations include significant versus non-significant identifiers and revision level.

The configuration ID correlates to sales catalog literature or the customer item and acts as the primary means of communication on acknowledgements, packing lists, invoices, and so forth. For the purposes of this book, the term configuration ID will be used as the unique identifier of a configuration.

Attributes of a configuration must be defined for the sales order line item. These configuration-specific attributes include weight, specification codes, sales classifications, and other user-defined fields.

Configuration Bill and Routing

A configuration for a make or subcontract custom product item represents an order-dependent bill specified from scratch. It consists of the same component types as a standard product bill. A configuration can be built with the following components, and the production process may generate by-products.

- Material components, designated as normal, phantom, reference, and/or customer-supplied material.
- Internal resources performing operations, where the resource type reflects capacity, scheduling, and costing characteristics (such as a single finite or pooled resource). A master operation may be used.
- External resources performing outside operations, where the resource type reflects no control (infinite resource) or complete control (finite resource) over scheduling the vendor's production. A master operation may be used.
- Tools, such as reusable fixtures.
- Documents, such as engineering or quality specifications or ECO notices.

The fields of critical component information (described in Chapters 5 and 6) apply to each type of component in a configuration: operation sequence, material required quantity or operation run-time, usage policy, and so forth. In particular, the operation sequence ties together a resource's routing operation and its required material and tools. Every configuration component can have an additional field—a markup percent—for using a cost-plus markup approach to price a configuration.

In addition to these component types, a configuration can also be built with a nonstock material component and a custom product component with its own configuration.

Nonstock Material Component   A nonstock material component can be purchased just for the configuration. The critical component information is very similar to an outside operation: operation sequence; a one-time part number, description, and purchase UM; a purchase quantity (and quantity type) and estimated purchase cost; a suggested vendor and possible additional information (such as text or reference designators). The nonstock material component provides the starting point for coordinating supply chain activities using a nonstock material purchase order.

Custom Product Component   A custom product item, defined as a component in a configuration, can have its own configuration. This can result in a multilevel configuration when the custom product component is make or subcontract. Some ERP systems do not support a custom product component and can only handle a single-level configuration.

A custom product component has a configuration ID and description. It requires specification of an operation sequence, required quantity (and quantity type), component type (of normal, phantom, or reference), and possibly scrap percent. It also has an estimated purchase cost for a buy or subcontract custom product item.

A custom product component provides the starting point for coordinating supply chain activities using another custom product supply order directly linked to the parent's order. The concept of a multilevel product structure is represented by linked supply orders. The item's primary source determines the type of the supply order, such as a custom product manufacturing order for a make item. A configuration's requirement for a phantom or reference component type does not result in a supply order.

A custom product purchase order is similar to a nonstock material purchase order, where the configuration's components provide reference information to the vendor. The custom product subcontract purchase order provides all of the advantages of the subcontract item approach (over the outside operation approach) to managing external production. In both cases, an additional field—an estimated purchase cost—must be defined for the component that reflects the item's unit of measure.

As noted earlier, each custom product component can have an additional field (a markup percent) for using a cost-plus markup to price a configuration. Each component for nonstock material, outside operation, and purchased configuration can also have an additional field (a sales price) for using a rolled-price approach to pricing a configuration.

ERP DESIGN ISSUE

Philosophical Differences in Defining a Configuration's Bill

ERP systems provide different approaches to defining a bill that also apply to defining a configuration's bill. These differences include the material-centric versus operation-centric approaches to defining a bill of material (described in Chapter 5), the bill of resources versus separate routing data approach to defining a routing operation (described in Chapter 6), and the subcontract item versus outside operation approach to managing external production (described in Chapter 4).

Other philosophical differences are involved with configurations. These differences include handling a configuration's inventory, revising a configuration's bill using a rules-based configurator, and saving (and reusing) previous configurations.

Approaches to Defining a Configuration's Bill

One approach to defining a configuration's bill is to start from scratch by adding components (materials, routing operations, and so forth) and modifying the components as needed. This is termed *direct definition*. Other approaches can be used to initially define a configuration, with subsequent modification by direct definition. These approaches assume that a starting point (a sales order or quotation line item) has been defined for a custom product item.

Copy a Previous Configuration   A previous configuration's bill can be copied into the current order or quote and modified via direct definition. This may take the form of copying some or all of the bill from one configuration or from multiple configurations, or even copying information from bills for standard products. Information about previous configurations should include quotes and actual orders and the configuration's attributes.

Create via a Template Configuration   A template configuration provides a variation of copying a previous variation, and supports the concept of option selection without using a planning bill.

Create via Option Selection from Planning Bill   A configuration's bill can be created by selecting options from the planning bill, and then modified via direct definition. The planning bill consists of predefined options that may comprise the entirety or majority of a configuration's components, and it may provide basic rules guiding option selection.

Create via Rules-Based Configurator   A rules-based configurator provides user-defined capabilities to prompt for responses and then to map the responses to the configuration's components. The prompts typically consist of a series of questions with branching logic. Responses to prompts may be fixed (e.g., choose option A, B, or C) or variable (e.g., enter a dimension between 1.0 and 10.0). Rules can be enforced so that prompts and responses provide a complete and correct definition. The mapping of responses to a configuration's components can include calculations about required quantities, identification of appropriate resources and materials, and operation descriptions with embedded variable information. The configuration can then be maintained via direct definition.

ERP systems provide varying degrees of support for rules-based configurators, especially in terms of three key issues. One issue involves reusing the configurator to revise a configuration. A second issue involves storing responses with a configuration and using the responses on external paperwork such as acknowledgements and invoices. A third issue involves using a smart part number as a shortcut to prompts and responses while still enforcing the rules.

ERP DESIGN ISSUE

Revising a Configuration Using a Rules-Based Configurator

Most ERP systems with a rules-based configurator provide a one-shot approach to defining the configuration. Revisions and modifications must be manually maintained, which defeats the purpose of using the rules-based configurator to enforce completeness and correctness. Further complications arise when a smart part number is used as the starting point for the rules-based configurator, since changes to the smart part number do not automatically update the configuration.

An ERP system that does support revisions to a configuration using a rules-based configurator must store the responses (and the version of the rules-based configurator) with the configuration. The responses (rather than the configuration's components) typically define the critical information to effectively communicate a configuration to the customer on order acknowledgements, packing lists, and invoices. This requirement to store responses has an impact on storing historical data about configurations.

As a final note, the use of planning bills typically becomes more difficult with a rules-based configurator because the product mix percentages are not easily determined.

Managing Changes to a Configuration

The initial definition of a configuration's bill and its ongoing changes may or may not require a standard approval procedure or an ECO approval process. A configuration for an internal prototype, for example, is typically very dynamic and formal approval procedures would be cumbersome. Conversely, a configuration based on customer specifications may require a formal approval for any change. As another example, the iterations of producing an acceptable first article typically require separate configurations reflecting an evolving design, where each configuration may require an approval procedure.

An approval process typically consists of several approval steps, with a sign-off requirement by relevant functional areas at each step. A template can be established for a standardized approval process; multiple templates are typically required to model different types of changes.

The critical issue is to identify the change in a configuration's bill and then communicate recommended actions immediately to functional areas affected by the change. Many custom products have a dynamic product or process design that requires continual changes, sometimes up to the moment of shipment. Changes in the configuration's bill may occur for many reasons, such as changing customer specifications, an evolving design, or finishing an initially incomplete design. An incomplete design may have used dummy or stubbed-in costs for cost estimating purposes, which must be replaced by specific components as the design is completed.

When a rules-based configurator creates a configuration, changes to a configuration may be managed by reusing the configurator to enforce correctness and completeness.

Tools for Analyzing and Maintaining Configurations

ERP systems provide different approaches to creating and maintaining a configuration, as described above. Additional tools make it easier to find and use a previous configuration, such as a finder capability. Bill analysis tools should apply to previous configurations, such as a where-used inquiry, bill comparison, summarized bill, costed bill, and lead time analysis for a configuration's bill.

ERP DESIGN ISSUE

Saving and Using Historical Information about Previous Configurations

Previous configurations may stem from quotations and sales orders. In some environments, only a small fraction of quotations become sales orders. This argues for storing historical information about previous configurations in a separate database from items and bills. The historical information, however, must be easy to find and use (e.g., via item finder capabilities). The historical information must also include attributes of the configuration and possibly responses from the rules-based configurator. As the amount of historical information grows, the approach to data retention may employ off-line storage that is readily and automatically available.

An alternative approach involves creating items and bills for every configuration related to a sales order (but not a quotation), rather than storing previous configurations in a separate database. This approach eliminates many of the differences between a standard product and custom product approach. It eliminates differences in the unique identifier, item attributes, multilevel bills, and inventory visibility. It also eliminates differences concerning item finder and bill maintenance and analysis capabilities. On the down side, the approach results in large numbers of item master and bill records, loss of change control in creating items and bills, and potential difficulties in differentiating a standard versus custom product. A fundamental flaw involves storing and using configurations related to quotations that do not have item or bill records, since this means the differences between items and configurations still apply.

Other Considerations for a Configuration's Components

Other considerations for a configuration's components include a mark-up percentage, sales price, usage policy, and forecast consumption.

Component Markup Percentage   Each component in a configuration's bill can have an additional field (a markup percent) for using a cost-plus markup approach to price a configuration.

Component Sales Price   Selected components in a configuration's bill can have an additional field (a sales price) for using a rolled-price approach to price a configuration. Some components have a purchase cost and sales price, such as an outside operation, nonstock material, and a custom product component for a buy or subcontract item.

Component Usage Policy   A component's usage policy can be issue or auto-deduct to reflect how you primarily report usage. A backflush location is generally required for auto-deducted material components.

Components and Forecast Consumption   Separate forecasts for an intermediate item (including purchased material) provide one method of anticipating demands. When specifying the intermediate item as a component in a configuration, the forecasted demand must be consumed by the actual demand, typically with an additional field to indicate forecast consumption.

Creating a Standard Product Bill from a Configuration's Bill   Some ERP systems support the creation of a standard product bill from a configuration's bill. This requires creation of new items in the item master for any configuration and nonstock material components. The new items typically require additional information about planning parameters, quality policies, cost data, and so forth.

Estimated Cost for a Configuration

A configuration's estimated cost is typically considered in the context of a make custom product item. It is based on the sum of the components' costs. Each component's costs can be segmented by cost element (material, labor, overhead, subcontract, and outside services) so that the total costs will be segmented by cost element.

A component can be a standard product material item or an internal operation for a resource item, where a set of cost data (typically standard costs) provides the basis for component costs. A component can be an outside operation with an estimated purchase cost. A configuration's components can also be a nonstock material item (with an estimated purchase cost) or a custom product (with its own configuration and estimated cost). These represent five sources of costing information; the costing implications of each source are described below.

Material Components

A configuration's material components are used to calculate total estimated costs for a make and subcontract custom product item. Total costs reflect the component type and required quantity for each component.

Component Type   The component type determines whether the component costs will be included in cost roll-up calculations: costs are added for normal, phantom, and tool components, ignored for reference and customer-supplied material components, and subtracted for by-product components.

Component Required Quantity and Scrap Percent   Costs reflect the component's required quantity, expressed per item or per order. The costs associated with a per order quantity are amortized over the order quantity to calculate a per unit cost. A component's scrap percent (if applicable) is normally included in the estimated costs.

Internal Operations

A configuration's internal operations are used to calculate incremental labor and overhead costs for a make custom product item. Incremental costs reflect the costs for internal resources, each operation's required time for the primary resource (and secondary resources, if specified), and operation yield percent.

Costs for Internal Resources   Costs for an internal resource reflect labor and/or overhead rates for operations performed at the resource.

Operation Required Time   Cost calculations reflect each operation's required time for the primary resource and possible secondary resources. Cost calculations include the required crew size for pooled resources. Aspects of the required time may represent a per order quantity (such as setup time), where costs are amortized over the order quantity (which acts as the accounting lot size) to calculate a per unit cost.

Operation Yield Percent   Costs normally include the operation yield percent (if applicable). This may impact the calculation of costs for material associated with the operation.

Outside Operations

An outside operation has a manually specified purchase cost (reflecting an outside service cost element) for a specified purchase quantity. It is normally defined per item for producing the configuration, although an operation UM (and UM conversion factor) may apply. A purchase cost expressed per order is amortized over the order quantity to calculate a per-unit cost.

Nonstock Material Components

A nonstock material component has a manually specified purchase cost (reflecting a nonstock material cost element) for a specified purchase quantity (and UM). It is normally defined per item for producing the configuration. A purchase cost expressed per order is amortized over the order quantity to calculate a per-unit cost.

Custom Product Components

The costs for a make custom product component reflect the costs associated with its own configuration, whether it is a normal or phantom component type. The required quantity is typically expressed per item but may be a per order quantity.

The component may be a buy or subcontract custom product item, which would require assignment of a purchase cost. The costs for a subcontracted configuration would also include its components.

Cost Data and the General Ledger

A configuration's costs are used for valuing cost of sales, which means general ledger account numbers must be assigned to identify each cost element (of material, labor, and so forth) for the custom product configuration. Other accounts must be assigned for internal and external work in process, variances, and possibly inventory of a completed configuration.

Estimated Price for a Configuration

A configuration's estimated price is typically based on the quantity ordered and the configuration's components. The most common pricing methods use either a cost-plus-markup approach or a rolled-price approach. Alternatively, a price book approach may be used for the custom product item (where the pricing ignores the configuration) or the pricing may be embedded in the rules-based configurator. These four approaches to pricing are explained below.

Cost-Plus-Markup Approach

The cost-plus-markup approach uses each component's cost and specified markup percentage to calculate a total estimated price. One variation to this approach uses a markup percentage by component type, such as a markup percentage for material components, internal operations, and outside operations. Another variation uses only one markup percentage that applies to the total estimated cost of all components.

Other variations could be considered. A nonstock material component, for example, may have quantity breakpoints in its estimated purchase costs. As another example, the costs for standard product items may be based on standard costs or another set of cost data.

Rolled-Price Approach

The rolled-price approach uses each component's price to calculate a total estimate price. A price book, specified for the sales order line item, can serve as the basis for pricing each material component and for each internal resource performing internal operations (expressed as a price per hour). The price for by-product components will be subtracted from the total. A separate sales price must be manually specified for each outside operation, nonstock material component, and purchased custom product component.

Pricing Based on the Custom Product Item

Pricing can be based on a price book for the custom product item, so that pricing ignores the configuration's components. The price book may define different prices reflecting quantity break points, and date effectivities apply to the price book. This approach often applies to situations where the configuration's components do not affect pricing, such as labels or color.

Pricing Embedded in a Rules-Based Configurator or Formula Pricing

Pricing can be based on the responses to prompts in a rules-based configurator, so that pricing ignores the configuration's components. This has also been termed *formula pricing,* since price calculations reflect some user-defined formula.

Supply Orders and a Configuration

The sales order for a configuration drives a custom product version of a supply order (a manufacturing order, purchase order, or subcontract purchase order) based on the item's primary source. An additional custom product supply order may be required to produce a configuration associated with a custom product component. In addition, a nonstock purchased material component (within a configuration) drives a type of purchase order.

Each type of custom product supply order requires coordination of supply chain activities. Major stages in the supply chain activities reflect an order life cycle, and the supply chain activities differ based on the type of supply order. Figure 9.1 illustrates the significance of each stage in the order life cycles for custom product supply orders.

A custom product manufacturing order represents the dominant supply approach supported by ERP systems and, therefore, forms the focus of further explanation. The custom product purchase order and subcontract purchase order will be touched on briefly.

A custom product manufacturing order is directly linked to a sales order, which drives the suggested order quantity, date, and configuration. The following box describes other implications of direct linkage. The order status starts with open, and it can be independently released for manufacturing purposes. Its start and due dates can also be scheduled separately from the sales order ship date.

Inventory of a completed configuration may or may not be supported by an ERP system. The lack of an item master record (for the configuration) precludes inventory in most ERP systems. Figure 9.1 illustrates the two choices: ship from WIP to customer or report receipts to inventory.

Status	Custom Product Manufacturing Order	Custom Product Purchase Order	Custom Product Subcontract PO
Planned Firm	N/A	N/A	N/A
Open	Suggested quantity/date and the configuration tied to sales order Override order start/due date	Suggested quantity/date tied to the sales order Override order start/due date Assign vendor	Suggested quantity/date and the configuration tied to sales order Override order start/due date Assign vendor
Released	Print MO paperwork Authorize production Issue material Report resource usage Reports units by operation Ship from WIP Or report receipts	Print PO paperwork Authorize delivery Ship from vendor Or report receipts	Print PO paperwork Authorize production and delivery Ship supplied material Ship from vendor (external WIP) Or report receipts
	To Customer or To Inventory	Inventory ▶ Issue material	
Completed	Prevent reporting Allow reopening Ignore remaining quantity	Prevent reporting Allow reopening Ignore remaining quantity	Prevent reporting Allow reopening Ignore remaining quantity
Closed	Prevent reopening Calculate manufacturing variances	Prevent reopening	Prevent reopening Calculate manufacturing variances

Figure 9.1 Life Cycle of a Custom Product Supply Order

ERP DESIGN ISSUE

Direct Linkage between a Custom Product Manufacturing Order and the Sales Order

Each custom product supply order has direct linkage to the sales order line item. The configuration is only built to a specific sales order. This has several implications.

♦ Changes in the sales order quantity and configuration's bill automatically update the custom product manufacturing order(s). The supply order quantity does not reflect MRP lot sizing logic (such as minimums or multiples), although it may reflect a yield percentage specified for the configuration.

♦ Changes in the sales order ship date automatically update the due date for the related manufacturing order(s). However, the supply order's start and due dates can be scheduled separately from the sales order.

♦ Changes in the sales order status, such as completed, cancelled, or hold, automatically apply to the related supply order(s).

♦ A completed configuration can be shipped from work-in-process, or issued to the next-level custom product manufacturing order, without recording a receipt or completion. The shipment can trigger backflushing of auto-deducted components. A completed configuration cannot be shipped to a different sales order.

♦ Lot tracking requirements can create complications for shipping a configuration from work-in-process, since the lot number must be preassigned to the supply order rather than during receipt into inventory.

♦ After sales order completion, there is no provision for tracking the configuration's available supplies (e.g., leftovers). This also applies to nonstock material components and configurations for custom product components.

♦ The order quantity for a custom product manufacturing order typically cannot be subdivided into multiple orders with smaller quantities.

♦ Custom product manufacturing orders for the exact same configuration cannot be combined into a single order.

ERP DESIGN ISSUE

Handling Inventory of a Custom Product Configuration

Most ERP systems require an item master record to handle inventory and provide stock status visibility. This precludes inventory of a configuration. A supplemental approach has been taken by some ERP systems to support receipts and provide inventory visibility of a configuration (and nonstock material). The supplemental approach has limitations: inventory is directly linked to the sales order line item; it cannot be moved or adjusted; and leftover inventory is ignored after order closure. As an alternative, an item master record for each configuration can be created (manually or automatically), thereby supporting inventory visibility.

A custom product configuration, by definition, is built and shipped to customer specification. It is not intended to be stocked in inventory and usable for other purposes. However, many firms need visibility of a configuration's location after it has been built.

Differences between a Configuration and Standard Product Item

Several factors define the differences in how ERP systems treat a custom product configuration and a standard product item. The key factors are summarized in Figure 9.2.

The critical differences between a standard product and custom product approach can be highlighted in terms of five key factors. Two of the factors—supply order linkage and inventory visibility—have been covered in breakout boxes, since differences are impacted by the design of an ERP system. The five differentiating factors include:

◆ Unique identifier of item number versus sales order line number. This involves several related differences about other identifiers, attributes, and the impact of an item's primary source.

◆ Product definition based on the order-dependent bill (inherited from the bill) versus a configuration's bill. This involves several related differ-

Factors	Standard Product Item	Custom Product Configuration
Unique Identifier	Item Number	Sales Order and Line Number
• Other Identifiers	Sales Catalog Item	Configuration ID
• Attributes	Attributes of Item	Attributes of Sales Order Line Item
• Primary Source	Make, Buy, Subcontract	Make*
Product Definition	Bill and Order-Dependent Bill	Configuration's Bill
• Nonstock Components	No	Yes (Custom Product**, Nonstock Material)
• Planned Cost	Standard Cost	Estimated Costs
• Multilevel Product	Multilevel Bill	Multiple Linked Supply Orders**
Supply Order Linkage	Indirect Linkage	Direct Linkage
Inventory Visibility	Yes (Receive to Inventory)	No (Ship from WIP)
Cost of Sales	Standard Cost + Variances	Actual Costs

*Many ERP systems only support a make custom product configuration.

**Some ERP systems only support a single-level configuration, and cannot support a custom product component with its own configuration.

Figure 9.2 Differences between a Standard Product Item and Custom Product Configuration

ences about the use of nonstock components, planned costs, and handling a multilevel product.

♦ Indirect versus direct linkage between the supply order(s) and sales order.
♦ Inventory visibility of a completed item versus a completed configuration.
♦ Cost of sales based on standard costs versus actual costs.

There are other differences in how an ERP system treats a configuration and a standard product item. These are summarized in Figure 9.3. The differences involve pricing, item finder capabilities, bill maintenance, bill analysis, and the approach to storing historical data. A separate breakout box covers the ERP design issue about storing and using previous configurations.

Many products could be modeled using either a standard product or a custom product approach. However, ERP systems frequently have a fundamental underlying design that will favor one approach or limit the usability of an approach. Some examples include the inability to handle a multilevel configuration, forecasts and planning bills, and attributes of a configuration. An ERP system's approach to handling the differentiating factors, identified in Figures 9.2 and 9.3, will often determine which approach works best.

Defining a Custom Product Planning Bill

A custom product family item can serve as the parent item for defining a planning bill, as well as the starting point of a configuration. Components in the

Other Factors	Standard Product Item	Custom Product Configuration
Pricing	Price Book for Item	Price Book for Custom Product Item
		Rolled Price of Components
		Cost Plus Markup for Components
		Formula Pricing
Item Finder Capabilities	Item Number and Description	Configuration ID and Description
	Item Attributes	Attributes of SO Line Item
		Sales Order, Customer, Custom Product Item
Bill Maintenance	Direct Definition	Direct Definition
	Copy Bill and Modify	Copy Configuration and Modify
		Use Configuration Template & Modify
		Option Selection and Modify
		Rules-Based Configurator
Bill Analysis	Where-Used (in Parent Items)	Where-Used (in Configurations)
	Bill Comparison	Configuration Comparison
	Summarized Bill	Summarized Configuration
	Lead-Time Analysis for Item	Lead-Time Analysis for Configuration
Storing Historical Data	Items and Bills	Previous Configurations
		Responses to Rules-Based Configurator

Figure 9.3 Differences between a Standard Product Item and Custom Product Configuration (Part 2)

planning bill typically represent options used in configurations. A planning bill can be used for forecasting or option selection or both. The family item may also support production planning when it represents a dedicated manufacturing cell (or key capacity constraint) involved in producing the custom product configurations.

Considerations about a custom product family item were covered earlier in terms of a starting point for configurations. The family item defines the internal unit of measure, the primary source of supply orders, and the planner or buyer responsibility for coordinating supply chain activities. Explanations of the planning bill for a custom product family item will use a case study to illustrate the key points.

Components in the Planning Bill

Components in the planning bill reflect the family item's production strategy. An assemble-to-order custom product, for example, must anticipate demand for material and resource components involved in final assembly. The planning bill for a make-to-order custom product, on the other hand, may only include long lead-time purchased material and a few critical resources (for capacity planning purposes). It may include some long lead-time manufactured intermediates. The planning bill for an engineer-to-order product may only contain a few critical resources for capacity planning purposes. This section will focus on the planning bill for an assemble-to-order custom product, since the concepts apply to other production strategies.

A planning bill for an assemble-to-order custom product is defined just like a standard product bill. It consists of the material components and internal operations that may be required to produce a configuration. In addition, it may have one or more custom product components, each with its own planning bill.

Material Components   Material components can often be grouped together to reflect optional or common components in a configuration. Each grouping can be given a name. A simplistic example of a toy car, shown in Figure 9.4, can be used to illustrate a planning bill and the concept of option groups.

The toy car has two required options (a body and wheels), one optional option (decals), and one common option (common parts such as axles and packaging). There are four color and size options for the purchased body, two size options for the manufactured wheel, and two options for the purchased decals. A phantom item represents the common parts. Each option within an option group has a product mix percentage.

The critical information for a material component in a planning bill is similar to that in a standard product bill, with two additional fields about configuration quantity and group name.

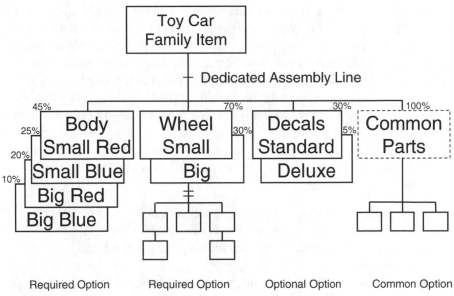

Figure 9.4 Case Study: Planning Bill for a Toy Car (Custom Product)

- ◆ *Component.* The component defines the item number.
- ◆ *Group Name.* The group name provides logical groupings of components.
- ◆ *Operation Sequence.* The component's operation sequence provides the linkage to the routing operation requiring the component.
- ◆ *Required Quantity.* The required quantity defines the product mix percentage expressed per item.
- ◆ *Typical Configuration Quantity.* The typical configuration quantity defines the average number of components in a configuration, such as four wheels in the toy car.
- ◆ *Component Type.* A material component may be normal, phantom or reference. In the toy car example, the phantom component type applies to the common parts. A normal component type applies to the other components. Other component types include customer-supplied material and by-products.
- ◆ *Component Date Effectivities.* The component date effectivities can identify when an option becomes available or is removed, or when mix percentages change. In the toy car example, new options for frame color and size can be phased in, and the current option for deluxe wheels could be phased out.

ERP systems sometimes support additional option group information for supporting a rules-based configurator. Further explanation of a rules-based configurator is outside the scope of this book.

Internal Operations   Each resource component represents a potential routing operation in a configuration, where the operation may be common or optional. Each resource component has a product mix percentage (indicating the probability of being used in a configuration) and a typical configuration quantity (indicating the average run time per item). This information supports capacity planning and option selection to define a configuration's routing. For illustrative purposes, the toy car example has only one internal operation performed on an assembly line dedicated to producing the toy cars.

The critical information for an internal operation in a planning bill is similar to that in a standard product routing, with two additional fields about configuration quantity and group name:

♦ *Component.* The resource component defines the primary resource, although optional secondary resources can also be specified.

♦ *Group Name.* The group name provides logical groupings of operations.

♦ *Operation Sequence.* The operation sequence provides the linkage to the materials required for the operation.

♦ *Required Quantity.* The required quantity defines the product mix percentage expressed per item, indicating the probability that the internal operation will be included in a configuration.

♦ *Typical Configuration Quantity.* The typical configuration quantity defines the average number of run time hours (or run rate) to produce a configuration. A pooled resource also requires a typical headcount requirement. Other time elements can be included, such as the setup time.

♦ *Operation Yield Percent.* An average yield percent may be specified for the internal operation.

♦ *Component Date Effectivities.* Component date effectivities identify when an internal resource becomes available, or when the factory layout changes. In the toy car example, a dedicated manufacturing cell may replace the labor-intensive assembly line as of a given date.

Additional information for an internal operation may reflect operation attributes, operation description, and text.

Custom Product Components   A custom product family item can be specified as a component in a planning bill in exactly the same manner as a material component. It has a group name, operation sequence, required quantity (indicating mix percentage), typical configuration quantity, component type, and date effectivities. When a planning bill gets used for option selection, each selected custom product component requires further option selection. Selection of a custom product component results in a separate custom product supply order when it has a normal component type.

ERP USAGE ISSUE

Modularizing the Bills to Support Custom Products

Many manufacturers with multiple variants of similar products can benefit from modularizing their bills to support custom products. There are warning signals for needed modularity: an explosive growth in the numbers of items and bills, overly complex bills of material, a perceived need for negative bill quantities, difficulties in anticipating demands, and longer-than-necessary delivery lead-times. Bill modularization leads the way for a custom products approach to defining and selling products.

Bill modularization starts with a detailed understanding of the product structure. One starting point involves deconstructing the product variants to identify common and unique items, and then restructuring the bill to reflect the new groupings of common and unique options. This typically results in disentangling an overly complex bill, isolating the unique items for usage late in the production process, and the use of phantoms for groups of common components. Another starting point involves lead time analysis of the multilevel product structures to identify the highest possible stocking level that supports the desired minimum delivery lead-time. The stocking level may be stated in the new groupings of common and unique options, typically leading to a reduction in the number of items to forecast.

Bill modularization typically impacts routing operations. Final assembly operations can be part of the configuration. Routing operations related to a group of common components can be defined for the phantom, with special attention to assignment of operation sequence numbers.

When bill modularization and a custom product approach replace a standard products approach, there are many implications for other aspects of the business. It requires changes to items and bills, item planning parameters, and the approach to sales and operations planning. It also requires changes to manufacturing documentation and drawings, sales literature and product pricing, order entry and delivery promises, paperwork (such as acknowledgements, packing lists, and invoices), and sales analysis.

Managing Change and Maintenance of Planning Bills

Planning bill maintenance becomes the joint responsibility of sales and master scheduling. Changes to the planning bill typically reflect new options, discontinuation of old options, and changes in mix percentages. Anticipated changes to a component's mix percentage can be defined using multiple occurrences of the component in the planning bill, where each occurrence defines the appropriate date effectivities. Changes in mix percentages may stem from introductions or deletions of options to the product family, or from changing demand patterns that reflect promotions, trends, seasonality or other reasons. The sum of the components' mix percentages within a group of required options is typically 100 percent. Any component's product mix percentage may be inflated to provide an inventory plan to buffer demand variations.

The same bill analysis and maintenance tools apply to planning bills. You can copy a planning bill to another item and make mass changes to a component based on its where-used information. The analysis tools include a where-used inquiry, bill comparison, costed bill, lead time analysis, and a material exposure profile.

Using the Planning Bill to Create a Configuration's Bill via Option Selection

Selecting options from the planning bill can create a configuration's bill. A planning bill consists of predefined options that may comprise the entirety or majority of a configuration's components. A multilevel planning bill contains a custom product component requiring its own configuration.

A sales order line item for the family item provides the starting point for a configuration, where selected options in its planning bill create the configuration's bill. The configuration is produced on a custom product manufacturing order linked to the sales order. A custom product component provides the starting point for another configuration, where selected options in its planning bill create the configuration's bill. The linked supply orders define the multilevel configuration.

Supply Orders and the Production Plan

A supply order provides one approach to defining a production plan for a family item. The supply order reflects the custom product item's primary source. A production plan's supply order has two stages in its order life cycle—planned and firm. MRP logic can use forecasts for the family item to calculate a planned supply order or suggested production plan. The suggested production plan can be manually overridden with different dates and quantities. Actual sales orders for configurations consume the production plan for the family item. MRP logic uses the unconsumed production plan and the planning bill to calculate a production forecast for each planning bill component.

The usefulness of a firmed up production plan expires as time elapses. It must be manually deleted in most ERP systems. A production plan expressed as planned supply orders will automatically be removed in most ERP systems. Manual (and automatic) removal must consider an item's demand management policies (especially forecast consumption) to determine when the usefulness of a production plan expires.

Common Problems Related to Custom Products

Limitations in ERP Systems Related to Configurations That Force a Standard Products Approach

The choice between a standard product and custom product approach for modeling a specific product is frequently constrained by capabilities within an ERP system. Most of these limitations are related to the factors differentiating standard and custom products, summarized in Figures 9.2 and 9.3. Examples of limitations include

Limited to Single-Level Configurations   The single-level limitation means that a standard product item must be defined to represent a configuration for an intermediate level. The supply order for the intermediate item is not directly linked to the sales order, which forces a manual approach to identifying linkage and a manual update to reflect changes in the sales order.

No Configuration Attributes   The inability to specify attributes of a configuration means that a standard product (with item attributes) must be used. These attributes may be related to production (e.g., production specifications, drawing number), shipping (e.g., weight and volume), sales analysis (e.g., classification codes) or other user-definable fields.

Lack of Inventory Visibility for Configurations   The lack of inventory visibility may require a standard products approach, especially in handling remnants or leftovers related to a configuration or nonstock material.

Inadequate Communication of the Configuration ID and Description   The ERP system may not consistently communicate information about the configuration ID, description, and attributes. This information is typically required on sales order acknowledgements, picking lists, packing lists, box labels, invoices, and related general ledger transaction detail. The information is also required on manufacturing orders, pick lists, receipts, dispatch lists, capacity requirement loads, lot trace and serial trace history, sales history, and recommended actions for procurement, production, quality, cost accounting, customer service, and shipping.

Inability to Handle Configurations for Purchased and Subcontract Item   The ERP system may only support custom product configurations for internal manufacturing, forcing the use of a nonstock material component and an outside operation to handle configurations for purchased and subcontract items.

Inadequate Support of Sales Forecasting and Sales Analysis for Custom Products   Some ERP systems only support sales history and forecasting of individual items. The sales history should include the unit volume for the family item, as well as a historical mix percentage and configuration quantity for each component. This reflects how many times and how much of the component was included in configurations. In support of forecasting, the sales history information should provide the basis for updating the planning bills. This may include seasonality and trend information related to planning bill components.

Planning Bills and Forecasts An order point approach must be used to anticipate demands for stocked components when an ERP system cannot support a planning bill and forecasts for a custom product family.

Part 3

Sales and Operations Planning

A firm's sales and operations planning (S&OP) process starts with the definition of all demands for the firm's goods and services. It formulates game plans that drive supply chain activities to meet those demands. More specifically, each product or product family requires an agreed-upon S&OP game plan that covers its demands. This frequently involves anticipating actual demands with forecasts and anticipating variations in actual demands (with inventory plans) to meet customer service objectives. It also involves interactions between the product's forecasted and actual demands, governed by demand management policies. Chapter 10 focuses on demands and demand management.

The S&OP game plan is expressed differently for different products, requiring a contingency approach, termed the *S&OP approach,* to sales and operations planning. The appropriate S&OP approach must consider the type of product, its production strategy, linkage between demands and supplies, and other factors. Each S&OP approach represents a slight variation to an overall framework for expressing a product's game plan. Chapter 11, Sales and Operations Planning, summarizes the contingency approach and uses the overall framework to explain two prevalent case studies: a make-to-stock standard product and an assemble-to-order custom product.

Chapter 11 covers general principles applicable to every S&OP approach. This includes making each game plan realistic based on an analysis of capacity and material constraints. It emphasizes the significance of an agreed-upon game plan that balances conflicting objectives, and provides near-term schedule stability and realistic delivery promises. It highlights the characteristics of a good S&OP game plan.

Chapter 12 provides additional case studies of S&OP approaches. Explanations of each S&OP approach use the same overall S&OP framework to describe how to develop and maintain a product's game plan.

Chapter 10

Demand Management

Demands provide the logical starting point for formulating a sales and operations planning (S&OP) game plan for each of the firm's products and services. The S&OP game plan drives the supply chain activities to meet those demands. The foundation of MRP logic is built on chasing demands, and demand-pull manufacturing philosophies are based on producing exactly to demand. This chapter starts by examining the sources of independent demands.

Some products can be completely produced to actual demands because the visibility of actual demands exceeds their cumulative manufacturing lead-time. In the same fashion, some products are completely designed and manufactured to order, such as internal prototypes, first articles, and one-time jobs built to customer specifications.

Other products must be completely or partially produced in advance of actual demands, such as make-to-stock standard products and assemble-to-order custom products. Many cases require inventories of long lead-time materials and selected intermediates or Kanban items to shorten delivery lead-times. This chapter explains how to anticipate actual demands, and demand variability, using forecasts and inventory plans within a product's S&OP approach.

The interaction between a product's forecasted and actual demands reflects its production strategy, and involves several demand management policies. This chapter explains the interaction, especially in support of make-to-order products, as part of the contingency approach to choosing a product's S&OP approach.

Identifying the Sources of Independent Demands

The sources of independent demand, both actual and estimated, can be viewed by functional area. Figure 10.1 illustrates the sources of independent demand for a single manufacturing plant. Some of these sources of demand may not apply to a given firm. The key concepts about sources of demand are that (1) demands can be categorized into standard product and custom product demands, and (2) actual demands can be viewed as sales orders. Using sales orders to express actual demands provides the basis for an ERP system to automatically consume forecasted demands.

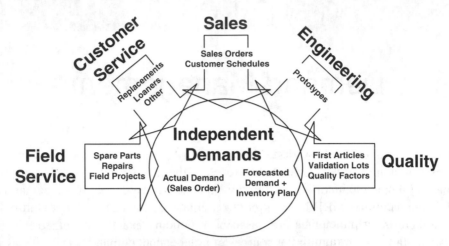

Figure 10.1 Sources of Independent Demand

Sales   Sales orders define actual demands for the firm's products and service, both standard and custom items. Sales order demands can be captured in a variety of ways, from internal personnel and Internet orders to customer Kanbans. Each item's production strategy determines the need for anticipating actual demands and variability in actual demands to meet customer service objectives.

Some demands involve interpretation. Customer schedules represent a combination of actual sales orders (in the near-term) and forecasted demands (in the longer term), and typically require interpretation before import into an ERP system. A warehouse order for a custom product configuration represents a sales order, where the initially-assigned internal customer becomes a real customer. Other sales order formats may reflect rented or leased items. Sales orders do not constitute demands when they have been cancelled. Orders placed on hold may or may not be considered actual demands. Quotations to prospects in the sales cycle do not represent actual demands, but can be used to forecast demand. A sales order can also be designated as an addition to forecasted demand.

Customer Service   Actual demands originating in customer service include the need for replacement items and possibly repair requests, as well as loaners, exhibition items, donations, and other miscellaneous requirements. It is typically necessary to anticipate these demands when they involve significant volumes of unexpected business.

Field Service   Actual demands originating in field service include the need for spare parts and for repairs and field service projects. Customer service objectives generally require anticipation of actual demands.

Engineering   Actual demands originating in engineering include prototypes, designed and built for internal or external customers. A prototype may involve requirements for material, nonstock material, and internal production resources, as well as engineering design resources. These actual demands represent custom product configurations and can be viewed as sales orders. Capacity planning for engineering and production resources provides one reason for anticipating demands.

Quality   Independent demands related to quality are often expressed as validation lots or first articles, especially during ramp up to production lot sizes. Quality's demands are also represented in repairs, replacements, and spare parts. Other quality factors can be embedded in the manufacturing database to affect calculation of required supplies. For example, the expected quality level of purchased material can be expressed as a yield percent. Expected quality levels in manufacturing processes can be expressed as component scrap and operation yield percentages.

Other Considerations   A multisite operation has additional sources of independent demand, such as demands from sister plants and demands to replenish inventory at distribution sites. Chapter 23, which discusses multisite operations, provides further explanation of these independent demands.

Many firms focus on sales order demands for current products, such as saleable end-items and custom product configurations. They do not adequately anticipate and capture other sources of demands in their ERP system, so that the demands represent surprises. Demand management requires that all demands be identified in an ERP system. For example, some firms neglect to identify demands for repairs and engineering design projects.

Anticipating Actual Demands with Forecasts

All manufacturers anticipate actual demands, as reflected in their people, equipment, and facilities. These resources represent an implicit forecast. Effective ERP system usage benefits from an explicit definition of forecasted demand. Forecasts can provide a single set of numbers determining capacity requirements, and replenishing stocked material (or Kanbans). The usefulness of forecasted demand increases as it extends beyond a minimum time horizon that represents each product's cumulative manufacturing lead-time.

Identifying What to Forecast

Forecasted demand should be expressed for saleable items in most cases, regardless of production strategy. The saleable item may be a standard product or a custom product family item. Forecasted demand is expressed by a quantity and date. MRP logic uses the product structure information to calculate requirements for all components, but only suggest supplies for stocked items.

Item planning policies (final assembly for a standard product and production plan for a family item) and phantom components ensure that demands blow through the product structure to the level of stocked components. For make-to-order products, this approach results in matched sets of components and provides visibility on requirements for resources involved in building to order. The matched sets of components provide the greatest flexibility in responding to demand variability while still achieving minimum delivery lead-time. Forecasting the saleable items typically involves fewer control points in comparison to separate forecasts (or order points or Kanbans) for many components. It also makes forecast consumption straightforward.

Forecasted demands should not be expressed for the saleable item in some situations. One exception involves forecasting a family of standard product items. Other exceptions involve forecasting common components used to produce many items.

Basis of Forecasted Demands

Forecasted demands define the management team's current predictions about a product's sales. Forecasted demands in an ERP system are generally expressed in terms of a projected shipping schedule. Forecasted demands should be constantly updated based on the latest-available information. Forecasts are not a wish list, nor a bookings measurement. A separate set of forecast data may be used for the purposes of performance measurement, sales quotas, motivation factors, or other reasons.

Forecasted demands can be based on many factors. Management's intuition acts as the primary factor in many smaller manufacturers. Other factors include predictions based on sales history, current quotations, customer schedules, and marketplace leading indicators.

Predictions Based on Sales History A product's sales history provides one basis for forecasted quantities and dates. The dates should represent the customer's requested ship date rather than the promised date or actual ship date. In addition, the predictions and sales history should account for returned goods, replacements, lost sales, cancelled sales orders, and outliers of surprise or spiky demands. Sales history may need to account for changes in sales orders. Few ERP systems correctly capture this type of information for sales analysis and forecasting purposes. In addition, sales history information does not generally apply to new products.

Off-the-shelf statistical forecasting packages can automatically fit a model to sales history data, and support manual overrides, for predicting demand of single standard products. They do not generally work for forecasting standard product families, unless they support calculations of aggregate demand by family and updates of mix percentages for saleable items in the family's planning bill.

Sales history data for a custom product requires information about the item, the components in each configuration, and possibly the responses to a rules-based configurator. Forecasted demands consist of dates and quantities for the custom product family item, as well as mix percentages and typical configuration quantities for options in the family's planning bill. Few forecasting packages support this approach, and few ERP systems support automatic updates to the planning bill. Manual updates to options in the planning bill can be based on a comparison between planned and actual mix percentages and configuration quantities.

Quotations Quotations for custom product configurations and standard products provide one basis for forecasted demand. Each quotation can be factored by a sales probability, where the probability may change based on the step in a structured sales cycle. The concept of reserving capacity for a quotation represents a special case, since the quotation could be treated as an actual demand rather than a forecasted demand.

Customer Schedules Customer schedules apply to a standard product, and represent actual demands (or sales orders) in the near-term horizon and forecasted demands in the longer-term horizon. Degrees of customer commitment, and policies about customer changes in the quantities, dates, and item mix, may even differentiate forecasted demands. A comparison between a new and current customer schedule can help identify changes, which argues for retaining versions of the customer schedule for comparison purposes. Customer schedules may be communicated via electronic data interchange (EDI). These schedules may require a manual review (e.g., to identify changes or validate requested delivery dates) prior to automatically updating forecasted and actual demands.

Other Factors Other factors can contribute to management's intuition about forecasted demands. These factors include knowledge of customer plans, marketplace leading indicators, and marketing promotions. The factors may also include Web page hits.

The need for forecasted demands applies to products and services related to other functional areas. For example, the forecasted demands for field service (spare parts, repairs, and field service projects) might reflect the installed base of equipment. Forecasted demands for customer service, especially replacements, will reflect previous experience.

Forecasted demands for engineering prototypes may be useful. Some firms use planning bills containing resource profiles to anticipate capacity requirements for prototypes. Other firms with partially defined bills for prototypes use stubbed-in modules to anticipate requirements for capacity and critical materials.

The management team's predictions about demands will change over time as they obtain additional information. Forecasted demands need to be reviewed and updated as part of each product's sales and operations planning process, typically in the context of a rolling forecast. As time progresses, management revises existing forecasts and adds forecasts for future periods at the end of the planning horizon.

Forecasted Demands by Item or by Customer

A forecast by item (or family item) makes sense when many customers buy a standard product. Any sales order will consume the item's forecast. A forecast by customer makes sense when you can identify projected item sales for a specific customer or a few customers. For example, this applies to the forecasted demands within a customer schedule. Only sales orders from the customer should consume the item's forecast by customer.

An item with mixed sources of demand, such as one major customer and many miscellaneous customers, can have forecasted demands for the major customer with the remainder by item. Only sales orders from the major customer should consume the forecast by customer, while all other sales orders will consume the item's forecast.

Using Forecasted Demands across the Company

Forecasted demands at any given time represent management's prediction of future business. An ERP system can provide visibility of this information across the company, so everyone works with one set of data. Accounting can project revenues, cash flows, budgets, and pro forma financial statements. Requirements for equipment and personnel can be calculated, thereby supporting equipment purchases and anticipating work force changes. Work force requirements include needed skill sets, temporary workers, overtime, and layoffs. Purchasing can use the visibility in vendor negotiations. Forecasted demands for one product (such as equipment) can be used to predict demands for other products and services (such as spare parts, repairs, and field service tasks).

A comparison between forecasted and actual demands requires a separate copy of the forecasts as of a given date. For example, a comparison may be made with forecasts that represent information at the start of a given year, quarter, or month.

Anticipating Variability in Actual Demands via Inventory Plans

Forecasted demands tend to be inaccurate by nature. This means demand variability must be anticipated to support customer service objectives. An inventory plan provides one approach to buffering against demand variability. Many firms book orders and make delivery promises as if they can provide 100 percent customer service, yet they seldom give themselves the benefit of an inventory plan. It is not surprising that the lack of an inventory plan (and poor forecast accuracy) shows up in unrealistic delivery promises, overloaded schedules, constant expediting, overtime, a hectic life style, and ultimately poor delivery performance and customer service.

The concept of an inventory plan applies to material and resources for supporting a minimum delivery lead-time. From a materials viewpoint, it applies to the highest possible stocking level within a product's bill of material. The stocked items reflect the production strategy: finished goods for a make-to-stock product, intermediates for an assemble-to-order product, and raw materials for a make-to-order product. From a resource viewpoint, it applies to make-to-order environments and the resources involved in building to order (such as final assembly operations).

An inventory plan should be expressed for saleable items in most cases, just like forecasted demands. This enables MRP logic to calculate requirements for all components, but only suggest supplies for stocked items. It results in matched sets of stocked components, provides visibility for resources involved in building to order, and involves fewer control points in comparison to setting many component safety stocks. It can also provide visibility of inventory plans for making delivery promises. Just like forecasted demands, exceptions to this general rule involve situations with common materials used to produce many items, and a family of standard products.

An inventory plan covers volume variability for standard and custom products. It must also cover variability in option mix percentages and configuration quantities for custom products, typically expressed in the planning bill (e.g., inflated mix percentages). The planning bill for a custom product represents matched sets of components, which provide the greatest flexibility in responding to demand variability while still achieving minimum delivery lead-time.

The identification of how much to inventory plan depends on the desired customer service objectives. Customer service objectives can be stated in various ways, such as percentage of orders shipped complete on the customer requested date, but the underlying trade-offs remain the same. Inventory investment and capacity requirements increase exponentially as service-level objectives are increased. Most firms recognize that a 100 percent service level is impossible, and an ideal inventory plan does not exist. A key issue with an inventory plan is that the management team agrees to live with the plan. How much can be based on management judgment. A starting point can be modified upward or downward over time.

CASE STUDY Use of an Inventory Plan

One company had a 60 percent level of accuracy in forecasted demands and no inventory plan, yet they booked orders and made delivery promises as if they could provide 100 percent customer service. Excessive expediting and overtime were used as the buffer, but still resulted in poor customer service and delivery performance.

A second company had an informal inventory plan undertaken by the scheduler and buyers. The inventory plan reflected their knowledge of the firm's products and demand patterns, but was never explicitly stated in their ERP system for each product line. The scheduler and buyers took responsibility for an inventory plan because nobody else would do it, and it seemed to reduce the headaches involved in expediting and overtime. The informal inventory plan could also be hidden from the firm's executives, who always emphasized minimal inventory. The informal plan was uncoordinated with product structure information: it frequently resulted in too much of one item and not enough of another. It was ignored in delivery promises anyhow. The lack of an agreed-upon inventory plan, defined within the formal ERP system, had the same results as with the first company.

A third company used formal inventory plans (expressed in the S&OP game plan for each product) that represented the best guess by the management team. The product structure and planning policies were reviewed to ensure that inventory plans (expressed for saleable items) were driving replenishment of stocked components. Most sales order delivery promises accounted for inventory availability, thereby reducing exceptions to a manageable level.

Interaction between Actual and Forecasted Demands

Independent demands for saleable items reflect a combination of sales orders and forecast. Sales orders consume forecasted demands to avoid doubled-up requirements. This interaction applies whether sales orders are directly or indirectly linked to supply orders. The combination of sales orders and forecasts reflects an item's production strategy, where the strategy has two primary determinants:

- The item's minimum delivery lead-time, measured in days. It is zero days for a make-to-stock product, the average production time using stocked components for a make-to-order product, and cumulative manufacturing lead-time for a completely make-to-order product.
- The visibility of an item's sold-out backlog of sales orders, measured in days of sales. The sold-out backlog is typically greater than the item's minimum delivery lead-time.

An ERP system often employs a demand management policy, termed a *demand fence* and measured in days, to represent these two determinants of production strategy and to govern how MRP logic should interpret item demands. An item's demands consist of sales orders with ship dates inside the demand fence, and a combination of sales orders and unconsumed forecast beyond the demand fence.

Controlling Demands via a Demand Fence

Use of a demand fence to control demands can be illustrated with another viewpoint on production strategies. Figure 10.2 illustrates four different production strategies for the same item, labeled product X, and the item's three-level product structure. The product structure is repeated for each production strategy to explicitly identify the level of stocked material and relevant lead-times. The lead-time analysis for this same product was provided earlier (see Figure 5.2).

Each case has forecasted demands that extend beyond the item's cumulative manufacturing lead-time (47 days), and the combination of sales order and forecast quantities are equal in each time period across the time horizon. The

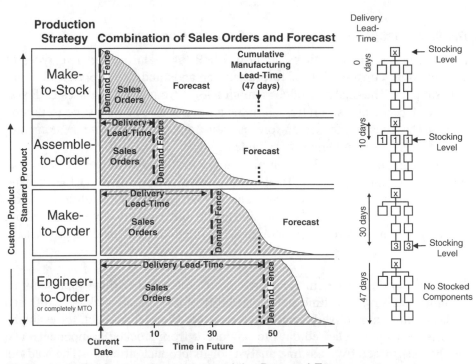

Figure 10.2 Production Strategies and the Demand Fence

level of stocked items (determining a minimum delivery lead-time) and the typical visibility of sold-out backlog (shown as the shaded area) differ for each case. Lead-time analysis is used to translate the level of stocked items into a specified number of days representing the demand fence.

- ◆ The demand fence for a make-to-stock production strategy is zero days based on the stocking level of finished goods.
- ◆ The demand fence for an assemble-to-order production strategy is 10 days based on the stocking level of level 1 components.
- ◆ The demand fence for a make-to-order production strategy is 30 days based on the stocking level of level 3 components.
- ◆ The demand fence for an engineer-to-order or completely make-to-order production strategy is 47 days with no stocked components

One implication of a demand fence is that forecasted demands drive replenishment of stocked components, and sales orders drive final assembly of the saleable item from stocked components. Furthermore, sales orders drive replenishment of make-to-order components not stocked in advance. The demand fence represents one of several demand management policies. MRP logic uses the saleable item's demand management policies, and the item's planning policy, to support the desired production strategy.

Demand Management Policies and Forecast Consumption

Demand management policies apply to MRP logic and impact two types of consumption: consumption of forecasted demands and consumption of available supplies. The dual role of consumption logic frequently confuses ERP system users, especially when framed in the terminology of forecast consumption policy. This section focuses on forecast consumption; a separate section summarizes consumption logic for available supplies.

MRP logic uses a combination of item master fields to model an item's demand management policies. To illustrate, three policies include the demand fence, forecast period and forecast consumption policy. Two additional fields, the consumed item and a UM conversion factor, may be needed when forecasting a family of standard products or common intermediates for standard products.

Demand Fence An item's demand fence (described earlier) represents its minimum delivery lead-time and the visibility of its sold out backlog, expressed in days. Minimum delivery lead-time for a make-to-order product, for example, reflects the average elapsed days to produce it from stocked components, and can be determined by lead-time analysis of its product structure. The sold-out backlog reflects a variable number of days reflecting current sales conditions.

Forecast Period   The forecast period provides a logical time span for MRP logic to compare forecasts to actual sales orders and to make assumptions about demands. The forecast period typically reflects the financial periods, but it can also be monthly or weekly periods. A sales order consumes the forecast within a forecast period based on its promised ship date, thereby avoiding doubled-up requirements.

As time progresses through a forecast period, the dates associated with an item's forecast may become past due. When sales orders have not consumed these past due forecasts, MRP logic assumes these yet-to-be-placed sales orders will arrive before the end of the forecast period. The yet-to-be-placed sales orders are included in the period's unconsumed forecast.

Treatment of these yet-to-be-placed sales orders in a period's unconsumed forecast is affected in two ways by the item's demand fence policy.

- The item's demand fence represents the minimum delivery lead-time, so MRP logic places this unconsumed forecast on the demand fence date (today's date plus the number of days in the demand fence). This assumes that sales orders arriving today will probably request ship dates for the minimum lead time.
- The item's demand fence represents the days of sold-out backlog, which creates an issue when the sold-out backlog extends into the next forecast period. As time progresses through the current forecast period, and the demand fence date progresses into the next forecast period, MRP logic assumes that additional sales orders will not materialize for shipment before the end of the current period. MRP logic assumes that all sales orders for the current period have been received, and additional sales orders will have a promised ship date in a future period.

When sales orders fall short of forecasted demands in a period, it raises the issue of how to handle unconsumed forecast. Does this represent a bad month in which sales orders did not materialize, or just a timing issue where the late arriving orders will materialize during the next period?

When sales orders exceed forecasted demands in a period, another issue involves how to handle the overconsumed forecast. Does this represent a good month, or just a timing issue where early arriving orders should consume forecasts in a future period? The demand management policy for forecast consumption defines the assumptions for these two issues.

Forecast Consumption Policy   The combination of an item's sales orders and forecasts within a forecast period becomes an issue when actual sales orders exceed or fall short of forecasted demand. The issue involves how to handle an overconsumed forecast or unconsumed forecast within a forecast period. An item's forecast consumption policy defines whether to ignore or roll forward

(1) an unconsumed forecast quantity and (2) an overconsumed forecast quantity to a future period.

A family item with a planning bill provides a simplified approach for forecasting many related standard products. Sales orders are placed for the end-items. This creates a problem when sales orders for one item (the end-item) must consume forecasts for a different item (the family item), especially when the two items have different units of measure.

A common raw material or intermediate item (or multiple items) may be used to produce many standard products, so that it may be simpler to forecast the common materials rather than end-items. Sales orders are placed for the end-items. This creates a problem when sales orders for one item (the end-item) must consume forecasts for a different item (the common material), especially when the two items have different units of measure. The problem becomes more complicated when a single sales order must consume forecasts for multiple items (multiple common materials).

In order to support these special cases of forecasting, the forecast consumption logic in an ERP system must handle designation of a consumed item (and possibly multiple consumed items) and unit of measure conversions.

Consumed Item and UM Conversion Factor An item's sales order normally consumes its own forecast. There are exceptions to this approach, as illustrated in the breakout box concerning forecasts for a standard product family and common materials. A solution approach to these exceptions requires two additional demand management policies to identify the consumed item and a UM conversion factor. In normal situations, the consumed item identifies the item's item number and the UM conversion factor is 1.

Some ERP systems use information in the planning bill to designate the consumed item (the family item) and the UM conversion factor. This approach does not support a family item representing input units (such as manhours), where detailed information about inputs may be embedded in the item's routing operations. It does not support forecasting of common material related to standard products, especially multiple common items.

Another exception to forecast consumption involves forecasting common material used to produce many custom products, where it gets included as a configuration's component. Forecast consumption must be designated for the configuration's component, rather than for the custom product family item on the sales order.

Suggested Rules of Thumb on Forecast Consumption

Several suggestions apply to forecast consumption and demand management policies. As a general rule of thumb, you should suppress any roll-forward effects to future periods in forecast consumption logic. The logic of impacting forecasted demands in future periods becomes very difficult to understand and track. If needed, you can manually adjust forecast quantities in future periods. This provides greater control and a simpler approach. It also means that an item's demands related to unconsumed forecasts seemingly disappear at the end of each forecast period (or when the item's demand fence date progresses into the next period).

A second rule of thumb involves the size of a forecast period. The financial period or monthly period generally works best. Sales orders throughout the period consume forecasted demands within the period. Weekly periods may apply when forecasted demands have been entered in weekly increments, and a slow month can be identified immediately by the pattern of sales orders. For example, the unconsumed forecast for the first week of the month should be ignored, since it appears to be a bad month based on early indicators of sales orders.

A warning applies to manually removing past-due forecasts. This may affect forecast consumption logic within a given period. Most ERP systems provide a mechanism for automatically removing past due forecasts.

Identifying Sales Orders That Add to Forecasted Demands

A sales order that was not anticipated in the item's forecast should (in many cases) be designated as an addition to forecasted demands. Without any intervention, these sales orders would consume the forecast and result in understated demands. In practical terms, the ability to identify a surprise demand may be very difficult, especially for clerical personnel in order entry. This means an ERP system should support designations of add-to-forecast after completion of sales order entry and prior to shipment.

Consumption Logic for Available Supplies

Demand management policies impact two types of consumption: consumption of forecasted demands and consumption of available supplies. Sales orders consume available supplies based on the consumed item and UM conversion factor. The other policies (demand fence, forecast period, and consumption policy) do not apply. Several illustrations provide further understanding of how consumption logic applies to forecasts and supplies.

- *Make-to-Stock Standard Product.* Sales orders for the end-item consume its forecast and master schedule (and inventory) of supplies.
- *Make-to-Order Standard Product.* Sales orders for the end-item consume its forecast. It does not consume any supplies, since the end-item does not have inventory or existing supply orders.
- *Custom Product Family.* Sales orders for the family item consume its sales forecast and production plan of uncommitted capacity.

- *Family of Make-to-Stock Standard Products.* Sales orders for the end-item can consume its production forecast and master schedule, or the family item's forecast and production plan of uncommitted capacity.
- *Common Material for Standard Products.* Sales orders for the end-item consume the forecast of common materials and their master schedules.
- *Common Material for Custom Product Configurations.* Sales orders for the custom product item do not consume forecasts, but the configuration's component can be designated to consume the forecast and master schedule of the common material.
- *Family Item Representing an Aggregate Capacity.* Sales order for an item can consume a different item's production plan (based on an additional consumed item and UM conversion factor) of uncommitted capacity. It does not consume any forecast, since the family item does not have any forecasted demand.

The dual nature of consumption logic must be considered in the sales and operations game plan for a product. The concept of forecast consumption and demand management logic is often misunderstood and implemented in different ways. The above extended discussion illustrates one approach and its considerations. Capabilities in an ERP system may limit the approaches for correctly consuming forecasts and supply availability.

Chapter 11

Sales and Operations Planning

Demand for saleable items provides a starting point to formulate each item's game plan, termed an *S&OP game plan,* for coordinating supply chain activities to meet demands. A given company will have multiple game plans to cover demands (both actual and forecast) for various saleable items. The S&OP game plan is expressed differently for different products, requiring a contingency approach to sales and operations planning. This is termed the *S&OP approach.* The appropriate S&OP approach must consider the type of product, its production strategy, linkage between demands and supplies, and other factors. An S&OP approach, for example, may involve a make-to-order custom product with direct linkage between a sales order and its supply order. In a given company, the saleable items can be categorized by the needed S&OP approach. Most firms typically use just a few basic S&OP approaches.

Various S&OP approaches can be explained using an overall framework. The framework provides an organizing focus to explain case studies of two prevalent S&OP approaches: a make-to-stock standard product and an assemble-to-order custom product. The next chapter uses the same framework to explain additional case studies of S&OP approaches.

Some general principles apply to every S&OP approach. One general principle involves aggregate or company-wide measures of demand, supply, and financial performance. Other principles involve making each game plan realistic based on material and capacity constraints, balancing conflicting objectives to derive an agreed-upon game plan, and making realistic delivery promises.

Some Basic S&OP Principles

Basic S&OP principles involve the minimum planning horizon for each game plan and the process of reviewing and updating game plans. The S&OP game plans may also coincide with a company-wide viewpoint on aggregate planning.

◆ *Minimum Planning Horizon for Each Game Plan.* A saleable item's cumulative manufacturing lead-time represents the minimum horizon to anticipate and respond to material requirements. In most cases, the planning horizon must be longer to respond to requirements for additions (or reductions) to equipment, tooling, people skills, headcount, facilities, warehouse space, and financing.

◆ *Reviewing and Updating Game Plans.* The process of reviewing and updating each S&OP game plan must be embedded into the firm's regularly scheduled meetings. Most firms already have established meeting patterns (weekly or monthly) that focus on looking ahead to plan and avoid problems in sales and operations.

Aggregate Planning and Product Families: Item Master Versus Company-wide Viewpoints

Product families and aggregate planning of finances, demands, and supplies provide a simplified view of running a manufacturing company from a top-management perspective. Detailed planning of hundreds (or thousands) of items becomes cumbersome and impractical for running the company from the top. Product families can be viewed from an *item master* or *company-wide* perspective.

The company-wide viewpoint on product families sometimes coincides with the item master viewpoint on family items. Aggregate forecasts of demand, for example, may apply to a custom product family or even a family of standard products with related demands. Aggregate measures of available supply (a production plan) may apply to a family produced in a dedicated manufacturing cell. Aggregate financial measures typically reflect the general ledger account numbers assigned to items or an analysis of item sales history.

The company-wide viewpoint on product families typically covers multiple items or multiple family items. It often represents what products do rather than how they are produced or forecasted. These situations involve reporting requirements to support summarization of financial performance, demands, and supplies. In some ERP systems, family items used only for production planning purposes can still represent the measures of aggregate supply. An ERP system's infinite capacity planning capabilities provide another way to calculate aggregate resource requirements.

An Overall S&OP Framework: Basic Elements

The basic elements of an overall S&OP framework involve demands, supply chain activities, and an S&OP game plan that coordinates supply chain activities to meet demands. Demands consist of sales orders and forecasts, and inventory plans. Supply chain activities must be coordinated in production, procurement, distribution, and customer service. The S&OP game plan consists of a master schedule (for stocked items) or final assembly schedule (for make-to-order items).

Use of these basic elements depends on the S&OP approach. A completely make-to-order custom product, for example, does not use forecasted demands or a master schedule. This represents a contingency-based approach to sales and operations planning, and a case study method will be used to explain contingencies affecting an S&OP game plan.

An overall S&OP framework, shown in Figure 11.1, provides the organizing focus for further explanation. The basic elements related to demand have been previously covered, but will be recapped here. Supply chain activities will be covered in future chapters, but the primary coordination tools can be summarized. An S&OP game plan puts the puzzle together for coordinating supply chain activities to meet demands. The pieces of this puzzle vary by situation, but the basic elements can be introduced here.

Demands

Independent demands represent a combination of sales orders and forecasts, where demand management policies govern interaction between the two. This interaction is shown as a two-headed arrow in Figure 11.1. An inventory plan represents a form of independent demand.

Sales Orders   Sales orders define actual demands originating from different sources, such as sales, customer service, field service, and engineering. Sales orders require delivery promises that reflect considerations within the S&OP game plan.

Sales Order Configurations   A sales order for a custom product requires a configuration.

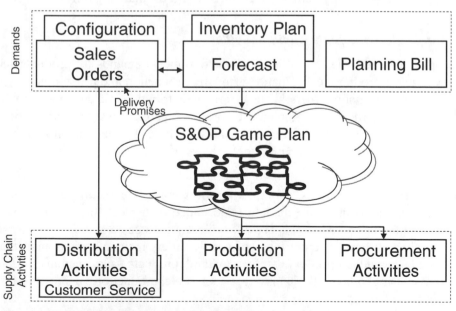

Figure 11.1 S&OP Framework: Basic Elements

Sales Orders and Their Impact on Demands and Supplies

Several aspects of sales orders impact demands. A sales order consumes forecasted demands to avoid doubled-up requirements. A sales order line item may be designated as an addition to forecasted demands. A sales order can be cancelled (or placed on hold), thereby affecting actual demands.

Other aspects of sales orders impact supplies. A sales order consumes available supplies to avoid doubled-up commitments. A sales order may be directly linked to the supply order(s). A custom product configuration contains information directly impacting production and procurement. A sales order may also contain information that impacts distribution (such as shipping specifications) and customer service (such as requests for expedited processing).

Forecasts   Forecasts can be used to anticipate actual demands. They are typically expressed for the saleable item. In some cases, the forecasted demands are expressed for a family of standard product items or for common material.

Inventory Plan   An inventory plan can be used to anticipate demand variability. An inventory plan (and forecasts) should drive replenishment of stocked items.

Planning Bill   A planning bill can be used to translate forecasts (and an inventory plan) for the family item into requirements for the planning bill components.

Coordination of Supply Chain Activities

Supply chain activities must be coordinated to meet demands for products and services. For products, coordination efforts in production and procurement typically focus on supply orders, while efforts in distribution and customer service focus on sales orders and shipments. Coordination efforts in service areas focus on service work orders and completions (rather than shipments). An ERP system provides various coordination tools for each area.

Production   The primary coordination tools consist of recommended planner actions, a production schedule (also called a dispatch list) by resource, and manufacturing orders. Paperwork typically includes a router-traveler and materials pick list. Different types of supply orders include normal and final-assembly manufacturing orders for standard products, and custom product manufacturing orders. Kanbans may coordinate production in an orderless environment.

Procurement The primary coordination tools consist of recommended buyer actions, a vendor schedule by vendor, and purchase orders. Purchase orders may be for normal material, subcontracted items (with supplied material), outside operations, a custom product configuration, nonstock material for configurations, and expense items. Kanbans may coordinate vendor replenishment in an orderless environment. Coordination in receiving can be aided by visibility (and tracking) of scheduled receipts related to purchase orders, customer-supplied material, and customers' returned goods.

Distribution The primary coordination tools consist of recommended shipping actions, a shipping schedule by area (identifying individual sales orders), and paperwork for each sales order (packing list and pick lists) and shipment (bill of lading and box labels). In addition to shipping product for sales orders, distribution may handle shipments from and to vendors, such as sending material to a subcontractor.

Customer Service Coordination of customer service activities (focusing on sales orders) consists of recommended actions for service representatives. The recommended actions may include follow-up on held sales orders, past due shipments (or service work order completions), customer requests for expedited processing, and warnings about projected late delivery.

Service Areas Coordination tools for service areas and production areas are similar: recommended planner actions, a schedule by resource, and paperwork for service work orders. The service areas may represent field service, design engineering, or another area. Service areas can be viewed as production areas and are not shown as a separate element in the S&OP framework.

Basics of an S&OP Game Plan

An S&OP game plan focuses on items at the highest levels in a product structure: saleable items down to the level of stocked components. It defines the supplies for these items, thereby coordinating supply chain activities for all lower-level components. It also considers possible constraints, sometimes expressed in a production plan.

Master Schedule The term master schedule applies to supply orders for standard products at the highest stocking level in the product structure. A master schedule applies to a make-to-stock end-item and to stocked components for a make-to-order product. The stocked item may be manufactured, purchased, or subcontracted. The master schedule provides visibility of an item's availability for making delivery promises.

Final Assembly (or Finishing) Schedule   The term *final assembly schedule* or *finishing schedule* applies to supply orders for make-to-order products, and has three different contexts:

 ◆ *Supply Orders for Custom Product Configurations Directly Linked to Sales Orders.* These typically consist of custom product manufacturing orders. Some ERP systems support a custom product purchase order or subcontract purchase order.
 ◆ *Supply Orders for Standard Products Directly Linked to Sales Orders.* These typically consist of final-assembly manufacturing orders. Some ERP systems also support direct linkage for a purchase order or subcontract purchase order.
 ◆ *Supply Orders for Standard Products Indirectly Linked to (but Driven by) Sales Orders.* These consist of normal manufacturing orders, purchase orders, and subcontract purchase orders.

Production Plan   The term *production plan* only applies to supply orders for family items, and may represent an aggregate capacity. The production plan provides visibility of uncommitted capacity for making delivery promises (when sales orders consume the production plan). The uncommitted production plan can also be used to calculate requirements for planning bill components. These requirements are termed *production forecast,* since they are projected or forecasted requirements to build generic family items.

Constraint (or Capacity) Planning   The term *constraint planning* represents the analysis of resource and material requirements for a given S&OP game plan, and the subsequent modification of availability or of the game plan to fit within constraints. The analysis of material requirements (also called material planning) identifies potential shortages. The analysis of resource constraints (also called capacity planning) identifies overloaded periods based on infinite loading. It may use finite loading to identify a capable-to-promise date or optimal schedule.

The formulation of an S&OP game plan, and the use of key elements in the overall framework, depends on the situation. The following two case studies provide context-sensitive explanations. The first case study focuses on a make-to-stock standard product: a single end-item with a printed circuit board component. The second case study focuses on an assemble-to-order custom product: an equipment unit with options. This case study involves a final assembly schedule and a production plan (and planning bill) for the family item.

S&OP Case Study: A Single Make-to-Stock Standard Product

The S&OP approach for a single make-to-stock (MTS) standard product represents a simple common scenario, especially with indirect linkage between supplies and demands. The case study involves a two-level product structure for an end-item. The end-item consists of a printed circuit board, a housing and other components that must be final-assembled and tested. A subcontractor produces the printed circuit board using supplied material. Lead-time analysis indicates a cumulative manufacturing lead-time of 40 days (8 weeks), which includes 10 days for final assembly and 20 days for the subcontracted printed circuit board.

Summary of Demand Management for the Case Study

The end-item's independent demands consist of forecasts and sales orders, and an inventory plan. Forecasts drive replenishment of finished goods. In this example, a monthly forecast (specified on the first of the month) indicates finished goods inventory should be available for sale by the specified date. Sales orders placed throughout the month consume the forecast. The unconsumed forecast is rolled forward throughout the month to keep anticipated demands visible, but then is dropped at the end of the monthly forecast period.

The inventory plan, expressed as a safety stock quantity for the end-item, represents protection against occasions when actual sales orders exceed the forecast. The end-item has on-hand stock of finished goods inventory to cover the inventory plan requirements, thereby reducing possible stock-out situations and unacceptable promised delivery dates.

The overall S&OP framework for an MTS standard product, shown in Figure 11.2, provides the basis for further explanation.

Key Aspects of the S&OP Approach

The end-item's master schedule currently consists of weekly manufacturing orders. The planner initially created firm orders (with end-of-week due dates) over a 12-week horizon, and released each order as time progressed. The firm orders were updated monthly. Capacity and material planning highlighted any projected constraints to the master schedule.

The planner subsequently changed the S&OP approach. The monthly forecast was segmented into weekly increments (with end-of-week due dates) over a rolling 12-week horizon, so that MRP logic automatically generated planned orders that could be easily firmed. The planner firmed the master schedule over the product's cumulative manufacturing lead-time (8 weeks), firming the eighth week on a rolling basis as time progressed.

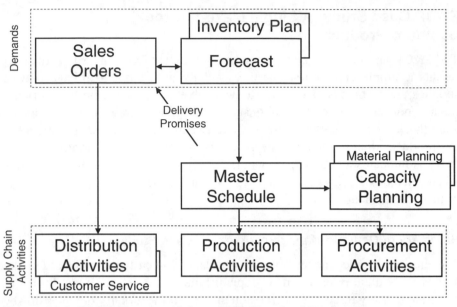

Figure 11.2 S&OP Framework for a MTS Standard Product

The planner is considering additional improvements in the S&OP approach.

- *Planning Fence for the End-Item.* The end-item's planning fence reflects its cumulative manufacturing lead-time. MRP logic provides an early warning about potential problems in the master schedule; it places unrealistic planned orders at the planning fence date.
- *Handling Wide Variations in Order Quantity.* The item's fixed lead-time does not model large variations in manufacturing order quantity. The planner is considering a calculated lead-time for the manufacturing order, or daily schedules (based on rate-based scheduling), to model a variable lead-time. The daily schedule approach has granularity advantages by providing the basis for improved coordination in production and procurement activities, as well as improved available-to-promise logic (which impacts daily activities in distribution).

How the S&OP Approach Affects Delivery Promises

Delivery promises on sales orders are based on the end-item's inventory and master schedule. Available-to-promise (ATP) logic for the saleable item provides an available date for a specified quantity, or an available quantity for a specified date. Actual sales orders consume the master schedule to correctly reflect availability.

Coordinating Supply Chain Activities

The promised ship dates on sales orders drive distribution activities to ship product. The end-item's master schedule (and product structure) provide the basis for coordinating supply chain activities in production and procurement. Use of planned and firm manufacturing orders enabled MRP logic to use the most-current bill information to calculate requirements for material and resource components. The order-dependent bills for near-term released orders lock in the latest bill information.

Only a small number of sales orders reflect unrealistic delivery promises, thereby reducing the number of exceptions in the supply chain that require expedited production and procurement activities.

The planner's ideas for improving the S&OP approach affect supply chain activities. The planning fence provides an early warning about potential problems in the supply chain, and daily schedules provide the basis for greater coordination in production, procurement, delivery promises, and distribution.

Master Scheduling without Visibility of Demands

Some situations do not provide demand visibility in a firm's ERP system. The situation usually occurs when the order entry system operates as a standalone application, or a corporate entity mandates the master schedule. These situations typically require a manual replenishment method and manually defined master schedules. MRP logic cannot use demand information to suggest replenishment; forecasts and sales orders do not exist. The master schedule reflects an implied forecast and inventory plan.

S&OP Case Study: An Assemble-to-Order Custom Product

The S&OP approach for an assemble-to-order (ATO) custom product represents a simple common scenario. It involves direct linkage between the sales order and a custom product manufacturing order. As shown in Figure 11.3, the case study involves an assemble-to-order equipment family made from stocked components. A configuration's bill consists of a selected base unit, optional controls, common parts, and other options. All configurations are produced on a dedicated assembly line. Lead-time analysis indicates a cumulative manufacturing lead-time of 35 days (7 weeks), and 5 days to produce a configuration from stocked components.

Summary of Demand Management for the Case Study

Anticipated demand for the family item consists of weekly forecasts. Using planned orders suggested by MRP logic, the planner firms up a weekly produc-

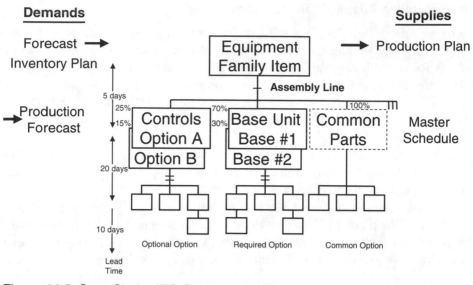

Figure 11.3 Case Study: ATO Custom Product for Equipment (Forecasting Viewpoint)

tion plan to represent the aggregate capacity (or run rate) of the assembly line. The production plan, expressed in equivalent units per week, is treated as "gospel" by the management team. Each sales order for an equipment configuration consumes the production plan, so that delivery promises are based on the unconsumed (or uncommitted) production plan.

To anticipate the yet-to-be-placed sales order configurations in each weekly forecast period, MRP logic uses the unconsumed production plan to calculate requirements for planning bill components. Requirements blow through phantom options to the level of stocked components. The inventory plan for the family item, expressed as a safety stock quantity to anticipate volume variability, is also used by MRP logic to calculate component requirements. These requirements, termed *production forecasts,* drive the master schedule for stocked components.

Each sales order defines a unique configuration using option selection from the planning bill. This sales order viewpoint is shown in Figure 11.4. Some configurations require direct definition to specify nonstock material components (such as a specialized decal) and even customer-supplied material. A custom product manufacturing order—directly linked to the sales order—forms part of the final assembly schedule for the assembly line. Each week's unconsumed forecast is rolled forward throughout the week, but then dropped at the end of the weekly forecast period.

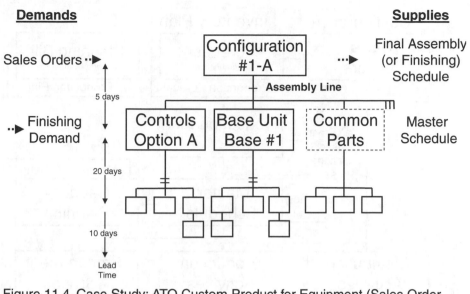

Figure 11.4 Case Study: ATO Custom Product for Equipment (Sales Order Viewpoint)

Key Aspects of the S&OP Approach

The overall S&OP framework for an ATO custom product, shown in Figure 11.5, involves more complexity than a single MTS product. As described earlier, sales orders consume the forecast and production plan, and MRP logic uses the unconsumed production plan to calculate production forecasts for planning bill components.

The final assembly schedule consists of custom product manufacturing orders directly linked to sales orders. The master schedule consists of supply orders for stocked components. The planner firms up each component's master schedule over a rolling 7 week horizon, since this represents the product's cumulative manufacturing lead-time. Material and capacity planning highlights potential constraints, especially in producing options.

The planner is considering improvements in the S&OP approach.

◆ *Planning Fence for Stocked Components.* MRP logic can generate an early warning when unrealistic demands would require additions to the master schedule within the planning fence horizon.

◆ *Inventory Plan for Option Mix Variability.* Inflating the option mix percentages in the planning bill provides greater flexibility to satisfy demand variations for long lead-time options.

◆ *Final Assembly for Options (Intermediates).* Some options are only produced to actual demand, and require a separate supply order because of

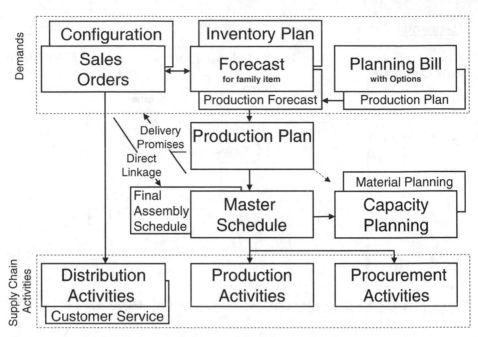

Figure 11.5 S&OP Framework for an ATO Custom Product

subcontract manufacturing, lot trace, or production purposes. These options need to be designated with a final assembly planning policy, so that forecasted demands blow through to stocked components, and actual demands (inclusion in a configuration) trigger a supply order for the option.

How the S&OP Approach Affects Delivery Promises

The production plan provides the primary basis for making delivery promises; the availability of selected options is a secondary basis. ATP logic provides an available date for a specified quantity, or an available quantity for a specified date. Sales orders consume the production plan, and a configuration's components consume the master schedule, to correctly reflect availability.

Coordinating Supply Chain Activities

The final assembly schedule (of custom product manufacturing orders and other orders for MTO components) and master schedule (for stocked components) provide the basis for coordinating supply chain activities in procurement and production. Although not mentioned in this case study, coordination may involve procurement of nonstock material purchases (specified in the configuration) and production of configured subassemblies.

Use of the planning bill for option selection provides close coordination between planned and actual demands for stocked components, especially since component effectivity dates can be used to enforce currently saleable options during option selection.

Sales orders drive distribution activities, and shipping paperwork (such as the packing list and invoice) can identify the selected options within a configuration.

ERP USAGE ISSUE

Significance of the Production Plan for a Custom Product

The production plan for a custom product family can represent two things: an aggregate measure of available material (expressed in matched sets of components in the planning bill) and available capacity (expressed in equivalent units). Its usefulness for aggregate capacity only applies when a custom product family reflects a dedicated manufacturing process, and the configurations have similar processing time requirements. The similar time requirements reflect the concept of equivalent units. Widely varying time requirements for producing different configurations often make the aggregate capacity measurement less useful.

Making the S&OP Game Plan Realistic

A product's S&OP game plan must be realistic and reasonably level-loaded. It does not need to be perfect. Execution of supply chain activities can be managed to handle the details. Making the S&OP game plan realistic involves identifying capacity and material exceptions that would constrain the plan, and then eliminating the constraints or changing the game plan. MRP logic can provide early warning signals about potential exceptions. One approach to developing a level-loaded S&OP game plan uses advanced scheduling logic.

Identifying Resource Capacity Exceptions

Capacity problems can be anticipated by infinite loading to identify overloaded periods, or finite loading to identify late supply orders that would result in missed delivery promises.

Infinite Loading   Infinite loading identifies overloaded periods to anticipate needed adjustments in available capacity or loads. MRP logic uses the S&OP game plan and bill information to calculate loads. MRP logic treats each resource as infinite (regardless of designated resource type) by assuming it can process multiple orders concurrently. The comparison of loads to available capacity identifies overloaded periods, using monthly, weekly, or daily periods. The period size corresponds to the purpose of capacity planning, ranging from rough-cut to detailed capacity planning. Figure 11.6 illustrates infinite capacity

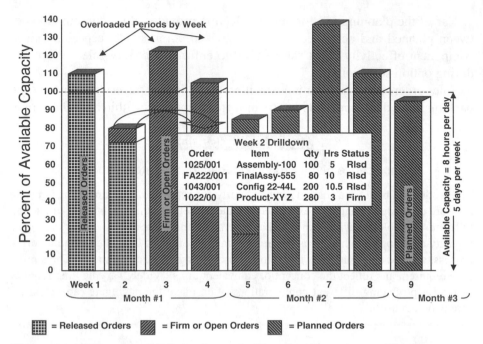

Figure 11.6 Example of Infinite Capacity Planning Resource = Final Assembly Work Center

planning using weekly period sizes to highlight overloaded periods, and the ability to drill down to detailed load information. A monthly period size would not indicate overloading in this example.

The analysis of capacity exceptions usually starts with bottleneck resources. The projection of overloaded periods typically leads to minor adjustments in available capacity, such as changes to available hours (overtime) or headcount (transferring personnel). The analysis of overloaded periods may lead to consideration of other courses of action that become increasingly difficult and expensive. As summarized in Figure 11.7, this may include adding people and equipment or adding shifts to adjust capacity. Adjustments in loads can also be considered, ranging from alternate operations to changing the S&OP game plans.

Infinite capacity planning can also identify projections of underutilization. The courses of action may involve adjustments to available capacity, such as reductions in temporary workers or reductions in working days. Conversely, loads can be adjusted by working ahead to reduce the sales order backlog or build inventory. Using what-if simulations can help identify the appropriate course of action for overloaded and for underutilized periods.

Finite Loading (Finite Scheduling) Finite loading (also termed finite scheduling) identifies late and unscheduled supply orders that would result in

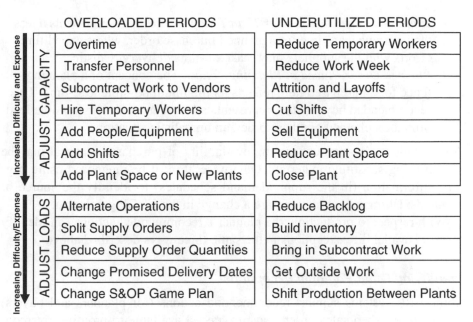

Figure 11.7 Courses of Action Based on Infinite Capacity Planning

missed delivery promises. Forward finite scheduling logic can calculate late orders, whereas backward finite scheduling logic calculates unscheduled orders. Finite scheduling logic recognizes finite resource types and treats available capacity as fixed. It results in adjustments to loads by rescheduling supply orders.

Finite scheduling logic may account for purchased material constraints, thereby identifying material items causing late or unscheduled orders. This analysis may lead to expedited purchase orders or use of alternate materials.

Identifying Material Availability Exceptions

MRP logic uses the S&OP game plan, bill information, and lead-times to calculate material requirements. It suggests recommended actions to expedite existing supply orders and suggest new planned orders. With respect to procurement, the buyer's recommended actions can identify material availability exceptions in at least three ways:

- *Calculated Need Date Earlier Than Today's Date.* This represents purchased material needed yesterday, an unrealistic situation. It applies to planned and current purchase orders. The need date for purchased material typically reflects lead-times for items higher in the product structure. The nature of these lead-times may provide some slack. For example, they may represent inflated fixed lead-time for make items.

◆ *Suggested Start Date Earlier Than Today's Date.* This represents a less than average lead-time for a planned purchase order, where expediting efforts with the suppliers may make on-time delivery realistic.

◆ *Planned Order Placed at Planning Fence.* The concept of a planning fence for a purchased item reflects its minimum possible lead-time. This recommended buyer action represents a less than minimum possible lead-time for a planned purchase order, an unrealistic situation.

An unrealistic situation concerning availability of purchased material may be solved using substitute materials. Otherwise, it must be diagnosed using pegging information (in the supply/demand schedules) to identify the source of demands. Ultimately, it may require a change in the S&OP game plan.

With respect to production, the planner's recommended actions can identify material availability exceptions in the same three ways described above.

Identifying Other Potential Exceptions

Some ERP systems support recommended actions (for planners and buyers) that identify when sales orders have exceeded available-to-promise, overconsumed the master schedule, or overconsumed the production plan. These messages provide an early warning that the S&OP game plan should be reviewed.

The recommended actions may also identify the need to replenish an obsolete item, suggesting that bill changes are required.

Past-due ship dates for sales orders represent unrealistic situations. These dates incorrectly communicate the need for shipping and supply chain activities. Past due ship dates must be changed to reflect best-available estimates.

Significance of an Agreed-Upon S&OP Game Plan

An effective S&OP game plan has several characteristics. First, it includes considerations about conflicting objectives. Second, it represents a reasonably realistic game plan based on analyses of capacity and material. Third, the management team understands and agrees with the game plan. Management commits to using the game plan to coordinate supply chain activities in distribution, production, and procurement. In particular, the sales management team must commit to making delivery promises based on the game plan. This can isolate and minimize the number of unrealistic delivery promises that require expediting.

Functional Areas and Conflicting Objectives

The development of each S&OP game plan represents a complex decision-making process that requires the management team to define and agree upon a plan that resolves conflicting objectives. Each functional area involved in the

S&OP process can be characterized in terms of their typical objectives. Even an integrated product team faces these conflicting objectives.

Sales and Field Service   The sales function focuses on customer service objectives. These objectives may be expressed in terms of meeting customer requested delivery dates or quantities with short delivery lead-times, zero stockouts, and high on-time shipping percentages. For custom products, the objectives include timely, accurate, and complete configurations for the purposes of cost estimating and pricing. Sales may require frequent sales order changes, dynamic changes to product designs, and the ability to handle spikes in the demand patterns to meet customer service objectives.

Engineering   The engineering function focuses on design improvement objectives. Design improvements may stem from efforts to lower product costs, or from marketplace and quality requirements. Engineering must be able to communicate planned changes to other functional areas. Frequent design changes can be facilitated by minimal inventory (reducing possible rework and obsolescence) and smaller lot sizes (reducing possible work-in-process impacts). For custom products, engineering's objectives include timely, accurate, and complete configurations. Engineering may require frequent design changes in the configurations, and communication of changes to other functional areas.

Cost Accounting   The cost accounting function focuses on cost reduction objectives. Cost reductions can be accomplished by engineering design improvements (reflected in bill changes) and by efficiencies in manufacturing and procurement. For example, the efficiencies may involve reduced setup times.

Production   The production function focuses on efficiency objectives. Stable designs and schedules, high throughput, and larger lot sizes make it easier to meet efficiency objectives. These approaches lead to lower product costs, but conflict with customer service objectives requiring frequent sales order changes, spiky demand patterns, and small lot sizes with fast turnaround. They also conflict with objectives involving dynamically changing product designs and minimal inventory.

Procurement   The procurement function focuses on efficiency-related objectives. For example, larger lot sizes often lead to lower purchase prices and stable schedules help avoid expediting fees. These approaches lead to lower product costs, but conflict with objectives involving dynamic changes to product designs and minimal inventory.

Inventory Management   The inventory management function focuses on objectives related to minimal inventory. Minimal inventory objectives can be facilitated by smaller lot sizes and stable demands, schedules, and product designs. However, customer service objectives typically require greater inventory to act as a buffer for anticipating demand variations and spiky demands. Efficiency objectives typically require larger lot sizes resulting in greater inventory.

Quality The quality function focuses on reducing scrap and yield problems, and introducing improved product and process designs. Larger lot sizes reduce scrap associated with setup and generally improve yields.

Accounting The accounting function focuses on objectives related to minimizing product costs and inventory, and to maximizing revenue and cash collection. Poor customer service leads to difficulties in cash collection.

Master Scheduling The objectives of a master scheduling function focus on maintaining each item's S&OP game plan. This requires an in-depth understanding of the firm's business to balance trade-off factors between conflicting objectives, an in-depth understanding of ERP system capabilities (and limitations), and enough stature to gain company-wide concurrence with the game plans. The basic trade-off factor for most master schedulers involves near-term schedule stability.

ERP Usage Issue: Near-Term Schedule Stability

Near-term schedule stability provides one solution for resolving many conflicting objectives. This enables production to achieve efficiencies for being competitive. It also supports objectives of other functional areas, such as procurement (reduced expediting time and fees) and cost accounting (reduced setup costs and expediting fees). Near-term schedule stability requires a basic trade-off with objectives requiring fast response and frequent schedule changes.

The primary approach to near-term schedule stability involves a frozen period, or multiple periods with degrees of "frozenness." The length of the frozen period should reflect a product's production strategy. Delivery lead-time and the inventory plan reflect agility in handling demand variations requiring fast response and frequent schedule changes. Manufacturing practices based on the just-in-time philosophy can facilitate improved agility. Hence, the frozen period may range from hours to days to months, depending on the product's context.

The critical issue is that management recognizes the need for a frozen period, and then carefully considers changes in near-term schedules. Anything is negotiable, but the cost of changes increases within the frozen period. The frozen period provides a stable target for coordinating supply chain activities and removes most alibis for missing schedules in production and procurement.

The related issue to near-term schedule stability involves delivery promises based on availability. The approach to delivery promises can reduce (and iso-late) the number of variations between actual demands and feasible plans. Con-sideration of feasible plans reflects management's commitment to near-term schedule stability.

ERP Usage Issue: Making Delivery Promises on Sales Orders

Realistic delivery promises provide coordination between actual demands and the product's S&OP game plan. Checking availability provides the key link be-tween actual sales and what the rest of the company has been working toward. The critical issue is to reduce the number of sales order exceptions requiring expediting.

Delivery promises based on available-to-promise (ATP) logic can reduce and isolate exceptions. A requested sales order quantity that exceeds availability should be entered as a delayed delivery or split delivery.

◆ *Delayed Delivery.* The sales order line item should identify the promise date and the customer's requested ship date. The difference in dates de-fines an exception condition, and provides the basis for recommended customer service actions to pursue expedited delivery. Delayed delivery can also be based on capable-to-promise (CTP) logic.

◆ *Split Delivery.* A split delivery is expressed with two sales order line items (or delivery lines) that split the order quantity. One line item identi-fies the partial quantity that can be promised as requested; the second line item identifies the remainder with the promised ship date. The second line item represents a delayed delivery, and isolates the exception condi-tion to a subset of the order quantity.

This suggested approach reduces and isolates the exception conditions requir-ing follow-up and possible expediting. In most cases, the customer has flexibil-ity in accepting a promise ship date that aligns with S&OP game plan. When exceptions do occur, further analysis and expediting can lead to changes in promised ship dates, just as changing conditions about demands and supplies may lead to subsequent changes in sales order promises.

Exceptions will occur. The intent of near-term schedule stability and delivery promises is to reduce the number of exceptions to a manageable level. Sales or-ders entered with unrealistic promise dates also represent an exception. Commu-nicating this exception to customer service and the item's planner or buyer pro-vides an early warning that a sales order will cause a disruption in current plans.

Characteristics of a Good S&OP Game Plan

A good S&OP game plan results in shorter delivery lead-times, fewer stock-outs and delayed deliveries, higher on-time shipping percentages, and a manageable amount of expediting. Figure 11.8 summarizes the characteristics of a good S&OP game plan.

A good S&OP game plan must cover all demands for the product. This includes actual and forecasted demands, as well as demands for a configuration's components. Sales orders cannot have past-due ship dates. The game plan may need to anticipate variability in demands with an agreed-upon inventory plan for the highest stocking level in the product structure.

A good S&OP game plan must be reasonably realistic, reflecting constraints regarding capacity and material. The game plan provides the basis for making delivery promises on sales orders and retains near-term schedule stability. The supply chain activities (in procurement, production, and distribution) work to the plan, with a manageable number of exceptions requiring expediting.

A good S&OP plan leads to improvements in performance. A comparison of actual versus planned performance for an S&OP game plan should be embedded in monthly review meetings. A typical S&OP comparison report focuses on monthly units of sales, production, and inventory for a product family, as shown in Figure 11.9. The report could also be expressed in units per day (based on working days per month).

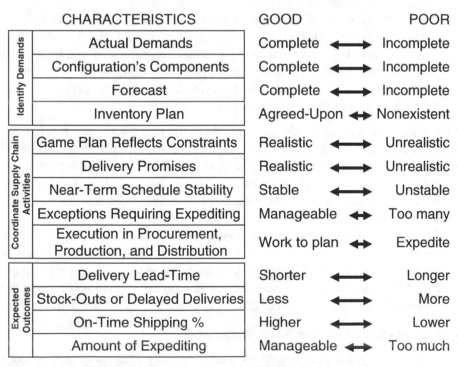

CHARACTERISTICS		GOOD		POOR
Identify Demands	Actual Demands	Complete	←→	Incomplete
	Configuration's Components	Complete	←→	Incomplete
	Forecast	Complete	←→	Incomplete
	Inventory Plan	Agreed-Upon	←→	Nonexistent
Coordinate Supply Chain Activities	Game Plan Reflects Constraints	Realistic	←→	Unrealistic
	Delivery Promises	Realistic	←→	Unrealistic
	Near-Term Schedule Stability	Stable	←→	Unstable
	Exceptions Requiring Expediting	Manageable	←→	Too many
	Execution in Procurement, Production, and Distribution	Work to plan	←→	Expedite
Expected Outcomes	Delivery Lead-Time	Shorter	←→	Longer
	Stock-Outs or Delayed Deliveries	Less	←→	More
	On-Time Shipping %	Higher	←→	Lower
	Amount of Expediting	Manageable	←→	Too much

Figure 11.8 Characteristics of a Good S&OP Game Plan

Product Family = Widgets

	Month 1	Month 2	Month 3	Month 4	Month 5	...
Workdays in Month	22	19	21	22	21	
Sales - Planned	100	90	94	88	92	
Sales - Actual	105	87	98			
Difference	5	(3)	4			
Cumulative Difference	5	2	6			
Production - Planned	95	95	95	95	95	
Production - Actual	96	97	93			
Difference	1	2	(2)			
Cumulative Difference	1	3	1			
Inventory - Planned	50	50	50	50	50	
Inventory - Actual 53	44	54	49			
Difference	(6)	4	(1)			

Current Date

Figure 11.9 S&OP Comparison Report: Sales Versus Production

Making Delivery Promises Using Available-to-Promise Logic

A critical S&OP issue involves making realistic delivery promises. This provides coordination between actual demands and the product's S&OP game plan. Delivery promises provide the opportunity to be honest with customers. Customers prefer honest and realistic answers (even if they are unpleasant) to unrealistic and inaccurate answers. This leads to customer trust and loyalty, and ultimately provides the best measure of customer service.

Delivery promises based on the S&OP game plans can be based on available-to-promise (ATP) logic. There are several variations of ATP logic for standard products and custom products. A quoted lead-time may also be used when an S&OP game plan does not exist, such as a completely make-to-order standard product. It typically represents the item's cumulative manufacturing lead-time. This simple approach ignores considerations about order quantity, available resource capacity, and current factory loads.

Available-to-Promise (ATP) Logic for a Standard Product

ATP logic can provide a promised date for a specified quantity or an available quantity for a specified date, or both. Checking availability for a specified quantity represents forward finite scheduling. ATP logic requires an S&OP game plan, with three variations that reflect a focus on the saleable item, the item's components, and the item's production plan.

- *ATP for the Saleable Item.* Availability is based on the item's uncommitted inventory and scheduled receipts, where these have been defined as part of the item's S&OP game plan.
- *ATP for the Item's Material Components.* Availability is based on the item's stocked components, plus the lead-time to produce the item from stocked components. The promise date reflects availability of the worst-case component.
- *ATP for the Item's Production Plan.* Availability is based on the uncommitted production plan related to the item.

A combination of ATP approaches may be used. Availability of a make-to-order product, for example, can be based on the item's components and the item's production plan. A customer may also request a combined shipment for multiple sales order line items on the same ship date, so that ATP logic must consider availability of the worst-case line item.

ATP Logic for a Custom Product

ATP logic for a custom product requires an S&OP game plan, with three variations that reflect a focus on the custom product family item and the configuration's components.

- *ATP for the Family Item's Production Plan.* Availability can be based on the family item's uncommitted production plan, where checking availability for a specified quantity represents forward finite scheduling. The production plan may include planned supply orders.
- *ATP for a Stocked Component within the Configuration.* Availability can be checked for each stocked component within the configuration. This may provide useful feedback to the customer, where option selection can accommodate customer preferences concerning availability. This approach does not support a promise date for the entire configuration (the sales order).
- *ATP for All Components within the Configuration.* Availability can be based on all stocked components within the configuration, plus the family item's average lead-time or a calculated lead-time. The promise date reflects availability of the worst-case component.

Using a combination of approaches also applies to a custom product, as well as the need for a combined shipment of multiple sales order line items.

Making Delivery Promises Based on Capable-to-Promise Logic

Capable-to-promise (CTP) logic can also be used to make delivery promises. It may be used in combination with an available-to-promise approach. It is frequently used when an S&OP game plan has not been formulated. CTP logic is typically considered in terms of a single sales order, using either a simple approach or a comprehensive approach. It may also apply globally to all orders.

CTP Logic for a Single Order

CTP logic for a single order can provide a promised date for a specified quantity of a standard or custom product using its bill and forward finite scheduling. This approach typically ignores scheduling rules involving multiple orders (e.g., sequencing of orders to minimize setup) because it focuses on a single order. For a single order, CTP logic has two major variations that reflect a simple or comprehensive approach to available capacity and scheduling rules.

* *CTP Using a Simple Approach.* Simple CTP logic calculates an available ship date by using infinite loading rules for each resource. Simplistic scheduling rules apply to a linear sequence of the item's routing operations. It may handle a linear sequence of supply orders when the item has a multilevel product structure.

   This simple CTP approach generally ignores current factory loads, so that it performs forward scheduling starting with today's date or a future date representing a frozen period. It does not typically consider material constraints, more comprehensive scheduling rules (such as alternate operations and secondary resources), or level-by-level netting logic. The simple CTP approach is sufficient for items with basic scheduling requirements, especially when the item and its components have little or no work-in-process.

* *CTP Using a Comprehensive Approach.* Comprehensive CTP logic calculates an available ship date using finite loading rules for each resource, a comprehesive model of each resource's available capacity, and more comprehensive scheduling rules. These scheduling rules may consider secondary resources, overlapping operations, alternate operations, and other factors. It may consider material constraints. The comprehensive CTP approach may perform scheduling with or without consideration of current factory loads. It can start with today's date and ignore current loads, or with the first open periods in an existing schedule.

Comprehensive CTP Logic for All Orders (Global CTP Logic)

Global CTP logic can be used to schedule all orders, thereby recognizing current factory loads and comprehensive scheduling rules involving multiple orders. When used for making delivery promises, a global CTP approach runs the risk of disrupting a previously optimal schedule. A frozen period may be used to avoid this problem.

Problems with Comprehensive CTP Logic

Comprehensive CTP logic requires the implementation of advanced planning and scheduling (APS) capabilities, and typically focuses on manufacturing activities. APS and its ability to support comprehensive CTP logic requires a comprehensive model of production. This includes each resource's available capacity, complete data about bills and routing operations, comprehensive scheduling rules, and timely reporting of actual production to identify remaining work. The idealism of these models and scheduling rules looks great in presales presentations. However, the practical realities of most manufacturing environments lead to failed implementations for the majority of firms. Implementations tend to fail because the model and scheduling rules become overly complex, data maintenance and reporting efforts become too time consuming, and users do not rigorously adhere to the suggested schedule.

Before undertaking an APS implementation with comprehensive CTP logic, ask the production scheduler the level of detail really wanted in a dispatch list. In many cases, the minute-by-minute detailed dispatch lists generated by the advanced scheduling capabilities are not needed, only the basic production schedules and visibility of overloaded periods. The production schedules should reflect near-term schedule stability and be reasonably level-loaded. A knowledgeable scheduler can mentally grasp the scheduling rules and the dynamics of available capacity to implement the details.

Other Common Problems Related to Sales and Operations Planning

What Happens When You Make Unrealistic Delivery Promises?

When an item's sales order quantity must be entered with an unrealistic promised delivery date, an exception condition must be communicated after-the-fact to the relevant person. These occasions may reflect automatic entry of sales orders via EDI (electronic data interchange). The item's planner identifies the person responsible for responding to the exception condition. The exception condition identifies that sales orders have exceeded available-to-promise, so that the planner can analyze the situation and take actions. The actions may involve expediting supply orders, delaying delivery dates on lower priority sales orders, or communicating a delay to the customer. Lack of action typically means poorly coordinated supply chain activities, a delayed shipment, and a breakdown in usefulness of the formal ERP system.

The Impact of Past-Due Ship Dates for Sales Orders

Past-due ship dates are wrongly viewed as the poor man's expediting tool. Sale order line items with past-due ship dates represent unrealistic promises. They create confusion just like any other unrealistic promise. The past-due ship dates must be updated to reflect the best estimate, which enables priorities to be correctly communicated through the supply chain. Ship dates also provide the basis for forecast consumption, so that updates may affect demand calculations.

Suggestions for Entering Master Schedules and Forecasts

Production frequency can be represented by master schedule due dates. Some rules of thumb apply to weekly, monthly, and intermittent production frequencies as illustrated by the following suggestions:

- *Weekly Production Frequency.* End-of-week due dates (e.g., Friday) denote the production quantity must be completed by the last working day within the week. As a corollary, the item's lead-time may be defined as one week, so that the defaulted order start date ensures component availability by the start-of-week date. Order start dates can be overridden to indicate short weeks.
- *Monthly Production Frequency.* One rule of thumb uses the last-working-day-in-month or the last-working-Friday as a master schedule due date. Unfortunately, MRP logic will schedule all production for month-end completion. As an alternative, a designated week rule of thumb can be used. The master schedules for different items can be designated for different weeks throughout each month, using end-of-week due dates.
- *Intermittent Production Frequency.* Intermittent production can typically use the designated-weeks rule of thumb, with end-of-week due dates.

Consistent use (and understanding) of master production schedule due dates can help the sales function interpret available-to-promise dates.

Related suggestions apply to forecast dates and quantities. Given a monthly forecast quantity, the master scheduler should use forecast quantities and dates that align with the anticipated production frequency. The forecast dates and quantities can reflect weekly segments or the designated week. Use of a planning bill (and lead-time offsets) can automatically generate production forecasts with weekly (or daily) quantities for a monthly production plan. A rate-based replenishment method can also generate daily schedules.

A monthly forecast could be entered with the first-working-day-in-month as the forecast date. For an MTS product, this denotes finished goods inventory must be ready to sell in the coming month. Unfortunately, this rule-of-thumb means MRP logic will try scheduling all production to meet the one demand date. Also, this rule-of-thumb does not segment demand quantities for the purposes of weekly (or intermittent) production frequency. The master scheduler would have to manually create manufacturing orders to represent weekly (or intermittent) production frequency, and MRP logic can generate a high noise level of reschedule messages trying to align supplies with demands.

Chapter 12

Sales and Operations Planning Case Studies

The basics of running a manufacturing company from the top involve a sales and operations planning (S&OP) process. As part of the process, a firm will employ multiple S&OP game plans—one for each saleable item or product family. The context of a specific product or product family defines contingencies affecting the appropriate S&OP approach.

Understanding how to run a manufacturing firm from the top starts with categorizing a firm's products and services by S&OP approach. Most firms can categorize their products into two or three S&OP approaches, so that an understanding of a given approach applies to many products. A manufacturer of make-to-stock standard products, for example, may also produce make-to-order custom products (such as prototypes). They can categorize their products into two S&OP approaches.

The type of product (standard versus custom) represents the primary contingency affecting the choice of an S&OP approach. There are other contingencies. The major contingencies include:

- Type of product
- The product's production strategy
- The need for direct linkage between sales orders and supply orders for the product, and the number of levels in the product structure that require direct linkage
- The use of a family item and its planning bill for forecasting purposes
- The use of a family item for production planning (and aggregate ATP) purposes
- Special cases, such as common materials to produce many products, project manufacturing, and field service tasks

The combinations of these major contingencies provide the starting point for a taxonomy or categorization of S&OP approaches. A categorization of S&OP approaches, illustrated in Figure 12.1, provides the organizing focus for presenting various case studies. It also provides a tool for helping firms identify the applicable S&OP approaches for their products.

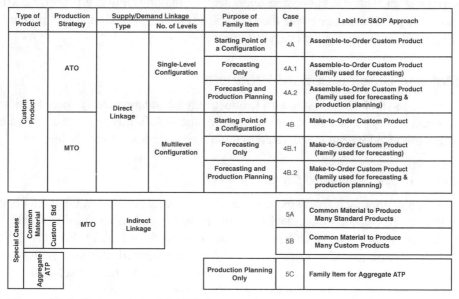

Type of Product	Production Strategy	Supply/Demand Linkage		Purpose of Family Item	Case #	Label for S&OP Approach
		Type	No. of Levels			
Standard Product	MTS	Indirect Linkage	n/a	n/a	1	Single Make-to-Stock End-Item
				Forecasting Only	1.1	Family of Make-to-Stock End-Items (for forecasting purposes only)
				Forecasting and Production Planning	1.2	Family of Make-to-Stock End-Items (for forecasting and production planning)
				Production Planning Only	1.3	Family Item for Aggregate ATP
	MTO	Indirect Linkage	n/a	n/a	2	Single Make-to-Order End-Item
				Forecasting Only	2.1	Family of Make-to-Order End-Items (for forecasting purposes only)
				Forecasting and Production Planning	2.2	Family of Make-to-Order End-Items (for forecasting & production planning)
		Direct Linkage	Single-Level Bill	n/a	3A	Single Assemble-to-Order End-Item (with direct linkage to sales order)
			Multilevel Bill	n/a	3B	Single Make-to-Order End-Item (with direct linkage to sales order)

Type of Product	Production Strategy	Supply/Demand Linkage		Purpose of Family Item	Case #	Label for S&OP Approach
		Type	No. of Levels			
Custom Product	ATO	Direct Linkage	Single-Level Configuration	Starting Point of a Configuration	4A	Assemble-to-Order Custom Product
				Forecasting Only	4A.1	Assemble-to-Order Custom Product (family used for forecasting)
				Forecasting and Production Planning	4A.2	Assemble-to-Order Custom Product (family used for forecasting & production planning)
	MTO		Multilevel Configuration	Starting Point of a Configuration	4B	Make-to-Order Custom Product
				Forecasting Only	4B.1	Make-to-Order Custom Product (family used for forecasting)
				Forecasting and Production Planning	4B.2	Make-to-Order Custom Product (family used for forecasting & production planning)

Special Cases	Common Material	Std	MTO	Indirect Linkage		5A	Common Material to Produce Many Standard Products
		Custom				5B	Common Material to Produce Many Custom Products
	Aggregate ATP				Production Planning Only	5C	Family Item for Aggregate ATP

Figure 12.1 Categories of S&OP Approaches

Each category has an assigned case study number, starting with number 1 for a single make-to-stock standard product. The numbering scheme for various case studies has significance: it reflects the additional contingencies of family items and levels of direct linkage. The case studies involving a family of make-to-stock standard products, for example, are designated 1.1, 1.2, and 1.3 to reflect the three variations in S&OP approach using a family item.

The special cases for S&OP approaches include common materials used to produce many products (case 5A and 5B). Other special cases are covered in subsequent chapters. These special cases include an S&OP approach for field service tasks, and S&OP approaches for several project manufacturing scenarios (such as project billing).

For purposes of presenting illustrative case studies, the categorization of S&OP approaches consists of five major categories:

- Make-to-stock standard products
- Make-to-order standard products
- Make-to-order standard products with direct linkage
- Custom products
- Special cases

Each S&OP approach can be characterized by the focus of forecasted demand, applicable demand management and supply management policies, the type of supply order, and the suggested approach for making delivery promises. The case study explanations cover these characteristics. Space limitations preclude illustrative case studies for every category.

Make-to-Stock Standard Products

A make-to-stock (MTS) standard product may be independently forecasted, or forecasted as part of a family of related products. A family may also represent items produced within a dedicated manufacturing cell or assembly line.

CASE #1: SINGLE MAKE-TO-STOCK END-ITEM

The S&OP approach for a single MTS end-item was covered in Chapter 11. In summary, forecasted demands drive replenishment of finished goods inventory, where the item's supply orders constitute the master schedule. From an ERP system viewpoint, this means the end-item has a normal planning policy and sales orders consume forecast and availability within the master schedule. The concepts for a single MTS end-item apply to the next two case studies.

CASE #1.1: FAMILY OF MAKE-TO-STOCK END-ITEMS (FOR FORECASTING PURPOSES ONLY)

The case study involves a family of spare parts used in many units of similar equipment. The case study's planning bill was described earlier in Chapter 5. A monthly forecast for the family item represents aggregate demand, in this case an approximation of total field units (or equipment population) at that point in time. MRP logic explodes the forecast through the planning bill to create a production forecast for each stocked service part. MRP logic suggests a production

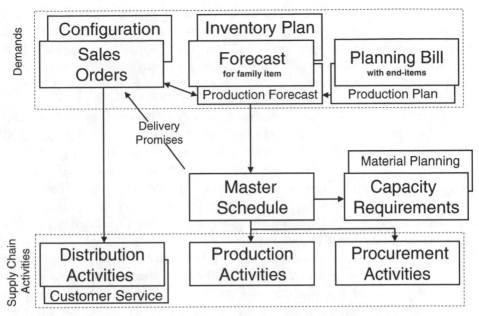

Figure 12.2 S&OP Framework for a Family of MTS End-Items

plan for the family item, but it has no significance when using the planning bill for only forecasting purposes. This concept is illustrated in the S&OP framework, shown in Figure 12.2, where the production plan box resides with other elements of demand. Sales orders consume the production forecast for end-items, thereby avoiding doubled-up requirements.

Supply orders for stocked service parts constitute the master schedule. In this case study, the stocked components reflect the spare parts in the planning bill. Some spare parts may be sold as a kit, or only produced to actual demand, as defined by the item's planning policy.

Delivery promises are based on each end-item's inventory and master schedule, and sales orders consume the master schedule to correctly reflect availability. The promised ship dates on sales orders drive distribution activities, and the master schedules provide the basis for coordinating production and procurement activities.

CASE #1.2: FAMILY OF MAKE-TO-STOCK END-ITEMS (FOR FORECASTING AND PRODUCTION PLANNING PURPOSES)

The case study involves a family of MTS end-items produced in a dedicated manufacturing cell. The end-items represent novelty consumer products with a high percentage of common materials, and some unique components that differentiate the products.

Demands for the product family consist of the combination of a forecast and sales orders. In this example, a weekly forecast has been entered. MRP logic uses the combination of sales order and forecasted demands to suggest a production plan, which is normally firmed up (over the item's cumulative manufacturing lead-time) to represent the production rate in equivalent units per week. Sales orders consume the family's production plan.

Demands for each product within the product family consist of the combination of the production forecast and sales orders. MRP logic calculates the production forecast based on the planning bill and the unconsumed production plan. That is, the production forecast anticipates the yet-to-be-placed sales orders using the planning bill mix percentages (and UM conversion factors) as a simplified model of forecasted demand. The inventory plan for the family item results in requirements for end-items, once again using the planning bill mix percentages to distribute requirements.

Delivery promises are based on availability of the end-item's inventory and master schedule, and on availability within the cell's uncommitted capacity (the family item's production plan). Supply orders for the family item represent the production plan: the aggregate capacity of the dedicated manufacturing cell. The concept of equivalent units provides one measure of aggregate capacity.

Make-to-Order Standard Products (with Indirect Linkage)

A make-to-order standard product does not necessarily imply a requirement for direct linkage between supply chain activities and sales order demands. Many MTO products can be produced with an indirect linkage. They may be completely built to actual demands or built from stocked components. The level of stocked components impacts the end-item's delivery lead-time.

A single MTO standard product can be independently forecasted, just like an MTS standard product, but the forecasts drive replenishment of stocked components (and not finished goods inventory). An MTO product does not have supply orders in advance of actual demands, so that delivery promises must be based on availability of stocked components and/or scheduling logic. Sales orders consume the end-item's forecasted demands to avoid doubled up requirements.

CASE #2: SINGLE MAKE-TO-ORDER END-ITEM (WITH INDIRECT LINKAGE)

A completely MTO standard product has a sold-out backlog that exceeds the item's cumulative manufacturing lead-time. In contrast, a partially MTO standard product is built from stocked components. The S&OP approach in this case study focuses on a partially MTO product. It requires consideration of (1) the minimum delivery lead time to build the item from stocked components, (2) the visibility of the item's sold-out backlog, and (3) which components should be stocked (based on forecasts) versus final-assembled to actual demands. The item's demand fence represents the first two considerations, and governs the combination of sales orders and forecasts in calculation of demands. A final-assembly planning policy for the saleable item, and for any MTO component above the level of stocked components, reflects the third consideration.

The case study involves the same product covered in Chapter 11: an end-item with a printed circuit board. Use of the same case study allows us to see the parallels in S&OP approaches between an MTS and an MTO product. The product consists of a two-level product structure and is made-to-order from first-level stocked components. Lead-time analysis indicates a delivery lead-time of 10 days to produce the item from first-level components, and this constitutes the demand fence for managing the combination of sales order and forecasted demand.

With a final-assembly planning policy, the end-item's demands related to forecasts and inventory plans blow through to the level of stocked components. However, the end-item's demands related to sales orders are used by MRP logic to suggest planned manufacturing orders comprising the final assembly schedule.

Note: The case study example could have reflected an MTO product built from second-level stocked components. In this case, the first-level make and subcontract components would be designated final assembly so that requirements blow through to the next lower level. The end-item's demand fence would change accordingly (to 30 days in this example). Alternatively, the first-level components could be designated as phantom component types to achieve the blow-through effect. However, this approach does not trigger supply orders for the first-level components.

In this example, a monthly forecast (specified on the first of the month) indicates stocked components should be available for producing the end-item 10 days before the specified date. Sales orders placed throughout the month consume the forecast. The unconsumed forecast is rolled forward throughout the month to keep anticipated demands visible, but then dropped at the end of the monthly forecast period. The inventory plan (expressed as a safety stock quantity for the end-item) represents protection against occasions when actual sales orders exceed the forecast. The requirements related to an inventory plan blow through the final-assembly item(s) to the level of stocked components.

The overall S&OP framework for a partially MTO standard product is shown in Figure 12.3.

Supply orders for stocked components constitute the master schedule. Manufacturing orders for the end-item, and any final-assembly component, constitute the final assembly schedule. MRP logic suggests planned manufacturing orders to cover sales order demands, with indirect linkage between the supply

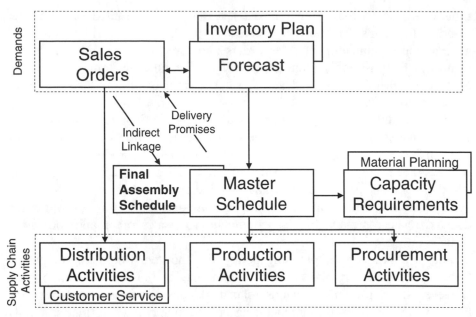

Figure 12.3 S&OP Framework for an MTO Standard Product

orders and sales orders. A planned manufacturing order for a final-assembly item reflects its lead-time and lot sizing logic.

In this example, the end-item is produced weekly because of capacity planning issues. The planner can segment the end-item's monthly forecast into weekly increments (with end-of-week due dates) over a rolling 12-week horizon, so that MRP logic automatically generates weekly planned orders for master scheduled items. The planner firms the master schedule over the product's cumulative manufacturing lead time (8 weeks), firming the eighth week on a rolling basis as time progresses.

The final-assembly end-item does not have supply orders until after sales order entry, so that delivery promises must be based on availability of stocked components or simple capable-to-promise for a single order.

Using Order Points to Replenish Stocked Components of MTO Products

An order point replenishment method can be used for some or all stocked components, rather than using forecasted demands and MRP logic. A Kanban method may also be used, which provides similar replenishment logic.

Order point replenishment methods are typically based on a fixed daily usage rate. Independent order points tend to create an uncoordinated approach to materials, especially with changing demand patterns, and provide no visibility on resource requirements. The resulting inventories typically do not represent matched sets of components that anticipate demands in the S&OP game plan. However, some ERP systems support order point logic based on a dynamic daily usage rate, as earlier described in Chapter 7 on item planning data.

Common Problem: Modeling an MTO Standard Product in ERP Systems without Final Assembly Logic

Many ERP systems do not provide the logic associated with a final-assembly planning policy, but generally support a normal and phantom item. A completely MTO product can be modeled with a normal end-item and components. Difficulties arise in modeling a partially MTO product built from stocked components. A phantom item approach works for products with short lead times such as hours or days, whereas a normal item (plus demand fence) approach works for products with longer lead-times such as weeks or months.

Phantom Item Approach. The end-item, and any MTO component not produced in advance of actual demand, is designated as a phantom. Forecasted demands blow through a phantom to the level of stocked components. Sales orders consume forecasts (avoiding doubled-up requirements for stocked components), and sales orders can drive a planned manufacturing order for the phantom end-item.

One limitation of the phantom approach is that MRP logic only suggests a planned order for the saleable end-item, and not for any MTO components. For many environments, the single supply order may provide the desired approach for managing supply chain activities. Other environments need supply orders for the MTO components. A second limitation is that a phantom's lead time is ignored by blow through logic, but recognized by the planned manufacturing order. This means that stocked components will be available earlier than necessary, which should not be a significant factor for short lead time products. In summary, the phantom item approach *explicitly* recognizes actual demands in suggesting a planned manufacturing order, and works best for products with short lead-times (hours or days).

Normal Item Approach (Plus Demand Fence). The end-item's demand fence represents the sold-out backlog, thereby providing MRP logic the basis for only suggesting a planned manufacturing order to cover actual demands in the near-term. The end-item's planned orders in the long-term (beyond the demand fence) reflect forecasted demands, and requirements for stocked components reflect a combination of forecast and sales orders.

This approach only works when (1) recommended planner actions about releasing planned orders can be filtered by a look ahead window expressed in days, and (2) the end-item's demand fence horizon is sufficiently long. The end-item's demand fence must exceed its days of supply horizon, its lead time, and its planning fence. The second factor ensures near-term planned orders only cover actual demands. The first factor ensures that the planner does not inadvertently release future planned orders (covering forecasted demands). One advantage of this approach is that forecasts drive planned supply orders beyond the demand fence. The planned supply orders provide visibility for ATP logic. Delivery promises place sales orders at the end of the sold-out backlog. In summary, the demand fence approach *implicitly* recognizes actual demands in suggesting a planned manufacturing order, and works best for products with longer lead times (weeks or months).

CASE #2.2: FAMILY OF MAKE-TO-ORDER END-ITEMS (FOR FORECASTING AND PRODUCTION PLANNING)

A family of MTO end-items may be used for forecasting and production planning, just like a family of MTS products. This case study uses an example from process manufacturing, where the family represents a common production process that can produce multiple items from a common intermediate bulk item. The family item's unit of measure reflects the aggregate capacity of the common production process. As shown in Figure 12.4, the family item's unit of measure is kilograms to reflect the weight capacity of a blending and packaging production line. The production line requires multiple resources to produce the bulk item (such as blending and cooking) and multiple resources to package the end-item (such as filling and packaging).

The saleable end-items have a unit of measure of each with different packaging sizes containing the common bulk material(s). The example in Figure 12.4 shows end-items containing 1, 2, and 5 kilograms of bulk material. Since the end-items and bulk material are only produced to actual sales orders, they have

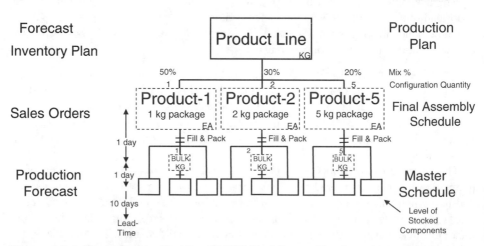

Figure 12.4 Case Study: Family of MTO End-Items (Produced on a Common Production Line)

been designated with a final-assembly planning policy (shown as a dashed box around each item). Each end-item requires unique packaging materials, and bulk material requires ingredients, which represent the stocked components.

The planning bill consists of end-items with a product mix percentage and UM conversion factor. An end-item's mix percentage represents its proportion of total weight produced by the blending and packaging production line. The UM conversion factor represents the amount of bulk material in each end-item. The amount of bulk material may need to be specified in the planning bill component (for planning purposes), in the end-item's bill (for manufacturing purposes), and in the end-item's demand management policies (for forecast consumption purposes).

Note: A similar approach can be taken for other types of process manufacturers. With liquids and chemicals, for example, the parent item has a volume unit of measure (such as barrels or liters) and the planning bill components reflect different packaging sizes (such as half barrel) with product mix percentages and a UM conversion factor.

Demands for the product family consist of the forecast (expressed in kilograms), which is consumed by sales orders for various products (entered in "eaches," but consuming kilograms of forecast). In this example, a weekly forecast has been entered (with end-of-week dates). MRP logic suggests a production plan, which is normally firmed up to indicate the intended production rate in kilograms per week. Sales orders for end-items consume availability within this production plan.

Demands for end-items consist of sales orders, which MRP logic uses to suggest planned manufacturing orders for the final-assembly end-items and bulk material. Demands for stocked components consist of the production forecast and dependent demands related to final-assembly manufacturing orders. MRP logic calculates the production forecast based on the planning bill and the unconsumed production plan. That is, the production forecast anticipates the yet-to-be-placed sales orders. The family item's inventory plan also results in requirements for stocked components.

Delivery promises can be based on ATP logic for the production plan to assess available capacity within the common production line. It can also be based on ATP logic for the end-item's stocked components to identify any missing components, especially the unique packaging materials.

Make-to-Order Standard Products (with Direct Linkage)

Similar S&OP approaches apply to MTO standard products with indirect and direct linkage to sales orders. The primary difference involves the interpretation of a final-assembly planning policy: one interpretation results in a supply order indirectly linked to the sales order (based on MRP logic), the other interpretation results in direct linkage. With direct linkage, the final-assembly schedule consists of final-assembly manufacturing orders rather than normal manufacturing orders. The illustrative case studies presented earlier also apply to MTO products with direct linkage.

Custom Products

The S&OP approaches for custom products reflect differences in the use of the family item and multilevel configurations. The S&OP case study presented in the last chapter, for example, focused on a single-level configuration and a family used for forecasting and production planning purposes. In many cases, the family item only serves as the starting point of a configuration. In other cases, the family item (and its planning bill) are used for forecasting purposes.

A multilevel configuration represents a more complex scenario than a single-level configuration. The variations in use of a family item (and planning bill) also apply to the multilevel configurations. A series of linked supply orders represents a multilevel configuration, as illustrated in the following case study.

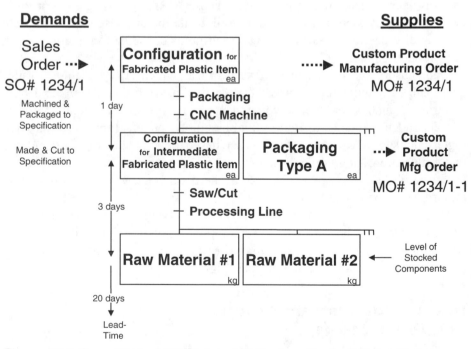

Figure 12.5 Case Study: MTO Fabricated Custom Product (Sales Order
           Viewpoint)

CASE #4B: MAKE-TO-ORDER CUSTOM PRODUCT (MULTILEVEL CONFIGURATION)

The case study involves a two-level configuration for a fabricated plastic item, as shown in Figure 12.5. The item must be made and cut to specification (an intermediate stocking stage) using stocked components, and then machined and packaged to specification.

The sales order configuration defines the packaging material components and a custom product component (an intermediate plastic item cut to specification) that can be packaged after machining it to specification. The configuration for the intermediate plastic item specifies the raw material ingredients that must go through a processing line and then be cut to specification. The sales order (SO# 1234, line 1 in this example) is directly linked to a custom product manufacturing order (MO# 1234/1), which in turn is linked to another supply order (MO#1234/1-1) for the intermediate. Lead times for producing the two configurations have been estimated as 1 day and 3 days.

This case study also illustrates use of a multilevel planning bill, and an aggregate forecast, to anticipate demands for stocked components. The multilevel planning bill consists of two custom product family items. The first family item has a planning bill consisting of one custom product, several mutually exclusive packaging options with product mix percentages, and the typical time requirements for machining and packaging of a fabricated plastic item. The second family item, a generic custom product intermediate, has a planning bill consisting of several common raw material ingredients with mix percentages and the typical time requirements for the processing line and the saw work center.

A monthly forecast for the custom product family item represents aggregate demand. The forecast and an inventory plan for the family item will blow requirements through to the level of stocked components in the planning bill. In particular, it blows through the planning bills of custom product components. Sales orders consume the forecast for the family item, thereby avoiding doubled-up requirements.

Supply orders for stocked components constitute the master schedule. Supply orders for custom product family items consist of the finishing schedule (also termed a final-assembly schedule) driven by sales order configurations. The finishing schedule consists of custom product manufacturing orders, where each one has direct linkage to a sales order and its configuration.

Special Case: Common Material Used to Produce Many MTO Items

Some manufacturers produce multiple MTO products from common material. The common material may be purchased items or intermediate items. Forecasted demands focus on the common material, whereas sales orders focus on end-items (for standard products) or configurations (for custom products). This requires a different type of forecast consumption logic.

◆ *Common Material for Producing Custom Product Configurations.* The sales order for the custom product family does not consume forecast. Rather, forecasts for the common material are consumed by including the material component in a configuration.

◆ *Common Material for Producing MTO Standard Products.* The sales order for an end-item does consume forecast, but the consumed item must be identified as the common material. Forecast consumption may also require a UM conversion factor to correctly account for UM differences between the end-item and common material component. The demand management policies for a saleable end-item must identify the relevant material components as the consumed items with appropriate UM conversion factors.

As a general rule, forecasting common material works best for producing custom product configurations. The common material represents the critical options that constrain production. However, some situations require finished goods inventory of a configuration so that a standard products approach must be used. Therefore, an S&OP approach for common materials must also apply to standard products. In both cases, the focus on forecasting the common material creates a dilemma on how to anticipate requirements for other material components as well as resources.

Special Case: Aggregate ATP

Many manufacturers could use an aggregate measure of capacity as a simple method for improving delivery promises. The key issue is to identify what represents a meaningful measure of aggregate capacity. In small manufacturers, a meaningful measure may be total factory capacity, but most factories can be viewed as having several meaningful segments. Easily identifiable examples include a dedicated manufacturing cell or assembly line. Other examples include the bottleneck work centers that constrain throughput. Most firms already have some sense of throughput, measured in equivalent units, volume or even value. For example, the value measurement may be dollars per day, so that a sales order backlog of "x dollars" represents a number of fully booked production days.

ERP systems provide several methods for measuring aggregate capacity. One method employs a resource item and routing information, so that the comparison between available capacity and calculated resource requirements highlights overloaded periods. This comparison is a cumbersome tool for making delivery promises. Capable-to-promise logic (with finite scheduling) can use the same information to support delivery promises, but finite scheduling using an advanced planning and scheduling (APS) application can quickly become complex. It represents overkill for making delivery promises in many situations.

A second method employs the production plan concept to provide a simple means for considering available capacity in delivery promises. It requires a family item to represent aggregate capacity, with a meaningful unit of measure. The family item's production plan defines available capacity, and the available capacity must be consumed by sales orders to provide meaningful delivery promises. Some of the S&OP approaches embody this production plan concept, such as a product family produced in a dedicated manufacturing cell. Other S&OP approaches can use a separate family item and its production plan to embody the production plan concept and provide simple ATP logic. However, it requires that sales orders consume this separate production plan to correctly calculate available capacity.

Part 4

Sales Management

Sales orders capture demands for the firm's products and services. Sales orders comprise a key element in two larger contexts: the sales and operations planning (S&OP) game plan and the customer relationship life cycle. Within a product's S&OP game plan, sales orders define actual demands so that the entire supply chain is customer demand-driven. Demands pull products through the supply chain. Customer demands, both actual and forecasted, become the driving force in forming S&OP game plans, and each S&OP game plan in turn provides the means to make delivery promises. Two different terms are used to refer to this context: *sales order management* and *supply order management.*

◆ Sales order management involves five basic steps (accept orders, configure orders, source orders, make delivery promises, and monitor status of orders and deliveries) that will be covered in this section's chapter on sales order processing. The fifth step—monitor status—often represents a customer service responsibility.

◆ Supply order management involves coordinating activities in procurement, production, inventory, distribution, and field service functions, as described in Part 5 with separate chapters for each function. Field services often represent a customer service responsibility.

Sales orders have a second, larger context: customer service across the customer relationship life cycle. Customer service starts with the initial customer contact, extends through the events of sales order entry and shipment, and continues with ongoing customer contacts and account management. The scope of customer service typically covers presale and postsale responsibilities as well as monitoring status of orders, deliveries, and accounts.

A basic success factor involves the extent to which an ERP system defines all independent demands for products, and the explicit sales order requirements impacting supply chain activities. Capturing these requirements includes use of textual instructions and other objects in ERP systems. These requirements often evolve dynamically, from quotations through sales orders to the time just prior to shipment, and involve collaborative work in the sales channel as well as the supply chain.

Chapter 13

Sales Order Processing

A key step in sales order processing—accept orders—captures actual demands for the firm's products and services. Sales orders may originate from one or more order streams: direct customer communication to order entry personnel, sales representatives, web-placed orders, electronically transmitted customer schedules, and any other source of external customer demand. The responsibility for accepting orders from external customers typically resides in the sales function. Demands from internal customers can also be defined as sales orders, possibly as the responsibility of someone outside the sales function. Sales order management ensures a single common database for identifying customers and all sources of independent demands.

Each sales order has a unique identifier and involves several stages in a life cycle. Each stage (or order status) has significance. Order status, such as open versus closed status, impacts demands and supply chain activities. Other issues may be involved in the treatment of sales order demands, such as designating a sales order as cancelled or hold.

Processing a sales order from an external customer typically involves five steps: accept order, configure order, source order, make delivery promises, and monitor status of the order and delivery. Information captured in these steps impacts demands and coordination of supply chain activities, as well as sales analysis. For example, sales orders may involve forecast consumption, hard allocations, and differences between promised dates and requested dates.

A basic success factor is the extent to which an ERP system defines all independent demands for products, and explicitly defines sales order requirements impacting supply chain activities. There are many common problems associated with this basic success factor, starting with identifying all sources of sales order demands. The common problems often involve the life cycle for a sales order and issues surrounding the treatment of demands. Definition of sales order requirements at each step in sales order processing impacts demands and supply chain activities. Many problems stem from using informal methods (such as descriptive text) rather than explicit means to communicate requirements through the formal ERP system.

Sources of Demand

A sales order represents an independent demand for products and services. It has a specified customer. Each company will have multiple sources of demand, also termed *order streams*. Many firms focus on order streams from external customers, but internal customers can also act as the source of demands. Figure 13.1 illustrates the sources of sales order demands from external and internal customers, segmented into demands for products and services.

Product sales to external customers constitute the primary source of sales order demands in most manufacturers. Other order streams may also be significant. Each firm categorizes these order streams differently, but illustrations include telemarketing, web-placed orders, and other sources identified in Figure 13.1. Some manufacturers have significant service sales to external customers, such as those related to field services and engineering design services.

Internal customers often represent a significant but overlooked source of independent demands. These demands can also be modeled as sales orders. A frequent example involves a prototype for internal R&D purposes, or a warehouse order to initiate building a custom product configuration prior to a sales order. Other examples reflect a multisite operation, where internal demand reflects a transfer order from a sister plant or distribution center. Capturing these demands in a common database provides the basis for sales and operations planning, and coordinating supply chain activities to meet demands.

	Product Demands	Service Demands
External Customer	Product sales	Installation services
	After-market spare parts	Onsite technical services
	Telemarketing	Predelivery services
	Catalog sales	Postsale maintenance services
	Customer schedules (and EDI)	Training or consulting services
	Web-placed orders	Repair diagnostic services
	International sales	Engineering design services
	Repair	
	Prototype for customer	
	Other: Replacement, loaner	
Internal	Prototype for R&D	Engineering design for R&D
	Warehouse order for configuration	
	Transfer orders in multisite operations	

Figure 13.1 Sources of Sales Order Demand from External and Internal Customers

Identifying Customers

Each external and internal customer is defined in a customer master file with a unique identifier. For external customers, the customer master file defines information for order entry, shipping, sales analysis, accounting, and other purposes. Only a few data elements have significance affecting demands and shipments.

- *Sold-to Customer.* The customer identifier generally represents the sold-to customer. Sales orders to the sold-to customer can consume forecasts by customer.
- *Ship-to Location.* A sold-to customer can have one or more ship-to locations for shipment purposes. Some ERP systems support a separate customer identifier to represent designated ship-to locations, where the sold-to and ship-to customers belong to the same hierarchy of customers (such as a corporate sold-to customer and multiple stores as ship-to customers). Taxing authorities apply to each ship-to location. The ship-to location (and taxing authority) may indirectly impact how sales orders are entered, since separate ship-to locations may require separate sales orders.
- *Customer Hold Status.* The customer hold status may prevent sales orders from being entered, or prevent shipments from being recorded. Placing a customer on hold (with a reason code) may result in automatically changing all relevant sales orders to a hold status. The effect reverses itself when reversing the customer hold. Credit management policies may also result in new sales orders being placed automatically on hold when the customer exceeds limits.
- *One-Time Customer.* Most ERP systems require a customer master record for sales orders to one-time customers, such as credit card sales.

Internal customers must also be defined on the customer master, typically with reduced information requirements. In a multisite ERP system, some internal customers, such as sister plants and distribution centers, may be defined in a separate file, and transfer orders replace sales orders as the means to define actual demands.

Identifying Demands and the Structure of a Sales Order

A sales order defines demand in terms of specified items, quantities, and delivery dates. As a generally accepted approach in ERP systems, the identifier for each demand consists of two data elements: a sales order number and line item number. A given line item may specify multiple delivery dates, so that the unique identifier may consist of a third element: the delivery date or delivery line number. These three data elements reflect the basic structure of a sales order.

A sales order number may be manually or automatically assigned (via a counter). Many firms use a significant sales order number, typically a prefix, to identify the source of independent demand, so that automatic assignment consists of a counter for each prefix. Often, each source of demand or order stream, illustrated in Figure 13.1, has a unique prefix. Some ERP systems provide a sales order attribute to identify the source of demand, so that a prefix is not required.

Life Cycle of a Sales Order

Each sales order has a life cycle of several stages represented by an order status. A simplistic life cycle viewpoint consists of an open and closed status. A life cycle generally applies to each element in the basic structure of a sales order: the overall sales order, each sales order line item, and each delivery line. A more comprehensive life cycle viewpoint must consider several key issues regarding the treatment of demands, as summarized in the breakout box.

ERP DESIGN ISSUE

Sales Order Life Cycle and Treatment of Demands

Several key issues regarding demands must be considered in the structure and life cycle of a sales order.

◆ *Handling Changes in Demands.* A sales order may be changed in several ways. The designated customer may change. The order may have additions or deletions to line items. A line item may be changed to a different quantity or date, or even to a different item. A custom product configuration may be changed, such as changes to the configuration ID or the configuration's components. A sales order may be changed to cancelled or hold, and back again. Some ERP systems enforce artificial limitations on changes, such as requiring a completely new order or line item to handle changes in demands.

◆ *Authorizing Shipment or Delivery.* A sales order (or line item or delivery line) should have an explicit means to authorize shipment or delivery, so that distribution or field service activities can be coordinated correctly. The authorization is commonly termed *released for shipment*. One line item may be released for shipment, while another line with a future delivery date should not be released. Only released lines should be communicated to distribution for recommended shipment.

◆ *Handling Demands with Different Delivery Dates.* Different delivery dates on sales order line items may reflect customer requests or user segmentation into multiple line items with dates that reflect delivery promises based on availability. These are termed split deliveries.

◆ *Handling Demands Designated as Cancelled.* A sales order (or line item) may be cancelled so that demands should be ignored and shipments stopped. The cancellation may be reversed. Information about cancelled sales orders should be available for sales analysis purposes, especially with respect to lost sales. This argues for designating a reason code for cancellations.

◆ *Handling Demands Designated as Hold.* A hold status indicates the sales order (or line item) should still be treated as a demand, but shipments may not be recorded. Distribution should not be notified of the need for shipment, or notified to stop activity on a previously released order. The hold status can be removed or changed. There are many reasons for a hold status. It typically represents an internal viewpoint, where manual assignment indicates required follow-up to review completeness, correctness, or credit approval. For credit management purposes, the hold status may be automatically assigned when a customer has been placed on hold or has exceeded a credit management policy. Removal of a customer hold, or the credit exception, should result in automatic removal of the hold status on relevant orders.

◆ *Handling Remaining Demands after Partial Shipment.* The unshipped quantity for a given line item typically represents a remaining demand, frequently termed a *back order* quantity. This situation commonly occurs when availability is not considered at the time of sales order entry, or at the time sales orders are released for shipment.

◆ *Handling Demands with a Combined Shipment/Invoice.* A shipment frequently requires an accompanying invoice. This requires invoice generation when the user designates a completed sales order shipment. In some situations, the shipment is the invoice, and the shipment number provides the basis for customer payment (and matching cash receipts to invoices).

◆ *Handling Point-of-Sale Demands.* A point-of-sale demand, or walk-in sale, involves a single transaction to represent the sales order, shipment, and invoice. The single transaction may also include payment via cash, credit card, or other method.

◆ *Handling Sales Orders for Internal Customers.* A sales order from an internal customer often represents a configuration for an internal R&D prototype, or a configuration being produced in anticipation of a getting the sale.

◆ *Handling Different Identifiers.* The sales order may be expressed for the internal item, the customer item, or a catalog item number. A configuration ID (or smart part number) may be specified a custom product configuration.

Proposed Stages in a Sales Order Life Cycle

The proposed life cycles stages for a sales order and line item are illustrated in Figure 13.2, along with the significance of each status. The line item stages are similar to the life cycle for a supply order line item, but the released status reflects an authorization for shipment rather than an authorization for production or procurement. A significant difference involves a *mass change* for all sales order line items, such as a single transaction that updates all line items for ship date changes, shipment authorization, cancellation, or completion. This concept of mass change does not apply to supply orders; each line item on a supply order is treated separately.

The proposed life cycle stages account for issues in treatment of demands and provide a unifying framework for further explanations about sales orders.

Status	Sales Order Status	Line Item Status
Open	Assign order number Assign or change customer Add or delete line items	Assign line number (automatically) Identify or change demands for item, quantity and date Define configuration (custom product only)
Released for Shipment	Authorize shipment and delivery for all line items Note: Automatically updated if all lines released	Authorize shipment/delivery for line item Print shipping paperwork (packing list, pick list) Record shipment/delivery

Shipment and Invoice Status

Status	Sales Order Status	Line Item Status
Completed	Ignore demands of unshipped line items Prevent recording of shipment and delivery of any line Prevent adding or deleting line items Note: Automatically updated if all lines completed	Ignore demands of unshipped remaining quantity Prevent recording of shipment and delivery Prevent changes to line item Prevent changes to configuration (custom products only)
Closed	Prevent reopening order	Prevent reopening line item

Figure 13.2 Life Cycle of a Sales Order and Order Status

Each order status and line item status has significance. An open or released line item identifies demand. A released line item represents an authorization for shipment and delivery, and the ability to print shipping paperwork and report shipping activity. The demands associated with a completed line item (or completed order) are ignored and further activity prevented. Figure 13.2 does not indicate every implication of order status. For example, it does not identify limitations on deletions after reporting shipping activity against a line item.

Shipping activity may result in a shipment and invoice. These are viewed as separate entities from the sales order, with their own life cycle. The shipment identifier, for example, represents the bill of lading. A shipment may contain line items from multiple orders. An invoice applies to the items shipped for a given sales order; multiple invoices may apply to the same sales order when items are shipped on different dates or shipments.

The stages in an order life cycle do not require a linear progression. Order status may be initially entered as released to indicate the need for immediate shipment. A completed order or line item may be reopened (re-released) to record changes or additional shipping activities. In addition, a hold or cancelled status may apply to line items and the entire order. This argues for a separate status field, termed the *hold/cancelled status*.

Some ERP systems focus on the life cycle for just the sales order, without a line item status. This design approach, termed an order-centric approach, has several limitations as explained in the breakout box.

Limitations of an Order-Centric Approach to the Sales Order Life Cycle

Some ERP systems provide an order-centric approach to the sales order life cycle. This approach generally makes simplifying assumptions about the sales order: (1) all line items will be shipped the same day, (2) sales order status applies to all line items, and (3) the order's hold/cancelled status applies to all line items. With an order-centric approach, the unshipped line items (or unshipped remainder on a line item) on a completed sales order represent a backorder condition. The ERP system typically creates a new sales order to identify the backorder, with the same sales order number and a suffix but a different delivery date. Several iterations of partial shipments will result in several iterations of backorders.

The order-centric approach provides a simple model of the sales order life cycle, especially when customers do not want partial shipments. However, it has limitations in selectively communicating information about line items, such as multiple delivery dates, authorization for shipment, and hold/cancelled status. This constrains the idea of using multiple line items with delivery dates reflecting availability. Multiple iterations of backorders may also cause difficulties in interpreting sales history data.

Hold/Cancelled Status and the Sales Order Life Cycle

An additional status for each order (and line item) can be used to designate hold or cancelled. The hold status can prevent shipment, and a cancelled status results in demand being ignored. The hold/cancelled status can be manually or automatically assigned, with a user-specified reason code. The hold/cancelled status (and reason code) provides the basis to communicate recommended actions and coordinate related supply chain activities.

Hold Status Manually placing a sales order on hold means that all line items are treated as hold. Alternatively, an individual line item can be manually placed on hold. A manually assigned hold typically reflects a problem that requires immediate attention or resolution before shipment, as defined by the reason code. Some ERP systems provide variations of open status (rather than a separate hold status) to support the hold concept. For orders with a hold status, the recommended actions could be (1) to customer service for resolving the problem causing the hold, or (2) to distribution to stop current shipping efforts. The hold status should prevent shipments from being recorded, possibly prevent (or display prominently on) printed paperwork, and suppress recommended shipping actions.

Placing a customer on hold may result in automatically changing the status of related sales orders to hold; removing the customer from hold results in automatic reverses. A customer hold (and reason code) typically reflects credit problems that must be resolved before shipment.

Cancelled Status A manually cancelled sales order means that all line items are treated as cancelled. Alternatively, an individual line item can be manually cancelled. A completed line item status provides the same functionality with respect to demands, but does not provide an alert or reason for the cancellation.

For a cancelled status, the recommended actions could be communicated (1) to customer service for diagnosing the problem causing the cancellation, (2) to distribution to stop current shipping efforts, or (3) to the planner or buyer to review affected supply orders. A supply order with direct linkage to the sales order should be cancelled automatically. With indirectly linked supply orders, MRP logic recognizes reduced demands and suggests recommended actions.

Accept Sales Order

The first step in sales order processing—accept order—defines actual demands. Sales order information can be manually or automatically entered. Automatic entry, for example, may reflect a web-placed order or an electronically transmitted customer schedule. The basic structure and critical information in a sales order remains the same.

Critical Information in a Sales Order

A sales order consists of three sections (a header section, a line item section, and a summary section) that define critical information about demands and coordination of supply chain activities. It includes other information, such as the bill-to-customer, customer PO number, currency, and so forth, that fall outside the scope of our focus on demands and supply chain coordination.

Sales Order Header Section The sales order header section defines the sold-to customer. Sales orders consume forecasts by customer on the basis of the sold-to customer. Demands can be affected by a cancelled status for the order.

The header section also defines information affecting supply chain activities in distribution (or service delivery). This includes the identifier for the customer's ship-to location, or a ship-to customer. It may include a consolidated ship-to identifier to support a freight-forward service, or a distribution center in a multisite operation. Shipping instructions may be specified, such as the carrier, free-on-board point, and/or textual information. Shipments can be affected by a hold status for the order.

Sales Order Line Item Section A sales order line item defines demands for the item in terms of quantity and ship date. It may also provide the starting point for configuring a custom product. The ship date affects consumption of forecasted demands and availability (if applicable), and a delivery date reflects the ship date plus transportation lead time. Multiple delivery lines with separate dates may be specified for a given line item. Demands can be affected by a cancelled status for the line item.

The line item section also defines information affecting supply chain activities in distribution and production and procurement. For example, shipments can be affected by a hold status for the line item, and textual information can be specified (such as shipping instructions).

Sales Order Summary Section   The summary section provides an automatic calculation for total order value and taxes. It may optionally provide automatic calculation of other totals (such as shipping weight and volume), and manual entry of information (such as estimated freight or special charges).

Sales Orders Versus Price Books, Quotes, and Contracts

Sales orders often use information from previously defined agreements. These agreements are typically defined in terms of price books, quotes, and/or sales contracts.

Price Book   The concept of a price book applies to standard products. In a typical ERP system, a price book has a unique user-assigned identifier and date effectivities. It defines prices for saleable items, typically with quantity breakpoints. The price book may specify item numbers or catalog item numbers. A price book can be defined and assigned to a single customer, thereby representing a contract price. A price book can also be assigned to a group of customers, such as defining prices for wholesalers and retailers. Multiple price books may be assigned to a customer, such as the regular price book, a summer special price book, or next year's price book. In some cases, a price book may serve to limit a customer's orders to authorized items in the price book.

In an ERP system, a price book can be explicitly identified for a sales order to define the basis for item pricing. Alternatively, an item's pricing may be inherited from the applicable price book based on the customer, item, item quantity, and date. This implicit approach may use the date ordered or date shipped as the basis for price book effectivity.

A price book typically supports pricing based on order quantities for individual SO line items. In some cases, pricing is based on the total order value, weight, or other aggregate measure. Pricing may require minimum order quantities or a minimum order value. Pricing may involve other rules, such as "buy 10 and get one free." These cases require rules-based pricing, which is considered outside the scope of this book.

Quote   The concept of a quote (or quotation) applies to both standard products and customer product configurations. A quote is typically viewed as a separate entity with a unique user-assigned identifier. It identifies the customer and agreed-upon prices for one or more items, typically with quantity breakpoints. A quote may also define payment terms and have effectivity dates (also termed a quote expiration date). A quote may reflect a response to a request for quote or prices that have been negotiated with the vendor. A quote does not represent actual demand.

ERP systems must provide different approaches to quotes as a result of differences between standard and custom products.

- *Quote for Standard Products.* A quote identifies prices for one or more standard product items. The quoted prices may draw on price book information. A designated price book on a sales order provides the same functionality as a designated quote.
- *Quote for a Custom Product Configuration.* A quote defines prices for one or more configurations. A quoted price for a custom product configuration typically reflects a cost-plus markup or rolled price approach or a negotiated price. Multiple prices may be quoted for different quantity breakpoints. There are a wide variety of requirements for presenting quote information, from a simple quoted price to detailed specifications on the configuration.

ERP systems provide different approaches for using a quote in a sales order. In one approach, the quote identifier must be explicitly specified on the sales order (or line item) to invoke the quoted price and configuration. In a second approach, the quote reflects a shopping cart or template order, with line items that can be selectively converted to a sales order. In a third approach, the line item status includes a quote status, which can be changed to open or released to selectively convert quotes to sales orders.

Sales Contract A sales contract has two variations: an item-specific contract and a non-item-specific contract. Each contract has a unique user-defined identifier. An item-specific contract is similar to a quote, and must be specified on a sales order to invoke the agreement. A contract provides additional benefits in terms of tracking expenditures by contract, and possibly limiting a customer's orders to authorized items in the contract. In contrast, a non-item-specific contract only provides the basis for tracking customer expenditures by contract.

Blanket Sales Order

A blanket sales order consists of one or more line items. Each line item defines an item, and possibly a configuration for a custom product. Each line item also defines a price, a maximum expected order quantity, and effectivity dates. Specific delivery dates and quantities can be made for each line. Each delivery date and quantity represents a release against the blanket sales order. Only the releases represent actual demands.

Other Steps in Sales Order Processing

Processing a sales order involves several additional steps beyond accept order. These include configure order, source order, make delivery promises, and monitor status.[1] Figure 13.3 summarizes the significance of each step in sales order processing.

Configure Order

The need for a configure order step applies to selected order streams and products. For example, it does not apply to electronically transmitted customer schedules for standard products. The configure order step has a broader context of tailoring products and services to meet customer requirements. This includes configuring a custom product to customer specifications. The following examples illustrate the significance of configure order.

- ◆ Configure a custom product. Configurations represent a broad spectrum of tailoring products and services. A simplistic configuration, for example, may identify customer selection of optional packaging variations. A

[1] Christopher Gopal and Harold Cypress, *Integrated Distribution Management,* Homewood, IL: Business One Irwin, 1993, pp. 50–58. Gopal and Cypress define these five steps and provide explanations for each step.

Steps in Sales Order Processing	Examples of Significance
Accept Order	Identify customer (sold-to, ship-to, bill-to) Identify item and order quantity Identify applicable quote, price book, or contract
Configure Order	Define custom product configuration Suggest related items or most appropriate items Identify order minimums and expediting fees Identify total weight and volume and transportation issues
Source Order	Designate ship-from site (based on availability or rules)
Make Delivery Promise	Use available-to-promise logic, split deliveries Use capable-to-promise logic
Monitor Status	Follow-up orders with hold status, requested expediting, or overdue shipment Provide status of order, shipment, or account

Figure 13.3 Steps in Sales Order Processing

complex configuration may require a rules-based configurator to be correctly defined.

◆ Assist the customer in buying the latest version of a product, or one that is compatible with the customer's previous purchases.

◆ Assist the customer in buying related products and services. The related items may be required, such as installation services or parts required for proper operation. They may be strongly recommended, such as approved supplies, display units, training, or service agreements. They may represent optional complementary products.

◆ Assist the customer in identifying the appropriate product for the application. This may simply be an alternate product. Alternatively, a decision tree or other rules-based approach may guide the customer through the application requirements and identify the existing item number(s) that would satisfy requirements. A slight variation involves lot attributes, where the customer's requirements represent acceptable values and existing inventory must be identified with lot attributes that meet requirements.

◆ Identify order minimums, expediting fees, or special charges that apply to the sales order or line item.

◆ Identify transportation considerations. This includes total weight and volume and estimated freight costs. This may also include shipping instructions, preferred shipping method, and so forth.

Some order streams and products lend themselves to automating the configure order step. Automation may assist sales representatives or the customers directly (such as web-placed orders).

Source Order (Designating a Ship-From Location)

The source order step only applies to multisite operations with distribution from more than one site. The site may represent a distribution center or manufacturing plant. It does not apply to single-site operations, a single colocated manufacturing and distribution site, or a multisite operation with a single centralized distribution center.

The source order step often involves designating a ship-from site based on predefined rules. For instance, one rule designates a predefined distribution center for ship-to locations within a geographic area. A more flexible approach may use predefined rules for suggesting a primary source, but support availability or transportation considerations. The designated ship-from site may be specified for the entire sales order, or for a sales order line item, depending on the ERP system.

Some situations require coordination of deliveries from multiple ship-from sites. A door manufacturer with multiple plants producing different door components, for example, requires coordinated delivery of knobs, hinges, frames, and doors to a commercial construction site. This requirement argues for a single distribution center for coordinating deliveries and a consolidated shipment.

Make Delivery Promises

The approach to making delivery promises depends on the product's S&OP approach and system capabilities. The approach typically reflects available-to-promise logic, based on availability of the saleable item, its components or its production plan. The approach may use capable-to-promise logic. Chapter 11, sales and operations planning, identified the contingencies affecting how to make delivery promises.

Delivery promises provide the key link between sales orders and what the rest of the company has been working toward. The critical issue is to reduce and isolate the number of sales order exceptions requiring expediting. With ATP logic, a requested date or order quantity that exceeds availability should be entered as a delayed delivery or split delivery. In most cases, the customer has flexibility in accepting a promise ship date that aligns with the S&OP game plan.

When a sales order demand exceeds availability, communicating this exception to customer service and the item's planner or buyer (responsible for coordinating the item's supply chain activities) provides an early warning that a sales order will cause a disruption in current plans.

Monitor Status of Orders and Deliveries

Customer service representatives generally have responsibility for monitoring the status of sales orders and deliveries. Recommended actions for customer service may include following up sales orders with hold or cancelled status, past due shipments, customer requests for expedited delivery, and warnings about projected late delivery. The next chapter provides further explanations of customer service responsibilities.

Sales Order Considerations That Impact Demands

The designation of cancelled status directly impacts sales order demands. Demands are impacted by other designations on sales orders. These include the promised ship date and additions to forecasts. Some considerations indirectly impact sales order demands, such as the treatment of customer schedules and key financial concerns.

Significance of Promised Ship Date

Sales order demands must reflect the current promised ship date based on the best available information. This date affects forecast consumption logic (within forecast periods), cash flow projections and financial analysis (within fiscal periods), and coordination of distribution and other supply chain activities. It should initially reflect a realistic delivery promise based on availability, with changes to reflect customer requests, anticipated scheduling delays, or missed shipments. A past-due date is unacceptable.

The promised ship date plus the transportation lead-time defines a promised delivery date. Internal coordination can be driven by the ship dates whereas external communications (such as acknowledgements) typically focus on the delivery dates.

The current promised ship date can be different than the original promise date or the customer request date. Differences in dates between current promise and customer requested dates identify the customer's request for expedited delivery. Performance metrics for on-time shipping can be viewed from three perspectives: against the current or original promised dates or the customer's requested date.

Designating a Sales Order as an Addition to Forecasted Demand

An item's sales order typically consumes forecasted demand, but a line item may represent abnormal demand that should be added to the item's forecast. Therefore, a separate field is required to designate a line item as an addition to forecast.

Interpretation of Customer Schedules

A customer schedule generally represents a combination of sales orders and forecasts. The difference may be explicitly identified in the schedules. Alternatively, predefined rules may be applied to the schedule, such as a rolling 2-week horizon that identifies sales orders in the near-term and forecasts beyond the 2 weeks. The interpretation of sales orders and forecasts may need to consider an item's demand management policies (especially forecast consumption logic within forecast periods) to correctly reflect the combination of demands.

Financial Concerns That Indirectly Impact Sales Order Demands

A sales order can be shipped in a single shipment or multiple shipments, where each shipment requires a separate invoice. The invoice identifies applicable taxes, payment terms and method, and the sales price specified on the sales order, but these financial concerns may indirectly impact demands as described below.

Sales or VAT Tax   The ship-to location determines the applicable sales or VAT tax. When the sales order header specifies the ship-to location, multiple sales orders must be entered to model multiple ship-to locations. Each invoice reflects the applicable tax.

Payment Terms and Payment Method When the sales order header specifies payment terms and method, multiple sales orders must be entered to specify different payment terms and methods. Each invoice reflects the applicable payment method.

Pricing and Special Charges An item's sales price is typically based on the quantity ordered for a sales order line item. When multiple sales orders reflect segmentation for tax or payment method considerations, it may affect pricing logic in an ERP system. Special charges related to an order or line item may also be affected by segmentation or by multiple partial shipments. The issue involves whether to invoice the special charges on the basis of the first shipment or prorated across multiple shipments.

Sales Order Considerations That Impact Coordination of Supply Chain Activities

Sales orders can specify information that impacts supply chain activities. This includes shipment instructions for distribution, delivery instructions for field service, and special orders for procurement. It also includes designating final-assembly orders and allocations.

Specifying Shipment Instructions (for Distribution)

Shipment instructions may be expressed in several ways. One method specifies textual instructions for the entire sales order (using text in the sales order header section) or for an individual line (using text in the line item section). For a standard product, a second method specifies packaging considerations using unique item numbers and bills that include packaging variations. For a custom product, packaging and shipping instructions may be specified as options in the configuration.

Shipping instructions sometimes impact coordination of production activities. The sequence of truck loading, for example, may drive the sequence of production scheduling.

Designating the Need for Direct Linkage between the Sales Order Demand and Its Supply Order

Some ERP systems support the need for direct linkage by explicitly designating a sales order line item as final assembly. Sales orders for a custom product configuration, or a standard product designated with a final-assembly planning policy, also have direct linkage, but do not require an explicit designation.

Designating Hard Allocations of Existing Inventory

Hard allocations represent one method for directly linking inventory supplies to a sales order. The need for hard allocations frequently stems from customer requirements for a specific lot (or lots) of material with attributes that match customer requirements. Hard allocations may also stem from distribution considerations, such as allocating limited supplies to customer demands, allocating inventory for shipment from a specific location, or moving material to the shipping area (such as into a waiting truck) prior to recording shipment. Hard allocations may be made during or subsequent to order entry.

Designating Special Orders (for Procurement)

Special orders represent customer requirements for an item not defined in the item master. ERP systems provide several ways to support special orders. One method to identify a special order involves using a custom product item labeled special order, and then specifying nonstock purchased material as configuration components. Each nonstock material component can have a sales price and estimated cost, and procurement activities can be coordinated to obtain the special orders. The sales order line item for the custom product can then be shipped after receipt of the special orders. Alternatively, the vendor may be instructed to drop-ship the nonstock items directly to the customer.

Identifying Customer-Supplied Material for a Sales Order

Customer-supplied material may be used to produce a custom product configuration or a standard product. It may be provided as a kit to produce the item or stocked on-site. ERP systems provide different ways to handle customer-supplied material. One method involves identifying customer-supplied material as a component (with a unique component type) in the configuration for a custom product, or in the bill for a standard product. This method also requires a designated inventory status that ties inventory of customer-supplied material to a sales order line item, as explained in Chapter 16.

Handling Repairs of a Customer-Supplied Item

A sales order for repairing a customer-supplied item, and sending it back to the customer, represents one type of repair activity. Other types of repairs may place the repaired item into stock. Repairs of a customer-supplied item are typically modeled with a custom product configuration. The repair may involve strip-down, repairing parts, and rebuilding the item.

Handling Field Service Tasks

A sales order for a field service task must be directly linked to the service work order to identify the customer requiring the service. Direct linkage applies to a standard service task or a configuration for a customized service task. Delivery instructions for a service work order are often specified as text or as operation descriptions in the routing for a standard service task.

Sales History and Sales Analysis

Sales history information generally focuses on sales orders, but may include quotations. It may cover bookings, or the rate of sales orders, which must account for order placement date and changes in sales order quantities.

Sales orders and shipments provide the foundation for sales analysis. Sales orders identify the items, order quantities, and ship dates (such as the three dates described above). For custom products, the sales order identifies the configuration ID and components, and possibly the responses to a rules-based configurator. In addition, the sales history should account for returned goods, replacements, lost sales, cancelled sales orders, and outliers of surprise or spiky demands.

Comparisons between sales history and a sales forecast require separate sets of forecast data. Each set represents the forecast as of a given date, and must be stored independently. Forecasted demands within an ERP system are constantly updated to reflect the latest available information. Forecasted demands can also be deleted automatically as they become past due.

The analysis of sales history becomes more complicated when using family items (with planning bills) for forecasting. For example, the sales history for standard product items must identify the relevant family item, and analysis must identify the actual mix percentages for comparison to the planning bill. The need for feedback on mix percentages (and configuration quantities) also applies to custom product planning bills.

Sales Order Considerations with Multiple Sales Channels

Explanations of sales order processing typically focus on a single sales channel: a direct sell to the customer. Internal sales and field sales personnel involved in the direct sell are employees of the manufacturing enterprise. The manufacturer's ERP system handles the major information flows (such as sales orders, shipments, and invoices) to the customer. The scope of this ERP system, illustrated in Figure 13.4 as ERP System #1, may be limited to the four walls of the manufacturing enterprise.

E-business initiatives enlarge the scope of an ERP system. These initiatives include EDI applications and customer access to directly process quotes or orders and verify status. Figure 13.4 illustrates the enlarged scope of ERP System #1 to support customer access.

The majority of smaller manufacturers use other sales channels in addition to (or in place of) direct sales by employees. The sales channels often involve independent sales agents and/or resellers, with various synonyms for each. A wide variety of business models applies to each type of sales channel. A few of the variations will be explained.

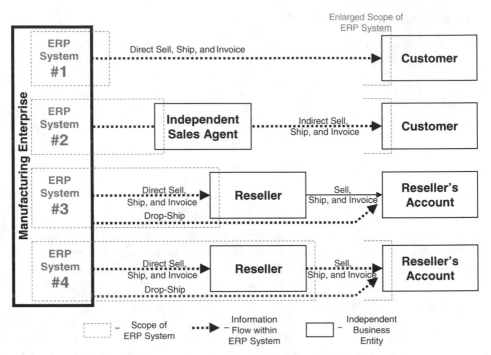

Figure 13.4 Sales Channel Variations and the Impact on an ERP System

Independent Sales Agents Independent sales agents are not employees of the manufacturing enterprise and are often employed by an independent business entity. They may sell products from multiple manufacturers as manufacturing reps. Their sales efforts represent an indirect sell for the manufacturing enterprise, with commissions payable to the individuals (or their business entity) involved in a sale. The commission calculations may become very complex, where considerations may include splits, payment basis (such as payment based on shipment versus cash receipt), and other factors. An ERP system must include these commission calculations and identify the business entities (and people) associated with independent sales agents.

The scope of an ERP system extends to these sales agents (and even to customers), as illustrated by ERP System #2 in Figure 13.4. The information flow related to sales, shipments, and invoices passes through the independent sales agents, so that the ERP system retains visibility of the customer.

Resellers with Standalone Systems A reseller, also referred to as a distributor or value-added reseller, represents an independent business that buys the firm's products and subsequently sells them to their customers (termed reseller accounts). The reseller stocks the manufacturer's products or has products drop-shipped directly to the reseller's accounts, using a standalone information system to manage their business. This becomes more complex with custom product configurations.

Some of the key issues from an ERP system viewpoint involve the scope of the manufacturer's ERP system and visibility of the reseller's account (the end-consumer). Scope and visibility typically stop with the reseller. The reseller represents the customer in the manufacturer's ERP system. The reseller's system handles information flows to the reseller's accounts. This makes it difficult to identify end-consumers and extend e-business initiatives to end-consumers. End-consumer information may be needed for warranty or lot-trace purposes, for example. Product configurators and status information within the manufacturer's ERP system cannot be easily extended to the reseller's accounts or integrated with the reseller's system. Figure 13.4 illustrates this scenario with ERP System #3.

Information captured by the reseller (such as drawings, specifications and configuration data) defines explicit sales order requirements impacting supply chain activities. This represents a critical success factor for the manufacturer's ERP system and requires some form of integrated systems across the sales channel. The integrated systems must support collaborative work (between the reseller, the reseller's account, and the manufacturing enterprise) and the evolving dynamic definition of sales order requirements.

Resellers Using an Integrated System The scope of the manufacturer's ERP system may be extended beyond the reseller to define explicit sales order requirements impacting supply chain activities and to support collaborative work. This coverage may range from simple quotation and order processing to complete support for all applications (including inventory and accounting) to manage the reseller's business. This approach supports visibility of the end-consumer as well as extending e-business initiatives to the end-consumer. This approach may provide visibility of inventory within the sales channel (typically valued at zero cost from the perspective of the manufacturer) to support demand management and distribution considerations. It may support lead tracking across the sales channels, and recognize sales cycle responsibilities beyond just a customer service rep. Figure 13.4 illustrates this scenario with ERP System #4.

Other Common Problems Related to Sales Order Processing

Many of the common problems in sales order processing have already been covered within this chapter. These problems include identifying all sources of sales order demands, based on order streams related to external customers as well as internal customers. The problems are sometimes related to system limitations, such as limitations in the sales order life cycle, treatment of demands, and the ability to correctly model price books, quotations, sales contracts, or blanket sales orders. These limitations reflect ERP design issues.

Many common problems involve the significance of promised ship dates on sales orders. Promised ship dates may have been entered incorrectly to start with (without realistic delivery promises), not updated, and frequently left as past due. This ignores considerations that impact demands and coordination of distribution and other supply chain activities. Other parts of the company often use informal systems because the formal ERP system does not provide useful information.

The use of multiple sales channels, such as resellers, introduces problems in the scope and visibility for the manufacturer's ERP system. In particular, the scope must extend beyond the reseller to capture explicit sales order requirements impacting supply chain activities.

Chapter 14

Customer Service

The scope of customer service extends across the entire customer relationship life cycle. Customer service includes every customer contact and customer-related event in an ERP system, such as sales orders and shipments. Each contact and its related activities offer the opportunity to meet and exceed customer expectations, thereby increasing customer satisfaction.

This chapter covers customer service using the framework of the customer relationship life cycle. The discussion segments customer service into presale and postsale activities. It reviews the use of a customer relationship management (CRM) application within the context of an ERP system. It also covers variations in handling returned materials.

Scope of Customer Service

The customer relationship life cycle provides a broader context for sales order management and customer service. The life cycle reflects how customers acquire and use a firm's products and services. As shown in Figure 14.1, the scope of customer service extends across each step in the life cycle.

The scope of customer service can be segmented into presales and postsales activities. Presales activities include handling initial customer contacts, identifying and qualifying leads, defining customer requirements, providing quotations, and processing sales orders. Postsales activities include answering inquiries on the status of orders and deliveries and account status, as well as account management of ongoing customer contacts. These activities also assist customers in integrating and monitoring product usage, upgrading and maintaining products, and transfer and disposal of products. Several key events across the customer relationship life cycle—quotations, sales orders, product shipments, service deliveries, invoices, and returned materials—represent basic transactions in an ERP system.

Applications supporting these customer service activities have typically been developed independently from an ERP system. They are labeled customer relationship management (CRM) applications, and they have variations in functionality. One variation, for instance, focuses on contact management. Using a separate CRM application package requires integration with the firm's ERP system. The ERP software vendor may already provide integration between

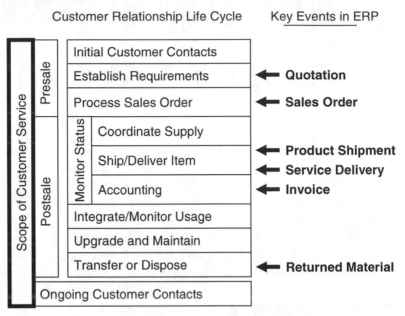

Figure 14.1 Scope of Customer Service

systems, but the degree of integration often varies. The next section highlights the nature and problems in integration. In other cases, the CRM application may be fully integrated, developed, and maintained by the ERP software vendor.

Customer Relationship Management (CRM) and ERP

A CRM application primarily supports customer service, and its capabilities can be similarly segmented into presale and postsale activities. Customer service personnel often use a CRM application to identify required follow-up activities related to customer contacts. Required follow-up activities (and status) related to quotations, orders, shipments, and customer status also originate within an ERP system. These can be communicated as recommended customer service actions. Integration between an ERP system and a separate CRM application involves several key integration points.

CRM and Presales Activities

Initial customer contacts may be initiated by the customer, or originate from sales efforts to proactively contact and identify potential customers. Potential customers can be classified as prospects or leads. A lead represents a potential customer with an expressed interest in the firm's products and services, whereas a prospect represents a name on a mailing or telemarketing list with a potential but unknown interest. In many firms, proactive selling starts with a prospect list to identify and qualify leads. A subset of leads become actual customers.

Presales activities focus on acquiring new customers and increasing penetration within the existing customer base. This typically involves defining marketing projects related to advertising, trade shows, mailings, telemarketing calls, and so forth. A specific campaign will be undertaken within a given marketing project, such as telemarketing calls to a purchased list of prospects, a direct mailing to the existing customer base, a particular trade show event, or a specific magazine advertisement. The aim of each campaign is to generate and qualify leads. Tracing leads (and sales orders) back to a given campaign provides a means to measure its effectiveness.

The basic elements of a CRM application, shown in Figure 14.2, support these presales activities. The basic elements include master files about prospects, leads, and customers, and identification of marketing projects and campaigns.

To generate and qualify leads, CRM provides marketing automation tools for direct mailings and telemarketing calls. CRM supports telemarketing calls to a prospect list, for example, by telemarketing queues (for automatic dialing) and sales scripts (to prompt personnel through lead qualification questions). Prospect

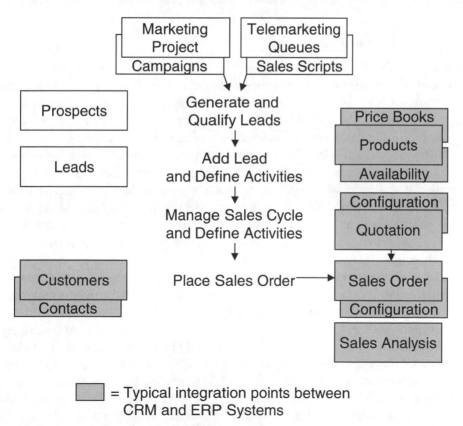

= Typical integration points between CRM and ERP Systems

Figure 14.2 CRM and Presales Activities

information can be converted to a lead, the contact recorded, and required activities assigned to designated employees. The required activities may involve a follow-up call, sending literature, a meeting, a "to-do" action item, or just an informative message or note about the contact. Most CRM applications use e-mail to communicate required activities and informative messages.

A qualified lead is the typical starting point for most sales cycles. CRM provides technology-assisted selling tools to manage the sales cycle and define further activities. That is, the CRM database contains a complete history and status of the account, including presale and postsale contacts. This enables sales reps to cross-sell and up-sell to new and existing customers. A structured sales cycle consists of user-defined stages with a sales probability for each stage, and provides greater sales predictability.

Selling tools within CRM include information about standard products and their price books, quotations for custom product configurations, and product availability. The conclusion of a successful sales cycle results in a customer and sales order, and possible custom product configurations. When unsuccessful, it results in a lost sale (and provides win/loss information for sales analysis).

CRM and Postsales Activities

Postsales activities focus on managing accounts, answering inquiries about status, and responding to customer requests for support. These typically involve recording each customer contact, and possibly defining required activities such as a follow-up call, a meeting, or to-do action item. In particular, the customer contact may identify a support incident requiring follow-up activity.

A support incident identifies a customer problem in product usage or service delivery. It may be reported in a wide variety of ways—from an e-mail to a phone call to a personal visit. Customer service personnel typically report a support incident, but customers can report one via web-based access. Many problems can be answered using a knowledge base of common questions and solutions, accessible by customer service reps and customers. Building a knowledge base requires time and internal expertise, but it can reduce the number of customer queries requiring customer service personnel time. It also provides competitive differentiation. Telephone support and knowledge base usage may require a service agreement with the customer.

A support incident may identify problems requiring material returns, leading to a returned material authorization (RMA) and possible verification of product warranty. It may also lead to a field service task and possible verification of the service agreement. The support incident, RMA, and warranty represent some of the basic elements in a CRM application, shown in Figure 14.3, to support postsales activities. Other basic elements include service agreements and the knowledge base.

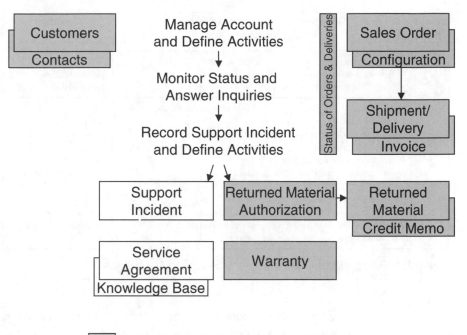

= Typical integration points between
CRM and ERP Systems

Figure 14.3 Sampling and Postsales Activities

Postsales customer service includes answering inquiries about the status of orders and deliveries and about account status. Access to status information can be placed on the Web (with restricted status) so that customers can view information on demand, without customer service assistance. Status information, shown as a separate element in Figure 14.3, can be drawn from the ERP database.

Recommended Customer Service Actions

Customer service personnel can be proactively contacting customers, and coordinating supply chain activities, based on the status of quotations, orders, shipments, and accounts. The basis for an action message may be elapsed time, an event, or a calculation. Figure 14.4 provides a sampling of recommended customer service actions.

Recommended customer service actions often reflect elapsed time, such as reviewing soon-to-expire quotations, authorizing shipment for soon-to-ship sales orders, and follow-up on past-due shipments. Other recommended actions are triggered by events, such as reviewing a sales order that exceeded available-to-promise, an order marked as hold, or orders marked for expediting to the

Message Basis	Recommended Action Message for Customer Service	Message Filter
Elapsed Time	Review quotation based on quotation expiration date Authorize shipment of sales order (release for shipment) Review sales order with past due shipment or service delivery	Look ahead days Look ahead days Days past due
Event	Review sales order that exceeded available-to-promise at time of order entry Review quotation flagged for follow-up Review sales order placed on hold Review sales order "released for shipment" – inventory is not yet available Review sales order that has been cancelled Review sales order with request for expedited delivery	 Reason code Reason code Reason code Requested vs promise date
Calculation	Review customer or order with credit exceptions Review sales order with insufficient profitability Review sales order with projected late delivery/shipment Review sales order with projected cost overrun	 Profit % or value Days late Cost % or value

Figure 14.4 Sampling of Customer Service Action Messages

requested ship dates. Some recommended actions reflect calculations, such as reviewing orders with projected cost overruns, late delivery, or insufficient profitability. In terms of credit management, the recommended actions can include reviewing a customer that has exceeded credit limits or credit policies or that has been placed on hold.

Integration between ERP and CRM

The key integration points between an ERP and CRM application are shown in Figures 14.2 and 14.3 as shaded items. They include master file data about customers (plus contact persons within the customer) and products. Product information includes price books and availability of inventory and schedules.

The integration points related to presales activities include quotations (plus custom product configurations), sales orders, and information for sales analysis. For postsales activities, they include status information (about orders, shipments, and accounts), returned material authorizations, and warranties for shipped products.

The integration points also include identification of required activities related to customer service, since they have two sources (from CRM customer contacts and ERP recommended actions). They typically have two formats (from CRM e-mail messages and ERP action screens). Recommended actions in ERP may overlap the required activities in CRM.

Integration between ERP and CRM remains a critical issue for most small manufacturers, and for most ERP software vendors serving these firms, until such time as affordable CRM functionality has been built into an ERP system.

Returned Material and Returned Material Authorizations

Returned material is a significant issue in some manufacturing environments. Returned material generally requires an authorization, termed a returned material authorization (RMA) or a returned goods authorization (RGA). A support incident often provides the starting point for an RMA.

In its simplest form, the customer reports a problem and requests replacement or full credit for a specified item and quantity. An RMA identifies the customer, the item and quantity, and expected return date. After receiving the item and quantity against the RMA, the replacement is sent on a new sales order at no charge, or a credit memo is issued at the original price. Inventory of the returned item is dispositioned as scrapped, or sometimes returned to the vendor. Most people will be familiar with this simple procedure because it is frequently used in retail sales.

RMA procedures become more complicated with variations in returns, replacements, inventory dispositions, and accounting. Variations in returned material procedures, summarized in Figure 14.5, can become very complex. Most ERP systems support only simple procedures. Figure 14.5 highlights the simple RMA procedure in bold type and provides the framework for describing variations in returned goods.

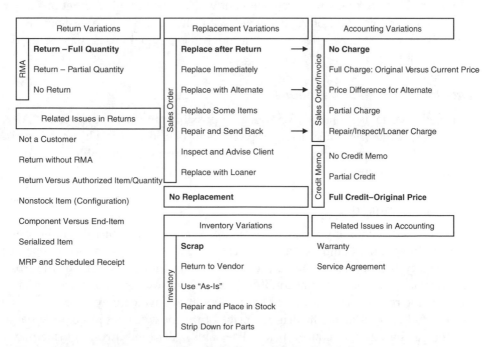

Figure 14.5 Variations of Returned Material Procedures

Return Variations

The returned goods ideally match the items and quantities on the RMA. A partial return (of partial quantities and/or items) may be predefined on the RMA to reflect scrapped material that will not be returned. If not, handling partial returns or no returns becomes increasingly complex, especially in recognizing RMA closure.

Several related issues can make returns more complex. The organization requesting the RMA may not be a customer, items are returned without an RMA, the returned items and quantities do not match the RMA's authorized items and quantities, the returned item represents a nonstock item (such as a configuration), the returned items represent the components of an end-item (and not the shipped end-item), the serial numbers of returned items do not match the RMA's authorized serial numbers (or they duplicate existing serial numbers), and MRP logic may or may not recognize scheduled receipts.

Replacement Variations

The two basic replacement variations, replace after return versus no replacement, can easily become more complex. The customer may require immediate replacement (before return), repairs to returned material (for sending back to the customer), or inspection of returned material (with advice on subsequent steps). The customer may want replacement with a loaner, replacement of some of the returned material, or replacement with alternate items. A replacement typically requires a new sales order, although the original order may be used when it is still open.

Inventory Disposition Variations

Returned material is frequently scrapped, or possibly returned to the vendor. Alternatively, it may be used "as-is," repaired and placed into stock, or stripped down for its component parts. These alternatives result in available inventory for MRP logic purposes.

Accounting Variations

The two basic accounting variations, no charge replacement or full credit, can easily become more complex. In many cases, the accounting variations depend on warranty and service agreement considerations, and the ability to link returned material to them. The accounting variations also reflect how sales orders modeled the replacement variations. The accounting invoice may reflect a sales order at full charges using the original price or the most current price, or at partial charges based on a reduced price. The sales order (and invoice) price may reflect the repair costs or the difference in prices when the replacement is an alternate item. Alternatively, the returned item may require a manual credit memo for partial credit.

A Simple RMA Supply Order

A simple RMA order should minimally identify the customer, the authorized items and quantities for return (and/or scrap with no return), the scheduled return date, the customer preference for replacement (credit or other), and the authorized price for replacement or credit. Other information may be considered, such as serial numbers, warranty or service agreement identifier, original sales order number, and special instructions. The RMA number provides a unique identifier, typically automatically assigned with a counter and possible prefix. The life cycle of the RMA order, and each RMA line item, reflect an order status of released, complete, and closed.

A simple RMA order represents a supply order, and is typically ignored by MRP logic. Upon receipt of the returned goods into on hold inventory, a simple RMA order could spawn a sales order for replacement, a credit memo for credit, or nothing. Variations for handling the other options involve increasing levels of complexity. For example, one option may involve repairing the returned item via a custom product configuration for sending it back to the customer, or via a rework order to place it into stock.

Common Problems Related to Customer Service

Common problems in ERP systems for customer service include the lack of recommended action messages, poor integration with a CRM application, CRM affordability, and complex procedures for handling returned material.

Lack of Customer Service Action Messages

Many ERP systems provide insufficient support for coordinating customer service activities. In particular, they provide little or no support for recommended action messages. Users must develop supplemental applications to highlight needed actions based on elapsed time, calculations, or events. An event manager may be used.

Lack of Discipline in CRM Usage

A CRM application offers the promise of a comprehensive database about each customer contact and coordinating required activities. However, it is very difficult to achieve the discipline in reporting customer contacts, and the actions taken on required activities. The difficulties tend to increase as the scope of CRM includes external personnel, such as resellers in the sales channel. This results in a partially complete database of customer contacts, and impairs coordination of required activities.

Integration between CRM and ERP Using Replicated Data

Integration between the two applications is often accomplished with replicated data. CRM typically serves as the primary information repository about contacts with prospects, leads, and customers, and management of the sales cycle. ERP typically serves as the primary repository about products, price books, availability, quotations, configurations, sales orders, shipments, and status.

Integration via replicated data involves dual constructs; the CRM and ERP systems often have different viewpoints of the same construct. For example, each application will have a different viewpoint on price books, the structure of a sales order, and the nature (and rules) of a custom product configuration. This creates problems for integration.

The expense of comprehensively integrating the two applications typically makes it unaffordable for most small manufacturers. The dual construct problem—and the resulting lack of integration—often requires manual maintenance of duplicate data and/or parallel systems.

Affordability of CRM for Smaller Manufacturers

The purchase cost of many CRM packages makes them unaffordable for most small manufacturers. Significant implementation-related costs, such as external assistance or tailoring the CRM package, magnify the affordability issue. Many smaller firms bypass the affordability issue by using a simpler CRM application, perhaps focusing on presales contact management.

Complexity of RMA Processing

Complex variations in handling returned materials involve increasing levels of complexity in modeling an RMA. A simple approach (via a simple RMA order) is often the best approach in an ERP system. More complex variations can be modeled through manual procedures and basic transactions. These basic transactions include sales orders for standard and custom products, invoices, credit memos, inventory, rework orders, and return-to-vendor transactions.

Part 5

Executing Supply Chain Activities

Supply chain activities can be broadly viewed in terms of five categories or areas: procurement, production, inventory, distribution, and field service. Procurement and production activities focus on supply orders, while distribution and field service focus on sales orders. Inventory may be linked to a supply order (such as purchase order receipts placed in receiving inspection) or a sales order (such as staged inventory or a custom product configuration). For explanatory purposes, quality management is viewed as a sixth area involved with supply chain activities, although its scope spans all ERP applications. These six areas provide the organizing focus for chapters within this section.

The nature of each area's supply chain activities depends on several basic factors, such as the type of product (standard versus custom), the linkage between sales orders and supply orders, and an order-based versus orderless manufacturing environment. These factors require a contingency approach to managing activities in each area. Differences in the design of an ERP system represent additional contingencies that must be considered. An ERP system's capabilities to support subcontract purchase orders and direct-linkage manufacturing orders, for example, impact the nature of procurement and production activities. Suggestions for ERP system usage must reflect a contingency approach.

Each chapter includes a framework that summarizes the key elements involved in coordination and execution of relevant supply chain activities. Each framework identifies the primary drivers of activities and key coordination tools, such as recommended action messages and schedules. The usefulness of action messages and schedules represents a macrolevel quality metric that characterizes the effectiveness of an ERP system. The usefulness is directly impacted by three basic success factors: the effectiveness of a firm's S&OP (sales and operations planning) game plans, the completeness and accuracy of the manufacturing database, and the extent to which sales orders explicitly define requirements.

Chapter 20 on quality management covers macrolevel quality metrics on ERP system effectiveness. It also covers the practical implications of quality concerns embedded throughout an ERP system and the impact of certification programs.

Chapter 15

Procurement and Receiving

A primary responsibility of procurement is to execute the supply chain activities driven by the firm's S&OP (sales and operations planning) game plans. Purchased material constitutes the majority of product costs for many manufacturers, and inventory of purchased material represents a significant portion of current assets. Procurement activities significantly improve bottom-line performance by supply chain coordination and cost reduction efforts, and improve agility through lead-time reduction efforts. Coordination efforts should improve the quality of purchased items and reduce production disruptions, even for operation-intensive products with minimal material content. Many products are dependent on tooling, customer-supplied material, or subcontracted manufacturing that requires coordination efforts in procurement.

Procurement activities for production-related items are directly impacted by two key factors: the effectiveness of S&OP game plans and the completeness and accuracy of the manufacturing database. One measure of these factors is the number of procurement activities initiated to meet requirements not driven by S&OP game plans. Other measures include the number of expedited purchases and the perceived need for a requisition approval process to purchase production-related items.

Procurement activities also reflect requirements for other items, such as capital equipment and expense items, not directly driven by the S&OP game plans. Purchase requisitions typically drive these requirements. While these items may represent a significant share of procurement activities, they fall outside the scope of this book.

A Contingency Approach to Procurement Activity

Procurement activities for production-related items involve different types of purchase orders. Almost all firms employ purchase orders for standard product items, with either frequent or infrequent replenishment. Some firms require outside processing, modeled with subcontract items or outside operations or both. Other firms require custom product configurations involving one-time purchase requirements. Procurement activities vary by type of purchase.

Procurement activities are structured around a purchasing cycle that minimally includes four basic steps: (1) identify item demand, (2) source the item by identifying and qualifying vendors, (3) negotiate and define an agreement, and (4) execute procurement activity. Every purchase goes through the basic steps. In an ERP system, the first step—identify item demand—reflects requirements driven by the S&OP game plans.

The other steps in a purchase cycle—identify source, define agreement, and execute—depend on the type of purchase. A critical inventoried item with frequent replenishment, for example, involves different steps than a configuration's requirement for a nonstock component. In the same vein, the supplier relationships typically differ: a one-time purchase reflects *ad hoc* contact, whereas frequent replenishment benefits from close working ties with an approved vendor. This argues for a contingency approach that structures procurement activity based on type of purchase.

Production-related purchases reflect standard products, custom products, and outside operations. Figure 15.1 illustrates several types of purchases within these categories, and a contingency approach to procurement activity. It does not include all types of purchases, such as Kanban replenishment and purchase orders directly linked to sales orders for standard products.

The type of purchase determines the applicable purchase order and the way to handle approved vendors, agreements, coordination, and receipts. A given ERP system may not support all types of purchase orders, and a given order type can be implemented differently in the design of an ERP system.

Type of Purchase			Freq	Identify Source	Define Agreement	Coordinate and Execute Delivery	Receipt
Procurement Activity (header)							
Standard Product		Normal PO	Frequent	Approved Vendor	Blanket PO or Contract	Vendor Schedule or PO	Into Inventory
Standard Product		Subcontract PO	Infrequent	Approved Vendor or Ad Hoc	Quote and PO	PO	Into Inventory
Custom Product	Component	Nonstock Material PO	One-Time	Ad Hoc	PO	PO	Into WIP
Custom Product	Configuration	Custom Product Subcontract PO	One-Time	Ad Hoc	PO	PO	Into Inventory
Outside Operation	Operation	Outside Operation PO	One-Time	Preferred Vendor	PO	PO	Into WIP

Figure 15.1 A Contingency Approach to Procurement Activity

Purchase Orders for Standard Products

Each standard product item has an item master record designating its primary source, such as buy or subcontract, with related planning data and standard costs. It can be purchased complete using a normal PO or externally produced using a subcontract PO with supplied material. Both PO types have the same purchase order life cycle and both record receipts into inventory. Procurement activities vary slightly between items purchased frequently versus infrequently.

- *Frequently Purchased Items.* A frequently purchased item typically has one or more approved vendors, with possible vendor item information. A blanket PO and contract often define agreements. Execution of procurement activities often involves releases against blanket POs. The PO provides coordination with the supplier, and vendor schedules can improve coordination and supplier visibility.
- *Infrequently Purchased Items.* An infrequently purchased item may have approved vendors and quotes defining agreements. Purchase order execution can draw on the quoted price. Otherwise, the PO itself defines the agreement and provides coordination.

Managing External Production Using a Subcontract PO Versus an Outside Operation PO

Production at external suppliers can be managed using two different approaches: an outside operation or a subcontract item approach. These approaches were previously compared. In summary, the outside operation approach requires coordination between two streams of activities for the manufacturing order operation and its related purchase order. The outside operation approach often works better for one-time operations, such as intermittent subcontracting of a make item, or outside operations in a custom product configuration.

The subcontract item approach provides a single coordinating mechanism by combining the concepts of a purchase order and a manufacturing order. A subcontract item represents one outside operation with a bill defining a kit of supplied material. The subcontract item approach has several advantages but does not work well for one-time operations to produce standard products, since it requires an item master record for the subcontract item and a separate level in the bill.

Purchase Orders Related to Custom Product Configurations

Custom product configurations may result in several types of one-time procurement activities, such as a nonstock material component and a subcontracted configuration for the saleable item. Figure 15.1 identifies these two types of purchases. Other types of purchases, such as a purchased configuration, are not shown for simplicity's sake.

These one-time requirements involve *ad hoc* source identification and quali-fication. The purchase order defines the agreement and provides coordination. A configuration's one-time requirements may require approved vendors and quotes, but the lack of an item master record creates modeling difficulties in most ERP systems.

The lack of an item master record also creates difficulties in handling pur-chase order receipts and inventory related to a custom product configuration. Nonstock material may be received into work-in-process (as shown in Figure 15.1), while a subcontracted configuration may be received into inventory (for subsequent shipment).

Purchase Orders for Outside Operations

An outside operation is defined in the context of a routing for a standard prod-uct or a custom product configuration. Most ERP systems support a preferred vendor, or even multiple preferred vendors, to identify the primary source for an outside operation. The purchase order defines the agreement and provides coor-dination, and the purchase order gets received into work-in-process (WIP). An outside operation may require quotes, but the lack of an item master record cre-ates modeling difficulties in most ERP systems.

Supplier Relationship Considerations

The concepts of supplier relationships generally apply to standard products with frequent purchases. Close working ties can focus on quality at the source, lead-ing to reduced reject rates and inspection requirements. It can also lead to shorter item lead-times (and improved agility in responding to changes), typi-cally using vendor schedules to provide visibility of planned requirements. It may also involve vendor-managed inventory or Kanban replenishment methods.

Procurement and accounting require identification of vendors, typically de-fined in a vendor master file with relevant information for purchasing and payables. Most ERP systems require a vendor master record for every type of purchase, even one-time suppliers. Vendor policies affecting supply chain activ-ities include a hold status and receiving inspection requirements for standard product items.

Dual Procurement Roles: Buyer and Vendor Scheduler

Procurement activities can be segmented into two roles, buyer and vendor scheduler, for managing each purchase cycle. The buyer role focuses on identi-fying and qualifying sources and negotiating agreements. The vendor scheduler role focuses on executing purchases and coordinating deliveries to meet re-quirements. In smaller firms, a purchasing agent typically performs both roles.

Within this book, the term buyer and recommended buyer actions apply to both roles.

Kanban Replenishment for Purchased Material

Kanban replenishment for purchased material typically applies to standard product buy items. The Kanban replaces a purchase order as the primary coordination tool. A blanket purchase order is frequently used to represent Kanban replenishment. Each Kanban delivery of an item represents a delivery line within a blanket PO line item.

ERP DESIGN ISSUE °

Direct Linkage between a Purchase Order and Sales Order for Standard Products

Some ERP systems support direct linkage between a purchase order and a sales order for standard products. This represents a different type of purchase order, since changes to the sales order quantity (and date) automatically update the purchase order. It could be called a final-assembly purchase order. Direct linkage provides the foundation for identifying drop-shipments in the sales order, and automatically communicating drop-ship information (via the final-assembly purchase order) to the supplier.

Purchase orders related to a custom product configuration, such as a nonstock component, a subcontracted configuration, or outside operation, also require direct linkage to the sales order.

A Framework for Procurement Activities

An overall framework for procurement activities applies to each type of purchase order. Purchase orders are driven by S&OP game plans and information in the manufacturing database, and optionally draw on sourcing and agreement information. Each purchase requires execution and delivery coordination, as well as receiving activities that impact accounting. These represent five major areas in a framework for procurement activities, shown in Figure 15.2, and provide the organizing focus for further explanation.

Drivers of Procurement Activities

The S&OP game plan acts as the primary driver of item demand, the first step in every purchase cycle. Each S&OP game plan is typically expressed in terms of master schedules for the highest level of stocked items or final-assembly schedules driven by sales orders. Using the S&OP game plans and information in the manufacturing database, an ERP system communicates recommended buyer actions to synchronize supplies with demands. The master schedules and final

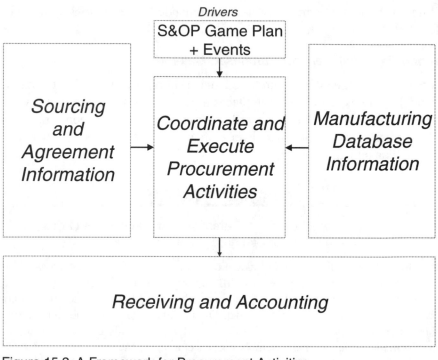

Figure 15.2 A Framework for Procurement Activities

assembly schedules represent an authorization to undertake procurement activities and eliminate the need for purchase requisitions and a requisition approval process.

Other drivers of procurement activities include events and time-based conditions, communicated through recommended buyer actions. A received short transaction, for example, serves as an event that requires buyer attention. Examples of time-based conditions include past-due receipts, follow-up on anticipated deliveries from a problem vendor, and follow-up on anticipated expiration of a blanket purchase order. An approved requisition for expense items or capital equipment also serves as a driver.

Review of Manufacturing Database Information Relevant to Procurement

Information in the manufacturing database is critical for translating S&OP game plans into recommended buyer actions. This information was covered in Part 2, which explained how to structure the manufacturing database. As summarized here, the information represents three key elements in the framework for procurement activity: standard product planning data, custom product configuration data, and information about subcontracted manufacturing.

Standard Product Planning Data

The critical planning data for each item includes the primary source, buyer responsibility, item lead-time, replenishment method, and lot-sizing logic for suggested order quantities.

Primary Source   A purchased item's primary source of replenishment, either buy or subcontract, is reflected in the item's bill and costs, and serves as the basis for suggesting replenishment.

Buyer Responsibility   A buyer field identifies the responsibility for item replenishment and provides the organizing focus for how ERP systems communicate the need to synchronize procurement activities. Suggestions about planned procurement for a buy or subcontract item inherit the item's buyer, which can be overridden on a purchase order. In this way, an ERP system can direct recommended actions concerning existing orders to the relevant buyers.

Item Lead-Time   The lead-time for a buy and subcontract item represents an average supplier notification period and turnaround time, respectively. By providing visibility on planned requirements, vendor schedules typically lead to reduced lead times (in comparison to surprise orders). An item's inspection lead-time can be used as a buffer against supplier inconsistency in on-time delivery. An item's planning fence can be used to identify the shortest possible lead-time. MRP logic may optionally consider a vendor-specific lead-time for a given purchase order.

Replenishment Method   The replenishment method for a standard product item is typically based on MRP logic. Other methods include rate-based scheduling, order-point, and Kanban. With normal planning, the suggested supply order is indirectly linked to a sales order.

Some ERP systems support replenishment directly linked to sales order demand. With direct linkage, the suggested purchase order quantity and need date are directly linked to the sales order quantity and ship date and do not reflect MRP lot-sizing logic.

Lot-Sizing Logic and Suggested Order Quantity   Replenishment methods based on MRP logic typically identify the desired delivery frequency, expressed as the days of supply, to calculate a suggested order quantity. A planned order quantity covers all demands during a frequency interval and may be subject to modifiers for quantity minimum and multiples (representing packaging, unit of measure, transportation, or other considerations). MRP logic can also suggest a fixed quantity or a daily schedule to cover demands, or an order quantity triggered by order point logic.

Planning Policy   A purchased item may be replenished to cover any demands, or only demands related to sales orders, based on the planning policy of normal or final-assembly.

Custom Product Configuration Data

Configuration data may result in three types of one-time procurement activities: a custom product component for a nonstock material item, a purchased configuration, or subcontracted configuration. The critical planning data varies slightly between the three types of purchases.

♦ *Nonstock Purchased Material Component.* A configuration's components can include a nonstock purchased material, with a one-time item number, description, planned cost, unit of measure (UM), and quantity. The responsible buyer can initially default to the buyer for the custom product parent item, or be manually specified on the purchase order. Purchase lead-time is initially unknown, although a suggested vendor may be identified.

♦ *Purchased Configuration.* Some ERP systems support a purchased configuration for a buy custom product item, where procurement activities parallel those for a nonstock material item. The configuration only provides specification information. It defines a one-time item number (the configuration ID) and description, where the UM reflects the custom product item. The buyer assigned to a PO can initially default to the custom product item's buyer and be overridden.

♦ *Subcontracted Configuration.* Some ERP systems support a purchased configuration for a subcontract custom product. The configuration defines a one-time item number (the configuration ID) and description, where the UM reflects the custom product item. The configuration's bill defines supplied material. The buyer assigned to a PO can initially default to the custom product item's buyer and be overridden.

Subcontracted Manufacturing and Supplied Material

A subcontract purchase order represents one approach for managing subcontracted manufacturing. Supplied material is defined in the item's bill or in a configuration's bill. Bill components may optionally indicate supplied tools or documents and specify the material to be obtained by the vendor (reference components). The item's description, or the configuration's description, indicates the desired outside processing.

Outside Operation Planning Data

An outside operation PO represents a second approach for subcontracted manufacturing. Routing data defines the critical planning data, such as the preferred vendor, a purchase quantity and UM, a turnaround time (expressed in days), and the responsible buyer. The operation description indicates the desired outside processing.

An outside operation may also specify requirements for the external resource to support scheduling and capacity planning. In an ERP system, this often requires two separate fields: one to identify the preferred vendor and one to identify the external resource. Additional complexities are involved when an ERP system supports an alternate operation for an outside operation.

Most ERP systems do not explicitly identify supplied material for an outside operation, since sending a partially completed product cannot be easily identified without an item number. Other components (with the same operation sequence number as the outside operation) could be identified for information purposes.

Sourcing and Agreement Information

ERP systems provide multiple ways to define a qualified source and agreements, typically reflecting differences in the type of purchase. The key elements of sourcing/agreement information include approved vendors, vendor quotes and contracts, and blanket purchase orders.

Approved Vendors

The concept of an approved vendor typically applies to frequently purchased items, whereas one-time purchases involve *ad hoc* sourcing. As a general rule, ERP systems implement the concept of approved vendor using different approaches for standard product items and outside operations.

Approved Vendors for a Standard Product Item   Approved vendors for a standard product item can be predefined, with optional specification of vendor item information. Each vendor item may have attributes affecting procurement and receiving activities, such as lead-time and inspection policy. ERP systems may limit an item's purchase orders to approved vendors.

Preferred Vendor for an Outside Operation   Qualified sources for an outside operation can be predefined in the routing operation as a preferred vendor. Many ERP systems only allow one preferred vendor to be predefined for an outside operation. Additional complexities are involved when an ERP system supports an alternate operation (and alternate preferred vendor) for an outside operation.

Price Quotes

The concept of price quotes applies to all types of purchases. A price quote identifies the vendor and agreed-upon prices for one or more items, typically with quantity breakpoints and date effectivities. A price quote may also define payment terms. A price quote may reflect responses to a request for quote, or prices that have been negotiated with the vendor. ERP systems provide several tools to support vendor negotiations, such as vendor performance reports and the value of all projected purchases from the vendor.

ERP systems must provide different approaches to price quotes as a result of differences between types of purchases. In most cases, a price quote has a unique user-assigned identifier and must be explicitly specified on a purchase order to invoke the quoted price. Other cases use an implicit approach to using price quote information.

Price Quotes for Standard Products   A price quote identifies prices for one or more standard product items. The quote identifier must be explicitly specified on a purchase order to invoke the quoted price.

Standard Products and Implicit Price Quotes   The price quote does not have an identifier and a purchase order automatically inherits pricing information based on the vendor, item, item's quantity, and date. A similar situation applies to sales orders and price books, where the sales order inherits pricing information based on the customer, item, item's quantity, and date.

Price Quotes for an Outside Operation, Nonstock Material, or Custom Product Configuration   An ERP system must provide a different approach to defining quotes when an item master record does not apply. The quote identifier must be explicitly specified on a purchase order to invoke the quoted price. Alternatively, the price quote may act as a template for creating a purchase order.

Purchase Contracts

A purchase contract has two variations: an item-specific contract and a non-item-specific contract. An item-specific contract is similar to an explicit price quote and generally applies only to standard product items.

Item-Specific Contract   The contract has a user-defined identifier and defines a vendor and pricing for one or more standard product items. It typically defines date effectivities, quantity breakpoints, and even payment terms. The contract identifier must be explicitly specified on a purchase order to invoke the pricing agreement. A contract provides additional benefits in terms of tracking expenditures and vendor performance by contract.

Non-Item-Specific Contract   The contract has a user-defined identifier and provides the basis for tracking vendor expenditures by contract. Non-item-specific contracts can be used to track expenditures for outside operations, nonstock material, and configurations.

Blanket Purchase Orders

A blanket PO generally applies to standard product items and consists of one or more line items. Each line item specifies an item number, an effectivity period, a total expected order quantity, and an agreed-upon price. Each release against a blanket PO line item defines a delivery line, specifying a delivery date and quantity.

A blanket PO line item with delivery lines can provide significant advantages in reporting supply chain activities:

- *Recommended Buyer Actions Identify the Blanket PO Number.* Taking the recommended buyer action creates a release against the blanket PO line item.
- *Reporting Supplied Material for Subcontracted Items.* Supplied material can be issued to a vendor against the blanket PO line item, rather than as a kit for each delivery line.
- *Cascading Over-Receipts.* Over-receipts recorded against one delivery line can optionally cascade to the next delivery line, thereby reducing its expected quantity.
- *Automatic Creation of Delivery Lines upon Receipt.* Delivery lines can be automatically created to reflect receipts against the blanket PO line item.

Using International Sources for Purchases

International sources of purchased material are becoming very common, even for small manufacturers. A foreign supplier may require pricing based on the foreign currency, and tracking of shipments through multiple steps prior to actual receipt. The multiple steps, for example, might reflect placing the goods onboard ship, receipt into customs, and so forth.

International sources of subcontract manufacturing are also becoming more common. In addition to the considerations mentioned above, additional paperwork for supplied material and completed items is required to cross international borders. The transborder material flow often requires other special reporting requirements. In some cases, the foreign subcontractor represents a wholly or partially owned subsidiary.

Coordinating and Executing Procurement Activities

ERP systems provide three key tools for executing and coordinating procurement activities: purchase orders, vendor schedules, and recommended buyer actions. A fourth tool—a pick list—provides coordination of supplied material for subcontracted manufacturing. In some cases, coordination may involve vendor capacity planning for purchased items.

Purchase Orders

Purchase orders represent the primary means of communicating requirements to suppliers and of coordinating deliveries to meet the promised dock date. Released purchase orders also serve contractual purposes and may draw on previously defined agreement information such as price quotes, contracts, or blanket POs. The S&OP game plans and manufacturing database information generate the need to execute different types of purchase orders, related to standard products, custom product configurations, and outside operations, and to coordinate deliveries that are synchronized to demands.

A subcontract PO requires a second coordinating mechanism—the pick list—to send supplied material to the vendor.

Vendor Schedules

Vendor schedules provide requirements visibility to suppliers for frequently purchased standard product items. A vendor schedule typically expresses requirements in the vendor item's UM. It consists of actual purchase orders in the near-term horizon and planned purchase orders over the longer-term horizon. The time horizon depends on the items being purchased. A vendor schedule typically shows weekly requirements over a 2 to 3 month horizon and monthly requirements thereafter, with identification of released purchase orders. Figure 15.3

Vendor:	Amalgamated Industries		Vendor Schedule as of Jan 11, 20XX			
Vendor Item#:	Part #12345 EA	Buyer: BOB	Lead-Time: 10 Days			
Internal Item#:	Part#XYZ EA					

	Jan 12	Jan 19	...	Mar 02	Mar 30	April 27
	Past-Due	Week 1	Week 2	...	Week 8	Wk 9-12	Wk 13-16
Released PO		100					
Firm/Open PO							
Planned PO					260	740	800
Total	0	100	0		260	740	800

PO Detail	PO# & Line#	Ordered	Received	Open	Due Date	Contract#
		---------- Quantity ----------				
	1003 / 001	280	180	100	Jan 12	AB2001

Vendor Item#:	Part #567 RL	Buyer: SUE	Lead-Time: 5 Days			
Internal Item#:	Part#ABC LB					

Released PO							
Firm/Open PO							
Planned PO					50	300	400
Total	0	0	0		50	300	400

Figure 15.3 An Example Vendor Schedule

provides an example vendor schedule. By providing visibility on planned purchases, vendor schedules typically lead to shorter item lead-times: a shorter supplier notification period for buy items and a shorter turnaround period for subcontract items.

The planned purchase orders to a given vendor reflect a source percentage defined with the approved vendor information. The approved vendor for a sole-source item, for example, would have 100 percent of the item's planned POs in their vendor schedule. The approved vendors for a dual-source item may have a 50-50 split of the item's planned purchase orders in their vendor schedules.

Effective use of a vendor schedule typically requires a close working relationship with the supplier and frequent (weekly) updates. In particular, a mutual understanding must exist on the significance of planned purchase orders, and possible time fence policies concerning acceptable changes. Vendor schedule information may be communicated in a variety of ways, such as mail, fax, e-mail, or secure web access. It may also be communicated via electronic data interchange (EDI), but this method is not generally required by suppliers of smaller firms.

The format for a vendor schedule may use the concept of an electronic schedule board when using web access by suppliers. An example schedule board format is included in Chapter 17 (see Figure 17.4).

Recommended Buyer Actions

ERP systems communicate the impact of S&OP game plans on procurement activities using recommended buyer actions. Recommended actions also reflect events and elapsed time conditions that affect procurement activities. Figure 15.4 illustrates several recommended buyer actions, segmented by message driver. The buyer responsible for item replenishment, or assigned to coordinate a given PO line item, provides the organizing focus for recommended action messages.

Some buyer action messages only apply to standard product items (indicated in Figure 15.4), such as items with order point replenishment. Some messages still apply to items with a Kanban replenishment method.

Message filters by buyer can reduce the noise level of unnecessary messages. A buyer's message filter may suppress a message entirely, and some messages have a basis for selective filtering (shown in Figure 15.4). A "Release PO" message, for example, can be based on a look ahead window, so that the recommended action appears a number of days before the PO start date.

Vendor Capacity Planning

Vendor capacity planning represents one more coordination tool for procurement. It generally applies to subcontractors that have been defined as external resources. A vendor's capacity requirements can be calculated on the basis of the

Message Driver	Recommended Buyer Action Message	Message Applies to		Message Filter
		Only Standard Product	Kanban Item	
S&OP Game Plans	Release purchase order			Look ahead days
	Release a delivery line within a blanket purchase order			Look ahead days
	Release purchase order based on order point logic	x		
	Release PO with unrealistic lead-time (planning fence)	x		
	Review recommended PO for phase-out/obsolete item	x		
	Reschedule purchase order earlier (expedite)			Days early
	Reschedule purchase order later (de-expedite)			Days late
	Cancel existing purchase order			
	Reduce order quantity of existing purchase order			
Event	Print PO for a newly released (or changed) order			
	Review item with ATP exceeded by a sales order	x	x	
	Follow up on purchase order that was received short			
	Follow up on PO received outside quantity/date tolerances	x		Over/under tolerances
	Close a PO based on suggested closure by receiving			Auto-close
	Cancel existing purchase order for item marked obsolete	x		
	Review purchase order placed on hold			Reason code
	Review existing subcontract PO because of bill changes	x	x	
	Review/define information for new item	x	x	
	Review information for item changed to buy	x	x	
Elapsed Time	Follow up on expected PO receipt from problem vendor			Look ahead days
	Follow up on past-due PO receipt			Look behind days
	Follow up existing PO with past-due supplied material	x		Look behind days
	Review blanket PO about to expire, or near maximum	x	x	Look ahead days
	Review contract about to expire, or near maximum	x	x	Look ahead days

Figure 15.4 Illustration of Buyer Action Messages

required times for the external resource specified in an outside operation. When using the subcontract item approach, an outside operation (with zero costs) must be added to calculate capacity requirements. In some cases, the capacity requirements related to outside operations can be used for finite scheduling purposes.

Receiving Activities

Receiving activities encompass purchase order receipts and other types of receipts. For purchase orders, the receiving process varies slightly based on the type of purchase (shown in Figure 15.1). A standard product item can be received into inventory, for example, while an outside operation is received into work-in-process. Each receipt transaction provides the basis for measuring vendor performance, building a buy card history, and updating payables and the general ledger.

Purchase Order Receipts

Receiving activities can be anticipated with a schedule of expected receipts. Actual receipts are recorded against released purchase order line items and receipts may be reversed, typically to identify corrections.

Receipts for outside operations go directly into work-in-process for the parent manufacturing order. Receipts for nonstock material and configurations may go into work-in-process or inventory, depending on the ERP system. Receipts for standard product items go into on-hand inventory, or into inspection inventory based on receiving inspection policies.

Receiving Inspection (and Quarantine Period)

Receiving inspection only applies to standard product items and represents one area of quality management responsibilities. The recommended actions for quality management identify items placed in inspection or on hold status, identified by purchase order and line number.

An item's inspection lead-time represents the average elapsed time between receipt into inspection inventory and its availability. It typically reflects the dock-to-stock activities that include inspection activities or a quarantine period. In terms of MRP logic, the material received into inspection will be available after the item's inspection lead-time (reflecting the quarantine period), and the quantity in inspection will be factored by the item's expected yield percentage to estimate the available quantity. Dispositions of inspection inventory may involve returns to vendor.

Multistep Receiving Procedures

Some manufacturing environments require a multistep receiving procedure prior to recognizing a PO receipt into inventory. The multistep receiving procedure typically reflects inspection requirements, but it could also reflect steps in transportation. A multistep receiving procedure consists of user-defined steps that provide tracking of receiving activities against a PO line item, without recognizing receipts into inventory or any impact on payables. MRP logic views availability in terms of the PO's promised dock date, and the receiving steps provide visibility about the expected receipt.

Returns to Vendor

Returns to vendor impact inventory and accounting, and must be linked to a specified purchase order and line number for each returned item. For a given PO, a return to vendor transaction typically identifies the quantity being returned for credit, the quantity being scrapped (and therefore not returned) for credit, and the quantity to be replaced (if the PO line item can be reopened). Since credit calculations may be incorrect, a manual entry of the credit amount may be necessary. The return to vendor transaction generally requires explanatory text and the authorizing RMA from the supplier.

Many ERP systems place restrictions on the return-to-vendor transaction. For example, the item must be in inspection or on hold status, and linked to a purchase order and line number. The item's lot number (if applicable) must be one received from the vendor. The PO cannot be closed or deleted from the system. This last restriction often means that returns must be recorded with inventory adjustments, and manual debit memos in payables.

Vendor Performance

Receipts provide the basis for measuring vendor performance, typically in terms of delivery, quality, and price. The delivery measurement has two dimensions, timeliness and correct quantity, with delivery tolerances for acceptable variations. Delivery tolerances can be defined for each item purchased from a vendor, or globally for all items purchased from a vendor. Vendor performance measures reflect all receipts during a specified time period, such year-to-date receipts.

Delivery Timeliness   Delivery timeliness can be measured by comparing the actual receipt dates (for a PO line item) against the promise date (at the time of receipt). Two promise dates may be considered: the original promise date or the current promise date. In an ERP system, the current promise date is continually changed for internal reasons (so that supplies align with demands) or external reasons (to reflect expected delivery problems). The measure of delivery timeliness is expressed as a percentage (divide the number of on-time receipts by the total number of receipts). Delivery tolerances, expressed as allowable days early or late, identify on-time receipts.

Delivery Quantity   Delivery of the correct quantity can be measured by comparing actual received quantities on the promise date against the PO's order quantity. Delivery tolerances, expressed as allowable over or under quantities, identify correct quantity performance. The measure is expressed as a percentage (divide the number of correct quantity receipts by the total number of receipts).

Quality   Quality performance can be measured by comparing the quantity of rejected items to the total quantity received. One method of identifying a rejected item is based on PO receipts placed into on hold inventory with a reject reason code. This method becomes more complex when an item's quality problems, and ultimate rejection, are not recognized until well after the PO receipt. The material must be moved to on hold status and relinked to the original PO line item to provide the basis for measuring quality performance. The measure of quality performance is expressed as a percentage.

Price   Price performance can be measured in terms of purchase price variances for standard product items and outside operations. The measure of price performance is expressed as a percentage, where the total value of purchase price variances is divided by the total value (at standard cost) of received items.

Vendor performance can be tracked by individual item (for standard products) and for all items received from the vendor. Vendor performance can also be tracked for each line item within a contract, and for all line items with a contract.

Buy Card History

Each receipt transaction provides the basis for a buy card history for a standard product item. The buy card history may also identify vendor performance measures for each receipt. This provides reference information for buyers considering the best source for a new purchase order.

Other Types of Purchasing Receipts

Receiving activities involve other types of receipts. For example, a subcontractor may return unused materials and by-products. Chapter 16, which covers inventory management, describes other types of receipts not related to purchasing.

Handling Vendor-Managed Inventory

The term *vendor-managed inventory* has several interpretations, but its primary application involves on-site inventory owned and managed by the supplier. The assumption is that the supplier takes responsibility for replenishing inventory and that a usage transaction correctly updates information. These assumptions have several implications for an ERP system:

- Visibility of an item's vendor-managed inventory in stock status inquiries. The inventory is treated as zero cost for general ledger purposes.
- Linkage between an item's vendor-managed inventory and a blanket PO line item defining the vendor and price.
- The usage transaction allows material to be picked from vendor-managed inventory for issuing to a manufacturing order.
- The usage transaction correctly updates the value of work-in-process inventory at standard cost.
- The usage transaction may reflect an accounts payable invoice, so it must correctly create an accounts payable invoice and update the general ledger payables account (based on the blanket PO price), and possibly update the general ledger purchase price variance account.

Analysis Tools for Procurement

Procurement personnel become involved in efforts to reduce costs, reduce lead times, and improve quality. ERP systems provide several analysis tools to assist in these efforts.

- *Costed Bill.* The costed bill identifies purchased items that significantly impact total costs, thereby focusing cost reduction efforts.

◆ *Purchase Price Variances.* Variances highlight purchase orders and buyer responsibilities for excessive costs, thereby focusing cost reduction efforts.

◆ *Lead-Time Analysis.* Lead-time analysis identifies purchased items on the critical path of cumulative manufacturing lead-time, thereby focusing lead-time reduction efforts.

◆ *Problem Vendors.* Vendor performance measures on quality and delivery can focus quality improvement efforts.

Symmetry between Procurement and Sales

Purchase orders represent the mirror image of sales orders. The terminology and constructs to model procurement and receiving activities have equivalents in modeling sales/shipment activities, as summarized in Figure 15.5.

Procurement and sales both involve differences between a standard products approach and a custom products approach. The various types of purchase orders map into two types of sales orders configurations: a sales order for a standard product and a sales order for a custom product. For procurement, the standard products approach provides some advantages in inventory visibility, types of agreements, vendor schedules, and buy-card history.

Item Type	Procurement	Sales
Standard Product	Normal purchase order Subcontract purchase order • Bill (Supplied Materials) • Send Supplied Material Price Quote – Implicit Quote – Explicit Contract – Item Specific Contract – Expenditure Only Blanket purchase order Vendor Schedule Purchase order receipt Returns to Vendor Vendor Performance Buy Card History	Sales order for a standard product • Bill (Customer-Supplied Material) • Receive Customer-Supplied Material Price Book – Implicit Quote – Explicit Contract – Item Specific Contract – Expenditure Only Blanket sales order Customer Schedule Sales order shipment Returned Material and RMAs Shipping Performance Sales History
Custom Product	Nonstock Material Custom product purchase order Custom Product Subcontract PO • Configuration (Supplied Material) Quote – Explicit Purchase order receipt (no inventory) Vendor Performance No Buy Card History	Sales order for a Configuration • Configuration (Customer-Supplied Material) Quote – Explicit (based on Configuration) Sales order shipment from WIP (no inventory) Shipping Performance Sales History of Configurations
Outside Operation	Frequent outside operation Infrequent outside operation	Sales order for a Standard Product Sales order for Custom Product Configuration

Figure 15.5 Symmetry between Procurement and Sales

Common Problems Related to Procurement

The common problems related to procurement activities often involve inflated lead-times, unrealistic lot-sizing logic, and unusable buyer action messages. The leading indicators of procurement problems include the perceived need for requisitions and the number of procurement activities initiated to meet requirements not driven by S&OP game plans.

Perceived Need for Requisitions for Production-Related Items

The S&OP game plan acts as the primary driver of purchasing requirements, the first step in every purchase cycle, for production-related items. The concept of purchase requisitions (to identify demand) does not apply to these items. The perceived need for requisitions typically starts with out-of-control purchases; it indicates more fundamental problems in an ERP system.

The Number of Procurement Activities Initiated to Meet Requirements Not Driven by S&OP Game Plans

This factor provides a leading indicator of out-of-control purchases. The S&OP game plan, expressed in master schedules and final-assembly schedules, is translated into purchasing requirements based on product structures and other information in the manufacturing database. Each purchase not driven by the S&OP game plans indicates a potential problem that must be identified and resolved. For example, the problem may stem from incomplete or inaccurate bills and configurations, or incomplete identification of demands for developing the S&OP game plans.

Inflated Lead-Times for Purchased Items

Many buyers use inflated item lead-times to provide greater visibility to suppliers via released purchase orders. This approach typically results in large numbers of recommended buyer actions for PO rescheduling to align supplies with demands. The early action to initiate purchase orders may not reflect finalized product structures in a dynamic environment. Long lead-times run counter to agile manufacturing precepts emphasizing shorter lead times. Use of realistic lead-times and planned purchase orders embraces agile manufacturing precepts. Planned POs automatically realign supplies with demands, thereby avoiding unnecessary buyer actions to reschedule existing POs.

Inflated lead-times for subcontract items create additional problems, where lead-time represents the turnaround time. It results in unnecessarily early requirements for material components and has a cascade effect on requirements for lower-level components. It results in unnecessarily early recommendations for PO release and material issues, leading to larger external work-in-process inventories. When buyers rely on informal systems (that recognize the true lead-time of subcontracted items) to complete and ship supplied material, the effectiveness of the formal system and recommended buyer actions is destroyed.

Unrealistic Lot-Sizing Logic for Purchased Items

Many buyers use unrealistic lot-sizing logic and replenishment methods that do not model their decision making. MRP logic generates planned orders that misrepresent anticipated purchases and communicate useless recommended buyer actions. Planned orders for subcontract items have a cascade effect on requirements for lower-level components. This frequently leads to a breakdown in use of the formal ERP system, since planned orders become meaningless and buyers ignore recommended actions.

Lot-sizing logic must reflect purchasing considerations. These considerations include delivery frequency, quantity minimum and multiples, yields, and possibly daily schedules.

Improving the Usefulness of Recommended Buyer Action Messages

The usefulness of recommended buyer action messages provides a leading indicator of an ERP system's effectiveness. Several steps can be taken to improve message usefulness. The steps also result in better vendor schedules.

The first step focuses on improving S&OP game plans. Exceptions requiring expediting can be reduced to a manageable level. The significance of an agreed-upon S&OP game plan becomes apparent in near-term schedule stability and realistic delivery promises.

The second step focuses on the manufacturing database, since MRP logic uses it to translate S&OP game plans into procurement requirements. It must model supply chain activities completely and accurately in terms of information about items, bills, and configurations. This includes realistic lead-times and lot-sizing logic, and using planned orders as much as possible to automatically align supplies with demands. The vendor schedule can communicate planned requirements.

The third step focuses on improving production schedules that impact procurement. In particular, the lead-time and lot-sizing logic for manufactured items must be realistic. The chapter on production (Chapter 17) provides suggestions for improving the usefulness of production schedules.

The fourth step focuses on global improvements under the direct control of procurement. These include lead-time reduction efforts (based on lead-time analysis), vendor schedules for selected suppliers, and supplier relationships that improve quality at the source.

A fifth step involves creative use of buyer codes, and the message filters associated with each code, to reduce the noise level in action messages. As a starting point, each purchasing agent should segment items (and purchase orders) within their responsibility into three ABC categories, and assign a buyer ID to each category.

- *The "A" Category Will Contain Critical Problem Items and New Items.* These require immediate attention. Applicable messages might include follow-up on anticipated deliveries (from problem vendors) and warnings about suggested replenishment of phase-out items. The "A" category does not typically reflect the accountant's version of ABC segmentation based on value.
- *The "C" Category Represents Items with Few Problems.* Some messages do not apply and message filters can be applied (such as tolerances for de-expedite messages).

An item or purchase order can be elevated (or demoted) in importance by assigning the appropriate buyer ID. In this way, the purchasing agent can set appropriate message filters by buyer ID and reduce the noise level of action messages. Other capabilities can reduce message volume, such as auto-releasing purchase orders for selected items or vendors.

Chapter 16

Inventory Management

Inventory of production-related items represents a significant portion of current assets. It also supports game plans defined in sales and operations planning. Inventory balances result from efforts to synchronize supplies with demands, and higher inventory turns reflect better synchronization.

The scope of inventory management responsibilities traditionally focuses on the stockroom. It frequently extends to receiving and distribution, work-in-process (WIP), subcontractors, floor stock inventory, spare parts inventory, customer returns, vendor returns, customer-supplied material, vendor-managed inventory, and some quality management concerns. These concerns include inventory initially received into inspection, or subsequently moved to inspection, for disposition by quality management.

This chapter covers the basics of inventory management from an ERP system perspective. It focuses on inventory related to standard product items, including the identification of inventory locations and inventory status. The distribution management aspects of inventory are covered in Chapter 18.

Inventory Locations

The starting point of inventory management involves the identification of inventory locations. Each inventory location represents a physical area that can store an item's inventory. A single-site manufacturing firm can have multiple inventory locations, typically identified by stockroom and bin. Most ERP systems allow users to predefine valid locations and then limit inventory transactions to valid locations. A standard product item can be stocked in one or more locations and a given location can contain inventory of one or more items. Some ERP systems do not limit inventory transactions to valid locations, so that a location may be created "on the fly."

A particular inventory location may have designated limitations. A common example involves a receiving inspection location that can only handle inventory balances with an inventory status of in-inspection. A similar example involves a material review location that can only handle inventory balances with an inventory status of on-hold or in-inspection. These examples introduce the concept of inventory status as an attribute of an item's inventory balance.

Some ERP systems support the concept of a nonusable or non-nettable location, so that limitations apply to any inventory balances placed in the location. Other limitations may be associated with an inventory location. These include considerations of capacity (such as weight or volume), material type (such as hazardous or liquid materials), or some other attribute of the item or inventory balance.

Inventory Status and Ownership

All ERP systems identify inventory balances with an inventory record. The basic inventory record defines an item number, location, and quantity. It includes lot number and serial number for lot-traced and serial-traced items. In addition, it may include information about inventory status and ownership.

Inventory Status

Inventory status represents an attribute of an item's inventory balance. The basic values for inventory status are on-hand, in-inspection, or on-hold. Inventory status impacts usability and MRP logic.

- *Inventory Status and Usability.* An on-hand inventory balance represents a usable supply; it can be issued to production or shipped to customers. An on-hold inventory balance is considered unusable. The disposition of an inventory balance in-inspection must be determined by quality management before it can be used.
- *Inventory Status and MRP Logic.* MRP logic ignores an on-hold inventory balance. The inventory placed in receiving inspection for a specified supply order represents an in-inspection inventory balance, but merits special consideration by MRP logic. MRP logic may factor the inventory by the item's expected yield (reflecting anticipated dispositions by quality) and consider availability based on the item's inspection lead-time.

Some ERP systems support other values for inventory status, and even support the addition of user-defined values. The key aspects of usability and MRP logic should apply to other values.

Ownership Status

The concept of inventory ownership is best illustrated by three common examples: receiving inspection inventory for a purchase order receipt, staged (or allocated) inventory for shipment, and work-in-process (WIP) inventory of components. Other examples can also be cited.

- *Receiving Inspection.* Receiving inspection inventory is linked to a purchase order receipt (or other supply order receipt). Dispositions by quality management refer to the supply order so that order closure and quality performance measures can be correctly interpreted.
- *Staged for Shipment.* Staged (or allocated) inventory for shipment is linked to a sales order. The inventory balance can only be used for the sales order shipment (unless it gets unallocated), and MRP logic only considers it available for the sales order.
- *Internal WIP.* WIP inventories of components are linked to a manufacturing order. Each inventory balance can only be used for producing the manufactured item.

Customer-Supplied Material   This requires stock status visibility of an item's normal inventory and customer-supplied material. The receipt into inventory of customer-owned material (valued at zero cost) can be linked to the parent item's manufacturing order.

Inventory Stocked at a Customer Site   The customer-site inventory is closely linked to a blanket sales order so that subsequent usage transactions pick up the agreed-upon sales price. Usage is limited to the blanket sales order. This is conceptually similar to the staged (or allocated) inventory for shipment. Replenishment of inventory stocked at a customer site typically represents a shipment of internally owned inventory. The usage transaction completes a two-step shipment process.

Inventory of a Custom Product Configuration   A completed configuration's inventory can be linked to the sales order number. Usage is limited to the sales order.

Receiving inspection inventory also applies to manufacturing orders and by-products associated with manufacturing orders. Work-in-process inventory also applies to subcontract purchase orders and custom product manufacturing orders.

Definition of WIP Inventory in an ERP System

Work-in-process (WIP) inventory is tied to a manufacturing order. In a typical scenario, a material component is issued from inventory to WIP for the manufacturing order. At the completion of the manufacturing order, the parent item is received into inventory and the ERP system automatically reduces the component's WIP inventory (based on the order-dependent bill). This is termed *relieving WIP inventory*. A component's WIP inventory may not be completely relieved by receipts at the time of order closure. With standard costing, the order closure process makes an assumption about the component's remaining WIP inventory. It assumes the remaining quantity must have been scrapped;

it zeroes out the component's WIP inventory balance and calculates an offsetting general ledger transaction (typically called a material usage variance). The overall effect is termed *clearing out the WIP accounts* for the manufacturing order. The same approach applies to subcontract purchase orders, where material components are issued to (and relieved from) external work-in-process.

Floor stock inventory of component materials, and inventory of parent items located in the production area, are still viewed as inventory by an ERP system. This inventory appears in stock status inquiries for the specified location(s).

Basics of Stockroom Inventory Management

The basics of stockroom inventory management involve complete and accurate reporting of inventory transactions, verifying accuracy, and detecting sources of error through cycle counting. Transactions may be reported via data collection systems. The basics include recommended stockroom actions, quality management concerns on inventory transactions, and several analysis tools.

Types of Transactions

Inventory transactions can be categorized into five basic types: receipts, issues, shipments, movements, and adjustments. The five basic types of transactions are illustrated in Figure 16.1 and explained below.

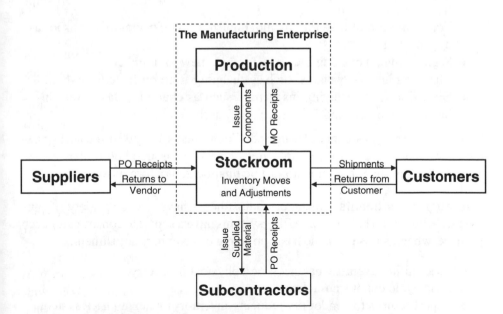

Figure 16.1 Basics of Stockroom Inventory Management

Receipts Receipts typically focus on purchase orders for standard products. Other purchase receipts include subcontracted items, outside operations, non-stock material, and configurations. Subcontracted items may also involve related by-products and returns of unused materials. Receipts also apply to manufacturing orders (and related by-products and returns of unused material), customer returns against an RMA, and customer-supplied material.

Component Issues and Backflushing Component issues and backflushing typically focus on manufacturing orders and custom product manufacturing orders. Component issues also apply to subcontract purchase orders. Ownership linkage may limit component usage, such as using customer-supplied material for producing a specific manufacturing order.

Shipments Shipments must be recorded against a sales order, for either a standard product or a custom product configuration. Ownership linkage may limit shipments, such as shipping allocated inventory to a specific sales order.

Inventory Movements Inventory movements have a wide variety of purposes, as illustrated below. Some ERP systems have a separate construct for each purpose, but they share the same basic principle of inventory movement.

- Physical movement of material from one location to another
- Replenishing floor stock material from the stockroom
- Replenishing a remote warehouse, or inventory stocked at a customer, from the stockroom
- Transportation of material, by moving from a stockroom to a transportation location
- Segmenting an existing lot, or assigning a new lot number
- Changing inventory status, such as changing from on-hand to on-hold
- Dispositions in receiving inspection, such as changing status from in-inspection to on-hand for a specified purchase order receipt

Some inventory types cannot be moved. Components issued to internal or external work-in-process, for example, must be reverse issued before they can be moved. Allocations for shipment must be unallocated before movement.

Inventory Adjustments Inventory adjustments have a wide variety of purposes, as illustrated below. Some ERP systems have a separate construct for each purpose, whereas it is the same basic principle of inventory adjustment.

- Load initial inventory balances, or a physical inventory
- Load cycle count transactions
- Report returns to vendor (by reducing inventory) when an ERP system doesn't support the return

- Report returns from customers (by increasing inventory) when an ERP system doesn't support the return
- Report receipts of customer-supplied material (by increasing inventory) when an ERP system does not explicitly support customer-supplied materials
- Report scrap of on-hold or in-inspection inventory (thereby reducing inventory). The inventory may have an ownership linkage (such as a purchase order receipt)

Some inventory types cannot be adjusted. For example, a component's WIP inventory cannot be adjusted.

The Arguments For and Against Negative Inventory Balances

A negative inventory balance indicates a problem in inventory reporting, such as a missing, erroneous, or duplicate transaction. Some would argue that transaction timing may cause artificial negative balances, but online transaction reporting minimizes this issue. Robust backflushing logic can handle one problem related to transaction timing, by remembering a component's unfinished backflush quantity and then finishing the backflush when inventory arrives in the backflush location. In most cases, the cause of a potential negative inventory should be fixed, rather than allowing negative balances.

Inventory Transaction Audit Trail

An ERP system should provide a complete transaction audit trail of every inventory receipt, issue, shipment, move, and adjustment of an item. The inventory transaction audit trail is typically limited to standard product items. A second audit trail should be provided in the general ledger to trace account balances to the detailed inventory transactions.

Cycle Counting

The primary purpose of cycle counting is to identify the source of inventory errors and then take corrective action to avoid future errors. A secondary purpose is to provide valid financial reporting of inventory value.

To achieve the primary purpose, the control group method provides a good cycle counting strategy. The control group consists of selected problem items (such as 20 to 30 items). Each item is counted daily to identify a source of inventory error as soon as possible after the event. The inventory transaction audit trail provides one diagnostic tool.

Most stockroom personnel can easily identify their problem items, such as items with errors caused by unit of measure conversion, backflushing, and floor stock usage. Periodic cycle counting of floor stock inventories, in particular, can minimize the impact of loose controls over reported usage. Any items with a perceived need for negative inventory balances are also good candidates. Items within the control group will change over time to focus on different problem areas.

To achieve the secondary purpose, one cycle counting strategy identifies a random selection of items and locations for each day's counting. The random daily counts can then cycle through all items and locations to avoid physical inventory counts. If errors are identified, the source of inventory error will probably be more difficult to diagnose.

Using Bar Code Data Collection for Inventory Transactions

The advantages of bar code data collection over manual transactions include speed and accuracy. An additional advantage of bar code data collection is that human engineering can be tailored to the task, rather than to the ERP system's design. A single bar code transaction, for example, may update several screens of information in an ERP system, or even update multiple systems (such as ERP and a standalone quality management application).

Other Inventory Control Considerations

Inventory control procedures can be employed to use up old material before using new material in support of planned engineering changes. The same concept applies to using FIFO (first in/first out) logic to issue or ship lot-traced inventory.

Lot-traced inventory may have lot expiration or retest dates. Lot control may be used to support remnant tracking, such as returning a partial roll of dimensional material to stock.

A logical kit pull can verify available inventory prior to actual kit pulls to issue components to a manufacturing order or subcontract purchase order, or to ship multiple line items on a sales order.

A tool crib may require issues and receipts of tools, much like materials in a stockroom. In most cases, tools reside on the factory floor so that inventory control represents overkill.

Recommended Stockroom Actions

Execution and coordination of several stockroom activities can be guided by recommended actions. These recommended actions, illustrated in Figure 16.2, support production- and distribution-related activities as well as warnings about inventory. Some messages only apply to standard products.

Quality Management Concerns about Inventory Transactions

Quality management policies about inventory transactions include lot- and serial-control policies, and receiving inspection policies. These policies must be enforced in inventory transactions, such as enforcing lot number assignment upon receipt.

Driver	Recommended Stockroom Message	Message Applies to Standard Product Only	Message Applies to Kanban Item	Message Filter
Production Related	Print pick list of components for manufacturing order			Look ahead days
	Issue components to manufacturing order			Look ahead days
	Move inventory to replenish floor stock location		x	
	Review past due component issue			
Distribution Related	Print pick list of components for subcontract PO			Look ahead days
	Ship supplied material for subcontract PO			Look ahead days
	Ship returns to vendor		x	
Warnings	Auto-deduction error for inventory of component item	x	x	
	Item (with inventory) marked as obsolete	x	x	
	Lot expiration or retest required for item & lot	x	x	Look ahead days
	Cycle count required for item or location	x	x	
	Received item must be issued immediately to supply order			
	Received item must be shipped immediately for sales order			

Figure 16.2 Illustrations of Stockroom Action Messages

Quality management also requires transactional control over inventory movement and adjustments that impact inventory status, especially in highly regulated environments. A drug manufacturer, for example, would need to limit who can approve material that resides in an in-inspection status. Example transactions impacting status include the following:

- An inventory move transaction to change inventory status related to in-inspection or on-hold, such as recording dispositions that move inventory from in-inspection to on-hand.
- An inventory adjustment transaction affecting inventory status, such as scrapping material from an in-inspection status.

This argues for screen level and/or field level security to enforce transactional control. Some ERP systems provide variations of the movement and adjustment screens to support limited access to inventory transactions that impact quality reporting.

Analysis Tools for Inventory Management

Some basic analysis tools include calculating ABC classifications, identifying excess or obsolete inventory, and assessing impacts of inventory revaluations.

Calculating ABC Classifications The accounting version of ABC analysis focuses on a value measurement (cost times inventory usage over a time period). Inventory usage may reflect historical data or projected usages driven by the S&OP game plans. The projected usage measurement is generally more useful because it factors in anticipated changes, such as changing demands and product structures.

Identifying Excess or Obsolete Inventory   A recommended action message identifying items marked as obsolete (or phase out) is one method. Another approach compares the items' projected requirements (driven by the S&OP game plans) to current inventory balances and identifies excess inventory. A third approach compares daily usage rates to inventory balances and identifies slow moving and excess inventory.

Anticipating the Impact of an Inventory Revaluation   Changes to the frozen standard costs result in inventory revaluations based on inventory balances. A cost comparison between two sets of cost data (between the frozen standard and next period standard, for instance) identifies the impact when it accounts for inventory balances. The impact can also be segmented by the inventory general ledger accounts assigned to items.

Other inventory management tools assist the accounting function, such as the information detail to support WIP inventory reconciliation (by order and by item).

Common Problems Related to Inventory Management

The common problems in inventory management include inventory accuracy and limitations in single-site MRP logic.

Poor Inventory Accuracy

Inventory balances are critical in MRP calculations. The lack of accuracy means the S&OP game plans cannot be translated into schedules actually used to coordinate supply chain activities.

Single-Site MRP Logic and Multiple Inventory Locations

MRP logic is not location sensitive in a single-site ERP system. Single-site MRP logic looks at an item's total inventory regardless of location within the site. It cannot differentiate an item's supplies or demands by location, such as a separate spare parts inventory, inventory stocked at a remote distribution center, or inventory stocked at subcontractors. This differentiation requires multisite or project MRP logic. Multisite MRP logic requires additional constructs and accounting capabilities, as described in Chapter 23 on multisite operations.

Chapter 17

Production and Production Activity Control

Production represents the heart of most manufacturers and their distinctive competency. A separate functional area, termed *production activity control,* is often responsible for coordinating the execution of production activities. These activities are driven by the firm's S&OP (sales and operations planning) game plans.

Different manufacturing environments have a wide range of production activities. Many of the variations in production activities can be modeled using resources and routing information. Other variations reflect order-based versus orderless approaches, with differing requirements for linking production activities to sales orders, defining component requirements, suggesting planned production, reporting actual production, and reporting completions. This argues for a contingency approach to modeling and managing production activity.

This chapter uses an overall framework to explain management of production activities. Using the framework as an organizing focus, the chapter reviews the primary drivers of production activities and summarizes relevant information in the manufacturing database. It explains the primary coordination tools for executing production activities, the ways to track production status, and record completions. The chapter also examines common problems related to production activity control.

A Contingency Approach to Modeling Production Activities

A manufacturing enterprise typically has several types of production activities. The formulation of each S&OP game plan reflects consideration of these variations. As described Chapter 11 on sales and operations planning, these considerations include the type of product, its production strategy, and linkage between sales orders and supply orders. These considerations reflect a contingency approach to sales and operations planning. The contingency approach extends to modeling and managing production activities.

The set of activities to internally produce an item is typically represented by a manufacturing order (MO). Other terms, such as work order, shop order, or

Item Type	Type of Production & Linkage to Sales Order	Characteristics of Production Activities				
		Source of Mfg Info	Replenishment Method		Report Production Against	Report Completion
			Trigger	Quantity		
Custom Product / Direct	Custom Product MO	Config	Linked to SO	Linked to SO Quantity	MO	Issue From WIP
Standard Product / Direct	Final-Assembly MO	Bill and Routing	Linked to SO	Linked to SO Quantity	MO	Issue From WIP
Standard Product / Indirect	Normal MO	Bill and Routing	MRP	Calculated Planned Order	MO	Receive to Inventory
Standard Product / Indirect	Blanket MO	Bill and Routing	MRP	Calculated Group of Daily Schedules	Blanket MO	Receive to Inventory
Standard Product / Indirect	Kanban (No MO)	Bill and Routing	Kanban	Calculated based on Daily Usage	Item & Resource	Receive to Inventory

MO = Manufacturing Order   Config = Configuration
SO = Sales Order   WIP = Work-in-Process

Figure 17.1 A Contingency Approach to Modeling Production Activity

production order, may be used, but manufacturing order (and its abbreviation MO) will be used consistently for further explanations. Differing types of manufacturing orders are used to model different types of production activities, as shown in Figure 17.1.

The major types of production listed in Figure 17.1 include four order-based approaches and one orderless approach. Each approach has been labeled and reflects several considerations: the item type, the linkage to a sale orders (SO), the source of manufacturing information, the replenishment method, the nature of production reporting, and completion reporting. The types of production provide an organizing focus for further explanation. The types of production in Figure 17.1 represent an illustrative list. Other types of production are not shown, such as rework orders or Kanbans directly linked to SOs.

Manufacturing Order for a Custom Product Configuration

Production of a custom product configuration, using a custom product manufacturing order, is directly linked to a sales order. The sales order configuration defines the source of manufacturing information and the production quantity and date. Production activities can be reported against the manufacturing order. A completed configuration is typically shipped from work-in-process (WIP). It may be issued from WIP to the next-level MO in a multilevel configuration.

Manufacturing Order for a Standard Product

Production of a standard product uses the item's bill and routing as the source of manufacturing information. Production of a standard product can be directly linked to a sales order, just like a custom product. Alternatively, the production of a standard product can be indirectly linked to demands, so that a single manufacturing order covers multiple demands. Production may be driven by an order-based or orderless replenishment method. There are four basic variations to managing production of a standard product.

Final-Assembly Manufacturing Order   A final-assembly MO is directly linked to a sales order, so that changes in the sales order date and quantity affect the manufacturing order. A single manufacturing order covers only one demand.

Production activities can be reported against the manufacturing order. A completed parent item is typically shipped from WIP to the sales order. It may be issued from WIP to the next-level MO for multilevel linked orders.

Normal Manufacturing Order   A normal MO is indirectly linked to demands and may have multiple line items for different items. A single manufacturing order line item may cover multiple demands. In terms of replenishment method, MRP logic suggests a planned order with a production date and quantity to cover unmet demands. Order-point logic also results in a normal MO. Production activities can be reported against the manufacturing order line item. A completed parent item is received into inventory.

Blanket Manufacturing Order   A blanket MO is indirectly linked to demands and may have multiple line items for different items. A line item may have multiple delivery lines, each specifying a date and quantity. A blanket MO is conceptually similar to a blanket purchase order. Production activities and receipts (to inventory) can be reported against the blanket MO line item. A blanket MO serves different purposes, such as supporting rate-based scheduling, inventory management of customer-supplied material, and modeling Kanban completions.

- ◆ *Rate-Based Scheduling.* A blanket MO line item represents a group of daily schedules (or schedule identifier), and each day's quantity and date represents a predefined delivery line.
- ◆ *Customer-Supplied Material.* Inventory of customer-supplied material (to produce a parent item) can be linked to a blanket MO line item, with reported usage tied to delivery lines.

Kanban (No MO) A Kanban represents a visible signal to replenish inventory and provides an orderless approach to managing production. It is indirectly linked to demands. Production activities can be reported against the parent item (to trigger backflushing) and completions go into inventory. In some cases, Kanbans may be directly linked to sales orders for final-assembly purposes, and shipments represent completions.

A Framework for Production Activities

An overall framework for production activities applies to each type of production. Manufacturing orders (and Kanbans) are driven by S&OP game plans and by information in the manufacturing database. Each type of production requires coordination and execution, including the reporting of material and labor. Some require tracking of production status. Item completions (receipts) impact inventory and accounting. These represent five major areas in a framework for production activities, as shown in Figure 17.2, and provide the organizing focus for further explanation.

Details within each of the five major areas differ between order-based and orderless production activities. The primary drivers of production activities, the S&OP game plans, apply to both order-based and orderless environments.

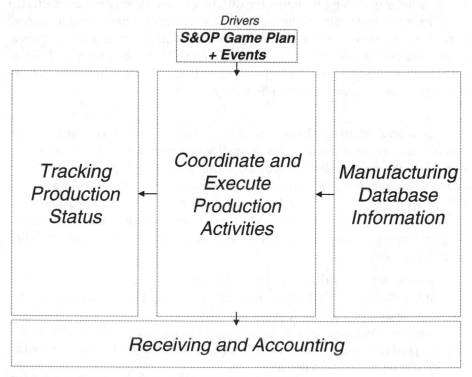

Figure 17.2 A Framework for Production Activities

Drivers of Production Activities

The S&OP game plans act as the primary drivers of production activities. Each S&OP game plan is typically expressed in terms of master schedules for the highest level of stocked items, and final-assembly schedules driven by sales orders. The significance of master schedule and final-assembly schedule varies by manufacturing environment in the types of manufacturing orders (and purchase orders) used.

- *Classic Job Shop Environment.* The master schedule consists of purchase orders, since only purchased material represents stocked items. The final-assembly schedule represents all production activities, and consists of custom product or final-assembly manufacturing orders with direct linkage to sales orders.
- *Make-to-Stock Standard Product Environment.* The master schedule consists of normal manufacturing orders for the saleable end-items. A final-assembly schedule does not apply.
- *Make-to-Order Standard Product Environment.* The master schedule consists of normal manufacturing orders (and purchase orders) for stocked components. The final-assembly schedule consists of final-assembly or normal manufacturing orders, depending on the need for linkage to sales orders.
- *Make-to-Order Custom Product Environment.* The master schedule consists of normal manufacturing orders (and purchase orders) for stocked components. The final-assembly schedule consists of custom product manufacturing orders with direct linkage to sales orders.
- *Orderless Standard Product Environments.* The master schedule consists of Kanbans for the highest stocking level in the product structure. A final-assembly schedule may apply, and may even be expressed by Kanbans.

An ERP system coordinates execution of production activities, and the coordination tools differ significantly between order-based and orderless environments.

- *Order-Based Coordination Tools.* An ERP system helps coordinate production activities using recommended planner actions, production schedules, and shop paperwork for manufacturing orders. In addition to the S&OP game plans, recommended planner actions are driven by events and time-based conditions. A sales order that results in overconsumption of availability, for example, serves as an event that requires planner attention. A past-due MO receipt reflects a time-based condition requiring planner attention.
- *Orderless Coordination Tools.* An ERP system helps coordinate production activities using Kanbans. Kanbans replace the order-based coordination tools, although some planner action messages still apply.

The ability to execute production activities in both order-based and orderless environments is directly impacted by the S&OP game plans.

Significance of Agreed-Upon S&OP Game Plans

The S&OP game plans can make or break production activities. The characteristics of a good S&OP game plan were described earlier (see Figure 11.9). In summary, a good S&OP game plan can be characterized by the complete identification of demands, consideration of constraints, realistic delivery promises, near-term schedule stability, a manageable number of exceptions requiring expediting, and execution of supply chain activities according to the plan. For example, production must assume that procurement works to the plan, and distribution must assume that production works to the plan. Sales order delivery promises assume that all areas work to the plan.

The significance of *agreed-upon* means that management understands and agrees with the resolution (and tradeoffs) of conflicting objectives expressed in the game plans. The lack of agreement and the corresponding commitment will ultimately destroy effective use of an ERP system to coordinate activities.

Coordinating and Executing Production Activities Using Kanbans

Kanbans coordinate orderless production activities of standard product items. The critical manufacturing database information focuses on the replenishment trigger and quantity for each item based on daily usage rates. As described earlier in Chapter 7 on item planning data, MRP logic can be used to calculate variable daily usage rates.

In an orderless environment, the minimum level of reporting involves parent item completions with component backflushing. Additional activities, such as resource time reporting, can be optionally reported against the resource and parent item. A time period, such as a day or week, provides the means to aggregate activities and costs. This results in a *period costing* approach to actual versus standard costs. Some ERP systems use a blanket manufacturing order to represent a time period, with line items defining items produced during the period. Each Kanban completion represents a delivery line.

Kanbans typically reflect indirect linkage to sales order demands. Kanbans may be directly linked to sales orders for final-assembly purposes. The final-assembly production schedule (identifying sales orders) serves as the basis for Kanbans. The minimum level of reporting involves sales order shipments from work-in-process with component backflushing.

Most firms involved with orderless manufacturing also require order-based approaches. These firms may be initiating JIT efforts, operating with both approaches, and/or have some activities (such as prototypes or configure-to-order products) that require an order-based approach.

Review of Manufacturing Database Information Relevant to Production

Information in the manufacturing database is critical for translating S&OP game plans into production schedules and recommended planner actions. This information was previously covered in chapters explaining how to structure the manufacturing database. As summarized here, the information represents six key elements in the framework for production activity: standard product planning data, custom product configuration data, bill of material and routing data, configuration bill data, resources, and employees.

Standard Product Planning Data

The critical planning data for each item includes the primary source, planner responsibility, item lead-time, replenishment method, and lot-sizing logic for suggested order quantities.

Primary Source An item's primary source of replenishment (make, subcontract, or buy) is reflected in the item's bill and costs, and serves as the basis for suggesting replenishment.

Planner Responsibility A planner field identifies the responsibility for replenishment of a make item, and provides the organizing focus for how ERP systems communicate the need to synchronize production activities. Suggestions about planned production inherit the item's planner, which can be overridden on a manufacturing order. In this way, ERP can direct recommended actions concerning existing orders to the relevant planners.

Item Lead-Time The lead-time for a make item represents an average elapsed time (in working days) to produce an average lot size under average load conditions. In some ERP systems, MRP logic may calculate a variable lead-time for a manufacturing order based on simplistic assumptions.

Replenishment Method The replenishment method for a standard product item is typically based on MRP logic. One variation involves MRP logic with rate-based scheduling to suggest a group of daily schedules. Another method involves order point logic. In all cases, replenishment is indirectly linked to sales order demand.

Some ERP systems support replenishment directly linked to sales order demand. This has been termed a final-assembly manufacturing order. One approach designates the need for direct linkage in the item master. The item designator, termed a final-assembly planning policy, means that a manufacturing order is only generated to cover a sales order demand. Other demands (such as forecasted demands) blow through the designated items.

Planning Policy The item's planning policy, such as normal or final assembly, determines whether MRP logic suggests a planned order to cover any demands or only demands related to sales orders.

Lot-Sizing Logic and Suggested Order Quantity Replenishment methods based on MRP logic typically identify the desired production frequency, expressed as the days of supply, to calculate a suggested order quantity. A planned order quantity covers all demands during the frequency interval, and may be subject to an item yield factor and modifiers for quantity minimum and multiples. MRP logic can also suggest a fixed quantity or a daily schedule to cover demands, or an order quantity triggered by order point logic.

Other Item Policies Other item policies affecting supply chain activities may include a usage policy (issue versus auto-deduct), order release policy (manual versus automatic) and yield factor.

Custom Product Configuration Data

The configuration data consists of a one-time item number (the configuration ID) and description, and a UM reflecting the custom product item. The planner and lead-time initially default to that of the custom product item and can be overridden.

Configuration Bill

A configuration's bill defines material and resource components. A material component may be designated as a phantom, and nonstock material components can be defined. Some ERP systems support custom product components, resulting in a multilevel configuration.

Standard Product Bill

A standard product's bill defines material and resource components, with component date effectivities. A material component may be designated as a phantom. Components in an order-dependent bill initially default to the item's bill, based on components that are in effect as of the manufacturing order start date. The order-dependent bill contains a phantom's components.

Resources and Employees

The resource master defines each type of resource performing internal operations and related costing, capacity, and scheduling data. It also defines external resources performing outside operations and related capacity and scheduling data.

The employee master defines individuals and pay rates. Average pay rates (tied to the resource labor pool) or individual pay rates may be used for charging labor time against manufacturing orders, and efficiencies calculated for individual employees.

Coordinating and Executing Production Activities

ERP systems provide three key tools for coordinating and executing production activities in an order-based environment: manufacturing orders, production schedules, and recommended planner actions. The manufacturing order's shop paperwork, the router/traveler and material pick list, provide additional tools to coordinate routing operations and inventory control. The production schedules reflect capacity planning and either manual or automatic scheduling. With long duration manufacturing orders, the production schedules need to reflect remaining work on existing orders based on reporting labor and resource usage and/or unit completions by operation.

A manufacturing order and its operations provide the basic building blocks that identify production activities. Therefore, they provide the logical starting point for explaining coordination tools.

Manufacturing Orders

A manufacturing order provides one of the primary means of communicating requirements to production. Different types of manufacturing orders model different types of production, and each type has an order life cycle. The shop paperwork for a released manufacturing order (a pick list of material and a router/traveler of operations) reflects the order-dependent bill, and provides additional coordination tools. The order-dependent bill may be modified to indicate material substitutions or alternate operations.

Material Components and the Pick List   MRP logic typically coordinates deliveries for components to produce a manufacturing order. As a precautionary measure, many planners verify component availability prior to MO release. This represents a logical kit pull and avoids problems associated with a physical kit pull. The planner can then make an informed decision about MO release when the logical kit pull identifies an anticipated material shortage. It must be emphasized that MRP logic has already identified the anticipated shortage, and communicated the need for expediting to the relevant planner or buyer via action messages. A pick list provides coordination of stockroom activities for picked components, and may also identify auto-deducted components for reference purposes.

Routing Operations and the Router/Traveler   A router/traveler of information about routing operations may or may not be required as a coordination tool.

Repetitive environments for standard products, for example, do not typically require a router/traveler. The router/traveler information may be available elsewhere (e.g., in electronic format), thereby reducing the need for accompanying paperwork.

The shop paperwork for a router/traveler is typically required for manufacturing a custom product configuration with unique routing requirements. It may also serve as a turnaround document to capture relevant production and quality information.

Capacity Planning

Capacity planning forms a key element in developing S&OP game plans, and making delivery promises, as explained earlier Chapter 11 on sales and operations planning. Capacity planning also represents a key coordination tool for production and provides the basis of realistic day-to-day production schedules.

An analysis of capacity requirements using infinite loading can identify overloaded periods for bottleneck resources. The courses of action based on infinite capacity planning were described earlier (see Figure 11.8). The desired result of infinite capacity planning is a reasonably realistic production schedule, where production personnel can work out the scheduling details. This represents a practical and simple approach to production schedules.

An analysis of capacity requirements may use finite loading to identify late or unscheduled manufacturing orders and to automatically calculate an optimal schedule. However, this requires implementation of APS (advanced planning and scheduling) capabilities. The advantages and disadvantages of implementing APS were described in Chapter 2.

Production Schedules

Production schedules coordinate production activities across multiple resources to meet scheduled MO completion dates. A production schedule, also termed a dispatch list or shop schedule, applies to each resource. It identifies manufacturing order operations in ascending sequence of priority, with the "hottest" operations listed first. Priority sequencing rules range from simple to complex. The most common and easily understood rule is based on operation due dates. A great advantage to using operation due dates is the automatic update based on changes to the manufacturing order quantity and/or scheduled completion date.

Production schedules can be expressed with a wide variety of formats. An example production schedule using a tabular format, shown in Figure 17.3, reflects sequencing based on operation due date, with ties broken by the MO due date.

The example production schedule in Figure 17.3 identifies individual operations, with information about each operation and its related manufacturing

Resource: Final-Assembly Work Center									Schedule as of Jan 11, 20XX	
	Manufacturing Order					Operation				
Operation Due Date	MO# & Line# Parent Item & Desc	Status	Order Qty	Due Date	SO Link Customer	Oper Seq	Units Completed	Remaining	Remaining Hours Setup	Run
Jan 10	1022 / 001 Product-XYZ	Released	280	Jan 12		20	180	100	n/a	3
Jan 11	1025 / 001 Assembly-100	Released	100	Jan 12		50	0	100	Complete	5
Jan 11	1025 / 002 Assembly-132	Released	100	Jan 15		30	0	100	1.5	12
Jan 12	FA222 / 001 FinalAssy-555	Open	80	Jan 15	GE	20	0	80	1.0	9
Jan 12	9822 / 001 Configuration	Hold	200	Jan 16	Allied	60	0	200	n/a	3
						Weekly Subtotal:			2.5	32
Jan 15	Product-STU	Planned	30	Jan 16		20	0	30	1.0	3
Jan 15	1043 / 001 Configuration 22-44L	Firm	200	Jan 17	Xerox	30	0	200	.5	10

Figure 17.3 An Example Production Schedule

order. Operation information includes the number of units completed (and remaining) and the remaining time. Information about manufacturing orders may identify the intended customer when direct linkage exists to the sales order. Direct linkage enables production to closely coordinate activities with shipping requirements for specific sequencing (such as truck loading).

The visibility of a production schedule depends on the environment, but typically covers at least a one-week horizon and includes planned, firm, and open manufacturing orders (in addition to released orders). Subtotals identify remaining work for a given time period, such as a week.

A production schedule may identify other information that proves useful to the planner or production personnel. This includes information about the prior operation and next operation, the operation UM for reporting unit completions, expected operation yield, the operation description, requirements for secondary resources, and so forth. Much of the information may be identified on the router/traveler, therefore minimizing the need for including it on the production schedule. The key concept is to provide a coordinating mechanism for each internal resource that correctly communicates requirements and responds to changes in requirements.

A second common format for a production schedule is a schedule board, maintained manually or electronically. An example schedule board, shown in

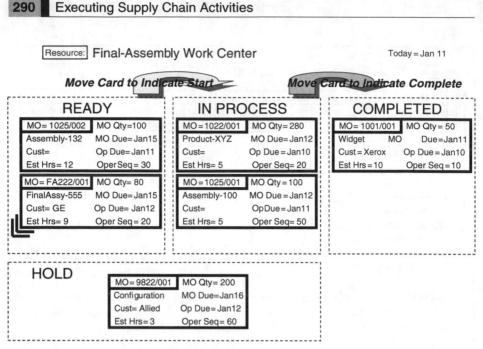

Figure 17.4 An Example Schedule Board

Figure 17.4, displays the same orders shown in the previous example. Each card or token represents a manufacturing order (rather than an operation). The schedule board identifies every resource. This example focuses on the final-assembly work center. Within a given resource, each card is placed (manually or via drag-and-drop) in the relevant area (ready, in process, completed, or on-hold) and moved to indicate start or completion. A ready card may come from the prior operation; a completed card may go to the next operation at another resource.

A third common format for a production schedule is a Gantt chart, maintained manually or electronically. An example Gantt chart, shown in Figure 17.5, displays the same orders shown in the previous examples. The Gantt chart displays sequencing of an order's operations across several work centers, using time periods along the horizontal axis. Each manufacturing order and its operations have their own color. The manufacturing order "1043/001," for example, has three operations: in the prep area (operation 10), the process line (20) and final assembly (30). The Gantt chart format does not typically include manufacturing orders placed on hold. The format can indicate parallel production in the same work center, illustrated in Figure 17.5 for the final-assembly work center.

Recommended Planner Actions

ERP systems communicate the impact of S&OP game plans on production activities using recommended planner actions. Recommended actions also reflect

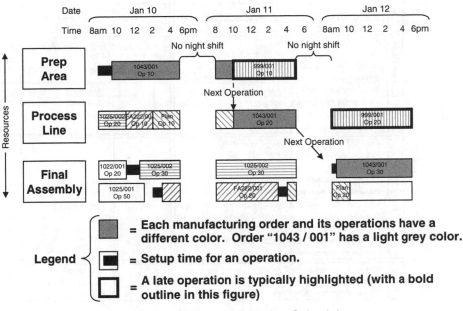

Figure 17.5 An Example Gantt Chart Production Schedule

events and elapsed time conditions that affect production activities. A sample of recommended planner actions are summarized in Figure 17.6. The planner responsible for item replenishment, or assigned to coordinate a given MO line item, provides the organizing focus for recommended action messages.

Some planner action messages only apply to standard product items, as indicated in Figure 17.6. This includes a message related to an item's replenishment based on order point logic, or related to an item's obsolete status. Some messages still apply to Kanban items.

Action messages driven by the S&OP game plans help coordinate production activities. The messages identify when to expedite and de-expedite orders, for example. Rescheduling an order later (de-expediting the order) can free up available capacity, and reduce WIP inventory if the order has not yet been released.

Message filters by planner can reduce the noise level of unnecessary messages. A planner's message filter may suppress a message entirely, and some messages have a basis for selective filtering, as shown in Figure 17.6. A "Release MO" message, for example, can be based on a look ahead window, so that the recommended action appears a number of days before the MO start date. The ability to auto-release orders may also be tied to the planner. The section on common problems related to production provides further suggestions for improving the usefulness of planner action messages.

Message Driver	Recommended Planner Action Message	Message Applies to		Message Filter
		Only Standard Product	Kanban Item	
S&OP Game Plans	Release manufacturing order			Look ahead days
	Release a delivery line within a blanket MO	x		Look ahead days
	Release MO based on order point logic	x		
	Release MO with unrealistic lead-time (planning fence)	x		
	Reschedule MO earlier (expedite)			Days early
	Reschedule MO later (de-expedite)			Days late
	Cancel existing MO	x		
	Reduce order quantity of existing MO	x		
Event	Print MO paperwork for a newly released MO			
	Review item with ATP exceeded by a sales order	x	x	
	Follow-up on MO that was received short			
	Review MO placed on hold (with reason code)			Reason code
	Review MO with projected late completion			Days late
	Close an MO based on suggested closure by receiving			Auto-close
	Cancel existing MO for item marked obsolete	x		
	Review existing MO because of bill changes	x		
	Review/define information for new item	x	x	
	Review information for item changed to make	x	x	
Time	Follow-up on expected MO receipt			Look ahead days
	Follow-up on past-due MO receipt			Look behind days
	Follow-up existing MO with past-due material picking	x		Look behind days

Figure 17.6 Illustrations of Planner Action Messages

Reporting Material Usage

The order-dependent bill defines the basis for a pick list and for reporting material usage. A material component can be issued or auto-deducted, typically on the basis of a component usage policy. Within the order-dependent bill, some components may be issued and others auto-deducted. Each approach offers several alternative means for reporting usage and different considerations.

Issued Components   The picking transaction can be manually entered or electronically entered via a data collection system (using various devices such as bar-code readers). A printed pick list may contain bar-code information. A picking transaction can be used to over- or underissue material, or return material to stock. It is especially applicable to lot- and serial-controlled items.

Most ERP systems limit picking transactions to components in the order-dependent bill, while some systems permit picking a nonauthorized component (with an automatic addition to the order-dependent bill).

Auto-Deducted Components   An auto-deduct or backflush transaction can be triggered by parent receipts and/or unit completions at pay-point operations. Backflushing logic deducts the theoretical issue quantity from inventory that is stocked in the component's backflush location. Auto-deducted material often consists of low-value, repetitive-usage, or bulky items.

Backflushing logic makes several assumptions about material usage. For example, it auto-deducts a material component on a prorated basis, even a per order component. It can optionally backflush component scrap based on component scrap percentages. It can optionally backflush lot-traced and serialized items on the basis of FIFO consumption. A reverse backflush transaction is also required. Over- and underissues must be reported via picking transactions, and some ERP systems require backflushing before reporting over- or underissues.

Reporting Labor and Resource Usage

The order-dependent routing defines the basis for a router/traveler. It also serves as the basis for reporting time and unit completions by operation. Reporting resource usage, in time and in unit completions, is critical when an operation's remaining work must be considered for scheduling, and when actual costs and operation yields are being tracked. Actual resource time and unit completions can be entered manually, or electronically entered via a data collection system (using various devices such as bar-code readers). The time reporting may come from a time and attendance system.

A resource's time can be issued or auto-deducted, typically on the basis of a resource usage policy. The concept of *issuing resources* (or *time reporting*) is symmetric to picking material components, without the requirement for inventory.

Reporting Time   Actual time can be reported via individual issue transactions, or the theoretical time can be auto-deducted based on unit completions reported for the operation or subsequent operations. Auto-deducted usage may also be triggered by parent item completions. Reporting actual time makes sense for some types of resources (such as a key machine or labor pool) and for certain conditions (such detailed cost data collection). Reported labor time can be costed on the basis of average pay rates or employee-specific pay rates. In many cases, the amount of time and effort expended on collecting and reconciling actual time far outweighs the benefits.

Reporting actual time may not make sense for resources such as manufacturing cells, since the operation's time requirements reflect the operating hours of the cell rather than individuals.

Reporting Unit Completions   An operation's unit completions can be treated as information only with no backflushing impact, or as a pay point that triggers backflushing of auto-deducted resources and material for the operation (and previous operations). The term *operation pay point* is often used to identify an operation that can trigger backflushing based on reported unit completions. The pay point policy should only apply to the primary resource for an operation.

Unit completions by operation can also be used to calculate remaining work, regardless of backflushing impact, for the purpose of production scheduling.

Tracking Production Status

The reporting of production activities can automatically update production status information. The typical measures of production status focus on the progress and costs of manufacturing orders, material shortages, and efficiency reports. ERP systems provide various ways to access and display this status information. For example, one approach uses an item's multilevel bill structure as the starting point to access progress information about supply orders for each component and to view progress-against-routing-operations data for each manufacturing order.

Manufacturing Order Progress

Progress associated with a manufacturing order has two measurements: receipts to-date versus order quantity, and progress against routing operations. The receipts to-date measurement applies to short-duration manufacturing orders, with elapsed production time in hours or days. The progress-against-operations measurement applies to long-duration manufacturing orders, with elapsed time in days or weeks. It also requires reporting time and/or unit completions by operation to provide meaningful measures of progress. The progress-against-operation measurements provide the basis for projecting an order completion date.

Manufacturing Order Costs

Actual costs associated with a manufacturing order can be viewed in three ways—total costs to-date, costs to-date by cost element, and costs to-date by component. Actual costs are based on reported material usage and resource usage and time, using either issue or backflush transactions or both. They may also reflect receipts of outside operations and by-products. Along with progress-against-routing measurements, actual costs to-date provide the basis for projecting costs (and variances) upon order completion.

Material Shortages

A material shortage represents the difference between actual component issues and the theoretical quantities in the order-dependent bill. Shortage reports have two basic variations: shortages by order and shortages by item. They represent a status report, since MRP logic communicates actual shortages as well as anticipated shortages via recommended action messages and schedules. An ERP system can also communicate the need for expedited processing of receipts (to cover actual shortages) at the time of receipt transactions.

Shortage reports are often treated as a key coordination tool when an ERP system ineffectively coordinates material requirements.

ERP DESIGN ISSUE

Interpretation of Material Shortage Reports

The definition of an actual material shortage is subject to various interpretations in an ERP system. A simple definition is the unpicked quantity for components of a released manufacturing order. This becomes confusing when there is a time delay between order release and order picking. The time delay may simply reflect elapsed time between order release and picking transactions. It becomes more complicated when some components involve delayed auto-deduction, or require delayed picking (caused by a component lead-time offset or materials linked to later operations). A component's unpicked quantity may even reflect a favorable material usage variance and not a shortage. Some ERP systems have attempted to overcome these gray areas with additional functionality, such as a pick complete order status. In most cases, the best and simplest approach depends on MRP logic to communicate time-phased material requirements.

Efficiency Reports

Efficiency reports compare actual time and unit completions against the theoretical times in the order-dependent routing. Efficiency reports have three basic variations summarizing information by employee, order, and resource. Each variation requires an audit report identifying detailed transaction history by time period.

ERP USAGE ISSUE

Usefulness of Efficiency Reports

Meaningful efficiency reports require comprehensive and accurate reporting of time and unit completions by operation, typically collected via a data collection system. In many cases, the amount of time and effort expended on collecting and reconciling actual time far outweighs the benefits. Witness the number of efficiency and audit reports that go unused, or provide minimal value-added to production activities. An equivalent effort expended on improving layout, reducing setup and breakdowns, analyzing and resetting operation time estimates, and other efficiency improvements would probably be more productive. The perceived need for collecting actual time, such as production of new standard products or poor routing information, can often be satisfied by a short-term "swat team" approach to collecting, analyzing, and resetting operation time estimates. This approach has a side benefit of focusing on improvements to efficiency, not just measuring it.

Receiving Activities Related to Production

Receiving activities reflect completion of parent items against manufacturing orders. However, the nature of receiving activities depends on the type of manufacturing order. This section reviews receiving activities in terms of three key elements. These elements consist of MO receipts, inspection, and manufacturing performance. Each element reflects differences in types of manufacturing orders.

Manufacturing Order Receipts

An MO receipt transaction serves several purposes. It signifies parent item completion, relieves work-in-process of components, measures MO progress, and provides the basis for closing an MO. MO receipts apply to by-products and tool returns related to an MO. Beyond this, the nature of receiving activities depends on the type of manufacturing order.

Normal MO   A normal MO line item can be received into inventory or inspection inventory.

Blanket MO   A blanket MO line item can also be received into inventory or inspection inventory. The receipt may reflect a predefined delivery line, or a delivery line created on the fly, depending on the use of a blanket manufacturing order.

Custom Product MO   A completed configuration is not typically received into an inventory location. It is typically shipped from WIP to the sales order. It may be issued to the next-level MO in a multilevel configuration. Both cases reflect an implicit MO receipt or completion.

Final-Assembly MO   A final-assembly MO can be received into inventory, since the parent is a standard product item, but this may break the direct linkage to the sales order. Alternatively, it may be shipped from WIP or issued to a next-level MO.

Inspection for Manufacturing Orders

Inspection for a manufacturing order is typically embedded in the routing, such as a routing operation performed by inspection resources. In some cases involving standard product items, however, the inspection operation should be modeled as a receipt to inspection inventory. This reflects a quarantine or holding period where inventory location must be specified, such as the fermentation period for alcoholic beverages in holding tanks. Receipts into inspection inventory apply to standard products. Inventory availability reflects the item's inspection lead-time. Dispositions by inspection are recorded as move or adjustment transactions.

Manufacturing Performance

Manufacturing performance can be measured by comparing actual costs to standard costs (for standard products) or estimated costs (for a configuration). Chapter 21 on cost accounting provides further explanation. Three other measures of manufacturing performance, delivery timeliness, quantity, and quality, are based on receipts.

Delivery Timeliness   Delivery timeliness can be measured by comparing the actual receipt dates against the due date assigned to an MO. Delivery tolerances, expressed as allowable days early or late, identify on-time performance. The measure is expressed as a percentage (divide the number of on-time receipts by the total number of receipts).

Delivery Quantity   Delivery quantity can be measured by comparing actual received quantities on the relevant due date against the MO order quantity. Delivery tolerances, expressed as allowable over or under quantities, identify correct quantity performance. The measure is expressed as a percentage (divide the number of correct quantity receipts by the total number of receipts).

Quality   One measure of quality performance compares the quantity rejected to the total received quantity for an MO line item. One method of identifying a rejected item is based on MO receipts placed into on-hold inventory with a reject reason code. This method becomes more complex when an item's quality problems, and ultimate rejection, are not recognized until well after the MO receipt. The material must be moved to on-hold status and relinked to the original MO line item to provide the basis for measuring quality performance.

Common Problems Related to Production Activity Control

The common problems include inflated lead-times, unrealistic lot-sizing logic, and handling scrap and rework. Other common problems involve scheduling without routing data and manually rekeyed schedule information. More serious problems involve the effectiveness of production schedules and planner action messages.

Inflated Lead-Times for Manufactured Items

Many planners use inflated item lead-times to provide greater visibility to production via released manufacturing orders. This approach typically results in large numbers of recommended planner actions for MO rescheduling. The early action to release orders may result in order-dependent bills that do not reflect up-to-date bill information. It may result in unnecessarily early requirements for material components, and a cascade effect on requirements for lower-level components. These impacts ultimately destroy the effectiveness of an ERP system for coordinating supply chain activities.

Use of realistic lead-times and planned orders embraces agile manufacturing concepts. Planned orders automatically realign supplies with demands, thereby avoiding unnecessary planner actions to reschedule orders.

Unrealistic Lot-Sizing Logic for Manufactured Items

Many planners use unrealistic lot-sizing logic that does not model their decision making. MRP logic generates planned orders that misrepresent anticipated production and communicate useless action messages. The planned orders have a cascade effect on requirements for lower-level components. Lot-sizing logic must reflect manufacturing considerations. These considerations include production frequency, quantity minimum and multiples, fixed order quantities, yields and possibly rate-based scheduling (with daily schedules).

Handling Scrap and Rework Related to a Manufacturing Order

Some manufacturing environments have significant scrap and rework issues. The nature of scrap and rework determines the appropriate solution approach. Several examples are summarized below.

- *Reusable Scrap.* Reusable scrap represents a by-product of a manufacturing order, often requiring a separate item number to differentiate the used material from new material.
- *Unusable Scrap Related to Setup.* The amount of material components that are scrapped during setup can be defined in the bill with per order quantities. Actual scrap can be recorded via picking transactions.
- *Scrap and Reworkable Scrap Related to a Completed End-Item.* The end-item can be received and then scrapped. Alternatively, a rework order can be created for reworkable end-item scrap, where the order-dependent bill must be manually defined (to build the item out of itself).
- *Rework Related to a Partially Completed End-Item.* This type of rework can be anticipated in a routing, typically with an additional operation. Actual rework time can be reported against the separate operation. In most cases, the partially completed item cannot be recognized in inventory because it lacks an item number.

Modeling some scrap and rework issues in an ERP system can become extremely complex, such as scrap related to a partially completed item. The general rule is to keep things simple. A solution approach should consider the cost accounting implications, the expected order receipts (for MRP logic purposes), component material usage, and remaining work for routing operations.

Scheduling without Routing Data

A production schedule normally reflects routing data: it lists manufacturing order operations performed at a given resource. Without routing data, a production schedule for final-assembly work centers may reflect the sales orders (and ship dates) segmented by an item attribute. The planner code for each item (and each MO) might be used to segment the final-assembly schedules.

The usefulness of a sales order ship schedule deteriorates when applied to the production of lower-level components. The planner code for each component item (and its MO) might be used to segment the production schedules for the relevant work centers. This provides a simple means to communicate production schedules without routing data.

Manually Rekeyed Schedule Information

Manually rekeyed production schedules provide an early-warning indicator of an ineffective ERP system. They generally reflect the informal system that has replaced the formal ERP system and a shortage report probably reflects a key coordination tool for materials.

In some cases, the ERP system provides effective production schedules but not in the desired format, such as a tabular, Gantt chart, or schedule board format. The desired format may involve user interaction, such as drag-and-drop capabilities. Further investigation may lead to workable solutions using supplemental applications to the ERP system that avoid manually rekeyed data.

Common Problems in Using Production Schedules

An ineffective production schedule can result from a number of factors. The most basic factor is that routing data does not model production activities. The second basic factor is that production personnel do not execute to the plan. They don't even start work according to the production schedule, but second-guess the schedule based on informal systems. A third basic factor involves long-duration manufacturing orders and the remaining work in production schedules. This requires feedback on actual production, such as parent receipts and unit completions at key operations. It does not necessarily require detailed time reporting by operation.

Effective production schedules are based on three assumptions. First, the S&OP game plans can be characterized as good. Second, the manufacturing database reflects the way products are built. Third, each resource works to their production schedule. The same three assumptions apply to the use of Kanbans for coordinating production activities.

Suggestions for improving the usefulness of production schedules parallel those for improving planner action messages.

Improving the Usefulness of Recommended Planner Action Messages

The usefulness of planner action messages provides a leading indicator of an ERP system's effectiveness. Several steps can be taken to improve message usefulness. The steps also result in better production schedules.

The first step focuses on global and continuous improvements within production. These include changes in factory layout, work simplification, lead-time reduction efforts (based on lead-time analysis), and quality improvements. Even small steps in simplifying the factory can make ERP systems easier to implement and use, since they do not have to model complex operations.

The second step focuses on improving S&OP game plans. The significance of an agreed-upon S&OP game plan becomes apparent in near-term schedule stability and realistic delivery promises. Exceptions requiring expediting can be reduced to a manageable level.

The third step focuses on the manufacturing database, since MRP logic uses it to translate S&OP game plans into production requirements. It must model supply chain activities completely and accurately in terms of information about items, bills, and configurations. This includes realistic lead-times and lot-sizing logic for manufactured items.

A fourth step involves using planned orders as much as possible to automatically align supplies with demands. This avoids unnecessary reschedule messages. Planned orders still provide visibility in production schedules. When necessary, orders may be firmed in advance of release so that up-to-date bill information can be used.

A fifth step involves creative use of planner codes, and the message filters associated with each planner code, to reduce the noise level in action messages. As a starting point, each scheduler should segment items (and manufacturing orders) within their responsibility into three ABC categories, and assign a planner ID to each category.

- The "A" category will contain critical problem items and new items. These require immediate attention. Applicable messages might include follow-up on anticipated deliveries and warnings about suggested replenishment of phase-out items. The "A" category does not typically reflect the accountant's version of ABC segmentation based on value.
- The "C" category represents items with few problems. Some messages do not apply, and message filters can be applied (such as tolerances for de-expedite messages).

An item or manufacturing order can be elevated (or demoted) in importance by assigning the appropriate planner ID. In this way, the scheduler can set appropriate message filters by planner ID and reduce the noise level of action messages. Other capabilities can reduce message volume, such as auto-releasing manufacturing orders for selected items.

Chapter 18

Distribution Management

The broad scope of distribution management covers the physical movement and storage of products in the supply chain. This includes inbound and outbound transportation, and multisite considerations such as interplant transfers and inventory deployment across the distribution network. It also includes inventory management within a distribution site.

A narrower scope of distribution management applies to a single-site manufacturing plant. It focuses on outbound transportation to customers and inbound transportation from suppliers. This chapter focuses on outbound shipments related to sales orders. This involves coordination of shipping activities to meet sales order requirements and execution of related activities such as packaging and transportation.

The basic types of shipping activities reflect differences in sales orders. A sales order can be for a standard or custom product, and a sales order can be directly linked to the supply order. This chapter provides a contingency approach and overall framework to basic shipping activities, and reviews some of the major variations in distribution management. It builds on information about sales order processing and inventory management covered in earlier chapters.

A Contingency Approach to Shipping Activities

Sales orders represent the dominant driver of outbound shipments in smaller manufacturing firms. Shipping activities differ when the sales order is for a standard product item versus a custom product configuration. An additional difference for standard products involves direct linkage between the sales order and supply order. This suggests three basic types of shipping activities driven by sales orders, as shown in Figure 18.1. There are differences in the source of item shipping information, the shipment source, allocations, and the nature of shipping variations.

The types of shipping activities driven by sales orders differ from those driven by purchase orders and transfer orders. These other types of shipping activities are included in Figure 18.1 (and briefly explained below) for illustrative purposes, but are outside the scope of this chapter.

Driver		Characteristics of Shipping Activities				
		Information Source	Shipment Source	Supply Order Linkage	Allocation or Staging	Other Variations
Sales Order	Standard Product	Item	Inventory	Indirect	Yes	Advanced Ship Notice (ASN) Kanbans Inventory Stocked at Customer Site
			WIP	Direct	No	Sequence Production for Truck Loading
	Custom Product	Configuration Sales Order Line Item	WIP	Direct	N/A	Packaging Options Special Order Parts
Purchase Order	Subcontract	Item's Bill of Supplied Material	Component Inventory	Indirect		Drop Ship Between Subcontractors Drop Ship Sales Order from Vendor
Transfer Order	Normal	Item	Inventory	Indirect		
	Subcontract	Item's Bill of Supplied Material	Component Inventory	Indirect		

Figure 18.1 A Contingency Approach to Shipping Activity

Shipping Activities Driven by Sales Orders

Sales orders drive three basic types of shipping activities, with several differences between each type.

- A sales order for a standard product is typically shipped from inventory. The item master defines shipping information such as weight or volume. One variation involves inventory staging or allocation; other variations involve advanced ship notices and Kanbans.
- A sales order for a standard product may be shipped from work-in-process (WIP) when it has direct linkage to the item's supply order. The direct linkage supports other shipping variations, such as sequencing production (based on visibility of sales orders) for truck loading purposes.
- A sales order for a custom product configuration is typically shipped from WIP, since it has direct linkage to the supply order. Shipping information must be specified for the configuration ID (the sales order line item) rather than using item master information. The concept of staging or allocation does not apply. The configuration may specify packaging options or special order components that affect shipping activities.

Shipping Activities Driven by Purchase Orders

A subcontract purchase order drives shipping activity to send supplied material to a vendor, as defined in the item's bill. The item master provides the source of some shipping information (e.g., component weight or volume). Components are shipped from inventory, and generally not staged or allocated. Variations include direct linkage between the sales order and a subcontract PO, drop-shipments between subcontractors, and drop-ship sales orders.

Other aspects of procurement require shipping activities, such as purchase orders for outside operations, subcontract purchase orders for a custom product configuration, and returns to vendor.

Shipping Activities Driven by Transfer Orders (in Multisite Operations)

A transfer order can be used to ship a standard product between sites in a multi-site operation. The two basic types of transfer orders, a normal and a subcontract transfer order, require different shipping activities. A normal transfer order involves shipping an item from one site to another. A subcontract transfer order involves shipping the supplied material components from one site to another, and a return shipment of the completed parent item. A move transaction between nearby sites does not require a shipment.

Some multisite operations use different ERP systems. Transfers can be modeled as a sales order (at one site) and a purchase order (at the other site).

Life Cycle of a Shipment for Sales Orders

A shipping transaction for a sales order serves several purposes. It reduces an item's inventory, and provides the basis for a packing list, invoicing, and closing a sales order line item. It may even provide the basis for backflushing components or relieving work-in-process for a custom product configuration. In a simple environment, a shipping transaction represents the completion of supply chain activities that started with a sales order. Other environments require further coordination of supply chain activities. A separate construct, a shipment, is frequently necessary to identity packaging and a bill of lading and to track the shipment through transportation to the ship-to location.

A shipment has a unique identifier and contains one or more sales order line items. It may contain items from multiple sales orders going to the same ship-to location (with the same carrier and freight payment method). It may optionally specify packaging. A transportation provider typically assigns a tracking number or other identifier to a shipment.

A shipment has a life cycle represented by a shipment status. A unique shipment identifier can be created upon the start of any shipment activity, such as recording packaging or shipping information, for a given sales order line item.

Once established, other sales order line items can be placed in the same shipment and the packaging information identified.

The shipment life cycle is different but related to the life cycle of sales orders placed in the shipment. The life cycles of sales orders and line items were covered earlier (see Figure 13.2). A sales order line item must be released for shipment prior to recording shipping and packaging information; it may be automatically closed after recording the quantity shipped. It may be manually closed when shipped short.

A shipment remains open so that other sales order line items may be placed in the shipment, until the shipment has been flagged as completed.

A shipment can optionally include packaging information. Each package is numbered, typically automatically. The contents of each package can be specified in terms of items and quantities. Each package can have a package type (such as box or carton), weight, volume, freight charge, value, and freight classification code (such as the National Motor Freight Classification codes). The packaging information provides the basis for a bill of lading, and the shipment identifier acts as the bill of lading number. A transportation provider typically assigns a tracking number (often termed a PRO number) to a shipment. Multiple shipments can be combined for freight forwarding purposes. This represents a consolidated shipment.

A Framework for Shipping Activities

An overall framework for shipping activities, shown in Figure 18.2, provides the organizing focus for further explanation. The framework emphasizes

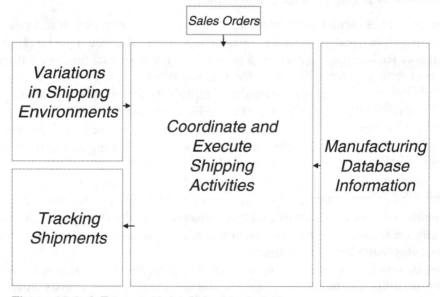

Figure 18.2 A Framework for Shipping Activities

coordination and execution of shipping activities related to sales orders and shipments.

The overall framework starts with sales orders that drive shipping activities. Shipping draws on information in the manufacturing database. Shipping action messages and ship schedules help coordinate shipping activities, where execution involves reporting the shipment and packaging information. Shipments can be tracked (and planned) through transportation providers. Several variations in shipping environments impact these activities.

Sales Order Requirements That Drive Shipping Activities

Shipping activities are driven by sales orders, where each line item identifies an item, a quantity, and ship date. The item may involve a custom product configuration. The assignment of realistic delivery promises reflects a key issue in sales order processing and the treatment of demands. Other issues include handling sales order changes, split deliveries to isolate expediting exceptions, cancelled and hold status, authorization for shipment, backorder quantities after partial shipments, and updating past-due ship dates. These issues, covered in Chapter 13 on sales order processing, can affect shipping activities.

Sales orders also identify other requirements that drive shipping activities. These include shipment, packaging or delivery instructions, special charges, special orders for nonstock items, and configuration components that specify packaging variations. A critical success factor involves the extent to which an ERP system explicitly defines these sales order requirements impacting supply chain activities.

Manufacturing Database Information Relevant to Shipping

Information in the manufacturing database supports several aspects of shipping activities. Much of the information was previously covered in the chapters on structuring the manufacturing database (Part 2), but can be summarized here. It represents four categories of information: standard product data, bills of material, custom product configuration data, and a configuration's bill.

Standard Product Data

Shipping information about standard products includes a primary stocking area, weight and volume, standard pack quantity, national motor freight code, and information about the customer item or catalog item. Other issues related to item data can impact shipping activities. These include revision level significance and unique item numbers to differentiate packaging variations. Correct handling of these issues can eliminate confusion in shipping.

Primary Stocking Area   An item's primary stocking area provides a means to segment the shipping schedule and recommended shipping actions. It supports a finished goods inventory segmented into zones for high volume shipping.

Weight and Volume   An item's weight and volume can be expressed per unit to support calculations of package weight and volume. It is often expressed per standard pack with a net and gross weight.

Standard Pack Quantity and UM   Some items are shipped in standard packs with a given UM (such as box or carton) and quantity per pack. It may be extended to a standard pallet quantity. It can be used to support automated packaging transactions within an ERP system to minimize manual data entry.

National Motor Freight Code   A National Motor Freight Code (or its equivalent) provides the basis for describing package contents on the bill of lading and packaging labels.

Other Identifiers   External paperwork such as packing lists can optionally identify the customer item or catalog item information rather than the internal item.

Standard Product Bill of Material

An item's bill of material may define the kit of parts for a sales order shipment. With direct linkage to a manufacturing order, a shipment from work-in-process may relieve work-in-process (and even backflush components) based on the order-dependent bill.

Custom Product Configuration Data

Shipping information about a configuration ID is specified in the sales order line item (rather than the item master). It includes the National Motor Freight Code, weight and volume, and customer item information.

Configuration's Bill of Material

A configuration's bill may serve several different purposes that impact shipping. The configuration's bill may:

- Specify packaging options for a sales order
- Specify special order components for shipment to the customer
- Define a kit of parts, where the parts may appear on packing lists

- ◆ Define user-selected options, where the selected options may appear on packing lists
- ◆ Define the basis for relieving WIP (and even backflushing components) when shipping items from work-in-process

The responses to a rules-based configurator typically define the configuration's bill and may provide critical information that should appear on packing lists.

Coordinate and Execute Shipping Activities

ERP systems provide three key tools for coordinating shipping activities: recommended shipping actions, a shipping schedule, and pick lists. In standard product environments, a shipment may be physically staged prior to shipment by moving material from its stocking location to shipping.

Shipment execution may simply involve recording the shipment of various sales order line items and generating a packing list for each sales order. It often involves packaging and generating package labels and a bill of lading for the shipment. Some environments enclose the invoice (or a pro forma invoice) with the shipment, while other environments send an invoice separately after shipment completion.

Recommended Shipping Actions

ERP systems communicate the impact of S&OP game plans on shipping activities using recommended shipping actions. Recommended actions reflect the primary drivers of shipping activities (sales orders) as well as warnings. A sample of recommended shipping messages is summarized in Figure 18.3.

Some recommended actions only apply to standard product items. Message filters by primary stocking area can reduce the noise of unnecessary messages. A message filter, for example, could be based on look-ahead days so that shipping can anticipate workloads, plan shipments, and arrange transportation.

Most shipping personnel segment their action messages to plan shipments and transportation. Sales order messages can be segmented by customer, customer ship-to, sales order number, carrier, ship date, or other characteristic. The shipping personnel, for example, might identify a subset of sales orders going out on a given carrier on a given date. The selected subset can then be used to print a consolidated pick list or a group of pick lists to prepare items for shipment.

Pick List

A pick list identifies the material to be shipped for a given sales order. It identifies the locations for finding the material, along with quantities (and lot or serial numbers if applicable). The locations may be displayed in a priority sequence based on location preferences or FIFO inventory.

Message Basis	Recommended Shipping Message	Message Filter
Sales Order	Ship sales order line item(s) released for shipment Print pick list for sales order	Look ahead days Look ahead days
Event	Stop shipping activity for order placed on hold Stop shipment activity for cancelled order Just received an item needed for immediate shipment Backflush error for component item of kit Automatic shipping resulted in problem Automatic packaging resulted in problem	
Elapsed Time	Review SO (or SO line item) with past due shipment Ship sales order line item(s) now due for shipment	Look ahead days

Figure 18.3 Illustrations of Shipping Action Messages

A consolidated pick list identifies the material to be shipped for multiple sales orders. It typically sorts items in location sequence to minimize efforts in picking material from stock.

Ship Schedule

A ship schedule consists of a subset of recommended action messages. It specifies the order line items requiring shipment. It may be segmented by item characteristics (such as primary shipping area) or order characteristics (such as customer, customer ship-to, carrier, and ship date) to coordinate shipping activities and plan shipments.

Shipment Staging

Some manufacturers of standard products will physically move material from the stocking area to the shipping area in preparation for shipments. The movement represents a hard-allocation to a given order and line item.

Execute a Shipment

Shipment execution may simply involve recording the shipment of various sales order line items and generating a packing list for each sales order. It often involves packaging and invoice creation.

Record Packaging and Print Labels An ERP system typically supports two approaches to packaging: standard pack and pick-and-pack. The standard pack approach only applies to standard products, using item master information as the basis for packaging. In the pick-and-pack approach, shipping personnel record the items placed in a given package (a box). They may be the same item, different items, and even items from different sales orders (to the same ship-to location). This defines package contents. A shipment may consist of one package or multiple packages.

A package can have a weight, volume, freight, value, and type (such as box, carton, or barrel). An ERP system can generate a package label for each package. Alternatively, an ERP system can be integrated with a freight application from a transportation provider such as UPS. The freight application can be used to weigh each package, automatically calculate freight charges based on the ship-to location, and generate a package label. Packaging information recorded in an ERP system provides the basis for a bill of lading.

A bill of lading generally accompanies each shipment. It reflects the shipment identifier and packages within a shipment. A standardized format typically applies to a bill of lading within the US transportation industry. The format includes the shipment identifier and information about the ship-from and ship-to locations, packages and weight, the carrier, and a tracking (PRO) number. It also includes instructions about collect-on-delivery (COD) and freight charges.

A consolidated bill of lading is often required for a freight-forwarder. Multiple shipments (to the same or different customers) can be consolidated into one large shipment for transportation to the freight-forwarding company. This company splits and delivers the individual shipments.

Record Shipment Each shipping transaction is recorded against a sales order line item. A shipping transaction can be reversed to indicate a correction. The shipping transactions serve multiple purposes. They reduce inventory, and provide the basis for packing lists, invoices, and closing sales order line items.

A packing list for a sales order summarizes the shipped versus ordered quantities for each line item, and identifies a shortfall as a backorder. The packing list may also identify the lot and serial numbers of shipped items, the components for a kit or custom product, text, and other information.

An invoice reflects shipping transactions and is closely tied to a sales order. The sales order defines the bill-to customer, prices, payment method, taxing authorities, and other relevant invoicing information. A sales order may have a single invoice (reflecting a complete shipment) or multiple invoices (reflecting multiple shipments). Multiple invoices are typically required when a sales order has line items with differing ship dates.

Tracking Shipments

Most smaller manufacturers use transportation providers (such as UPS) to track shipments. The transportation provider assigns a separate tracking number, termed a PRO number, to each shipment. This supplements ERP system capabilities in responding to shipment inquiries and tracking shipments.

A customer inquiry about shipment status typically centers on three basic questions: When will the sales order be shipped? What was shipped? Where is the shipment? An ERP system provides the basis for answering all three questions, typically using the tracking capabilities provided by transportation providers to answer the third question.

A shipment log summarizes every shipment during a specified time period. It includes information from the sales order and packing list (such as items shipped and backordered), as well as packaging information.

Shipping performance is normally measured by on-time shipping percentages across a given time period. On-time shipment can be measured for each sales order line item, using either the original promised ship date, the revised promised date, or the customer's requested date. Tolerances may be considered for days early or late and shipped versus ordered quantity. The measure may reflect individual line items or sales orders.

Variations in Shipping Environments

Manufacturers have a wide variety of shipping environments. Some of the variations include sales order allocations, Kanbans, and advanced ship notices (ASNs).

Sales Order Allocations

Sales order allocations represent a logical staging rather than a physical staging of inventory. From a sales viewpoint, an allocation may reflect customer requirements for a specific lot of material or a specific ship-from location. These allocations are typically assigned manually for individual sales orders at the time of order entry. Allocations must be correctly communicated to shipping personnel to ensure the correct inventory is sent to the customer.

Allocations serve a second purpose for distribution management. They reflect allocations of scarce inventory when demands exceed availability. Allocations are typically assigned automatically to a group of sales orders after order entry and prior to shipment. They are subject to user-definable allocation rules, such as customer priority. The set of allocations may be manually overridden or deallocated. The set of allocations (with manual overrides) may be used to automatically deduct inventory balances. This has been termed a *mass ship* transaction. Any mass update transaction requires feedback on errors, which can be provided by shipping action messages.

Mass Ship Transactions

High volume shipping environments frequently need to minimize transaction processing efforts. One approach uses automated packaging and shipping transactions, also termed mass ship transactions. Automated packaging applies to standard pack items, where an ERP system can make assumptions about packaging. With automated shipping, an ERP system assumes that all designated sales order line items were shipped. Any mass update transaction requires feedback on errors, which can be provided by shipping action messages.

Advanced Ship Notices and Bar-Code Labels

Advanced ship notices (ASN) and bar-coded shipping labels are an increasingly frequent requirement for many smaller manufacturers. Customers may specify that their shipments must have bar-coded shipping information labels, or advance ship notification, or both.

Bar-Coded Shipping Labels   Industry standards for bar-coded shipping labels have been established for the consumer product and automotive industries in the U.S. These reflect the Uniform Code Council (UCC) and Automotive Industry Action Group (AIAG) standards, respectively. A variety of other industry and proprietary standards are in use throughout the world.

Bar-coded shipping labels are typically used to identify packages (cartons) and pallets within a shipment. They include data elements about the shipment number, ship-to identifier and address, customer PO number, and contents (such as items and quantities). Additional references may be required by the customer to aid them in receiving and processing the materials.

Advanced Ship Notices (ASN)   An ASN can be as simple as sending a facsimile of the packing list and bill of lading to the customer at the time of shipment. An ASN is more commonly sent as an electronic (or EDI) transaction, with categories of information defined in a hierarchical format. The format standards typically reflect the ANSI X-12 856 Advance Ship Notice or the EDIFACT DESADV Dispatch Advice. The hierarchical format defines data about a shipment and its contents. The shipping approach determines whether items in a package are variable (the pick-and-pack approach) or fixed (the standard pack approach).

The ASN information includes several categories of information, as summarized in Figure 18.4. It includes basic data about the shipment number and customer PO number(s) included in the shipment. It includes content data about items (for the standard pack approach), or about pallets, cartons, and items within cartons (for the pick-and-pack approach). These represent the basic variations in hierarchical data structure; the details vary by customer.

Category of Information		Key Identifier	Typical Information
Basic Data	Shipment	Shipment Number	One for each shipment E.g., Carrier Total packages & weight Address information
	Order	Customer PO Number	One for each customer PO included in a shipment

Package Contents Unknown (Pallet, Carton, Item)   Package Contents are Known (Item + Optional Pallet/Carton)

Category of Information	Pick-and-Pack			Category of Information	Standard Pack		
	Key Identifier	Typical Information			Key Identifier	Typical Information	
Content Data — Tare	Pallet Label Number	One for each pallet e.g., weight of pallet Packages on pallet		Content Data — Item	Item Number	Item quantity per shipment Qty of pallets/cartons for item YTD cumulative qty for item	
Pack	Carton Label Number	One for every carton e.g., weight of carton		Tare	Optional Pallet Number	Summary of total pallets Weight of pallet	
Item	Item Number	Item quantity per carton		Pack	Optional Carton Number	Summary of total cartons	

Figure 18.4 Summary of ASN Information

Combination of ASN and Bar-Coded Labels   The combination of ASN and bar-coded labels enable customers to quickly process material receipts (via bar-code scanning) and then reconcile actual receipt information to what was expected (defined by the advanced ship notice information). The automation may provide additional benefits beyond speed and accuracy. ASN information about package measurements, for example, enables warehouse space to be preallocated for the expected receipt. Another example involves sending received material directly to the appropriate production area based on reference information.

Impact on ERP Systems   An ERP system may not support all data requirements for ASNs and bar-coded labels. These incremental data requirements may be stored in a supplemental database. The supplemental data may be captured when processing customer schedules, with additional data defined at time of shipment. The supplemental data can then be used to create bar-coded labels and advance ship notices. An alternative approach uses preprinted bar-code labels reflecting preassigned package quantities, and a preassigned label number. These are sometimes termed smart labels. The preassigned bar-coded label number is used to record packaging and shipping activities.

Chapter 19

Field Services

Field service provides a critical support function in some smaller manufacturers. A typical example involves a manufacturer that sells equipment and then performs installation and maintenance. Representative equipment includes computer products, communication systems, home appliances, and equipment for medical applications, the office, and the factory (such as robotics and numeric control machines). The nature of smaller firms generally means a limited amount of field service activity, although the market niche for some firms focuses entirely on field service rather than manufacturing.

The service call, or service work order, is the basic field service transaction.[1] A service call often involves installations, deinstallations, preventive maintenance or other scheduled activity. The required materials and resources for performing these types of field service activities can often be predefined. A service call may also represent an emergency situation that cannot be scheduled in advance. It often requires response times in hours and minutes, and required material and resources are difficult to predefine.

The service parts required for performing field service activities often represent a constraining factor. Too many service calls are not completed the first time because the right parts were not available. Service parts can be a large inventory investment. They tend to be slow moving, have short life cycles and highly variable demand, and have high carrying and obsolescence costs. The same parts may also be needed for production or for spare parts sold directly to customers. A smaller manufacturer may combine this inventory in a single site (the manufacturing plant) to minimize inventory investment. The use of overnight deliveries minimizes the impact on fast turnaround for emergency service calls.

The people resources required for performing field service activities can also be a constraining factor. These personnel often require advanced skill sets and experience. They cannot be easily hired and trained to meet overloaded situations, and extended periods of underutilization represents significant expense.

---

[1] Arthur V. Hill, *Field Service Management: An Integrated Approach to Increasing Customer Satisfaction,* Homewood, IL: Business One Irwin, 1993, pp. 63–68. Hill describes variations of service calls, and provides more detailed coverage of field service issues.

An ERP system can help anticipate requirements for materials and resources to perform field service tasks, whether they represent scheduled or emergency service calls. The use of S&OP game plans and a common manufacturing database can help coordinate and execute field service activities, and track status and costs. This chapter starts with an S&OP case study for an equipment manufacturer that performs field service installations. A summarized review builds on the previous explanations and highlights differences concerning sales order processing, production, and distribution.

CASE STUDY Field Services for Equipment Installation

An equipment manufacturer provides on-site equipment installations. Each equipment unit consists of a unique combination of features and options. Each installation is unique and requires a project manager and technician(s) to perform the installation tasks. The majority of installation activities represent predefined service tasks. Each service task identifies the required materials, operations, tools, and documents.

A sales order defines the configuration of anticipated service tasks to install an equipment unit. It also defines estimated time requirements for a project manager and technician. The configuration provides the basis for estimated costs and pricing, and the custom service work order is directly linked to the sales order.

The material and resource requirements must be anticipated prior to sales orders. The availability of skilled technicians and long lead-time materials are critical to customer service. With a planning bill, forecasted demands (for the number of equipment installations per month) can be translated into material and capacity requirements. The planning bill identifies the product mix percentages for service tasks. It may also define the average time requirements for a project manager and technician (expressed as a typical configuration quantity) to perform an installation. The planning bill uses component date effectivities to identify the introduction of new service tasks. The planning bill also supports option selection to configure the majority of service tasks.

Differences between Field Service and Production Activity Control

The coordination and execution of field service activities are very similar to production activity control. The symmetry between field service and production activities is reflected in the manufacturing database information, the primary coordination tools (orders, schedules, action messages, and capacity planning), the reporting of activities, and the tracking of status. Detailed explanations of these elements were provided in Chapter 17 on production activity control.

Differences between field service and production activities can be clarified and highlighted, as summarized below.

- The manufacturing database defines standard service tasks (or items), and the bill of materials and routing to perform each task. From a planning data viewpoint, these tasks can be directly linked to a sales order (a final assembly planning policy) and lot-sizing logic does not apply. The manufacturing database also defines custom service tasks (family items) that serve as the starting point for planning bills and configurations.
- Delivery schedules are similar to production schedules: they define responsibilities for performing service work orders. The responsibilities may be assigned to specific people or to labor pools.
- The order-dependent bill for a service work order defines the basis for a pick list, and issuing materials, tools, and documents to perform service tasks. The dynamic nature of service tasks frequently requires unanticipated materials (with usage reported after the fact) and returns of unused material. This means that picking transactions should not be limited to components in the order-dependent bill.
- Reporting the execution of field service activities often occurs after the fact. Most service work orders represent short-duration tasks for a quantity of one. This affects the nature of status reporting, such as tracking progress and material shortages.
- Tracking delivery performance of service work orders typically focuses on timeliness and quality. Quality measurements may be based on internal checklists and customer satisfaction questionnaires.
- The completion of a service work order represents a combination of production and distribution activities. Work order completion triggers generation of an invoice. An invoice often includes travel expenses for field service personnel.
- Recommended field service actions reflect the direct linkage between sales orders and work orders. They communicate the impact of sales orders and other exceptions (such as events or elapsed-time conditions) to the scheduler responsible for field service.

Variations in Field Service Environments

There are wide variations in field service environments, especially with larger companies. The nature of smaller manufacturers generally limits the scope and variations in field service. Two of the variations include tracking the configuration of installed units and remote inventory.

Some field service environments require bill of material information about an installed unit of equipment. Field service tasks for maintenance and upgrades result in changes to the unit's bill of material. These environments require a separate database containing the bill for each installed unit. The lot and/or serial numbers of components may need to be tracked, with warranty information tied to components rather than the entire unit.

Some environments require inventory stocked at field service locations. The location may be stationary (such as the field service office) or mobile (such as a van). This involves reporting inventory usage and replenishment mechanisms for service parts at the field service locations.

Chapter 20

Quality Management

The scope of quality management has evolved significantly with respect to an ERP system. The evolving scope partially stems from the emphasis on total quality management (TQM) and a continuously improving organization. The fundamental concepts and principles of TQM are the same as supply chain management. Both view the supply chain, from suppliers through manufacturing to customers, as part of a single interdependent system. Both emphasize the need for an integrated ERP system and work-flow processes for coordinating activities across the supply chain. A subset of criteria used in quality awards, such as the Malcolm Baldrige, Deming, and European Quality awards, focus on systematic approaches for improving company performance. These criteria include specifications for product and process design, business processes for managing internal and external production, and measures of performance (financial, operational, and supplier). An ERP system directly addresses these quality criteria.

Quality management has been impacted more recently by Six Sigma considerations. Many view Six Sigma Quality as an extension of TQM continuous improvement efforts that employ data-driven statistical analysis. It represents a problem solving technique to improve operations; other techniques include JIT and lean manufacturing strategies. From a managerial perspective, it emphasizes project-centered efforts that improve customer satisfaction and bottom-line results with rapid completions (3 to 6 months). Typical projects might focus on improving on-time delivery, supplier quality, purchased material costs, and manufacturing cycle times. An ERP system directly addresses these problems. In addition, an ERP reimplementation project (to improve operations) meets the Six Sigma criteria for impacting customers and the bottom line in a short time frame.

The practical implications of quality management in an ERP system are often skimmed over. Aspects of quality management are embedded throughout an ERP system, and do not necessarily manifest themselves as a standalone quality management module. The practical implications start with item master policies and how to structure the manufacturing database to reflect quality management concerns, and extend through other supply chain activities. The impact of quality concerns on an ERP system is best illustrated with a case study of a manufacturer in a highly regulated environment.

Other practical implications for an ERP system include the coordination of quality activities, structuring work-flow processes, the impact of ISO 9000 and other certification programs, and integration with specialized quality management applications. This chapter focuses on the practical implications of quality management in an ERP system, starting with macrolevel quality metrics.

Macrolevel Quality Metrics and an Effective ERP System

The concept of quality metrics forms the heart of Six Sigma and other quality philosophies. It can be extended to macrolevel quality metrics concerning the effectiveness of an ERP system. This has been termed process control charting at the 30,000-foot level, and reflects infrequent sampling to identify the big-picture capabilities of a system or process. Macrolevel metrics can be used to assess the effectiveness of a firm's ERP system.

Several ERP usage characteristics provide the basis for macrolevel metrics. Five usage characteristics have served as the organizing focus for explanations in this book. Figure 20.1 lists these five usage characteristics and examples of a macrolevel quality metric.

Quality Implications for an ERP System

Quality management concerns are embedded throughout an ERP system. They include item differentiation and enforcement of materials management policies, such as lot and serial control. They include quality factors in production processes, such as material scrap and operation yield percentages. The con-

Usage Characteristic	Examples of a Macrolevel Quality Metric
Does ERP define the way each product is *really used*?	How many exceptions in item planning data and bill and routing accuracy can be identified by comparing actual practices to data in the ERP system? Pick any three representative products.
Are the S&OP game plans realistic?	What percentage of current sales orders have realistic promised ship dates? What percentage of recently shipped products required expediting?
Do sales orders *explicitly define requirements* that impact supply chain activities?	How many requirements on a sales order are identified by text? How many sales orders are not configured correctly (including items, prices, configurations, etc)? Pick any ten sales orders.
Are schedules *actually used* to coordinate supply chain activities?	What percentage of purchase orders are initiated to meet requirements not specified by buyer action messages (or vendor schedule)? What percentage of manufacturing orders are started based on the production schedules? What percentage of sales orders are shipped according to the shipping schedule (reflecting promised ship dates)?
Does the system *update accounting correctly*?	What percentage of products (or configurations) have correct costs? Pick ten. How many hours are expended each accounting period to reconcile cost data from manufacturing?

Figure 20.1 Macrolevel Quality Metrics for an ERP System

cerns also include quality authorizations for changes to bills of material and routings.

Item Master Data Relevant to Quality

Item master information applies to almost every aspect of ERP systems, and represents a key control point for quality management. An item's lot control and serial control policies, for example, must be enforced in material transactions. Additions of new items, and changes to existing items, frequently require authorization by quality. These considerations are explained below.

Item Identifier   Problems in item identification often lead to quality problems. The need for differentiation often requires a unique item identifier, as described in Chapter 4. For example, unique item numbers can help differentiate stages of manufacturing and new versus used material. An item's revision level may or may not provide differentiation, depending on its significance in an ERP system.

Item Status   An item's status (preproduction, production, phase out, or obsolete) directly impacts allowable transactions in an ERP system. An item's status involves related issues, such as completing design specifications for new items and material use-up of old items.

Receiving Inspection Policy   Receiving inspection policies still apply to items while undertaking quality initiatives to reduce or eliminate inspection requirements. Inspection policies normally apply to a purchased or subcontracted item, since inspection for a manufactured item can be specified in a routing operation. In some cases, the inspection operation should be modeled as a receipt to inspection inventory. For example, this may reflect a quarantine or holding period.

An item's receiving inspection policy identifies whether a receipt must have 100 percent inspection, no inspection, or a statistical sample. The policy can be set by item, by vendor, or by vendor item to focus inspection efforts on problem areas. Inspection procedures for the item can be defined as a text object and subsequently viewed at the time of receiving inspection. Some ERP systems provide a special type of routing for purchased items that defines inspection operations. From a receiving inspection viewpoint, an item may undergo several receiving inspection steps prior to recognizing the item in inventory and available for usage.

Inspection Lead-Time   An item's inspection lead-time represents the average elapsed time between receipt into inspection and availability. It typically reflects the dock-to-stock activities or a quarantine period. In terms of MRP logic, the material will be available after the item's inspection lead-time (reflecting the quarantine period), and the quantity in inspection will be factored down by the item's expected yield percentage.

Expected Yield Percentage   An item's yield percentage represents the expected level of quality pertaining to supply orders and inspection inventory. MRP logic factors down the quantity of a scheduled receipt, and the quantity in inspection inventory, by the yield percentage. MRP logic will also inflate the quantity of a planned order by the yield percentage to ensure demands can be covered.

Item Lot Control Policy

Quality management requires lot control for regulated or high-risk products, such as medical devices, measuring and testing equipment, food and beverage products, and pharmaceutical products. A lot control policy mandates the specification of the item's lot number in reporting receipts, issues, and other supply-related transactions. Lot number assignment occurs upon receipt into inventory, although a lot number can be preassigned to a supply order. Purchased material can have a vendor lot number and an internal lot number, where multiple receipts of the same vendor lot can be differentiated by separate internal lot numbers.

Quality management may require fixed lot sizes in manufacturing orders, or batch-specific bills of material, to support stringent lot-trace requirements. Shelf life and retest periods (expressed in calendar days) can be used to suggest when an item's lots should be removed from available inventory or retested.

An ERP system automatically builds a lot-trace history (or genealogy) starting with receipt of a lot-traced item and ending with shipment. An item's lot receipts are tied to a supply order number, and lot usage is tied to a supply order or sales order number. Lot usage reflects a pick transaction or backflushing. An issued lot can be reverse issued for an order, and a received lot can be reverse received or returned to the vendor against a purchase order. In all three cases, an ERP system ensures lot integrity by validating that the reversed lot matches the original lot for the order. An item's lots may be combined, and a lot may be split.

Each transaction for lot-traced material builds a link in the chain of lot-trace history. Lot-trace history can be viewed from the top-down for a specified item, lot number, or order number. It can also be viewed from the bottom-up. A problem related to a specified sales order shipment, for example, can use the top-down viewpoint to identify component lots used to produce the item. Alternatively, a problem related to a specified lot of purchased material can use the bottom-up viewpoint to identify shipments (or supplies) of items that used the lot as a component.

A lot number of material can have multiple user-defined attributes serving quality and materials management purposes. Lot numbers differentiate supplies, and lot attributes (such as manufacturing date or potency) affect usage of supplies. A customer requirement, for example, may mandate specific lot attributes. The lot numbers provide a linking point to other quality management applications.

Item Serial Control Policy

Quality management may require serial control for selected items and their components. A serial control policy mandates the specification of a serial number for any supply-related transaction, with serial number assignment upon receipt. A serial control policy for make items may mandate manufacturing orders with a quantity of one to support stringent serial-trace requirements. Some ERP systems support serial number assignment after-the-fact, which relaxes the requirements of supply orders for one. There are several approaches to after-the-fact serial number assignment. One approach (the simplest approach) only assigns end-item serial numbers upon shipment. It may be augmented by after-the-fact assignment of serial numbers to serialized components. A second approach assigns serial numbers after parent item completion (and before shipment), with after-the-fact assignment of serial numbers to serialized components.

The history data for serial-traced items can be built upon receipt or after-the-fact. Just like lot-trace history, serial-trace history can be viewed from the top down for a specified item, serial number, or order number. It can also be viewed from the bottom up.

A serial number of a given item can have multiple user-defined attributes serving quality and materials management purposes. Serial numbers differentiate supplies, and attributes of a serial number may affect usage of supplies. The serial numbers provide a linking point to other quality management applications.

Serial control can serve several purposes. It may be used for managing engineering changes by end-item serial number or for validating a warranty period. Serial numbers of component items may be critical for field service upgrade purposes.

ECO Procedures and Quality Approval

Most firms require a standard procedure for adding new items and changing bills. The procedure ensures justification of a new item (e.g., to avoid creation of duplicate items), complete definition of critical information, and assignment of an item number. This standard procedure is typically referred to as an engineering change order (ECO) or engineering change notice (ECN) approval process.

Bills of Material

A bill of material identifies the required quantity of each material component and possibly the amount of planned scrap. The identification of planned scrap varies between the material-centric and operation-centric approaches to bills of material.

Changes to a bill of material, both one-time exceptions and planned changes, may require approval by quality. The planned changes may reflect continuous improvements in procedures (document components) or in scrap reduction.

Routing Operations and Resources

Resources related to quality management may reflect inspectors (a pooled resource) or an elapsed time requirement such as quarantine or burn-in (an infinite resource). Routing operations can identify requirements for quality-related resources and operation descriptions. Each routing operation may have a planned operation yield percentage, with a cumulative effect across multiple operations. Routing operations may include setup time and attributes (such as sequence-dependent setups) that can reduce scrap and improve operation yields. Routing operations may identify anticipated rework performed during work-in-process.

Changes to a routing, both one-time and planned, may require approval by quality. Planned changes may reflect continuous improvements in processing times, setup times, rework during work-in-process, operation yields, and factory layout.

Supply and Planning Data

Quality concerns may be reflected in planned supply orders, such as item yield percentages or fixed lot sizes (to satisfy stringent lot-trace requirements). A supply order may have a preassigned lot number for reporting quality data during work-in-process. Completed material placed into inspection requires disposition by quality management.

Quality is normally involved in identifying approved vendors. The development of a close supplier relationship can focus on quality at the source, leading to reduced reject rates and inspection requirements.

Product Costing

Quality factors can be included in product cost calculations. These factors include the item's yield percentage, component scrap percentages in the item's bill, and operation yield percentages in the item's routing. These three factors can also be excluded from a cost roll-up calculation, so that a cost comparison between sets of cost data (one with and one without quality factors) provides one cost of quality measurement.

Custom Product Configurations

Quality concerns can be built into the approaches for defining a custom product configuration. Option selection from a planning bill, for example, can reflect date effectivities of option availability and basic option selection rules. A rules-based configurator can provide a greater degree of quality management. The rules can ensure that the configured product meets the customer's application requiremnts, and reflects a valid and complete combination of options. Some rules-based configurators apply to managing ongoing changes related to a configuration. The initial definition of a configuration and its ongoing changes may or may not require an approval by quality.

Case Study: Impact of Quality Concerns on ERP in a Regulated Environment

A highly regulated environment, such as production of pharmaceutical products or medical devices, involves more stringent quality criteria. These quality criteria reflect good manufacturing practices and require compliance to regulations. As design specifications with appropriate test plans, the quality criteria provide the basis for a validation audit. In many cases, the validation audit must be performed retroactively against an existing ERP system. A validation audit for a given site provides written documented evidence that an ERP system will provide accurate, reliable, and consistent data, and is maintained under user control. A test failure requires written corrective action. It is the end-user's responsibility to provide this documentation, often with the professional assistance of the software vendor or other external consultant.

One example of a regulated product is a solid oral pharmaceutical product. Starting with various lot-controlled ingredients, a batch is mixed, made into tablets, and then packaged in a bottle with a label. Tablets are treated as phantoms, since production flows from the tablet machine immediately into packaging. There are several packaging variations.

The quality criteria in this regulated environment impact an ERP system in several ways. System security plays a larger role, and extends across the impacts on the manufacturing database, procurement, inventory transactions, production, and shipping.

Impact on System Security

System security can provide separation of responsibility by limiting the ability to update (versus query) data. The ability to add a sales order and customer, for example, may need to be separated. System security also involves an audit trail of every transaction affecting the ERP database and separate databases associated with supplementary applications. The transaction audit trail itself, typically an offline archive file with identification of what, when, and who, requires secure access. An electronic sign-off may be required before-the-fact to perform a transaction. An event manager may be used to identify unusual transactions after-the-fact, such as unauthorized users or larger-than-normal inventory adjustments.

Impact on Manufacturing Database

A lot-controlled item may have extended inspection requirements, a lot number mask, and user-defined lot attributes. The lot master and lot-trace genealogy require limited access to prevent falsification of data. Selected locations may be limited to a certain inventory status, such as the locations for receiving inspection or a material review board. Bills of material (and order-dependent bills) require limited access to enforce authorized changes.

Impact on Procurement

The quality management function defines an item's approved vendors. This often involves responsibility for vendor item information, quality specifications and inspection procedures. The approved vendors must be enforced upon PO creation for the item.

Impact on Inventory Transactions

Inventory disposition transactions must be limited to quality personnel. This typically requires limited access to inventory movement and adjustment transactions affecting item status. Strict label control is typically required, especially since mislabeling is a frequent cause for recalls. Label control starts with artwork, and extends all the way through 100 percent reconciliation of label inventory.

Impact on Production

The assignment of a manufacturing order or lot number often reflects an authorized *batch number.* The batch records associated with the batch number include electronic and paper-based information. The paper documents include labels from material components, shop paperwork with textual instructions and procedures, data collection on key variables and use of equipment, and written sign-offs. The electronic records typically focus on lot tracking and attributes of lots.

Quality testing may result in a *conditional release* of a given lot, such as a given batch. A conditional release typically reflects a delay in obtaining complete test results, such as a 7-day microbial test for a batch. Based on preliminary testing, the component's lot can be used in subsequent production activities and even packaged, but the end-item's lot cannot be shipped until the components' conditional releases have been cleared. This requires a review of the end-item's lot genealogy prior to shipment.

Impact on Distribution   Distribution personnel specify the lot numbers of end-items being shipped. Shipments should be prevented until all conditional releases have been cleared for the end-item and its components. Customer returns must be identified by lot number and placed on hold.

Coordination Tools in an ERP System for Quality Management Personnel

An ERP system can provide several coordination tools for quality management personnel. These include a production schedule for each quality-related resource, a dispatch list for dispositions of inspection inventory, and recommended actions for quality.

Production Schedule for a Quality-Related Resource

The production schedule identifies routing operations to be performed by the quality resource. The quality resource may include a labor pool of inspectors, a burn-in area, or other resource under quality management control. This may require time reporting (or unit completions by operation) to correctly reflect progress against the routing, availability for the next operation, backflushing, or actual costs.

Dispatch List for Dispositions of Inspection Inventory

The dispatch list identifies material placed into inspection or hold inventory. It may also identify the lot or serial numbers and the related supply order number. The disposition of inspected material typically involves an adjustment transaction to report scrap, or a move transaction, that must identify the applicable supply order (and lot or serial number).

A move transaction represents a logical move (from an in-inspection status to an on-hand or on-hold status) and possibly a physical movement to another location such as the stockroom. Dispositions of purchased material may involve returns to vendor.

Recommended Action Messages for Quality

Recommended action messages for quality include retesting lot-traced material based on the lot retest date, or removing lot-trace material based on the lot expiration date. Figure 20.2 provides further illustrations of recommended actions for quality management.

Work-Flow Processes and an ERP System

Quality management emphasizes work-flow processes across multiple functional areas, and documenting these processes. Each ERP system has an underlying or natural work flow. Many ERP software packages provide tools for user-

Recommended Quality Action Message	Message Filter
Review material placed in receiving inspection	Reason code
Review material placed on hold	Reason code
Perform retest on lot of material (based on retest date)	Look ahead days
Review lot of material based on lot expiration date	Look ahead days
Review manufacturing order with high scrap or low yield	Scrap percentage or value
Incomplete or missing data for item	Item attribute value
Incomplete or missing data for configuration	Configuration attribute value

Figure 20.2 Illustrations of Quality Management Action Messages

defined work flows, and for embedding the documentation of organizational procedures as context-sensitive help. Part of the user-defined work flows may also be embedded in a data collection system that prompts the user for specified information.

Upgrades to an ERP software package do not update the user-defined work flows and online organizational procedures. These must be updated separately to reflect new software package capabilities. The emphasis on continuous improvement translates into work flows and organizational procedures that reflect date effectivities, with ties to a specific software package release.

Impact of ISO 9000 and Other Certification Programs on an ERP System

An emerging trend affecting manufacturers involves a quality certification process. Purchasers are increasingly requesting certification from suppliers. One such certification option is registration of a manufacturer's quality system to ISO 9000 standards. ISO 9000 is a series of evolving standards used to document, implement, and demonstrate quality assurance systems. The standards are generic and enable a company to assure (by means of internal and external third-party audits) that it has a quality system in place that meets the published standard. Three of the five standards in the ISO 9000 series define different quality system models and deal with contractual obligations between buyer and seller.

The ISO 9000 standards have two key impacts on an ERP system. First, they involve documenting organizational procedures and work-flow processes, and ensuring the firm follows those processes and procedures. Second, they involve working to the game plans. An ERP system communicates the game plans across the company to provide accurate, reliable, and consistent information. It provides the logical framework for documenting procedures and work flows that can be incorporated directly into the system. The certification process involves a comparison between actual and documented procedures and work flows.

Integration of Specialized Quality Management Applications

Certificate of Analysis

Many regulated manufacturers require a certificate of analysis to accompany each shipment of lot-controlled material. It provides a statement that the product meets specifications and provides test results to prove it. A certificate of analysis typically contains some variable data that reflects the lots and lot attributes of the shipped material.

Material Safety Data Sheet

A material safety data sheet (MSDS) may also be required to accompany a shipment. It typically includes safe practices for handling material and other warnings. The MSDS generally contains fixed information pertaining to the end-item.

Statistical Process Control

A statistical process control (SPC) application provides a structured way to identify problems in order to improve performance. It involves identification of causes and effects of problems, with data collection and analysis to examine problems. Data may be reported in a variety of formats (graphs, histograms, Pareto charts) and tracked over time (control charts) to determine process variations. After making process changes, further data collection and reporting can highlight process improvements.

The key linkages between an ERP system and an SPC application typically focus on lot-traced material items or routing operations. Attributes of lot-traced material (or attributes of a routing operation) provide the basis for collecting data and SPC analysis.

Laboratory Information Management System

A laboratory information management system (LIMS) provides a separate database about materials. An LIMS application, for example, typically contains sample information about each lot. A physical sample may be retained for periodic stability tests. The key linkages between an ERP system and an LIMS application typically focus on lot numbers of lot-traced items.

Calibration Management

Some production environments have equipment requiring periodic calibration, such as scales and electronic testing equipment. A calibration management application identifies the equipment, schedules the calibrations, and records the calibration results. The key linkages between an ERP system and a calibration management application typically focus on preventive maintenance tasks that enforce use of calibrated equipment.

Part 6

Accounting and Reporting

Cost accounting forms one of the cornerstones for managing manufacturing operations. The best approach to cost accounting, such as standard costing or actual costing, depends on the situation. Standard costing with variances represents the most common approach for standard products manufacturers. It also addresses some of the difficulties associated with actual costing. The chapter on cost accounting (Chapter 21) reviews both methods.

Accounting applications fall outside the scope of this book. However, the chapter on cost accounting includes a summary of integration between manufacturing and accounting applications. It also includes a case study on interfacing an ERP system with a separate accounting system.

ERP systems support a wide variety of management reporting requirements. Not all requirements can be anticipated, so that user access to the ERP system database is critical. The chapter on management reporting (Chapter 22) provides a selective review of the basic reports and screens related to coordination, analysis and performance measurement of supply chain activities. It also provides illustrations of summarized management data across the enterprise, such as cash planning and an executive information system.

Chapter 21

Cost Accounting

The topic of cost accounting in manufacturing generally receives scant coverage. Yet product costing and cost accounting represent two aspects of managing manufacturing. The practical implications of cost accounting responsibilities have been covered in part by earlier chapters on developing product costs (Chapter 8) and estimating costs for custom product configurations (Chapter 9). This chapter focuses on cost accounting responsibilities for tracking actual costs, and valuing an item's inventory and cost of sales. It covers the practical implications of using a standard costing versus actual costing approach, and suggests contingencies on which approach works best.

Standard costing represents the dominant cost accounting approach used by manufacturers of standard products, with calculation of variances for each supply order. The variances highlight areas with good and bad performance. The standard costing approach avoids problems in actual costing, although actual costs can be calculated for comparison purposes using a separate set of cost data.

An actual costing approach generally applies to manufacturing a custom product configuration. The configuration's actual costs provide the basis for cost of sales and can be compared to its estimated costs. A custom product manufacturer, however, has standard purchased materials (and even standardized manufactured items) where a standard costing approach should be used. There are also situations where a configuration's planned cost (rather than its actual cost) should be used as the basis for cost of sales.

This chapter reviews the use of standard costing and actual costing for standard products, and covers actual costing for custom product configurations. It highlights problems with each approach. The chapter also covers the integration between an ERP system and general accounting applications.

Standard Costs and Variances

An item's standard cost reflects its primary source (make, buy, and subcontract) and provides the baseline for meaningful interpretation of variances. The concepts of standard costing and a frozen period were covered earlier in the chapter on product costing. Variances represent the difference between an item's standard cost and the actual costs incurred on a supply order. Variances apply to each type of supply order: manufacturing order, purchase order, and subcontract purchase order.

Variances also apply to a group of daily schedules (a schedule ID or blanket MO line item), a rework order, and even a logical period (for period costing purposes in orderless environments).

Variances Related to a Manufacturing Order for a Make Item

A manufacturing order line item (or a group of daily schedules) represents a single entity for variance calculation purposes. The total variance related to a manufacturing order for a make item can be segmented. One approach to segmentation reflects the baseline of standard costs and three different levels of comparison. These levels of comparison and identification of variances, illustrated in Figure 21.1, are summarized below.

The total variance for a given manufacturing order is graphically represented in Figure 21.1 as the distance between two lines: one line represents the parent item's frozen standard cost and the other line represents actual costs for the manufacturing order. The difference (distance) between frozen and actual involves two other levels of comparison. These are termed the *released standard cost* and *current planned cost*. These four different levels provide the basis for segmenting variances.

Frozen Standard Cost   The frozen standard cost for a make item reflects its bill as of a given point in time. For explanatory purposes, we will focus on a 12-month frozen period (starting January 1) with a cost roll-up calculation as of

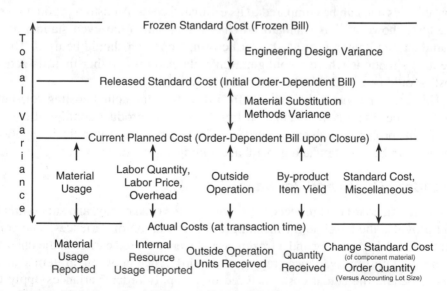

Figure 21.1 Standard Costs and Variances

January 1. The cost roll-up calculation retains the basis of its calculations, sometimes termed the *frozen bill.*

Released Standard Cost   The released standard cost reflects the initial order-dependent bill. The initial order-dependent bill consists of the item's components, such as material and resources, in effect as of the manufacturing order start date (say March 1). Differences between the initial order-dependent bill and the frozen bill reflect planned engineering changes defined by component effectivity dates. Differences may also stem from corrections to item information (such as item yield percent) and component information (such as corrections to component quantity). The value of these differences is termed an *engineering design variance.*

Current Planned Cost   The current planned costs reflect the order-dependent bill and the supply order quantity upon order closure. Changes to the initial order-dependent bill reflect additions and deletions of material components and routing operations, and other changes (such as the required component quantity). The values of these differences can be termed *material substitution variance* and *methods variance,* respectively.

Actual Costs   Actual costs for a manufacturing order reflect the reporting of production activities and the costs at transaction time. Differences between the current planned cost and actual costs can be segmented into several variances.

♦ *Material Usage Variance.* The reported material usage differs from the order-dependent bill.

♦ *Labor Quantity, Labor Price, and Overhead Variances.* The reported internal resource time differs from the order-dependent bill in terms of hours or hourly rate, where labor and/or overhead costs are tied to the resource.

♦ *Outside Operation Variance.* The reported receipts of the outside operation differ from the expected quantity in the order-dependent bill.

♦ *By-product Variance.* The reported receipts of good by-products differ from the expected receipts for the supply order.

♦ *Item Yield Variance.* The reported receipts of good parent items differ from the expected receipts (the manufacturing order quantity factored by the item yield percentage).

♦ *Standard Cost Variance.* The standard cost of a material component at the time of reported usage differs from the cost at time of order closure, reflecting a change in standard costs.

♦ *Miscellaneous Variance.* Additional variances can be calculated. For example, a difference between the manufacturing order quantity and the item's accounting lot size will change the amortization of per order costs. These are termed miscellaneous variances.

Backflushing components in the order-dependent bill minimizes the type of variances between actual costs and current planned costs. However, some variances may still apply, such as standard cost, yield, by-product, and miscellaneous variances. The key concepts of standard costing are that an item's standard cost plus variances equals its actual cost, and that variances can highlight problem areas in the supply chain activities.

Variances are typically calculated as part of an order closure process after order completion. However, variances can only be calculated when a manufacturing order satisfies cost accounting closure criteria. These closure criteria may include a wait period (after reporting order completion), dispositions of material in inspection, complete reporting of by-products and customer-supplied material, and tolerances on usage variances.

CASE STUDY   Cost Accounting Problems with Standard Costs

Difficulties with a standard costing approach may stem from system usage and system design, as illustrated in one firm's experience with manufacturing order variances. Difficulties in system usage reflected four common errors:

◆ Continuous updates to frozen standard costs for existing items were caused by daily cost roll-up calculations, resulting in a changing baseline for measuring variances.

◆ Manually maintained costs for a manufactured item were used as the frozen standard cost, resulting in a meaningless baseline for measuring variances.

◆ The order-dependent bill for a new manufactured item often reflected incomplete bills and routings (and phantoms with incomplete bills), resulting in a meaningless baseline for released standard costs. Meanwhile, the new item's frozen standard cost was continuously updated based on the latest bill.

◆ Variances were not calculated for completed manufacturing orders for several months after system implementation (due to lack of user understanding). The resulting variances were difficult to interpret (due to the above mentioned factors). Closure criteria often meant that variances could not be calculated; incorrect reporting on disposition of inspection inventory prevented closure.

Difficulties in usage were compounded by the ERP system design. The ERP system did not retain historical variance data; it generated a one-time hard-copy variance report at time of closure. The hard-copy variance report did not provide sufficient detail to clearly analyze the source of variances. Some of the resulting variances were combined for general ledger posting purposes, making it difficult for meaningful segmentation of material, labor, and overhead-related variances in the general ledger.

Variances Related to a Purchase Order for a Buy Item

The purchase price variance for a buy item represents the difference between the item's standard cost (for value-added material) and the PO purchase price at time of receipt. A second purchase price variance may be identified (during accounts payable invoice entry) when the vendor invoice price differs from the PO purchase price.

Note: A purchase price variance also applies to an outside operation PO, where the routing operation defines the standard cost.

Variances Related to a Subcontract PO for a Subcontract Item

A subcontract PO represents a combination purchase order and manufacturing order. The purchase price variance for a subcontract item represents the difference between the item's standard cost (for value-added subcontracting) and the PO purchase price at time of receipt. Most of the variances related to a manufacturing order also apply to a subcontract PO. The variances related to resource components (methods variance, labor quantity/price and overhead variances, outside operation variance) do not apply.

Variances Related to a Rework Manufacturing Order

A rework manufacturing order has a user-defined order-dependent bill defining the current planned costs, so that variances only identify differences with actual costs. The other variances do not apply.

Variances and Mixed Supply Orders

Additional complexities in variance analysis occur when a supply order does not represent an item's primary source. A purchase order to buy a complete make item for example, has a purchase price that must be compared to the item's total rolled cost (rather than to value-added material) to calculate a purchase price variance. A full explanation of these additional complexities is considered outside the scope of this book.

Historical Variances and Supply Orders

The calculated variances for each closed manufacturing order provide the basis for historical variance analysis. The historical data can be viewed by parent item, type of variance, or component, where the component could be material, by-product, machine resource, or labor pool. The same historical data can be retained for subcontract purchase orders. Many ERP systems delete closed manufacturing orders (based on data retention policies) to "clean up" the database, which argues for a separate database of closed orders and their variances.

The historical analysis of purchase price variances, related to a purchase order, subcontract PO, and outside operation PO, is also valuable. Many ERP systems delete closed purchase orders (based on data retention policies) to clean up the database, which also argues for a separate database of closed orders and their variances. This data is sometimes retained in accounts payable.

Recommended Action Messages for Cost Accounting

Variances provide one foundation for communicating recommended actions to cost accounting. Projected variances can identify projected cost overruns in a manufacturing order for a standard product. Actual variances (calculated after order closure) may also require follow-up activities by cost accounting. These represent recommended action messages for cost accounting, as illustrated in Figure 21.2.

Actual Costing for Standard Products

Actual costing is a broad term that encompasses several methods, such as last actual cost and average actual costs. Supply orders provide the basis for updating actual costs regardless of method. For example, actual costs can be updated based upon PO price (at time of order receipt) for a normal purchase order, and the total manufacturing cost (at time of order closure) for a normal manufacturing order.

One approach to actual costing for standard products uses a separate set of cost data; the set of cost data for frozen standard costs is still used for valuing inventory transactions. The separate set of actual cost data is updated based on supply orders, while frozen standard costs are used to calculate variances. This approach supports comparisons between standard and actual costs.

A second approach updates the set of cost data used for valuing inventory transactions; it replaces the use of frozen standard costs. As a general guideline, standard costs provide a more reliable means of inventory valuation because of problems in actual costing.

Recommended Cost Accounting Action Message	Message Filter
Review manufacturing order with projected cost overruns (variances)	Allowed variance percent or value
Review manufacturing order with actual variances	Allowed variance percent or value
Review custom product MO with projected cost overrun	Allowed percent or value
Review manufacturing order that cannot be closed	
Review cost estimate for custom product configuration	Configuration attribute value
Review sales order configuration with insufficient profitability	Profit percent or value
Incomplete or missing cost data for new item	Item attribute value

Figure 21.2 Illustrations of Cost Accounting Action Messages

Problems in Actual Costing

Recognizing actual costs upon order closure ensures that all activities have been reported against a manufacturing order, and provides the simplest calculation logic. In the same way, use of the PO price on a normal purchase order (rather than waiting for an invoice) provides the simplest calculation logic. The delay involved in waiting for a vendor's invoice, or in waiting for order closure, creates problems when the item gets used immediately. Any approach to "chase down" actual item usage (possibly through multiple bill levels) and apply actual costs becomes extremely complex.

Recognizing actual costs upon receipt of a manufacturing order involves timely transaction reporting and many assumptions, and requires more complex calculation logic. It has perceived advantages in avoiding delay problems, but typically becomes too complex to implement effectively.

Regardless of whether actual costs are recognized upon order receipt or closure, additional complexities are introduced when an item's replenishment involves different types of supply orders. For example, a purchase order, a manufacturing order, and a rework order for the same item would result in updating different cost elements for the same item.

Illustrations of Actual Costing Methods

Two actual costing methods, last actual cost and average actual costs, can be represented by a separate set of cost data. In a third method, actual cost by lot, actual costs are carried on the inventory record rather than as a separate set of cost data. These methods are summarized below.

Last Actual Cost   The last actual cost method takes a simplified approach. It uses the PO price (upon receipt) for a buy item, total manufacturing costs (upon closure) for a make item, and PO price plus material costs for a subcontract item (upon order closure). It ignores other supply orders that do not match the item's primary source, and always ignores a rework order. By definition, it ignores existing inventory. A separate set of cost data can be automatically updated by the last actual cost.

Average Actual Cost   The average actual cost method typically requires consideration of existing inventory to calculate an average cost. When material is used immediately after receipt, delays in recognizing actual costs (until order closure) mean that its calculated actual cost is inaccurate. In addition, a small amount of existing inventory can result in calculating an inflated (or deflated) average item cost. Use of different supply orders for the same item can also result in unusual actual costs (by cost element).

Actual Costing by Lot   Actual costs by lot requires a lot number assigned to each receipt, with actual costs carried on the inventory record rather than as a separate set of cost data. A given lot can only be associated with a single supply order, and has one actual cost. This eliminates the need to perform average costing (with existing inventory), and supports a mix of supply orders for an item. However, the delay involved in waiting for order closure creates problems when a manufactured item is used immediately.

Two of the actual costing methods, last actual and average actual, can be represented by separate sets of cost data. Hence, a cost comparison can be made between actual costs and standard costs, and costed bills can be viewed with one of the cost types.

Using Standard Costs Versus Actual Costs

An item's standard cost plus variances equals its actual cost for each supply order. The vast majority of manufacturers involved with any type of standard product (purchased and manufactured) can benefit from standard costing, since it highlights variances and potential problem areas in supply chain activities. It also avoids the typical problems in actual costing: valuing inventory before order closure, averaging costs (upon order closure) across a small amount of existing inventory, handling different types of supply orders for the same item, and increasing levels of system complexity. A separate set of cost data for actual costs, such as last actual or average actual, does provide benefits in terms of comparisons and development of the next period standard costs.

Custom product manufacturers, on the other hand, typically require a combination of standard and actual costing. Standard costing applies to the standardized purchased and manufactured components. Actual costing applies to one-time components and each custom product configuration.

Actual Costs for a Custom Product Configuration

The supply order for a configuration provides the basis for collecting actual costs, where actual costs reflect reporting of actual supply chain activities.

Actual Costs for a Custom Product Manufacturing Order

The calculation of actual costs reflects reported labor time, usage of material components, and other components. The significance of actual costs depends on the type of component in a configuration.

Material Components   Actual costs for a material component are calculated as the reported usage quantity times its standard cost (at the time of reported usage). Backflushing can auto-deduct the material's theoretical usage quantity.

Actual costs for by-product material (e.g., designated as a by-product component) are calculated as the total quantity received times its standard cost and are subtracted from the configuration's total cost.

Internal Operations Actual costs for an internal operation reflect the actual reported time at the primary resource and optional secondary resources. For each resource involved in an internal operation, actual costs can be based on the standard labor and overhead rates (at the time of reported usage). Labor transactions, on the other hand, can be valued based on the person's actual pay rate (at the time of reported usage) or the average rate for the labor grade.

Outside Operations Actual costs for an outside operation are calculated as the quantity received times the purchase cost (at the time of reported receipt).

Nonstock Material Purchases Actual costs for a configuration's nonstock material components are calculated as the quantity received times the purchase cost (at the time of reported receipt).

Custom Product Components Actual costs for a make component that is also a configuration can be based on two different approaches. A configuration's actual costs can reflect all reported activity, or just the configuration's planned cost. Difficulties arise in actual costing when some activities have not been completely reported against the configuration's supply order. In particular, usage (or partial usage) may occur prior to complete reporting for all components.

Actual Costs for a Custom Product Purchase Order

Actual costs for a custom product purchase order are calculated as the quantity received times the purchase cost (at the time of reported receipt).

Actual Costs for a Custom Product Subcontract PO

Actual costs for a custom product subcontract PO are calculated as the quantity received times the purchase cost (at the time of reported receipt), plus the actual costs for the components. Actual costs for components were described above (for a custom product manufacturing order).

Problems in Actual Costing for Configurations

Difficulties arise in actual costing when some activities have not been completely reported against a custom product manufacturing order. The configuration may need to be used or shipped before all activities are reported. Recognizing actual costs at time of shipment involves timely and complete transaction reporting, and partial shipments create additional complexities.

Partial shipments may involve assumptions about how to calculate projected actual costs based on the yet-to-be-reported activities.

One alternative to actual costing uses the configuration's planned costs to value cost of sales at time of shipment, with variances between actual and planned costs calculated at the time of order closure.

ERP and General Accounting Applications

General accounting applications include the general ledger, payables, receivables, payroll, and fixed assets. This section highlights the manufacturing transactions that impact these general accounting applications.

Integration with General Ledger

Numerous manufacturing transactions impact the general ledger. These transactions include PO receipts and returns, subcontract PO issues and receipts, outside operation PO receipts, MO issues and receipts, custom product MO issues and completions, variance calculations upon order closure, sales order shipments, returned goods, inventory adjustments, and changes to standard costs.

Integration with Payables

Information about purchase order receipts, reverse receipts, and dispositions by receiving inspection are passed to payables for matching accounts payable invoices to receipts. Returns to vendor may also result in debit memos.

Integration with Receivables

Information about sales order shipments, reverse shipments, and customer returns are passed to receivables for generating invoices (and credit memos).

Integration with Payroll and Human Resources

Information about labor time expended on internal operations may be captured in a variety of ways. A time and attendance system, for example, supports audits and reconciliation of each employee's actual time prior to updating the ERP database and payroll database. Alternatively, two separate streams of data may be collected: summarized data for payroll purposes and detailed data (by operation) for manufacturing order purposes. The payroll information can be used to update the general ledger on a periodic basis.

Integration with Fixed Assets

A purchase order for a piece of capital equipment may update a fixed assets application upon PO receipt. The depreciation schedules can be used to update the general ledger on a periodic basis.

Interfacing an ERP System with an Accounting System

Some manufacturers require an interface between their ERP system and a separate accounting application. The rationale for a separate accounting application varies widely. For example, the separate accounting application may be a corporate mandate, it may handle country-specific accounting requirements, or it may be a legacy system.

An interface involves synchronization of master file information, such as customers, vendors, and general ledger accounts. Other information residing in both systems, such as tax codes and payment methods, may also require synchronization. Synchronization of data may be done manually or electronically.

An interface also involves one-way communication (from the ERP system to the separate accounting application) of costed manufacturing transactions to the general ledger, purchase order receipts and returns to payables, and sales order shipments and returns to receivables.

Several factors can complicate the interface between the two systems. First, the master file information in each system may not have a one-to-one mapping. The customer master in one system, for example, may have capabilities (such as a hierarchy of customers or currency conversion) that have no equivalent in the other system. Second, the one-way communication can become convoluted or complex. For example, some accounting applications require complete replication of the purchase order information to support payables.

Chapter 22

Management Reporting

The management reports associated with an ERP system cover a wide spectrum of functional area and company-wide requirements. Many ERP systems have hundreds of predefined reports and inquiry screens. For the accounting functions, there are many agreed-upon standards for financial statements, cost and variance reports, budget reports, aged statements, and account inquiry screens. The reports and inquiry screens for other functions, such as sales and operations, have some generally agreed-upon basic requirements, but often require tailoring.

The basic reports and inquiries in an ERP system should be built with a commercially available user-friendly report writer so that they can be easily tailored. These reports include key documents such as purchase orders and packing lists. The basic reports are too numerous to cover within the scope of this book. However, several report categories involve coordination tools, action screens, supply and demand analysis, performance measurement, and summarized management data. This chapter summarizes various reports within these categories, and includes several illustrative examples.

Every ERP system must support user access to the ERP database, since user requirements cannot be entirely anticipated with predefined reports. Many commercially available tools, such as spreadsheets, data managers, and report writers, support end-user access to data without requiring a high degree of IT (information technology) sophistication. These tools can also be used to provide decision support systems (DSS) and executive information systems (EIS).

Management reporting frequently requires summarized data, rather than detailed transactional data, over extended time periods. Use of a data warehouse and data marts offers one approach to support management reporting and business intelligence.

Basic Reports and Screens in an ERP System

The basic reports and screens in an ERP system can be grouped into several categories. The categories of interest within this book focus on coordinating supply chain activities, especially action screens and schedules. Other categories include performance measurement and summarized management data. This section provides a brief overview of these categories and illustrative examples in each.

Coordination Tools in an ERP System

An ERP system supports coordination of activities across multiple function areas in order to meet the S&OP game plans. The key coordination tools vary by area, but generally consist of a key construct, action messages, and schedule. The production area, for example, coordinates activities using manufacturing orders (the key construct), planner action messages, production schedules, and capacity planning. Figure 22.1 illustrates key coordination tools for various functional areas. An orderless environment typically uses Kanban cards (or their equivalent) to coordinate supplies.

Examples of several coordination tools have been included in this book. These examples include capacity planning (Figure 11.9), a vendor schedule (Figure 15.6) and three variations of a production schedule: tabular (Figure 17.5), schedule board (Figure 17.6), and Gantt chart (Figure 17.7). An example buyer action screen is covered in a case study as part of the next section.

Action Screens

Action messages represent the nervous system of an ERP system. Action messages communicate needed activities based on the S&OP game plans, sales orders, events, elapsed time, calculations, and other factors. The primary engine for generating action messages varies by ERP system, and represents one of the most critical design issues. It typically involves MRP logic, but a given ERP system usually employs multiple programs to communicate action messages.

Area (Responsibility)	Key Coordination Tools			
	Key Construct	Action Messages	Schedule	Orderless
Procurement (Buyer)	Purchase Order	Buyer Actions	Vendor Schedule Receiving Schedule	Kanban
Production (Planner)	Manufacturing Order	Planner Actions	Production Schedule Capacity Planning	Kanban
Shipping (Stockroom)	Sales Order Pick List	Shipping Actions	Shipping Schedule	Kanban
Inventory (Stockroom)	Manufacturing Order Pick List Subcontract PO Pick List	Stockroom Actions	Cycle Count Schedule	Kanban
Field Service (Planner)	Service Work Order	Field Service Actions	Delivery Schedule Capacity Planning	
Customer Service (Service Rep)	Sales Order Return Materials Authorization (RMA)	Customer Service Actions		N/a
Quality		Quality Actions	Inspection Dispatch List	
Cost Accounting		Cost Accounting Actions		
Engineering (Engineer)		Engineering Actions		

Figure 22.1 Summary of Coordination Tools

All ERP systems generate some form of recommended action messages, typically focused on coordinating procurement and production activities. Each system provides a mechanism to view the exception conditions, ranging from hard copy to online and detailed to summary. Some ERP systems provide action-oriented screens that enable the user to view exceptions, perform drill-downs for further analysis, and take action from the same screen. The case study on a buyer action screen illustrates this concept.

An expanded view of action messages involves coordinating activities in other functional areas beyond procurement and production. Illustrations of these recommended action messages have been presented throughout this book, and are summarized in Figure 22.2.

The summary of recommended action messages highlights several key points. First, recommended actions can be used to coordinate multiple functional areas. Second, the messages may be driven by the S&OP game plans, sales orders, elapsed time, calculations, events, and other factors. Third, message filters may be applied to reduce the noise level of recommended action messages. Finally, the primary engine for generating action messages is not limited to MRP logic and the synchronization of supplies and demands.

The concept of user-defined action messages can extend the logic built into an ERP system. An *event manager* provides one approach to user-defined action messages. An event manager consists of a software application with if-then rules: if an event occurs, then communicate an action message to person X. An

Area (Responsibility)	Example Action Message	Message Basis	Message Filter
Procurement (Buyer)	Release purchase order	S&OP Game Plan	Look ahead days
	Reschedule purchase order earlier (expedite)	S&OP Game Plan	Days early
	Review blanket purchase order about to expire	Elapsed Time	Look ahead days
	Purchase nonstock material for a configuration	Event	
Production (Planner)	Release manufacturing order	S&OP Game Plan	Look ahead days
	Cancel existing manufacturing order	S&OP Game Plan	
	Review item with available-to-promise exceeded by sales order	Event	
	Review manufacturing order affected by changes in the bill	Event	
Shipping (Stockroom)	Ship sales order now due for shipment	Event or Time	Look ahead days
	Stop shipping activity for order placed on hold	Event	
Inventory (Stockroom)	Issue components to released manufacturing order	Event	
	Auto-deduction error for inventory of component item	Calculation	
	Cycle count required for item	Calculation	
Field Service (Planner)	Perform service work order for customer	S&OP Game Plan	Look ahead days
	Review service work order with past-due delivery	Elapsed Time	
Customer Service (Service Rep)	Review sales order placed on hold	Event	
	Review sales order with projected late delivery	Calculation	Days late
	Review quotation about to expire	Elapsed Time	Look ahead days
Quality	Review material placed in receiving inspection	Event	
	Review lot of material about to expire	Elapsed Time	Look ahead days
Cost Accounting	Review manufacturing order with projected cost overruns	Calculations	Value or %
	Review manufacturing order that cannot be closed	Calculation	
Engineering (Engineer)	Take action on step in ECO approval process	Event or Time	Look ahead days
	Review item with missing data	Calculation	

Figure 22.2 Illustrations of Recommended Actions

event may represent an ERP transaction (e.g., a shipment), elapsed time (e.g., a shipment missed its ship date), a calculation (e.g., the sum of shipments was greater than X), or other condition. Most event managers support e-mail communication of action messages.

The concept of action messages has often been implemented with e-mail. Event managers and CRM (customer relationship management) applications typically use e-mail to communicate required activities. This approach has a fundamental advantage in that e-mail has become an integral part of the current work culture. It has a fundamental disadvantage in that it is very difficult to take action on the e-mail screen; taking action requires use of the ERP system. The integration between ERP action messages and e-mail messages is still evolving.

The concept of work flows generally applies to action messages. Each message requires one or more steps to analyze the exception and take action. A user-defined work flow can structure these steps, thereby walking the user through the organizational procedures and system(s) to get the job done.

CASE STUDY Buyer Action Screen

The buyer action screen provides an organizing focus for how ERP systems communicate the need to synchronize purchased supplies with demands. The various recommended buyer actions were covered in Chapter 15 (procurement). An example buyer action screen, shown in Figure 22.3, illustrates how an ERP system can communicate these recommended actions.

In this example, the recommended buyer actions have been sorted in vendor sequence so that the buyer can resolve issues in a single conversation with each vendor. The messages reflect a 5-day look ahead window so that upcoming events, such as the need to release a planned purchase order, can be anticipated. The messages also reflect message filters, such as tolerances for reschedule messages.

Buyer: Tom

Current date = Jan 10
Look ahead window = 5 days

Action Message	Vendor	PO#/Line#	Status	Item	Open or Suggested Order Qty	Need Date	Promise Date
Release PO	Acme		Plan	Part #1	100	Jan 26	Jan 26
Reschedule	Acme	123 / 1	Rlsd	Diode #22	300	Jan 15	Jan 22
Cancel PO	Baxter	156 / 1	Firm	Part #34	80		Jan 19
Past Due	Baxter	225 / 2	Rlsd	Cap #73	144	Jan 10	Jan 09
Close PO	Champs	107 / 1	Rlsd	Insert #3	2	Jan 10	Jan 10
Follow-up	Champs	118 / 2	Rlsd	Part #22	50	Jan 12	Jan 12

Figure 22.3 Case Study: Buyer Action Screen

One method of making a buyer action screen more useful is to allow the buyer to enter actions (and related information) on the screen itself. The action fields pertaining to each recommended action are shown in Figure 22.3 as boxes. A buyer can take action on the first message, release a purchase order, by entering the vendor, PO number, and status field (to change a planned PO to a released PO). The buyer can take action on the second message, reschedule a PO, by changing the promise date. The buyer can also cancel or close a PO line item by changing its status. The fourth message indicates a receipt shortfall; the remaining open quantity of "2" for the "Close PO" message may require vendor confirmation. The fifth message indicates follow-up on an anticipated receipt.

Analysis Tools for Supplies and Demands

ERP systems provide several analysis tools for understanding the logic behind recommended actions. One of the key tools is termed *supply/demand analysis*. An item's supply/demand analysis provides the detailed information about calculations made by MRP logic. In many cases, the detailed calculations must be reviewed to understand recommended actions, or to diagnose possible solutions to problems with supplies and demands. An item's supply/demand analysis can be viewed in two basic formats: a summarized horizontal format and a detailed vertical formal.

The horizontal format for supply/demand analysis displays summary information in monthly, weekly, or daily periods. The example in Figure 22.4 shows a weekly period size for Product X, a saleable end-item that has forecasted demands.

The forecasted demands for Product X started with 100 units per week, with supply orders of 100 per week. Sales orders (with ship dates during week 1 and week 2) have consumed the item's forecast and the master schedule, thereby reducing the available-to-promise quantity.

Item: Product X

Current Date = Jan 10
Period Size = Weekly

Inventory = 0

| | Jan 12 | Jan 19 | Jan 26 | Fe |
	Week 1	Week 2	Week 3	W
Remaining Forecasted Demands	40	80	100	
Remaining Sales Order Demands	60	20	0	
Remaining Manufacturing Demands	0	0	0	
Supplies	100	100	100	
Projected Available Balance	0	0	0	
Available to Promise (ATP)	40	80	100	
Cumulative ATP	40	120	220	

Figure 22.4 Supply/Demand Analysis: Horizontal Format

The vertical format for supply/demand analysis displays detailed information about each supply and demand. The example in Figure 22.5 shows the same information for Product X as the horizontal format.

The vertical format displays the source of a supply order and the source of a demand. This is termed *pegging information.* For example, the source of the scheduled receipt on January 12 can be pegged to a manufacturing order. The source of demands on January 12 can be pegged to the item's unconsumed forecast and to two sales orders. MRP logic has generated planned manufacturing orders to cover demands on January 19 and 26.

Supply/demand analysis also applies to resource items. The supply in this case is represented by the resource's available daily capacity. A capacity planning screen (see Figure 11.9) provides a graphic summary of a resource's demand and supply, with drilldown capability to detailed loads.

Performance Measurement

Performance metrics represent a basic tenet of quality management. The typical metric varies by functional area, as well as the typical performance measurement report. Figure 22.6 illustrates some of the performance measurement tools that have been touched on in previous chapters.

Summarized Management Data across the Manufacturing Enterprise

An ERP system maintains detailed data that can be summarized for global views across the manufacturing enterprise. Examples include sales analysis,

Item: Product X					Current Date = Jan 10
Date	Gross Requirement	Scheduled Receipt	Proj Avail Balance	Planned Order	Pegging Information
Jan 10			0		Inventory
Jan 12		100	100		Mfg Order #1234
	40		60		Unconsumed Forecast
	35		25		Sales Order #762
	25		0		Sales Order #770
Jan 19			100	100	Planned Manufacturing Order
	80		20		Unconsumed Forecast
	20		0		Sales Order #783
Jan 26			100	100	Planned Manufacturing Order
	100		0		Unconsumed Forecast

Figure 22.5 Supply/Demand Analysis: Vertical Format

Area	Performance Measurement	
	Typical Metric	**Typical Report**
Procurement	Quality Delivery Price	Vendor Performance Subcontract PO Variances
Production	Quality Delivery Costs	Manufacturing Performance MO Variances Actual Versus Estimated Costs Efficiency Reports
Shipping	On-Time Shipping %	Shipping Performance
Inventory	Inventory Accuracy %	Cycle Count Report
Field Service	On-Time Delivery % Customer Satisfaction	Delivery Performance Actual vs Estimated Costs Efficiency Reports Customer Survey Results
Customer Service	Valid Delivery Promises Customer Satisfaction Returned Goods	Customer Survey Results
Engineering	Bill Accuracy % Routing Accuracy %	MO Variances Manual Audits

Figure 22.6 Summary of Performance Measurement Tools

variance history on manufacturing orders, and financial reports. Cash planning represents one example that combines manufacturing and accounting data into a global viewpoint. Figure 22.7 provides a cash planning example for a smaller manufacturer.

The cash planning example starts with a summary view of various sources of cash (such as receivables and current sales orders) and uses of cash (payables, unvouchered payables, and current purchase orders). The example shows expected cash receipts and outlays in weekly periods (it could be another time period such as monthly) and calculated amounts for a weekly net movement, an anticipated cash balance, and a comparison to budget. The expected cash receipts, for instance, reflect the invoice terms for receivables and the ship dates plus terms for sales orders.

The cash planning example indicates a large amount of expected cash in coming weeks from sales orders that haven't even shipped yet. This requires further analysis using drill-down capabilities. The first drill-down focuses on customers, and identifies Acme Limited as the primary source of cash in week 1. The second drill-down focuses on sales orders, and identifies order num-

SUMMARY	Month 1 Week 1	Week 2	Week 3	....
Receivables	47,320	125,211	140,322	
Sales Orders	182,005	54,299	89,276	
Payables	23,736	31,866	29,831	
Recvd: No Invoice	2,001	4,500	1,465	
Purchase Orders	52,781	63,329	50,101	
Payroll	101,400	0	101,400	
⋮				
Net Movement	50,401	79,815	46,801	
Cash Balance	698,344	778,159	824,960	
Cash Budget	650,000	750,000	850,000	
Variance	48,344	28,159	-25,040	

#1 Drill Down

CUSTOMERS	Month 1 Week 1	Week 2	Week 3	....
Acme Limited	144,577	1,200	2,381	
Baker Company	433		1,299	
Cedar Inc.		2,341		
⋮				

#2 Drill Down

SALES ORDERS	Month 1 Week 1	Week 2	Week 3	....
#2300	2,000		2,381	
#2522	1,578	1,200		
#2601	140,999			

Figure 22.7 Cash Planning Example

ber #2601. Further investigation of this order may indicate a COD payment, or a sales order with a past-due ship date.

Executive Information Systems

An executive information system (EIS) is designed to provide a combination of regular executive-level reports plus on-demand access or drill-down to underlying data. The data reflects transaction detail as well as summarized information, where summaries can be based on data warehouse information (explained in the next section). The results are presented in a variety of formats, ranging from lists and tables to graphs and charts, using various reporting tools. An EIS system can provide key indicators of company performance (based on information in the ERP database) and external factors (based on information about customers, the industry, and the economy).

Indicators and trends of financial performance include the cash balance, days of receivables, gross profit by product line, aged receivables (with drill-down to customers), and aged payables (with drill-down to vendors). Other financial indicators can be identified that reflect information in the profit-and-loss statements and balance sheets.

Indicators can also be identified for sales performance and manufacturing performance. For example, indicators of manufacturing performance include on-time shipping percentages, past-due shipments, inventory and bill accuracy, vendor performance for delivery, quality, and price, and variances related to manufacturing orders.

The definition of requirements for an EIS may overcome a tendency of executives to focus on available data rather than important data. In other words, the natural tendency of executives is to use whatever is available. If they receive reports that focus on internal efficiency variables, they will focus on these variables. The design of an EIS (by the executives who will use it) provides an opportunity to get the right mix of effectiveness and efficiency variables.

CASE STUDY EIS for an Industrial Products Manufacturer

The CEO and CFO at an industrial products manufacturer use an EIS to monitor critical business indicators on a daily basis. The EIS uses data extracted from their ERP system, and a PC-based data management and report generator package to display information graphically. The company spent approximately $10,000 on software and consulting assistance, and about 1 week elapsed time, to implement their EIS, far less than other alternatives that they investigated.

The EIS provides an electronic dashboard with dials of information that show business conditions as they change and develop. With user-specified alarm conditions (which indicate status with colors of critical red, warning yellow, and normal green) for more than 100 indicators of financial, sales, and operational performance, the executives can focus on trouble spots. At one point in time, the critical indicators included gross profit by product line and on-time shipment percentage. For each indicator, the executives used their own PCs with downloaded data to view the 12-month history graph of trends and access detailed data to diagnose the source of the problem. Then they met with accounting and manufacturing personnel to take corrective action.

Once they had a baseline EIS operational, the company executives wanted additional indicators (including some from external sources such as government and economic figures). The changing information requirements for EIS reflected an evolving sophistication among the executives about how they run the business. Rather than focus on easily obtained data such as financial measures and efficiency reports, the EIS implementation prompted the management team to rethink what they should measure.

Data Warehouse and Data Marts

Management reporting often involves the analysis of summarized data with the ability to drill down to detailed data. An EIS application (described above) typically uses summarized data to graphically highlight key performance metrics. The volume of detailed transaction data and the size of the database for an ERP system, however, may require unacceptably long computer processing time to summarize data, especially when *ad hoc* analyses require fast response time. Replicated data and a degree of data summarization provides one solution approach. The terms *data warehouse* and *data mart* refer to this data summarization and the ability to analyze the data. The terms reflect a shopping analogy, where management can shop for needed information from the store of information. The term *data mining* is also used.

A data mart (or data store) can be simplistically viewed as a table of summarized data for a specific subject. A table about monthly sales by item, for example, includes a row of summarized information about each month's shipments for each standard product item. Each row might simplistically contain information about the customer, item, quantity, and amount. A row may reflect multiple sales orders for the same item from the same customer in a given month, and a row would not be required when an item has zero sales for the month. The table of summarized data requires periodic updates. This involves extracting information from detailed transactions, and transforming it into rows of summarized data. This summarized data provides the basis for reporting and analysis.

Management reporting involves multiple data marts, one for each subject, that together comprise a data warehouse. A coordinated data mart approach ensures consistent interpretation of business constructs (such as customer or product line) and consistent data. Additional attributes (table columns) and data marts reflect reporting requirements. For example, the table about monthly sales by item may require additional attributes to identify the salesman and ship-from location (for a multisite operation), and an additional data mart may be required to identify monthly returned goods by item. Each attribute often requires additional information, such as characteristics of the customer or salesman.

The data mart contents and degree of summarization reflect an analysis of management's reporting requirements. The software vendors for ERP systems and data warehouse packages typically offer predefined approaches reflecting their analyses of best practices, thereby supporting faster implementation. These predefined approaches include data extracts and transformations from the ERP system, loading summarized data into data marts, and predefined models and reports. The data marts can be incrementally updated over time while still preserving historical data.

Decision Support Systems and User Access to Data

The availability of user-friendly report writers and database management systems have made decision support systems (DSS) affordable and easy to develop. Creative DSS applications are often topics at user conferences for ERP software packages. Examples of DSS applications can be found in every functional area, and across functional areas.

Part 7

Variations in Manufacturing Environments

Major variations in manufacturing environments reflect contingencies that must be considered in ERP system design and usage. Much of the variation can be attributed to three factors—the type of product (standard versus custom), the manufacturing strategy, and the linkage between sales orders and supply orders. Additional variations include multisite operations and project manufacturing.

Multisite operations involve varying degrees of coordination, ranging from autonomous sites to an integrated network of manufacturing plants and distribution centers. Many small manufacturers start as single-site operations and grow to multiple sites. Many larger manufacturers with multiple sites operate them as autonomous business units. The chapter on multisite operations reviews various alternatives to coordinating multiple sites. It also reviews the impact on ERP systems to support multiple sites and distribution requirements planning (DRP). It includes a case study of one firm that grew from a single site operation into multiple sites requiring close coordination.

Project manufacturing capabilities in an ERP system allow supplies and demands to be identified by project. Project sharing rules apply to the supplies. The chapter on project manufacturing operations explains the impact of project MRP logic in synchronizing supplies with demands, and the impact of project costing calculations. It also includes several case studies covering project manufacturing, progress billing, and repair and overhaul.

Other variations in manufacturing environments may be considered, such as the requirements for international operations and industry-specific operations. These variations fall outside the scope of this book.

Chapter 23

Multisite Operations

A multisite operation provides manufacturing, distribution, and/or customer delivery services from different physical locations. Each physical site may represent an autonomous financial entity (or strategic business unit) with a separate general ledger. Alternatively, a strategic business unit may consist of a combination of physical sites.

There are wide variations in the requirements to support multisite operations, and in the capabilities of ERP systems to support these requirements. This chapter reviews some of the variations in multisite operations. Some multisite environments are best modeled as autonomous sites, with minimal coordination requirements. Other environments require a multisite ERP system to coordinate supply chain activities across multiple sites. One such environment involves multiple distribution centers and distribution requirements planning (DRP) logic.

Physical Sites in a Multisite Operation

Each physical site in a multisite operation typically represents a manufacturing plant, a distribution center, or a customer delivery center. A given physical site may reflect a combination of the roles, such as a manufacturing plant and distribution center that coexist in one location. They may operate as one financial entity or as separate financial entities.

Manufacturing Plants

Multiple manufacturing plants may be required for different purposes. A plant's physical location may be placed in close proximity to suppliers or customers. The location may provide cheaper production or transportation costs, or greater availability of raw material and human resources. There may be political, technological, or competitive marketplace forces for multiple plants. A new plant may represent an acquisition. There may be a management bias toward focused factories or plant replication to keep operations small.

Multiple plants often represent vertical integration, with material flow between sites. One plant acts as the supplier (the supplying plant), while the other plant acts as the customer (the consuming plant). Material flow between sites generally reflects a transfer complete, although some environments involve a subcontract manufacturing situation where one plant supplies components so that the other plant can produce and return the completed item.

Distribution Centers

Multiple distribution centers may be required for proximity to customers or other reasons (mentioned above). A distribution center typically requires a separate inventory management function. Inventory can be replenished from a manufacturing plant or another distribution center, or from external suppliers. Inventory stocked at a distribution center can be sold and shipped to customers. Information about historical and future sales is maintained by distribution center, and the site provides the logistics function for deliveries to its customers.

A distribution center may also provide final assembly capabilities. This reduces the need for finished goods inventory and postpones value-added activities until customer requirements have been defined. Final assembly may involve a standard product or a custom product configuration. Alternatively, it may involve supplied material with a drop-shipment to the customer. By providing final assembly capabilities, a distribution center acts like a manufacturing plant.

Multiple distribution centers may reflect a supply chain or network of inventory stocking locations. Distribution requirements planning (DRP) applies MRP logic to the distribution function. Forecasted (and actual) demands by distribution center can be netted against supplies, so that DRP logic calculates requirements for sourcing sites further back in the supply chain.

In some cases, a distribution center may act as a stockless distribution point or a way station in product delivery. One scenario involves cross-docking, in which material arrives ready to be shipped for an existing sales order. The distribution center serves as a point of transfer, from one type of transportation (such as a long-haul full truckload) to another (such as local delivery trucks). A second scenario involves a consolidated shipment for many customers that must be changed to individual shipments. Inventories are not kept at the distribution site, therefore minimizing the need for a separate inventory management function. The distribution site provides freight-forwarder capabilities in this case.

Customer Delivery Centers

A customer delivery center consists of the facilities, people, and vehicles that perform final delivery of products to customers. It typically requires an inventory management function much like a distribution center. For example, it may involve delivery truck inventory, service parts inventory, or final assembly at the customer location.

Selective Coordination of a Multisite Operation

The nature of coordination between sites depends on the situation. At one extreme, each site represents an autonomous plant producing unique products for a unique set of customers. This scenario requires a minimal level of coordination between sites—typically just a consolidated general ledger. Other multisite scenarios require selective coordination of activities across sites. The following scenarios illustrate how an ERP system might handle selective coordination of engineering, procurement, distribution, production, sales, and accounting activities.

Consolidated General Ledger for Autonomous Sites

An autonomous site has profit-and-loss (P&L) responsibility as a separate financial entity, represented by a separate general ledger application. Coordination between sites typically involves budgeting and financial reporting based on a corporate standard for general ledger accounts. An ERP system can enforce a single standard for a general ledger (G/L) account number format and assignment of account numbers. Alternatively, an ERP system may allow different formats and account number assignments for each site, with a mapping between the local G/L account number and the corporate G/L account number.

The ERP system at each site periodically generates a consolidated G/L file, using the corporate G/L account numbers. The corporate general ledger processes the consolidation files from each site to create company-wide financial reports. Each site may operate with a different local currency, so that the consolidation file must be converted to the base currency of the corporate entity. The consolidation file may be in summary format, or contain the details of all G/L transactions. A multitiered corporate environment requires consolidation at several levels, such as a division level and then a corporate level.

CASE STUDY Multinational Appliance Manufacturer and Consolidated G/L

A multinational household appliance manufacturer sets up an autonomous plant in each region or country in which it does business. The plants make almost identical products, with tailoring to the local market. There is very little interplant material movement, as components are sourced locally. The management team has a strong bias toward smaller autonomous operations, so that a given plant never exceeds 200 employees. A regional plant that reaches 200 employees, for example, will be replicated in another country as an autonomous operation with its own P&L responsibility. Each plant uses a single-site ERP system to locally manage its business—from sales order processing through purchasing, production, and accounting. Each site provides consolidated G/L information (in summary format) to the corporate entity on a periodic basis.

Common Material Items across Multiple Sites

A multisite operation requires a corporate standard for identifying common materials, such as finished goods or purchased items, enforced by an ERP system. The common item identification supports the ability to calculate aggregate requirements for purchased material, communicate interplant requirements, and perform centralized sales order processing. The corporate item identification information includes the item number, description, unit of measure, selected attributes (e.g., item classification codes), and selected material management policies.

Each site requires item master information applicable to the local operation, such as replenishment policies and costing data. Each site also requires unique routing and bill of material information for a manufactured item, although some environments require corporate standards for bills of material (such as the ingredients for a pharmaceutical product).

Coordinating Procurement Activities across Multiple Sites

Coordination of procurement activities across multiple sites starts with a corporate standard for identifying vendors and common material items enforced by a multisite ERP system. Coordination by a corporate procurement function typically focuses on selection and qualification of approved vendors and negotiation of agreements. Within an ERP system, this involves identification of approved vendors by item, calculation of aggregate requirements by item and vendor, and definition of price quotes, purchase contracts, and blanket purchase orders.

The procurement function at each local site typically coordinates and executes day-to-day procurement activities for common material. The local site utilizes the sourcing and agreement information defined by the corporate procurement function.

Some environments require centralized purchasing personnel to perform day-to-day coordination for selected common materials. For example, vendor scheduling may involve transportation considerations (such as train cars or overseas shipments) for deliveries to several sites.

Multiple Sites and Variations in Order Entry

Coordination of order entry and shipping activities across a multisite operation starts with a corporate standard for identifying customers and common material items. Several scenarios can be considered. In one scenario, a local order entry function only takes sales orders for shipment from the local site. In a second scenario, it may take sales orders for shipment from other sites as well as the local site. This requires revenue recognition policies for determining whether the order entry site or the shipping site gets revenue credit for the sales order. In a third scenario, a corporate order entry function takes sales orders for drop-shipment from various sites. This also requires revenue recognition policies, especially when the order entry function represents a separate company.

Centralized Accounting for Autonomous Sites

Some manufacturers operate autonomous plants but perform centralized accounting for payables, invoicing and receivables, and/or general ledger. A corporate standard applies to identification of vendors and customers. The corporate accounting system requires information about shipment, receipt, and costed manufacturing (G/L) transactions for each site. The corporate accounting function typically generates a separate invoice for each shipment. However, some environments require a consolidated invoice for multiple shipments (from multiple sites). The corporate accounting system also processes cash receipts that apply to invoices from each site.

Logical Sites for Financial Reporting Purposes

A logical site may be used for financial reporting or tax purposes. In one scenario, a foreign and a domestic company may be established for the same physical site. Inventory passes from the domestic company to the foreign company to the customer, with revenue recognition by the foreign company and transfer pricing between the foreign and domestic companies.

Interplant Transfers between Sites Using Different ERP Systems

Material movements between autonomous plants can be modeled as a transfer order within a multisite ERP system, as described in the next section on distribution requirements planning. However, the autonomous plants in many multisite operations often use different ERP systems. These cases involve modeling an interplant transfer as a *sales order/purchase order* relationship between two sites. The supplier plant sells and ships material, whereas the customer plant buys and receives the material. The ownership of in-transit material may transfer upon shipment or receipt.

The normal flow of accounting activities would involve an accounts receivable invoice and cash receipt (for the supplier plant), and an accounts payable invoice and payment (for the customer plant). These can be replaced with G/L transactions for an intercompany payable and receivable based on transfer of in-transit ownership. The use of a vendor schedule (at the customer plant) provides forecast visibility to the supplier plant. The customer plant may provide supplied material, modeled with a subcontract purchase order.

Managing Multisite Operations with a Bias toward Autonomous Plants

Many multisite operations reflect a management bias toward autonomous plants treated as separate financial entities. An autonomous plant oftentimes reflects a focused factory, a stand-alone acquisition, or a stand-alone operation in a foreign location. Each plant requires its own tools, including an ERP system, to meet its objectives.

One approach to autonomous plants uses the same single-site ERP system for each plant. The single-site ERP system clearly identifies the responsibility for successful implementation. Users tend to take ownership of implementation and the smaller scale reduces the risk of project failure. The system can be tailored to match the business processes within the business unit, with an implementation tailored to local personnel. This approach reduces the need for consensus building between business units—and between corporate headquarters and a business unit. A side benefit to a single-site ERP system is the ability to add (or sell) a business unit free of system complications.

There may be requirements for selective coordination between sites. Some scenarios can be handled easily with single-site ERP systems, such as a consolidated general ledger or aggregate purchasing requirements. Other scenarios, such as extensive interplant transfers and distribution requirements planning, require a multisite ERP system to provide the necessary integration.

Multisite Operations and Distribution Requirements Planning

Distribution requirements planning (DRP) logic works in tandem with a multisite ERP system. DRP logic provides the primary means to coordinate supply chain activities across a network of interrelated plants and distribution centers. Much like MRP logic, DRP logic uses forecasted (and actual) demands by distribution center to suggest replenishment and calculate requirements for sourcing sites further back in the supply chain. DRP logic minimally involves two additional constructs, an interplant inventory move transaction and an interplant transfer order, to manage the flow of materials between sites.

ERP systems have implemented multisite capabilities using a wide variety of approaches. The capabilities typically include the definition of sites, the use of item/site identifiers in the manufacturing database, and constructs to manage the flow of materials between sites. These represent additional capabilities and complexities in comparison to a single-site ERP system.

Identification of Sites

Each site or plant has a unique identifier. Multiple stocking locations can be defined within a given site. Each site can be defined as a financial entity, or a combination of sites can be defined as a financial entity.

Impact on the Manufacturing Database

Item Identifier   The combination of item number and site, or item/site for short, defines a unique item identifier. The item/site identifier reflects authorized sites for an item; these sites can maintain inventory (and handle supply orders) for the item. In particular, the primary source for an item/site can be transfer and subcontract transfer. These represent additional primary sources (to make, buy and subcontract) in comparison to a single-site ERP system.

The item master information can be segmented into item and item/site information. The item information includes lot- and serial-control policies, internal unit of measure, and various user-defined attributes.

Bill of Materials The bill of material for an item can vary between sites, so that the bill must be defined for an item/site. The bill typically assumes all components are from the same site as the parent item. However, the planning bill for a standard product family may have components from different sites to support sales and operations planning across multiple sites.

Resources and Routings The same resource can be in different sites, so that the combination of resource item number and site define a unique identifier. The routing operations for an item can vary between sites, so that the routing must be defined for an item/site. The routing typically assumes all operations (resource components) are performed at the same site as the parent item.

Item Planning Data An item's planning data varies by site, as expressed in the item/site's primary source, replenishment method, and planning policy. In addition, a transfer item can be sourced from multiple supplier sites just as a buy item can have more than one vendor source. Source mix percentages can be used by DRP logic in suggesting replenishment.

The two additional replenishment sources (transfer and subcontract transfer) require two additional types of supply orders (a transfer order and a subcontract transfer order) to manage the flow of material between sites. A multisite operation also requires a simple inventory move transaction.

Interplant Inventory Move Transaction Moving inventory between two sites requires a different type of move transaction, typically termed an interplant inventory move. This transaction handles the possible financial impact of moving inventory between financial entities and provides a simple method to record movements between two nearby sites without the complexities of interplant transfers. These complexities include shipping paperwork (such as a bill of lading), tracking in-transit inventory, and separate transactions to record shipment and receipt at each site.

Transfer Order A transfer order represents a combination purchase order/sales order with the additional ability to manage in-transit inventory. Hence, a transfer order has a dual nature: it represents a supply to the customer site and a demand to the supplier site. The life cycle of a transfer order has two parallel paths to handle each site's supply chain activities. The two paths require different responsibilities for coordinating supply chain activities: the buyer at the customer site and the customer service representative at the supplier site.

A planned transfer order notifies the supplier site of demand for an item. At this point, an interplant inventory move could be recorded, bypassing the complexity of a transfer order. This represents the simplest approach for nearby sites that do not require shipping paperwork and tracking of in-transit inventory. Ownership transfers immediately.

As an alternative, the supplier site could release the planned transfer order (and assign an order number), print shipping paperwork, and record shipment. The transfer order tracks in-transit inventory, and the receipt transaction relieves in-transit inventory. This represents a simple approach for nonlocal sites with simple authorization policies on material transfers. Ownership can transfer upon shipment or receipt.

Other variations may be considered. Some multisite operations want more control over material transfer authorizations. For example, they want a separate confirmation from the supplier site and a formal delivery authorization from the customer site.

Subcontract Transfer Order A subcontract transfer order represents a combination of a subcontract purchase order (with supplied material) and a sales order for a product with customer-supplied material. An order-dependent bill is created upon opening and releasing the transfer order, and supplied material can be shipped (from the customer site) and received (at the supplier site).

Other variations of transfer orders can be considered. This includes a custom product transfer order, a final-assembly transfer order (with direct linkage to the sales order), and a subcontract transfer order that does not get returned (the completed item is stocked at the supplier site).

Product Costing The cost of an item can vary between sites, since the item's primary source and bill and routing may vary by site. When the primary source for an item/site is transfer, a transfer can be treated at cost (the supplier site's cost equals the price on a transfer order). This approach does not recognize any profit for the supplier site. Alternatively, the price on a transfer order can reflect an incremental up-charge relative to cost at the supplier site. The incremental up-charge reflects a separate cost element termed *transfer costs*. The incremental transfer costs for an item/site can be used in cost roll-up calculations, and to calculate a price variance on transfer orders.

Custom Products The approaches taken by ERP systems to support custom products in a multisite operation vary widely. With a basic approach, the planning bill (or bill of options) for a custom product family item can only be specified for a given site, where all components are assumed to be from the same site. A sales order for a custom product defines the item and supplier site, and the configuration's components must be from the same site. Changes to the supplier site (on a sales order line item) are typically prevented, since the configuration identifies operations and component materials that are unique to the supplier site (with site-specific costs).

Impact on S&OP and Sales Order Processing

Forecasted demand by item and site, and each item/site's replenishment method, provides the basis for inventory planning across multiple distribution centers. DRP logic provides level-by-level netting to calculate requirements for each supplier site (based on source mix percentages), going backward through the supply chain.

A sales order (or each sales order line item) defines the ship-from site. The designated ship-from site may reflect sourcing rules, such as proximity to the ship-to site. In many cases, the ship-from site may reflect availability to meet delivery date requirements. This requires available-to-promise information across multiple sites to identify the designated ship-from site.

Forecast consumption is based on the designated ship-from site, subject to the demand management policies for the item/site.

Impact on Distribution Management and Other Supply Chain Activities

The designated ship-from site on a sales order drives distribution activities related to customer shipments. Replenishment of inventory at distribution centers also drives distribution activities. Replenishment reflects source mix percentages for each item/site, so that planned requirements are spread across supplier sites.

Distribution management has the responsibility for transportation planning to replenish inventory at distribution centers. This often involves transportation management and route management applications as part of the ERP system. These applications can help manage trucks and containers, truck loading, consolidations, continuous runs, and backhauls. They may support cross-border regulations, customs and export documentation, and monitoring of shipments.

CASE STUDY Autonomous Sites Versus DRP Approach to a Multisite Operation

A small U.S. industrial products manufacturer started with a single manufacturing plant and a single-site ERP system. It outgrew the original facility, so that a nearby warehouse was used for finished goods inventory. The inventory of a completed end-item was moved to the separate warehouse. This situation is shown in Figure 23.1, using solid black lines to indicate their single-site ERP system. This figure identifies the inventory move between two locations as "#1."

Over time, a separate distribution center was established in Mexico to serve customers in Latin America. This site represented an autonomous business unit with its own single-site ERP system (shown in gray in Figure 23.1), and its own customers. It used a Spanish-language version of the software and a base currency of pesos. Material movements between sites reflected a sales order/purchase order relationship, identified as #2 in Figure 23.1.

At one point in time, the Mexican site started performing subcontracted manufacturing for the U.S. plant. It used some supplied material (with local sourcing for the other components), and returned the completed subassemblies to the U.S. site. Material movements between sites reflected a subcontracted purchase order/sales order relationship, identified as #3 in Figure 23.1.

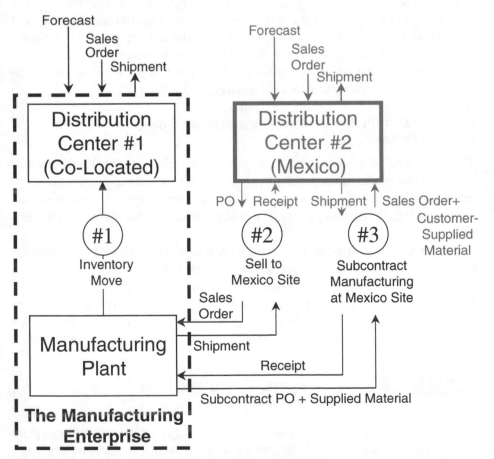

Figure 23.1 Case Study: Autonomous Sites in a Multisite Operation

The company is now considering several changes for future operations. One change involves a new multisite ERP system for all three sites: the original manufacturing plant, the distribution center #1, and the Mexican site. The same end-items can be stocked in each site; the same components can also be stocked at the U.S. and Mexican manufacturing facilities. This requires differentiating items at different sites using the item/site identifier. DRP logic and transfer orders would coordinate material movements between sites.

Chapter 24

Project Manufacturing Operations

Some firms require an ERP system with project manufacturing capabilities. A common example involves products for the aerospace and defense industries. Project manufacturing capabilities can be broadly segmented into project MRP and project costing. Project MRP provides one method to support multilevel linkage between supplies and demands, and applies to every production strategy, for custom products and standard products (with direct and indirect linkage). Project costing involves estimating and tracking costs by project.

This chapter provides a brief overview of project MRP and project costing capabilities. It includes three case studies of project manufacturing environments: one for make-to-order end-items, one for progress billing, and another for repair and overhaul environments.

Project Master

The starting point is a project identifier. A project identifier may require further segmentation, such as work breakdown structures and tasks. A project can optionally be assigned to a contract. We will focus on the project identifier for simplicity's sake.

The project identifier can be assigned to demands, so that project MRP logic can calculate requirements for project-specific supplies. However, several rules (assigned to each project) govern the ability to use other supplies. These are termed *project sharing rules* or *shareability rules*. Two basic sharing rules include (1) the ability to use general inventory and supply orders that are non-project related, and (2) the ability to use another project's inventory and supply orders. An item master field, indicating an item is general versus project-controlled, helps differentiate items.

The second basic rule has several implications. First, a project identifier can have a specified list of projects with sharable supplies. Second, it can be assumed that all projects within a contract have sharable supplies. Third, a given supply order, such as a purchase order or manufacturing order, may be created to cover demands from multiple projects. This third implication impacts project costing, as will be discussed shortly.

Each project may have a project status, such as open and closed, and a hold or cancelled status. The project status can affect project MRP logic (for instance, by ignoring project demands for a closed or cancelled project) and transactions (by permitting transactions to finish orders in process).

Project MRP and an S&OP Case Study

The use of project manufacturing capabilities applies to every S&OP game plan. For illustration purposes, an S&OP case study will be explained for make-to-order standard products. The example products, shown in Figure 24.1, consist of a two-level product structure.

Two different end items (End-Item A and End-Item B) are required for two different projects (Project #123 and Project #XYZ) with the same ship date. Both end-items require Assy #1 and Part #1. Each project allows use of general inventory but requires separate supply orders for project-controlled items. Demands for the general item Part #2 can be satisfied by general inventory. Demands for the project-controlled items Assy #1 and Part #1 require separate manufacturing orders and purchase orders, respectively.

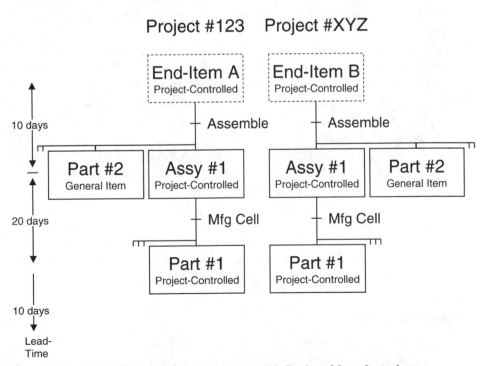

Figure 24.1 Case Study: MTO End-Items with Project Manufacturing

Summary of Demand Management for Case Study

Forecasts and an inventory plan can be defined without a project identifier, thereby anticipating actual demands and driving replenishment of stocked components. This approach assumes that a project's sharing rules allow use of general inventory or supplies. Otherwise, a project-specific forecast may be used to anticipate a project-specific actual demand.

Sales orders are assigned a project identifier. The combination of sales orders and forecasts define the demands used by project MRP logic to calculate demands and suggested supplies throughout the product structure.

When demands are not used to drive supply chain activities, the project identifier can be assigned to a manufacturing order, typically for the item at the highest level in the product structure.

Key Aspects of the S&OP Approach

Project MRP logic includes level-by-level netting calculations and the rescheduling assumption, so that sharable supplies will be considered before suggesting planned supply orders. In our example of Project #123 and #XYZ, the supplies for other projects are not considered sharable. Planned supply orders for project-controlled items are directly linked to demands via the project identifier.

A given supply order may cover demands for multiple projects. In particular, project MRP logic suggests a planned order to cover demands for multiple projects when the projects' sharing rules coincide. Inventory can also be moved between projects, with a warning when the move breaks rules about shared supplies. Some environments require tracking of this inventory, and it is termed a *borrow-payback* capability.

Supply orders for stocked components constitute the master schedule. Stocked components typically represent general inventory, although project-specific forecasts may drive replenishment of project-controlled stocked components.

Supply orders for final-assembly end-items and components constitute the final assembly schedule. A given supply order may be for one project, or for multiple projects when permitted by sharing rules. The project identifier provides visibility of the sales order (without having direct linkage between the supply order and sales order).

Project Costing

A project may have one or more cost estimates, with estimates for specific items being produced for the project. A project's actual costs reflect purchase prices for project-specific purchase orders, and actual costs charged to project-specific manufacturing orders. The actual costs may also include material and labor charges not directly tied to a manufacturing order, project-to-project transfers, cycle counts, accounts payable invoices tied to the project, and miscellaneous direct charges.

Actual costs associated with a project-specific manufacturing order become more difficult to interpret when the order serves multiple projects. Actual costs can be theoretically split between projects based on the parent item's quantity per project. However, delayed recognition of actual costs, and item usage prior to closure, creates difficulties in allocating actual costs between projects.

A project's estimated and actual costs can be summarized according to project segmentation, such as the work breakdown structure, and by cost element. The status of all project-related activities can also be reviewed, such as project-related sales orders, manufacturing orders, purchase orders, and inventory.

Progress billing is frequently based on a project's actual costs or the status of project-related activities. The activities frequently represent milestones. With customer-specified development of a new product, for example, the three major milestones may represent completion of engineering design, completion of first working prototype, and completion of a successful production-rate lot of material (with appropriate yields). These three major milestones each have a different S&OP game plan, explained in the case study on progress billing.

CASE STUDY Progress Billing and an S&OP Case Study for Project Manufacturing

The segmentation of project costs and activities can frequently be aligned to a S&OP game plan and serve progress billing purposes. In this case study of new product development, the progress billings (and S&OP game plans) reflect three phases. The three phases correspond to completion of engineering design, completion of first working prototype, and completion of a successful production-rate lot of material (with appropriate yields).

Phase 1: Completion of Engineering Design. The S&OP game plan uses an MTO custom products approach to define a configuration with only engineering-related resource components. A project management application may be used to schedule milestones and resources. Actual times and costs can be collected for the configuration. Completion (or shipment) of the configuration triggers invoicing (progress billing) for Phase 1.

Phase 2: Completion of First Working Prototype. The S&OP game plan uses an MTO custom products approach to define a configuration with various resource and material components. The resources reflect internal production as well as engineering resources. The material components include standard products (both project-controlled and general items), nonstock material, or custom product components with their own configurations. Actual times and costs can be collected for the configuration. Completion (or shipment) of the configuration triggers invoicing (progress billing) for Phase 2.

Multiple prototypes may be needed to satisfy customer specifications for a working prototype. Each prototype iteration can be modeled as a separate configuration, possibly created by copying the previous configuration.

Phase 3: Completion of a Successful Production-Rate Lot of Material. The S&OP game plan uses an MTO standard products approach to define a standard bill (and standard costs) at production volumes. Items may be project-controlled or general. Sales orders drive the final assembly schedule, although forecasts may be used to anticipate requirements (especially when multiple production iterations are required). Actual material and resource usage can be reported (with variances highlighted) and actual costs summed for the project. Shipment of the sales order line item triggers invoicing (progress billing) for Phase 3.

Multiple production iterations may be needed to satisfy customer specifications for a production-rate lot of material. Each iteration represents a sales order for an internal customer, where the customer may be changed upon successful completion.

CASE STUDY Repair and Overhaul of Transportation Equipment

Transportation equipment, such as airplanes, buses, and train cars, typically requires repair and overhaul, where a project can be created for tracking all activities related to a specific piece of equipment. Repair and overhaul activities to refurbish equipment can be modeled using a custom products approach. As shown in Figure 24.2, the configura-

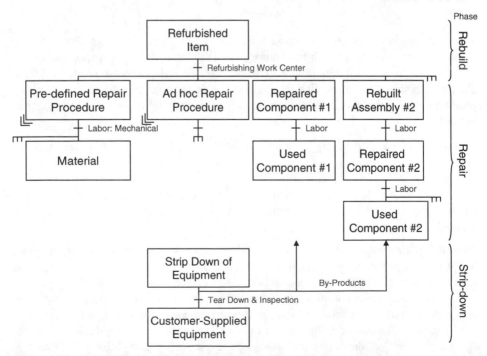

Figure 24.2 Case Study: Repair and Overhaul of Transportation Equipment

tion of a refurbished item consists of predefined repair procedures (with new component material), *ad hoc* repair procedures (identified during inspection and strip-down), repaired and rebuilt components, and refurbishing operations.

A piece of customer-supplied equipment goes through three major phases (strip-down, repair, and rebuild) to become a refurbished item. The starting point is a sales order for the custom product item (the refurbished item) with a specified project identifier.

Strip-Down Phase. The customer-supplied item goes through an inspection survey and strip-down process. Some ERP systems support a strip-down bill of material. The disposition of each component can be use-as-is, repairable, or scrap. The strip-down process often involves a multilevel bill, where the strip-down activity initially identifies a repairable assembly that must be stripped down even further. In this example, the repairable components include Used Component #1 and Used Component #2. The second used component goes into an assembly that was stripped down. Used components may be serialized. A defect code may be assigned to each used component, where the defect code can have an associated repair scheme.

The inspection survey may also identify additional repair procedures for the end-item, defined as additional components in the configuration.

Repair Phase. Used components can be repaired. In this example, the Repaired Component #1 is built from the Used Component #1, along with some other material and labor. Used components may be repaired, and then rebuilt into an assembly (that was previously stripped down into parts). In this example, the Repaired Component #2 is used to rebuild Rebuilt Assembly #2.

Rebuild Phase. The refurbished item gets rebuilt from repaired components and rebuilt assemblies in a refurbishing work center. Predefined and *ad hoc* repair procedures also require material and resource components.

Actual project costs reflect the reported material and labor for multiple manufacturing orders and rework orders. An estimated project cost to refurbish a piece of equipment can also be based on the detailed configuration data.

Part 8

Summary

This book focused on suggestions for improving the effectiveness of ERP system usage, particularly for smaller manufacturers. It used case studies to illustrate common situations and common problems. The suggestions reflect a contingency approach that accounts for major variations in manufacturing environments and system capabilities. The suggestions primarily apply to the ERP project implementation team in a manufacturing firm, with particular relevance to managers involved in production, procurement, engineering, and quality. The Summary chapter identifies the book's significance to these various target audiences.

Chapter 25

Summary

The starting point of this book was that most manufacturers do not effectively use their ERP system to run the business; its central theme was to provide practical suggestions for maximizing effective system usage; its target audience was the management team responsible for system implementation in smaller manufacturers. To this end, the practical suggestions account for variations in manufacturing environments and ERP software packages.

Variations in manufacturing environments and ERP software packages affect system usage and must be considered in a contingency approach to practical suggestions.

- Much of the variation in manufacturing environments reflects five basic factors: the type of product (standard versus custom), the production strategy, linkage between sales orders and supply orders, the extent of lean manufacturing practices, and the need for advanced scheduling capabilities. Additional variations are involved with multisite operations and project manufacturing. These represent the primary differences (there are others) underlying a contingency approach to ERP usage. This book identified contingency approaches to ERP system usage, and conceptual frameworks that apply across differing types of manufacturing environments.
- Variations in ERP software packages reflect underlying design philosophies and capabilities. These differences manifest themselves in key design issues that shape and limit usage. They are embedded in the software's conceptual framework and programs and are not readily apparent to the average user with limited familiarity of a single system. This book identified more than 20 major ERP design issues affecting usage in differing types of manufacturing environments.

Note: The contingency viewpoints on design issues and usage are especially apparent in efforts to reimplement an ERP system by knowledgeable users. These users are willing to reexamine and simplify business processes with consideration of the capabilities and limitations of their ERP system. Implementations are easier when users can view and model the business in terms paralleling the system's underlying design rather than in a way that runs counter to the underlying design.

The organizing focus for practical suggestions covered five basic areas in running a manufacturing enterprise: structuring the manufacturing database, developing S&OP game plans, processing sales orders, coordinating and executing to plan, and integrated accounting. Characteristics of ERP system usage in each area provide the basis for macrolevel quality metrics on system effectiveness. In most cases, these macrolevel metrics confirm management intuition about an ineffective ERP system. The justification for system reimplementation or replacement can be based on bottom-line results, improved customer satisfaction, and other intangible benefits.

A summary of the book identifies its significance to various target audiences. The target audiences start with the emphasis on smaller manufacturers.

Significance for the Project Implementation Team in Smaller Manufacturers

Effective usage of an ERP system requires a vocabulary and conceptual models that are foreign to many managers. This basic understanding enables management to model their manufacturing environment. All too often, system implementation focuses on replicating current practices, which run counter to the fundamental logic within an ERP system. As described in this book, the basics start with understanding how to structure the manufacturing database and develop S&OP game plans to run the business.

Significance for Executives of Smaller Manufacturers

The chief executive or CEO of a smaller manufacturer normally focuses on running the company from the top, with limited participation in (and understanding of) the particulars of ERP system implementation and usage. They usually assign responsibility for the details of an ERP system to their management team. The majority of this book covered the details of an ERP system to assist this management team, and was meant to be a tool that the chief executive can provide to the team. The book covered some CEO issues, such as the justification of ERP investments and major trends affecting manufacturers and ERP. It also suggested use of several macrolevel metrics for gauging ERP system effectiveness.

Significance for Larger Manufacturers

The vocabulary and conceptual models of an ERP system apply to large and small manufacturers. The depth and breadth of system functionality apply to both. A contingency approach to modeling the manufacturing environment applies to both. Larger firms have more people involved in implementation, affecting the scope, duration, cost, and project management of an ERP implementation (or reimplementation). In particular, the larger firm frequently deals with multisite contingencies. Variations in multisite operations range from autonomous sites to corporate coordination across a network of manufacturing plants and distribution centers. Many larger firms have a bias toward autonomous sites. This book focused on ERP systems for autonomous sites.

Significance for Production and Procurement Managers in Coordinating Supply Chain Activities

Coordination of supply chain activities typically involves action messages. Unfortunately, the promise of improved coordination is not realized in most manufacturers. Action messages are often characterized as unrealistic. They represent information overload and a high noise level that obscure the real needs for taking action. This book addressed how to improve the effectiveness of action messages, especially for buyers and planners. It expanded the scope of action messages for coordinating other functional areas such as customer service, cost accounting, inventory management, and shipping.

Coordination extends beyond action messages. It involves capacity planning and scheduling, and a contingency approach for using various coordination tools. For example, this book provided an integrated viewpoint on order-based versus orderless manufacturing environments, and how to support coordination for both in a single system.

Significance for Engineering Managers

The engineering function in smaller manufacturers often has responsibility for maintaining the primary contents of the manufacturing database—the items, bills of material, resources, routings, and custom product configurations. The manufacturing database provides the baseline for modeling a manufacturing enterprise and determines the extent to which an ERP system models the way each product is really built. Bills of material reflect more than just product design; the information is used for costing, material planning, material usage reporting, lot tracking, stages of manufacturing, and sales of end-items and configurations. Routings reflect more than just process design; the information is used for modeling factory layout, calculating value-added costs and capacity requirements, production scheduling, labor and machine reporting, and shop floor tracking of end-items and configurations. The bills frequently require consideration of modularization (especially to support configure-to-order custom products) and product families, and the corresponding impacts on drawings, marketing literature, pricing, quotations, and sales order processing. These considerations represent significant responsibilities—and the need to understand the implications of an integrated ERP system—for the engineering function beyond just an engineering parts list.

Significance for Quality Managers

The practical implications of quality management in an ERP system are often embedded throughout the system, and do not necessarily manifest themselves as a stand-alone software module. The practical implications start with item master policies and how to structure the manufacturing database. They also start with the initial customer contact and extend through the sales cycle and supply chain activities. The configure order step in sales order processing, for example, involves defining customer requirements accurately and completely, and eliminating errors and confusion, before sales orders are even entered. Other practical implications of an ERP system include coordination of quality activities, structuring work-flow processes, the impact of ISO 9000 and other certification programs, managing highly regulated environments, and integration with specialized quality management applications. This book highlighted these practical implications for the quality manager.

Significance for ERP Software Vendors

Many of the employees within ERP software vendors have an incomplete picture of what an ERP system entails. Their understanding of ERP, especially its conceptual models and vocabulary, is often colored by the specifics of their software package. Actual field experience of working with manufacturers to implement the software package is typically limited to the presales and postsales consultants, and specialization within these ranks often means a limited overall understanding. This book is intended to provide a broad yet comprehensive understanding of the depth and breadth of an ERP system, and what it takes to model the contingencies of various manufacturing environments.

Significance for Business School Curricula

The curricula in most business programs tend to skim over ERP systems, especially for smaller firms. The relevant disciplines—operations management, information systems, marketing and sales, and accounting—tend to focus on leading edge developments and technologies (rather than the basics), big-picture perspectives (rather than the details), and larger firms. An interdisciplinary advanced class in ERP systems is required that can bridge the theoretical and practical aspects of ERP systems, and delve in sufficient detail to cover a contingency-based approach to system implementation and usage.

Curricula in many vocational and technical colleges and industrial engineering schools also cover ERP systems. These classes have been hampered by the lack of textbooks that provide a broad yet comprehensive understanding of ERP systems and what it takes to model the contingencies of various manufacturing environments. One intent of this book is to fulfill this need.

Final Note

The scope of this book precluded treatment and suggestions for implementing (or reimplementing) an ERP system. A successful implementation process involves change. The first step requires recognition of the need to abandon old ways of doing business for new ones. Understanding the new way provides a starting point for recognizing limitations of the old way. This book focused on explaining the basics of ERP systems with the vocabulary and conceptual models that represent a new way of thinking for many smaller firms. The concepts themselves are not new.

An implementation (or re-implementation) process involves a detailed plan for putting the new way of thinking into place. This means substituting unfamiliar practices with familiar practices. The basic guidelines for a successful implementation process have been covered elsewhere. These guidelines include allocating priorities and time to make key personnel available for the project team; empowering the project team to make real and lasting changes to business processes; and making a commitment to training and ongoing improvement. The project team typically overlaps with the existing management team in smaller firms. This enables the smaller manufacturer to make decisions today and take decisive action tomorrow on maximizing the effectiveness of their ERP system.

Bibliography

Brands, H. W. *The First American: The Life and Times of Benjamin Franklin.* New York: Anchor Books, 2000.

Breyfogle, Forrest, James Cupello, and Becki Meadows. *Managing Six Sigma.* New York: Wiley-Interscience, 2001.

Carter, Joseph. *Purchasing: Continued Improvement Through Integration.* Homewood, IL: Business One Irwin, 1993.

Clement, Jerry, Andy Coldrick, and John Sari. *Manufacturing Data Structures: Building Foundations for Excellence with Bills of Material and Process Information.* Essex Junction, VT: Oliver Wight Publications, 1992.

Davis, Gordon B., and Scott Hamilton. *Managing Information: How Information Systems Impact Organizational Strategy.* Homewood, IL: Business One Irwin, 1993.

Edwards, Peter, Melvyn Peters, and Graham Sharman. "The Effectiveness of Information Systems in Supporting the Extended Supply Chain." *Journal of Business Logistics,* Vol. 22, No. 1, 2001, pp 1–28.

Flaig, Scott. *Integrative Manufacturing: Transforming the Organization Through People, Process, and Technology.* Homewood, IL: Business One Irwin, 1993.

Fleming, Quentin, John Bronn, and Gary Humphreys. *Project and Production Scheduling.* Chicago: Probus, 1987.

Gopal, Christopher, and Harold Cypress. *Integrated Distribution Management.* Homewood, IL: Business One Irwin, 1993.

Greenberg, Paul. *CRM at the Speed of Light.* New York: McGraw-Hill, 2001.

Hill, Arthur V. *Field Service Management: An Integrated Approach to Increasing Customer Satisfaction.* Homewood, IL: Business One Irwin, 1993.

Hitt, Lorin M., D. J. Wu, and Xiaoge Zhou. "Investment in Enterprise Resource Planning: Business Impact and Productivity Measures." *Journal of Management Information Systems,* Vol. 19, No. 1, Summer 2002, pp. 71–98.

Hunt, V. Daniel. *Managing for Quality: Integrating Quality and Business Strategy.* Homewood, IL: Business One Irwin, 1993.

Kemps, Robert R. *Fundamentals of Project Performance Measurement.* San Diego, CA: San Diego Publishing, 1992.

Kremers, Mark, and Han van Dissel. "ERP System Migrations." *Communications of the ACM,* Vol. 43, No. 4, April 2000, pp. 52–56.

Ling, Richard C., and Walter E. Goddard. *Orchestrating Success: Improve Control of the Business with Sales and Operations Planning.* Essex Junction, VT: Oliver Wight Publications, 1991.

Luber, Alan D. *Solving Business Problems with MRP II.* Boston: Digital Press, 1995.

Mabert, Vince A., Ashok Soni, and M. A. Venkataramanan. "Enterprise Resource Planning: Measuring Value." *Production and Inventory Management Journal,* Vol. 43, No. 4, Third Quarter, 2001, pp. 46–51.

Mabert, Vince A., Ashok Soni, and M. A. Venkataramanan. "Enterprise Resource Planning Survey of US Manufacturing Firms." *Production and Inventory Management Journal,* Vol. 41, No. 2, Second Quarter, 2000, pp. 52–58.

Markus, Lynne M., C. Tanis, and P. C. van Fenema. "Multisite ERP Implementations." *Communications of the ACM,* Vol. 43, No. 4, April 2000, pp. 42–46.

Martin, Andre J. *Distribution Resource Planning: The Gateway to True Quick Response and Continuous Replenishment.* Essex Junction, VT: Oliver Wight Publications, 1995.

Orlicky, Joseph. *Material Requirements Planning.* New York: McGraw-Hill, 1975.

Peter, J. Paul. *Marketing for the Manufacturer.* Homewood, IL: Business One Irwin, 1993.

Plossl, George W. *Manufacturing Control: The Last Frontier for Profits.* Reston, VA: Prentice-Hall, 1973.

Plossl, George W., and Oliver W. Wight. *Material Requirements Planning by Computer.* Falls Church, VA: American Production and Inventory Control Society, 1971.

Proud, John F. *Master Scheduling: A Practical Guide to Competitive Manufacturing.* Essex Junction, VT: Oliver Wight Publications, 1994.

Ragowsky, Arik, Niv Ahituv, and Seev Neumann. "Documenting the Benefit an Organization May Gain by Using Information Systems." Communications of the ACM, Vol. 43, No. 11, November 2000, pp. 303–311.

Ragowsky, Arik, Niv Ahituv, and Seev Neumann. "Identifying the Value and Importance of an Information System Application." *Information & Management,* Vol. 31, No. 2, November 1996, pp. 10–22.

Ragowsky, Arik, Myles Stern, and Dennis Adams. "Relating Benefits from Using IS to Organization's Operating Characteristics: Interpreting Results from Two Countries." *Journal of Management Information Systems,* Vol. 16, No. 4, Spring 2000, pp. 175–194.

Rosenthal, Stephan R. *Effective Product Design and Development: How to Cut Lead Time and Increase Customer Satisfaction.* Homewood, IL: Business One Irwin, 1993.

Schorr, John E. *Power Purchasing.* Essex Junction, VT: Oliver Wight Publications, 1992.

Shunk, Dan L. *Integrated Process Design and Development.* Homewood, IL: Business One Irwin, 1993.

Slemaker, Chuck M. *The Principles and Practice of Cost/Schedule Control Systems.* Princeton, NJ: Petrocelli Books, 1985.

Stuckey, M. M. *Demass: Transforming the Dinosaur Organization.* Cambridge, MA: Productivity Press, 1993.

Taylor, David, and David Brunt. *Manufacturing Operations and Supply Chain Management: The Lean Approach.* London: Thomson Learning, 2001.

Umble, Michael, Elizabeth Umble, and Larry Von Deylen. "Integrating Enterprise Resource Planning and Theory of Constraints: A Case Study." *Production and Inventory Management Journal,* Vol. 42, No. 2, Second Quarter, 2001, pp. 43–48.

Van Everdingen, Yvonne, Jos Van Hillegersberg, and Eric Waarts. "ERP Adoption by European Midsize Companies." *Communications of the ACM,* Vol. 43, No. 4, April 2000, pp. 27–31.

Vollman, Thomas E., W. L. Berry, and D. C. Whybark. *Manufacturing Planning and Control Systems.* Homewood, IL: Dow Jones-Irwin, 1988.

Vollman, Thomas E., W. L. Berry, and D. C. Whybark. *Integrated Production and Inventory Management: Revitalizing the Manufacturing Enterprise.* Homewood, IL: Business One Irwin, 1993.

Wantuck, Kenneth A. *Just In Time for America.* Southfield, MI: KWA Media, 1989.

Wight, Oliver W. *The Executive's Guide to Successful MRP II.* Englewood Cliffs, NJ: Prentice-Hall, 1982.

Wight, Oliver. *Manufacturing Resource Planning: MRP II.* Essex Junction, VT: Oliver Wight Limited Publications, 1984.

Womack, James P., and Daniel T. Jones. *Lean Thinking.* New York: Simon & Shuster, 1996.

Index

About the Author

Scott Hamilton, Ph.D., has specialized in ERP systems for manufacturing for more than 30 years. A top consultant, developer, user, and researcher, Dr. Hamilton has consulted with more than 1000 firms, conducted more than 200 executive seminars, and designed several influential ERP application software packages. He has published more than 30 articles in professional journals and is coauthor of *Managing Information: How Information Systems Impact Organizational Strategy*, the APICS CIRM textbook on information systems for manufacturing.